World Beer Guide

WORLD BEER GUIDE

— Andrea Gillies —

BLOOMSBURY

First published 1995 by Bloomsbury Publishing Plc,
2 Soho Square, London W1V 6HB

A copy of the CIP entry for this book is available from the British Library

ISBN 0 7475 2156 5

10 9 8 7 6 5 4 3 2 1

Text design by AB3
Typeset by Hewer Text Composition Services, Edinburgh
Printed by Clays Limited, St Ives plc

DEDICATION

To Calum, my tasting partner

Acknowledgements

Thanks are due to all those retailers who so generously contributed bottled and canned beers for the tastings. And to all those breweries across Britain and the world who were so generous with their time and information. Many thanks to you all.

Contents

Introduction

IF SOMEBODY WERE to disparage the whole world of wine as 'all the same; wine's just wine', not worthy of serious attention, and snort with derision at the very idea of wine appreciation and wine journalism, we would immediately mark them down as hopeless and ignorant philistines. Yet the very same attitude to the equally (if not more) complex global beer culture is expressed without fear of social embarrassment. Indeed, it's the serious beer lover who is called upon to be defensive and explain such eccentric tastes . . .

I wrote the above in 1988, shortly after starting my stint as editor of the *Good Beer Guide*, which (if you aren't already intimate) is a 5000-strong pub guide to establishments that offer good cask ale. At the time, two facts about 1996 would have seemed easy to predict: that world beer tasting would still require a passport, and that Mrs Thatcher would still be leading the Conservative Party. But it's a funny old world. As I write, my desk is piled high with competing press releases, all proclaiming the greater virtues of rival beer brands, many of them new to our shores. Equally significantly, Oddbins is beginning to take a serious and informed interest in expanding its world beer range, and we all know what happened (to wine-buying) when they Discovered Australia. There's also masses of anecdotal evidence that attitudes are changing. A friend who represents the voice of the post-modernist, post-sundried tomatoist, dedicated young hedonist, as well as any randomly picked *Independent on Sunday* reader (okay, so not that random), recently declared herself shamed by being spotted with a four-pack of a well-known brand of lager in a well-known supermarket. She had longed for a brown paper bag – in fact two: one for the beers, one for her head. She had felt as bad as if she had been caught buying Lambrusco. Aha!

Aha? you echo. Merely a handful of years ago, this selfsame person, believing a beer is a beer is a beer, would have had no such hang-ups, as all beer drinking was on one social level then: whatever brand or bottle she picked, she would have been slumming it. (Unless she'd been a classic 1980s beer-fashion victim, cramming her trolley with yellow Mexican beer, perhaps) Whereas now, knowing that beer has gourmet potential, she is self-conscious. Of course, as a food page addict, she's too dogmatic in her aversions. There's still a place for tins of lager – the better ones at least – and that is cluttering up the fridge for when the lust for a cold glass of something should strike. (It could just as easily be a box of South African white wine, on a summer evening.) But the point is this: there's also a place in the cellar, alongside the dusty cases of red picked up in Corbières last year, for some fine bottled ales of endless variety from all over Britain, and, from the rest of the world, perhaps some sharp and fruity Belgian lambics, yeasty wheat beers, soft and oaky bières de garde, classic abbey beers and an Australian sparkler. There's also a place in the bottle-rack under the stairs, or in the larder, for an extraordinarily diverse collection of bottled world beers made for drinking now.

This guide takes the form of a complete world beer kit. It prepares you for tasting by explaining how beer is made, and with what; introduces the beer styles of the world, how and where they're produced, their ingredients and characteristics. There's also a guide to beer flavours, how to go about tasting, and which foods to partner with which. Having set out the basics, the guide goes on to list, taste and rate the imports currently available, A–Z by country. In addition, the British section includes not only the bottled and canned beers available in major retail outlets, but also cross-references with a complete directory of British Breweries, which for the first time in any beer guide details the bottled, canned and draught brands each brewery produces. There's even an index of beers, so it's easy to find your way around.

There are already many interesting and delicious beers from all over the world available in our national supermarkets and off-licences. But in world beer terms, these are but a trickle of imported products. The trickle is growing stronger, though, and with any luck will become a deluge by the end of the century. Meanwhile, there are, no doubt, good bottled imports on sale in Britain that have escaped the clutches of this first edition, simply because there is now a huge network of importers and wholesalers at work that bypasses the high street altogether. Ferreting out more of them, their outlets and their more unusual beer finds is a goal already set for the second edition.

If you know of other bottled or canned British and world beers available in British retail outlets (but not pubs and other venues), you can help make the second edition more comprehensive by sending details of stockists, their address and a note of the beers they stock to the **World Beer Guide**, c/o Bloomsbury Publishing Plc, 2 Soho Square, London W1V 6HB. I'd also welcome details from the importers and specialist outlets themselves.

Andrea Gillies

How to Use This Guide

By beer we mean . . .

It will swiftly become obvious that the term *Beer* is used in its correct international sense in this guide, to encompass both ales and lagers of every kind, from whatever corner of the globe. By beers we don't mean bitters. We mean milds, pale ales, India pale ales, brown ales, red ales, old ales, strong ales, stouts and porters, Trappist and abbey beers, wheat beers, lambics, fruit beers, bières du garde, lagers, export lagers, pilseners, dark lagers, vienna lagers, bocks, double bocks, smoke beers, stone beers, rye beers . . . and, of course, bitters.

Finding a bottled or canned beer

To be listed in this guide, a beer must clear the initial hurdle of being available in British retail outlets. Most (but not all) of the beers listed here have earned a national listing in our supermarkets, off-licences and wine multiples.

Otherwise, simple. If you know which country it's brewed in, just look it up under that country's listings. Beers are listed under their common titles, in alphabetical order. If a beer has a proper name of its own, like Golden Promise, Tiger or Tanglefoot, it's listed under that. If it only has a generic name, like Bitter, Wheatbeer or IPA, say, you'll find it under its brewery name.

However, there is a slight complication. Where a well-known beer brand genuinely originates from overseas, but is in this case brewed in Britain under licence, it's listed under its country of origin, and not as British. It's then made clear in the tasting note that it's actually brewed here. Thus all the Carlsbergs, Guinnesses and so on are kept together and not split up all over the place.

If you don't know which country it comes from, just look it up in the index first.

Finding a british brewery

In addition to the main listings, there's a handy reference list at the back, the British Breweries Directory. Here, breweries are listed in alphabetical order, and all their brands, whether draught, bottled or canned, are listed underneath. So, if you taste a beer from a particular brewery, and like it, you can look it up and find out what else the brewery makes. Sadly, there is only room to do this for the British contingent. A world breweries directory would take several heavy volumes . . .

Reading the listings

- The beer name is followed by the star rating (if any)
- Then the subtitle of the beer, as on the label, and the brewery name
- Whether the product is bottled or canned, and its alcohol content, expressed as an abv (alcohol by volume) percentage
- The tasting note, and a guide to drinking temperature
- The beer's availability in national retailers (Many beers will also be available in specialist, regional and corner shops)

Cask, keg, bottle and can

The main listing includes bottled and canned beer brands. The Breweries Directory also lists draught products, thus:

cask	draught, cask-conditioned (real) ale
keg	draught keg ales and lagers (filtered/pasteurized)
bottled	bottled beer, not bottle-conditioned unless:
bottled BC	Bottle-conditioned, contains active yeasts
can	canned beer
PET	large plastic screw-top party-size bottles

Star ratings

no stars	no redeeming features
*** one star**	mediocre, but better than a 0
**** two stars**	absolutely fine, but not exciting
***** three stars**	really good drinking, true to type
****** four stars**	world class beer, outstanding

Chilling guide

room temp	of a cool room, not a centrally heated one
larder cool	cooler, but not fridge cold
light fridge chill	fridged, but not thoroughly chilled
fridge cold	thoroughly fridge chilled

Store abbreviations

Retailers listed in the main beer listings are as follows (it should be obvious which is which):

Asda, Beer Cellar, Co-op, Majestic, Marks & Spencer, Oddbins, Safeway, Sainsbury's, Somerfield (Gateway), Spar (Landmark), Tesco, Thresher, Victoria Wine, Waitrose.

Widely: Beers listed as available *widely* are either ubiquitous national brands or mass-market imports to be found at several or most of the above outlets.

The Beer Cellar

You may not be familiar with the Beer Cellar. They are a beer by mail order, catalogue-based company, found at 31 Norwich Road, Strumpshaw, Norwich NR13 4AG Tel (01603) 714884. Catalogues are freely available, and contain mouthwatering listings/descriptions of over 200 beers from 40 countries. Beers are sold by the case, and cases can be mixed.

A word about tasting notes

The tasting notes in this guide are entirely original and are based on a six month beer tasting programme. Inevitably, some beers will have been deleted (or indeed, added) subsequent to going to press. The aim of the tastings was to assess the flavours, quality and drinkability of the products as they might be perceived by someone coming to them for the first time, with no preconceptions or specialist beer knowledge. They are *not* a definitive comment; merely the notes that emerged from a single tasting of the products, compared to other similar products, from a particular can or bottle on a particular day.

Some British breweries produce bottled and canned products that, for whatever reason, were not available in the high street retailers at the time of writing. Some are only available in pubs. Some are tiny breweries which only produce bottled beers in small quantities. Whatever the case, these are listed under that brewery's entry in the Breweries Directory. More mysteriously, there are UK brands tasted in the main listings that don't appear in the Breweries Directory – presumably because whoever makes them doesn't want to admit to them!

Alcohol by volume

This has now become the standard international alcoholic strength unit, though a beer's O.G. (original gravity), the system the breweries still use, is also often listed on a product. The average strength of International Lager Brands has now reached a level of 5% abv, which is the most common abv seen on imported bottled beers. However, this is still considered to be a pretty high figure in the world of British ales (and home-produced lagers, to an extent); a 5% abv bitter is considered of 'special', 'premium', 'strong' or even 'extra strong' calibre, depending on the brewery's own range and scale. Yet it is not considered strong at all in Belgium.

British Beer Trends

Pale Golden Ales look set to increase their fashionability even further in 1996. Their popularity has something to do with our increasing education about the world's beer styles, and our thirst for paler, refreshing but still tasty and full-bodied beers. Contact, at home and abroad, with some of the pale and interesting Belgian, Dutch and German beers is becoming influential, though the idea that ales can be creamy, fruity and refreshing is yet to have its day here. Our native pale beer trend is producing straw-coloured ales of the hoppy – perhaps even super-hoppy – and clean-edged (though also slightly toffeeish) sort. The West Country, which really kickstarted the pale golden ale revival in the 1980s, had better crack on with developing its bottling. Caledonian Brewery, up in Edinburgh, has already grabbed a huge amount of attention, here and abroad, with its newest product, Caledonian Pale. More products to follow, no doubt.

India Pale Ales are also enjoying a huge following, and with any luck there will be more delicious bottled IPAs on the retail shelves by summer 1996. IPA is a term that's become too loosely used, often just indicating a hoppy, pale bitter (and sometimes not even that), but more and more breweries are looking back into their old brewing books and rediscovering recipes from the past that produce beers of great complexity and finesse. More please.

Still on the Pale Trail, it wouldn't be remotely surprising to see a host of British **Wheat Beers** appear on the scene (or rather, on the mass market, as many breweries are already producing them), and the establishment of a native wheat beer style to take its place alongside the Belgian and Bavarian in our affections. But bottled and yeasty, cloudy versions, please, not tinned and filtered. (And if you think the idea of a canned wheat beer is fanciful, take a peek under S for Somerfield.)

Porters have been fashionable for a while, but could be potentially even more so if breweries pursue the softer, chocolatey and coffeeish style that's been emerging in the past two years. This has taken porters even further from their sibling ale the Stout, by reducing their bitter, roasted barley and burnt flavours and upping the softly fruity, light, gently dry, mocha and coffee notes. **Dark Beers**, of the light-textured and dry-finished sort are in general due for renaissance, as we enjoy more German, Czech and Slovakian dark, soft and chocolatey bottled lagers.

Lagers made in the traditional way, with good wholesome ingredients, and cold-stored ('store' is after all what lager means) until properly matured and mellowed could easily become a new preoccupation of the British brewery scene as our experience of mainland Europe, both in a bottle and at first hand, increases in scale and complexity. The more delicious our imports grow, the less impressive our home-produced efforts look.

Real Lagers II: The emergence of a peculiarly British hybrid (though actually Americans are also making them) of lager and ale may point the way forward for British solutions to the delicious imports problem. These **Real Lager Ales** are already being made here, albeit in isolated pockets so far. Some of these use traditional lager ingredients, but are warm conditioned (ale style) and served with active yeasts at cellar temperature, with no added carbon dioxide. A cult following is developing.

Directions in **Wine Fashion** could also influence the kind of beers we want to drink. Presently, there's a move away from big, beefy New World richness and boldness, and towards a wine style that marries it with a European elegance, creating wines that are tasty and rounded, but also subtle, clean and light. Beer fashion is already following a similar course, as the huge impact of fresh but tasty wheat beers on the British buying public in the last 18 months has shown. The now well-established fashion for varietal-based wines, rather than those named simply after their estate or regional style, is also beginning to make its presence felt in our draught beer world: Whitbread were the biggest, but not the only, brewery to announce recently a range of 'single varietal' ales. Bottled beers which make much of their **Single Malt** content (including pale golden ales), or name their hop varieties prominently on the label will probably follow.

Seasonal Ales are now, as many a weary and over-stretched microbrewery has confirmed, becoming just about obligatory. Summer, autumn, winter and spring beers are also an ideal chance for breweries to try out new ideas, particularly of the single malt, double malt, or single hop variety sort. With any luck some of the national breweries will go on to introduce more interesting ales into their permanent range, inspired by the success of these beers. The larger regionals are beginning to show much more confidence, with Specials as well as Seasonals, taking their lead from the enterprising Marston Brewery and its Head Brewer's Choice initiative.

Sorry to be negative, but . . .

There are two trends in British beer that need a good kick in the shin. The first is the dreaded **Widget**, which can take the credit for transforming previously merely appalling canned ales into undrinkably repellent ones, with a shaving foamy, whipped-up into a frenzy, super-creamy texture that no longer tastes of beer at all. But these cans will soon be spot on in declaring they recreate the taste of real draught beer, as widget technology has led to 'mixed gas' kegging, and the launching of new products like John Smith's Extra Smooth.

The other trend is **Crude Name Syndrome**, the by no means mandatory but nonetheless horrifyingly common microbrewery habit of giving unspeakable names to their beers. It starts with fairly harmless public bar machismo, with names like Brewer's Droop, Willie Warmer and Son of a Bitch. It goes on to develop a Thrash Metal Tendency, of the Ninjabeer, Whistle Belly Vengeance, Nettlethrasher, Gothic and Ripsnorter sort. Then, able to resist its urges no longer, it goes straight for The Dog's Bollocks or, worst of all, 'Recked 'Em, a beer produced by Reckless Eric's Brewery. This 'sniggering tendency' presumably knows its loyal local market will continue to find ordering a pint of Rectum hilarious for years and years. Meanwhile the rest of us are running in the other direction. Not because we're prudish and blush in the presence of Anglo Saxon, but because it's crass and embarrassingly unfunny.

British Brewery of the Year

PICKING THE WORLD beer of the year would be an impossible task. There would be more than 15 winners, all in their own categories, like the Oscars. Homing in on the British breweries that are producing outstanding beers at the moment is a lot easier, particularly if the field is limited to bottled beers.

There are four outstanding breweries making complete ranges of bottled beer at present: Bateman, Caledonian, Marston and Sam Smith. In addition, there have been single bottles from other British breweries that have proved particularly memorable in the *Guide* tastings: King & Barnes Festive, Fullers ESB, Ushers IPA and Black Sheep Ale among them. Two excellent bottled beers are produced by Nethergate, of Suffolk: Old Growler and Old Nethergate Special Bitter, and Nethergate is hereby officially crowned the *World Beer Guide* Small British Brewery of the Year 1996. Some much-deserved recognition must also go to McMullen, of Hertfordshire, who currently brew the beers for Nethergate.

If there must be one overall winner in the competition, it has to be Caledonian Brewery, of Edinburgh, makers of Deuchars IPA, Golden Pale, Golden Promise, Merman, and 70/- and 80/-, among others. Individually, these are all superb beers. Lined up together, they create a range of bottled beers of unrivalled quality and versatility. What is especially cheering is that they're never afraid of flavour, in an industry that too often opts for toning down and flattening out its beers' characters. Good ingredients (suppliers fight hard to get the Caley contract) and a brewing technique that refuses to cut corners and costs shine through. Added to which, they're absolutely delicious beers, identifiably a range, but all individuals in their own right. The greatest testament to them is possibly this: that at the end of a gruelling day, to find one last unexpected bottle of something Caledonian at the back of the cupboard makes the spirits lift.

Caledonian Brewery: *World Beer Guide* British Brewery of the Year 1996

Glossary

... of beer styles, beer language, beer labels ...

Abbey/Abbaye
Generally a beer made in Abbey-style rather than Abbey-brewed. Can be a completely secular reference to the Trappist style, or else describes beers made under licence by a secular brewery

ABV/Alcohol by Volume
Literally the percentage of alcohol in the volume of liquid. Has more or less replaced the old O.G. (original gravity) beer strength system on bottles and tins

Adjuncts
Non-traditional fermentable cereals, sugars and other grocery ingredients used to bulk out a beer and make it cheaper. Non-malt sugars are adjuncts. So are other 'natural' ingredients like rice, flour, maize grits and torrefied wheat. Non-natural ingredients are called *Additives*

Ale
A sort of beer (*see also* **Lager**) which very broadly describes the **Top-Fermenting** brewing method, and takes in a huge range of British and international beers, of many colours, styles and flavours. Wrongly used in some areas of the USA to denote any beer of a strength over 5% abv

Altbier
German term for an **Ale**, a **Top-Fermenting** beer. It's an 'Old Beer' because it is made using the ancient brewing style, before lager-brewing was invented. Altbiers are associated with Düsseldorf, and classically get their mellow flavours from being **Top-Fermented** and cold-conditioned

Ambrée/Amber
Generally a fruity, malty, gently or robustly caramel-sweet, occasionally sour-oaky, top-fermenting beer with a characteristic copper-amber-orangey-brown colour

Attenuation
The degree to which yeast consumes the available sugars and turns them into alcohol (and carbon dioxide) is the 'degree of attenuation'

Barley Wine
A beer so strong in alcohol (perhaps 8% abv, or even 10 or 12) that it's felt to have toppled over into the wine-made-from-barley category, though it is actually still a conventionally brewed beer

Bayerische
Bavarian

Beechwood
Ancient Bavarian ingredient, or rather agent, of beer production, revived in the USA by Anheuser Busch, who mature their major brands (Budweiser, Michelob) over beechwood chips, both for flavour, and to aid in clarification of the beer. This process is not unknown in other breweries

Belgian Ale
Belgium, like Britain, still has a strong tradition of brewing by the old **Top-Fermenting** method (though Belgium also makes **Lagers**, and neighbouring Europeans also make **Ales**)

Bière Blonde, Bière Brune
Common French descriptions of the pale and brown beer styles

Bière d'Alsace
Now commonly refers to pale 5% abv lagers from the Strasbourg area of northern France, bordering Germany. Almost always from Fischer Breweries when spotted on ten-packs of little bottles

Bière de Garde
Beers 'for keeping', classically of a characteristically rusty-auburn hue and sour-sweet oak character, from the northern French brewing area. Traditionally they are strong, **Top-Fermented** and **Bottle-Conditioned**, though many modern examples are filtered, and some even **Bottom-Fermented**

Bière des Flandres
Beer from French Flanders. In Britain, seen mostly on the packaging of rather dull 5% abv pale lagers in dinky little bottles

Bitter
Traditionally, an English **Ale** with a pronounced hop character, though the term is also used to describe only mildly hoppy beers intended for 'session' drinking. Can be described as 'ordinary', to distinguish it from special bitter. Some European and American producers are now using the term 'bitter' for particularly hoppy **Lagers**

Bock/Bok
In German, a strong beer, classically of the **Bottom-Fermenting** (**Lager**) style, whether pale, red or dark. Outside Germany, often a dark beer, though it's also a term used with internationally made strong golden lagers affecting Germanic associations

Bohemian
Authentically, from that area of the Czech Republic which spawned the clear, golden **Bottom-Fermenting** Pilsener Lager style, but now a term widely used by a motley crew of breweries all over the world to imply allegiance to old Czech traditions

Bottle-Conditioned
Bottle-conditioning (aka bottle-fermentation) carries on the maturation of a beer by means of residual (or in some cases, added) yeasts and sugars. The living beer continues to develop flavour and alcohol (and carbon dioxide) in the bottle, and produces a sediment in the process

Bottom-Fermented
Beers are either bottom-fermented, or **Top-Fermented**, depending on whether the yeast sits on the bottom of the tank, or floats on top of the beer. Bottom-fermentation is the newer method, a cold brewing technique used to make the **Lager** family of beers

Brasserie
In French, a brewery (as well as a café-bar)

Brew Pub
Public houses that make their own beers. Originally they only made beer for themselves, but brew pubs are increasingly brewing for other outlets, too

Brewery Conditioned
Beers that have been filtered and pasteurized at the brewery, giving them stability and longevity; the opposite of Bottle- and cask-Conditioned beers, which live on and mature with the help of active yeasts

Brown Ale
Sweet, mildish, low in alcohol, dark brown in colour, *or* (specifically in the north east of England) a drier, stronger, orangier malty beer. The 'brune' beers of Flanders are sourer in character

Brussels Lace
The filmy, lacy residue left on the sides of a glass

Cerveza
Latin for beer

Cream Ale
A common label in America for a pale, creamy **Ale** that perhaps looks more like a **Lager**; occasionally the two are literally combined. Bland in texture and flavour in big brewery hands; more exciting and complex when made by the **Micros**

Decoction
An extremely thorough mashing system that removes part of the mash each time, heats and returns it. Triple decoction is its most rigorous form. Think of it as systematically squeezing all available tea flavour out of the tea bag

Diat Pils
A low-sugar beer, not intended for those on a low-calorie 'diet', because they are actually high in calorific alcohol (or were until they were reined back to average strength). For 'diat' read 'diabetic'

Doppelbock/Double Bock
As the translation suggests, even bockier than a regular **Bock** beer. Traditionally, made in a German springtime. Names of modern examples often end in -ator (Coronator, Jubilator, and so on). Elsewhere in the world, commonly used to mean 'it's awfully strong'

Dortmunder
Most literally, a beer made in Dortmund, but used internationally to describe a beer in the style of the traditional Dortmund product, the Export, a strongish, full-bodied **Lager**

Draught Canned Beer
Either contains a nitrogen-bearing **Widget** at the bottom of the can, foaming up the beer as it is poured *or* involves the (less gassy) Nitrogen Flush system, in which the beer is just packed with the gas in suspension *or* the beer is passed through an assault course of plastic openings to increase aeration as it emerges from the tin

Dry Beer
Started out as a bland Japanese super-diat pils, was adopted (and further neutered) by the American market, and has now become a global marketing tag-line. Typically, little up-front flavour, and a curiously tongue-drying texture. Marketed on the basis that it's super-clean and has ridded itself of the burden of the 'bitter aftertaste'

Dry-Hopping
Adding hops to the cask. Gives a distinctive aroma, texture and flavour to the beer. Late Copper Hopping (or dry hopping at other points in the brewing process following the 'hop boil') is often also done

Dunkel
German for 'dark'

Eisbock
Literally, an Ice-Bock beer, made by applying the **Ice Beer** technique

Ester
Unpredictable byproduct of fermentation, creating fruity, heady, winey and other (unpredictable) flavours and aromas

Filtered
Most bottled, and all canned beers are filtered and pasteurized before being packaged, to increase stability and shelf life. The degree of filtering and pasteurization varies widely: some bottled beers are only lightly filtered, so that some life and natural sparkle remains. Those which are unfiltered and unpasteurized will go on to some form of **Bottle-Conditioning** (or in the case of draught beers, cask conditioning)

Frambozen/Framboise
Raspberry beer, traditionally, but not necessarily, created from a **Lambic** base. Belgian in origin

Gueuze
The name for a blend of young and old **Lambics**

Harvest Ales
Bottled beers (though some breweries also produce them on draught) made once a year, in the autumn, using that season's new malt, hops and other materials.

Haute Fermentation
French for **Top-Fermentation**

Hefe
German for 'yeast', denoting that an active yeast sediment remains, and that the beer is **Bottle Conditioned**. Most prominently seen on wheat beer labels of the Hefeweissbier or Hefeweizen sort. 'Hefetrub' means yeast sedimented

Hell/Helles
Pale, in German, and in the café-bar used to mean a quaffing lager. Often used to differentiate it when a sibling brand of similar name and label is a **Dunkel**

Herb
German for dry

Hock
Revived name for a **Mild**

Ice Beer
Modern process in which the beer is chilled to the point at which the water in it turns to ice and can be removed, so concentrating the alcohol levels (and, according to the advertising, also the flavour)

IPA/India Pale Ale
Historic beer style developed for the better transporting of beer to thirsty British officials of Empire. Masses of hops were used, and alcohol levels were high, to preserve the IPA en route. Today, also misused to describe standard **Bitters**

Kräusened
('kroy-sunnd') Traditional German technique in which a little wort is added to the beer at maturation stage. The wort (the malt-sugar water with which all brewing starts) works with yeasts in the beer, creating natural carbonation

Kriek
A cherry beer (Kriek is Flemish for cherry), traditionally but not necessarily made with a **Lambic** base. Belgian in origin

Krystall/Kristallklar
In German a filtered ('crystal-clear') version of a traditionally sedimented **Hefe** beer, a process which can leave previously opaque wheat beers looking like particularly golden lagers. Increasingly fashionable in mainland Europe

Kruidenbier
Belgian (Flemish) for a herb-spiced beer

Lager
Mostly British term for **Bottom-Fermenting** beers, usually restricting itself to the pale or golden type. In mainland Europe it's sometimes used to denote a table beer of no great ambition, and is increasingly used everywhere on the labels of beers intended for export. As, incidentally, is **Beer**, for the benefit of Americans (who use 'beer' and 'lager' interchangeably, as we do 'beer' and 'ale')

Lambic
Wheat beer traditionally brewed using only spontaneous fermentation from an area close to Brussels. Straight, newly made lambics can be almost undrinkably sour, and are blended with older, mellower ones to make **Gueuze**. Also the traditional base for **Krieks**.

Light Ale
Traditional name for bottled **Bitter**. Now increasingly used to indicate a mild-mannered bottled or canned product. In Scotland, the weakest of a brewery's bitter range (aka 60/-)

Lite Beer
In America, traditionally a low(ish) alcohol, bland pale **lager**, but it's a term that might also be used to describe the high **Adjunct** lagers of whatever strength, thin and light in texture thanks to low malt content, that are so popular in the United States (and around the world)

Low Alcohol
Low alcohol (or L.A.) beers are usually dreadfully tasteless (or even positively nasty) purpose-made weak lagers of between 0.05–2.5% abv. At 0.05% or lower, they are considered to be alcohol-free. The best-tasting beers are those that successfully use technology to remove the bulk of the alcohol from an otherwise tasty, premium lager (most notably Clausthaler, from Frankfurt). Arrested fermentation methods are more popular in Britain – the beer is brewed only until it reaches the prescribed alcohol level, and then the process is halted

Malt/All Malt
Beers described as all-malt or pure malt brews have derived all their fermentable sugars from malted grain (All Barley Malt, in appropriate cases) and not from sugars or other **Adjuncts**

Malt Liquor
American term for a strong lager, usually the strongest beer in the brewery range, whatever its malt (or indeed hop) character. Being high in alcohol is usually its main point

Microbrewery
Small brewery

Mild
Traditional draught ale, occasionally bottled/canned, relatively low in alcohol (3.5% abv is typical), and characteristically dark and malty in character, though paler, fruitier milds, and even mildly hoppy ones also exist

Munich Style/Münchener
Traditionally, a Munich lager has meant a dark (dunkel) lager, but the term is also used to describe the typically soft and malty pale Bavarian lager style, often described as Münchener **Hell**

Natural
Becoming more widely used on labels, but the lack of artificial additives, preservatives and the like is no guarantee of quality. 'Natural' also embraces

Adjuncts of the corn, rice grits and torrefied wheat sort (among other ingredients)

Oatmeal/Oat Malt
A traditional Scots style now enjoying a mini-revival. Or rather two styles: the first using pinhead oatmeal, the second malted oat grain

Obergärig
German for top-fermenting

Organic
Beers accredited by the Soil Association (or their international equivalents) as being made with organically grown grain and hops

Original Gravity
The old system of expressing alcoholic strength of beers, which is now being replaced on labels by **Alcohol by Volume** percentages. Works on the basis that water has a gravity of 1000 degrees; an O.G. of 1045, say, has been achieved by adding 45 parts of fermentable material (malt sugars or otherwise)

Pale Ale
Pale compared to a standard brown **Bitter**, that is. Classically, rather orange coloured, thanks to the kind of malt used

Pasteurized
see **Filtered**

Pilsener/Pilsner/Pils
Much abused term which can be found on the labels of all manner of **Lager** beers, but should properly be restricted to medium-bodied, well-made and tasty lagers with a characteristically dry, perhaps floral, hay-like or herbal character, particularly in aroma and finish

Porter
Originated in London as a lighter, less black and bitter stablemate to stout. Modern versions are growing even more coffeeish, fruity and refreshing. Porters (and stouts, though stout is a word rarely used abroad) from other nations can be **Bottom-Fermented** and are frequently higher in alcohol

Premium
Brewing hyperbole which appears to have originated in Germany, but has spread across the world like a rash. No guarantee of anything at all

Pure Beer Law
see **Reinheitsgebot**

Rauchbier
In German 'smoke beer', which gets its distinctive flavour and texture from the use of smoked malts

Reinheitsgebot
The splendidly exclusive Bavarian pure beer law, established 1516, and still upheld there, despite the decision of the European Court that Germany had no right to ban imports on an 'impurity' basis. The rest of Germany doesn't routinely apply it to exports either, but Bavaria still insists that beers be made from hops, malt, yeast and water only

Saison
Summer refresher, traditionally medium strong and prepared in the spring, made in the French-speaking area of Belgium

Scotch
Traditionally, a super-smooth, highly alcoholic, deeply malty, pond-dark beer, though a modern Scotch might just as easily be merely moderately strong, soft and fruit-oaky malty. But malty

Stark
German for strong

Steam Beer
Both a unique style and a company trademark, reserved for use by the Anchor Steam brewery of San Francisco. They use lager yeast at ale temperatures in unusually shallow vessels

Stock Ale
Like **Bière de Garde**, a beer to put by, to keep, to store. Originally a term used in Britain for ales made in spring, to put by for summer drinking. Now being revived by American **Microbreweries**

Stout
Chocolate-black, densely textured, but refreshingly dry, (usually) **Top-Fermented** beer, typically of around only 4% ABV. Dark, chocolate and black malts, together with generous hopping, are the secret of its flavour and body. English sweet stouts are propelled by lactose (milk sugars)

Top-Fermented
The most ancient of beer styles, in which the yeast settles on top of the warm infant beer in a great duvet-like crust. Beers made in this way are technically **Ales**, and develop a fruity character through warm fermentation and conditioning

Trappist
A beer label only permitted on the fine bottled products of just six monastic breweries, five of them Belgian and one Dutch. Strong, **Top-Fermenting,** complex, **Bottle-Conditioned Ales**

Triple/Tripel
Dutch term, widely used in the Netherlands and Belgium to denote the strongest beer of a brewery range, but especially an **Abbey/Trappist** one. Unlike the Dubbel/Double, usually quite pale in colour.

Vienna Style
A particular staging post in the kilning process produces an orangey-red malt with its own character, once considered exclusive to the **Lagers** produced in Vienna. Now pops up all over the place, but rarely in Vienna itself

Weiss/Weizen/Wit/Blanche
Wheat beers, often also referred to as White Beers, probably because of the pale milky translucency created by the suspension of tiny bits of wheat protein in the unfiltered versions. A speciality of both Germany and Belgium

Widget
see Draught Canned Beer

How Beer is Made

THIS IS ALL THE BUSY home-brewer needs to know. The basic recipe is as follows: crush up some barley malt and make into an infusion with hot water. Strain off, boil up with hops and strain off again; add the yeast and leave to ferment. Use top-fermenting yeast for ales, and at a temperature of about 20°C; bottom-fermenting for lagers, brewing at 5–10°C, and maturing in conditions cold as an Alpine cave . . . say three months at 0°C. It might be better to stick with ales, in which case leave for about a week. Separate from most of the yeast, and leave to mature. Sounds simple? Then I've misled you. For a truer picture of this extraordinarily complex process, and its equally complex ingredients, read on.

First take some barley. Let it germinate, or sprout, by moistening and warming it, before putting an end to its ambition by tipping it into a kiln to cook. Gently now, for a nice pilsener malt of palest hue. A higher temperature for a British pale malt, the basis of British ale brewing. Take it further and to a higher temperature to bring a strong amber-red blush to the Vienna malt style; further still for the brownish malt often still described as Munich style. A moist kilning produces 'crystals' and a ripe, perhaps buttery fullness we recognize as crystal malt. And there are other staging posts along the way. For chocolate and burnt black malts turn the temperature dial yet higher. These have been kilned to the point where there's little fermentable sugar left, so this must be compensated for elsewhere. Every beer recipe has its own signature combination of pale and 'coloured' malts, though there's presently a trend for 100% pale malt in British ale brewing. Some recipes also contain roasted barley, which means unmalted barley grains, roasted like coffee, and often tasting coffeeish too.

The malt is then coarsely crushed and pounded in a mill, and the resulting 'grist' put into a vat called a mash tun. It's also fairly common to add non-malted adjuncts at this point, most commonly corn or rice. Now the process becomes rather like making a good pot of fine leaf tea. Hot water (the liquor) is added, and left to infuse. Next, the water is let out of the sieve-like base of the tun. The liquor, now containing dissolved malt sugars, is called wort. More tea is squeezed out of the pot, by giving the remaining sludgy porridge another blast of hot water. If this is a delicate pale lager, dependent on malt character for much of its flavour and body, there might be a spot of triple decoction at this point: this is the process which removes part of the mash at a time, heating and thrashing the sugars out of it.

Now hops are added to the wort, in a copper or kettle, and brought to a rolling boil, typically for an hour or two. Not all the hops need be put in at once; some may be added shortly after, or kept to the very end. If sugar is to be used, it's probably added now. Once the hops are strained off, the wort is ready for the fermenting vessel, where (other than in the case of Belgian lambic beers, which are made with airborne yeasts) the yeast is added. This is the moment when ales and lagers fundamentally diverge.

A note about ales and lagers

Ale and lager are the common terms used to divide the whole world of beer into two camps. They're misleading, because they're just easier ways of saying top-fermenting and bottom-fermenting, which is how the world's beers really divide. Top-fermenting takes in ale, but also a whole load of other beers, such as wheat beers, that might not be obvious members of the ale fraternity. None the less, ale is the word we use. Bottom-fermenting beers are even more badly served by the catch-all term lager. This group includes the obvious lager-beers of the world, but it also embraces more unusual and complex ones. Some of the more interesting foreign stouts and porters are made by the bottom-fermenting ('lager') method, for instance. So the ale and lager polarity is a lot more convenient than it is appropriate. It is also very slightly complicated by ales that are cold-conditioned for mellow flavours (like Germany's Altbier), and more seriously complicated by irreverent Americans who do things like brewing with lager yeasts at ale temperatures (like the makers of Anchor Steam Beer). But this is how the two types of beer fundamentally divide:

Lager yeast is bottom-fermenting, and lagers are cold-fermented. Bottom-fermenting because the yeast settles at the bottom of the vessel, where it works slowly and thoroughly on the cold beer. Such yeasts attenuate much further than ale yeasts, and so create clean, crisp drinks. After fermentation, the beer is run off from most of its yeast and stored (store is what lager means) for anything between three weeks and three months. Three months is the classic maturation period for cold conditioning.

Ale yeast is top fermenting, and ales are warm-fermented. Top-fermenting because the ale yeast sits on top of the beer in a thick, crusty duvet, reacting with the warm air and gobbling whatever sugars it can find in the liquid below, turning them into alcohol and releasing carbon dioxide gas. The days pass: traditionally these include a Sunday, so the beer can be blessed by the Sabbath. Eventually, the yeast eats itself to death, and sinks to the bottom of the vessel. Or, more accurately, some is skimmed off, some sinks away.

The fresh 'green' ale is now left to mature, mellowing and refining its flavours. Finings (a fish byproduct) collects the superfluous yeast and sinks it. During conditioning, extra sugar may be added, to stimulate a 'secondary fermentation' in the cask or bottle; caramel is also commonly used for flavour and colour. 'Dry-hopping', which is simply the adding of fresh hops to the conditioning beer, adds its own vivid, fresh aromas and flavours. Fermentation and maturation in wood (and particularly oak) during brewing also make a huge impact on the flavour.

If all this takes place in a traditional tower brewery, there is also the great satisfaction of seeing the malt go in at the top, and the finished beer roll out at the bottom.

Real ale

Real Ale is beer that contains living, active yeast, and so goes on maturing in the pub cellar, where skilful cellarmanship brings it, through judicious contact with the air, to the peak of drinking perfection, before it is hand-pumped, or in some cases electric pumped to the bar. Alternatively, the barrel is brought upstairs, and the beer drawn direct from the tap, by gravity dispense. In Scotland, fermenting traditionally takes place at a lower temperature, and the cask is likely to be connected to an air pressure system leading to the tall fount on the bar.

Keg, canned and bottled

Keg beer is filtered and pasteurized before being pumped into airtight kegs with added gas, traditionally carbon dioxide, though 'mixed gas' (meaning carbon dioxide and nitrogen) is becoming increasingly common. Keg beer contains no active yeast, and has been processed for a long life. Most bottled beers are strictly speaking 'keg beers', though some are still unpasteurized. Premium (well-made) bottled beers often get the chance to mature longer than keg beer; if they are also only lightly filtered, and remain unpasteurized, they are obviously going to be of much higher quality (and much nicer to drink) than their canned equivalents. All canned beer is keg beer.

Bottle-conditioned beers contain (to varying degrees) residual or added yeasts and sugars, like a draught real ale. Sometimes a different yeast is added. It's not unknown, (in fact it's very common) for a bottle-conditioned beer to have been first pasteurized and filtered for safe handling before being reseeded with yeast and sugar during the bottling process. This might even involve a bottom-fermenting yeast being used to condition a top-fermented ale. It will sit politely at the bottom of the bottle.

Ingredients

A brewery's house style, and the character of its individual beers is not (usually) achieved by accident. It's done by arriving – through experimentation and instinct – at a point at which the sweetness of the barley malt, the richer character of darker malts and raw roasted grain, the sweet and savoury character of unmalted cereals, the herbal, floral, dry and bittering qualities of the hops, and rich fruits and acids of the yeast are all in the desired balance and proportion.

But it's not simply a matter of having the right basic components and technique. Ask any brewer who has tried to mimic the beer style of another country, or even of the next town. There are mysterious and elusive factors at work, ineffable forces similar to those that make a west coast malt whisky taste pungently of the peaty landscape, the briny Atlantic, the very heather-filled air. It may be the brewery water, perhaps the ancient mash tuns and coppers, fermenting and maturation vessels. Less elusively (but not completely – brewing is an art, as well as a science) it's also down to the exact ingredients.

Barley is beer-making's grape, in so far as it is the ideal source of fermentable sugar for brewing. Like the grape, barley has a natural sweetness. Like the grape, barley is as various as the soil and weather, and varies enormously from state to state, county to county: Maritime and Continental barley are barely the same grain. In general, ale makers favour winter barley, lager makers favour spring barley. In Britain, Halcyon (barley variety) malt is commonly used, though the once ubiquitous Maris Otter, which fell out of favour for many years, is now making a comeback in England, as is Golden Promise (to a lesser extent) in Scotland. These premium, traditional brewing barleys are now being appreciated and revived by a new generation that favours quality over cost.

Malt was originally produced using the floor-malted method: spreading the grain thinly over a huge great floor, and turning it repeatedly to ensure it was properly aired. Floor Malted Barley still has status in the industry, because it's intensive, time- and space-consuming – and, perhaps, produces a superior product? – but modern malting is increasingly done in an aerated vat or rotating drum. Modern kilning uses hot air, whereas in the old days malts were made over an open fire. This is still done in some parts of the world, notably Franconia in Germany, and you can taste the smoke in the Rauchbiers of that region. In Britain, some porter and stout makers are reviving the use of old-fashioned Brown Malts, and recreating the (thin but distinctive) texture and flavour of a beer made with the 'brown-roasted' malt as used in the days before the present high-temperature roasting technique was developed. It is a feature of stouts and porters particularly that they use both malted and raw-roasted barley. Most other ale styles use pale malt, together with varying percentages of crystal malt, and perhaps also some chocolate and black malt. But rich flavours can be produced by using pale malt alone: many breweries around the world set out to caramelize the malt by leaving it on an extended boil with the hops. At least one strong old English ale is made this way. Malt sugars are also responsible for the body and texture of a beer, as well as its flavour. If a yeast isn't allowed to attenuate very far, the remaining malt sugars will create body and flavour, even at low alcohol levels. This is typical of the better dark milds, many traditional Scots malt ales, and of beers like Guinness.

Wheat is a noble ingredient in many European beer styles, most obviously wheat beer itself. Unmalted wheat grain is used in Belgian wheat beers, but is not permitted in German ones, where the *Reinheitsgebot* allows only malted cereals. Wheat is also much (and increasingly) used both malted and unmalted in Britain and across the world, in all sorts of other beer styles. It's not a short cut or an easy option, because wheat is difficult to work with, unlike barley, which, with its detachable husk that falls and forms a natural filter in the vessel, seems almost designed for brewing. Wheat, however, brings a distinctive light creaminess to beers, principally because it forms tiny particles which remain in suspension. Flavours can be bready and yeasty, straightforwardly cereal-wheaten, appley, even citrussy. Torrefied wheat is a different matter (*see* Adjuncts, below). Oats and, to an even lesser extent, rye, are also used in brewing. Like wheat, they have a tendency to swell and clog and mush, but unlike wheat, only a tiny amount is needed to make an enormous impact in flavour. Hence they are usually restricted to speciality beers.

Adjuncts of an unmalted sort provide cheap bulking-out of beer body (malting is an expensive process), and a cheap source of sugars. Rice and corn are the most traditional 'all natural' adjuncts added, and the rice-and-corn approach has its world headquarters in the USA. Corn is used all over the world, to great excess in some quarters, and it makes its presence all too plain in all too many cheaply made, thin yellow lagers. Corn is also used in ale brewing, usually in the recipes of the big breweries producing national keg and canned beers. McEwans beers from Scotland get their sweet, thin texture this way.

It's less easy to be dogmatically damning of sugar in brewing, as many fine beers in Britain and across the world are made with it. It's a question of degree, and appropriateness; fundamentally, it's down to whether the use of sugar has been part of creating a great beer, or whether it has just been part of making a cheap and easy one. Sugar, in its various guises, is a direct and simple source of food for the yeast, and in many ways the most useful and tempting of all adjuncts. Why bother malting barley (or paying for it) when you can just open the sugar bag? But sugar is a crude substance, and can make crude beers unless used with flair. Ordinary sugar is sometimes used, but more often it's added in liquid or syrup form, or toasted, as the orangey-coloured caramel (though don't assume all orange beers contain it, or that all caramel flavours derive from it – they don't). Belgian trappist ales use candy sugar, which can give them a rum flavour. American and Australian brewers frequently add cane sugar. Cheaply made, mass market beers might be 40% non-malt, or more.

If you set out to make a sweet beer, the yeasts must be demobilized at some point to stop them eating all the available sugars, though yeasts, like other organisms, can eat themselves silly and be overwhelmed by their own alcohol. Hence sweet, bottled beers are pasteurized to preserve the sugars intact. (Lactose is a milk sugar that's not fermentable, and its use gave milk and cream stouts their great wave of popularity.) If yeasts were allowed to ferment out all the available sugars, the resulting beer would be high in alcohol, harsh and very thin-textured.

Torrefied wheat is made by heating wheat grains until they swell like popcorn. It's added mostly to aid head retention (or so they say).

Hops are elusive and fragile in character, but are not only useful for their floral, herbal aroma, dry, bittering flavour, and oily, resiny texture. They are also excellent natural preservatives, and help clarify beer. It's the hop 'flowers' (or blossoms) that are used, decorative little fruits whose shoots are still eaten by some as a side vegetable. Despite frequent references in this guide to the use of 'fresh hops', the whole hop blossoms are in fact routinely dried before being sacked up and sent to breweries, though there are occasionally instances of beers made with 'green', that is undried, hops direct from the autumn harvest. There are also breweries which use hops primarily for their preservative qualities, and intend only the subtlest hop character to get into their beers – lambic beers, for instance, which are yeast-led in flavour and texture. In these cases, mature whole hops are used. Hops are mortal, and quickly lose their magic. 'Whole' and 'fresh' are used to distinguish merely dried hops from the more modern, pelletized (cleaned-up, compressed and vacuum-packed) sort. Some breweries go further and use hop extract, an even more factory-friendly, whole-hop derivative.

There are upwards of a dozen hop varieties on the international best-seller list, with many more growing or in development in particular niches of the world. A beer might have just one hop variety in it, but it's more common to use two or three, or in some instances even six or seven, in as many 'additions' (at as many stages of boiling and brewing) as desired. Some are particularly prized for aroma, some for flavour; some for their bitter dryness, some for their generous resins. East Kent Fuggles and Worcester Goldings are the classic British combination; Kent and Worcester are the sites of the two great hop gardens of England. Challenger is now challenging this supremacy, along with Northern Brewer, Northdown, Progress and Target, and, increasingly, Bramling Cross, an old variety now enjoying a great revival for its distinctively lemony fruitiness. Saaz is the Czech classic, and is proudly listed on the front of many a modern non-Czech lager can; it's true that Saaz can add a dash of authentic pilsener class even to otherwise mediocre beers. Its German equivalent is Hallertau Mittelfrüh. Other German perennials include Hersbruck and Tetnang; Perle is a more modern, robustly bitter variety. Brewers Gold and Record (a Northern Brewer/Saaz hybrid) are also commonly used in Belgium. America is fast developing a great hop reputation, with varieties like Willamette and Mounthood cropping up more and more in British lists, and a whole new generation on the horizon, thanks to the demands of the American microbrewery revolution. Cluster and Cascade are otherwise the Fuggles and Goldings of America, and similarly, prized for bitterness and aroma respectively (though even an 'aroma hop' brings its own flavour and texture to bear in a beer). Australia is still dominated by Pride of Ringwood, but its ubiquitousness is ripe for challenge.

Yeast is often the forgotten ingredient in brewing. Not forgotten by the brewery, but by the keen beer-taster. Yet yeast is vital – not just yeast in general, but the particular, individual strain of yeast the head brewer keeps, at optimum temperature, under closely guarded lock and key. It's common for breweries to keep the seed culture at a professional laboratory, which will mail a bit for the brewers to culture up on site should anything tragic befall the current batch. As well they might, because the brewery's whole house style depends on the flavour and character, the rich, fragrant fruit, the clean acidity, the ripe, fat texture, the generous 'bloom' their very own yeast imparts. Some old breweries are still using the descendants of the original yeasts their great-great granddaddy brewer used.

Originally, of course, all yeasts were of the top-fermenting sort, and it was an ale yeast that first obligingly sank to the bottom of the vessel when beers were transferred to Bavarian Alpine caves in the beer-spoiling humidity of summer. Specialist lager yeasts better suited to the job have been purpose-bred since. Bottom-fermenting (lager) yeasts are terrifically stable, predictable yeasts, keen to conform and do the right thing, and the beers they make can too easily reflect this. Top-fermenters are more wilful; potentially mavericks, and like all mavericks, often much more alluring characters.

Water Water, or rather liquor, as practitioners always call it, is not a blank canvas in brewing. Water brings its own character, its own flavours, aromas and textures. Brewers like to have their own water source, be it an old well, a mountain spring, whatever, and can be almost as paranoid about their liquor as they are about their yeast. If breweries use tap water, it's frequently treated to make it less disgusting first. Or a brewery will add salts of various sorts to mimic the brewing liquor of another place. Most often this place is Burton-upon-Trent, whose mineral-rich water made it the brewing capital of Britain and, at the time of Empire, the world. The gypsum salts in Burton water are especially flattering to a pale, hoppy beer style still called India Pale Ale. The chloride-rich water of London, on the other hand, which is suitable for brown ale but not for IPA, was the main reason London was prevented from stealing Burton's thunder.

How to Taste Beer

The glass

In Belgium there's a glass for every beer. Not just every kind of beer, but every *brand* of beer. Such shenanigans needn't detain us here, though basic glass sense dictates that tall champagne flute type glasses are better than a pint mug for a Kriek. Actually most glasses you can think of flatter a decent beer more than a pint mug does. The standard tasting glass shape is a generous, rounded bowl with, ideally, a slight tapering-in top, to concentrate the flavours and aromas. It should be of generous proportions, to facilitate lots of enthusiastic swirling without getting the beer on the carpet, and have enough room for you to thrust your snout in and breathe deeply without choking half to death.

Good looks and aromas

It's pretty common for a bottled beer to release a slightly unpleasant odour when first opened. Give it a minute and the benefit of the doubt. Don't assume the beer should be sparkling clear. It might be of a brewing style that requires it not to sparkle; it might be of a brewing style that is happy to be cloudy, bottled with residual yeast, and/or tiny bits of wheat protein or another grain in suspension. But it *should* be appetizing, whatever its denomination. It should aspire to at least a modicum of vitality and life. Ditto the aromas (the 'nose'), which should inspire appetite. Swirl the glass about gently, get your nose in there and inhale.

Tasting

Nose, Front, Middle, Finish, Aftertaste.

Some beers, especially canned ones, taste exactly the same all the way through. The flavour you get when the beer first hits your tongue is the same as the one you get 'in the middle' of the sip, and in the 'finish'. In the case of many cheaply made beers it's likely that the flavour, such as it is, will die away completely by the time the finish should have arrived, and that the 'aftertaste' will be slightly unpleasant. There may be warnings of cheap ingredients on the nose, typically followed by a watery, grain husky flavour with acrid notes appearing in the finish and aftertaste, or a sweet, cloying and caramelly follow-through in the case of cheap ales padded out with sugar.

The nose should hold the promise of good flavours to come, but can also transmit early warning signals.

Structure is vital to a successful beer, and one that shows a pleasing development through all five sections of the tasting process can rightly be honoured as complex. Complexity is vital to the satisfaction rating of a fine beer; even apparently simple, clean-edged lagers can have a degree of development in their taste structure (at the better end of the market at least) albeit incredibly subtle in tone. Typically, a complex beer will have not just various strands of flavour chiming in all at once, like a musical chord, but flavours that are introduced at one point of the tasting process and then recede. Classically, these appear either in the finish (as the beer goes down), or late in the middle (also known as 'the back'). A fruity-nosed ale may offer a good but orthodox balance of malt and hop flavours at the front, intensify these but introduce a new, sharper note in the middle, go on to flower dramatically into a fat, yeasty, fruity fullness in the back (as the nose had predicted), before restating the hop and malt balance in the finish and aftertaste.

Some beers come up with surprising new flavours that were not predicted in anything that's come before, and just occasionally produce something really wild and wacky; a white rabbit from a hat. There's at least one lager with a fairly conventional front and middle, but then the clearest, most unobscured apricot juice note in the finish. This kind of experience is what makes tasting new beers for the first time so full of suspense.

When tasting, only give the mouthful a little bit more probing attention than you would when drinking. Working it too much with your tongue, and flattening the beer against the roof of your mouth, will only serve to accentuate bitterness, and will bring out the adjunct flavours in a cheaply made beer even more than usual. Temperature is important, too. Ales tasted when too cold will keep all their potential complexity well under wraps.

It's not just flavours and aromas the taster seeks. The texture of a beer is just as important to its success. Too thin and watery, and good flavours run away too fast; too rich and cloying in the mouth, and good flavours can grow sickly and outstay their welcome. Beer writers often refer to 'good mouthfeel' or 'malt in the mouth'. Some beer styles are intended to be super-clean and refreshing, but most aim to provide a malty body to their beers to some degree, with body-making malt sugars designed to survive the rapacious yeasts. Many good examples of pale beer styles manage to be both clean-edged and satisfying, retaining just enough pale 'textured' malt – described as textured because it provides not just flavour, but a creaminess of texture, perhaps even a slightly (pleasantly!) tongue-furring quality. Dark beers might have malts on their team so highly roasted that very little fermentable sugar remains, and so a dark, rich malt body results. Many dark beers of potentially overwhelming flavour are redeemed and reined in with a controlling, firm dryness, that cleans up the finish with prickling, bitter hop flavours. A slightly sparkling, lively texture cleans up chocolatey dark lagers. Potentially over-sweet, rich and buttery amber beers, packed with lots of luscious crystal malt, are tempered by drier pale ale and robust hop flavours. The super-clean, smooth and mellow, but still oddly textured 'mouthfeel' of the ice beer (even seeming, occasionally, like a very fine sieved puree) provides its distinctive structure.

Judging beers

The most important question to ask of a beer is 'Do I like this, and do I want some more?' There's precious little point ploughing on with a beer you just don't like, no matter how great its international status. But it's also important to attempt a little objectivity, and separate out the question 'Do I like this?' from the quite independent question, 'Does this beer achieve what it set out to do – is it good at being what it wants to be?' It might seem like an obvious point, but all the various world beer styles have equal rights to occupy a bottle; it's not just a case of good British ales, good European pilseners, plus a host of eccentric others. The smoke beer tastes a bit like a processed smoked cheese on purpose; the wheat beer's palate is supposed to feature apples and cloves; the stout's burnt currant notes are true to its style; the dark Trappist ale is meant to be so densely opaque and sherryish. You may not like it much, but the head brewer is very happy.

The Flavour Wheel

... from fresh mown hay to TCP ...

There are really too many aspects of flavour development in beer tasting to express as slices of a conventional pie chart. Instead, here's a plain Flavour List, in which the main categories of beer flavour – dryness, sweetness and so on – are listed, followed by the more common nuances of flavour that lead from them. It's one of the particular joys of beer tasting that there is no one experience of dryness, sweetness, or anything else for that matter. Complex ingredients and brewing methods lead to complex flavours, and, as in wine tasting, each individual's tastebuds read them differently. Pinning down the flavours is half the fun.

Beers still made under one of the surviving national pure beer laws, most famously the German *Reinheitsgebot* of 1516, are made from just the four classic ingredients: hops, malt, yeast and water. However, this apparently simple recipe results in not four flavours but *hundreds*. The four ingredients are themselves elaborately various: hop varieties differ enormously in character, and the use of pellets, oils and extracts brings yet more variation. Fresh (or rather, freshly dried) whole hop flowers can produce a wonderfully perfumed, floral quality. Malted barley isn't one product either: its flavours and textures depend on the extent of the malting, and the point at which it is halted, resulting in anything from the palest white malt to the darkest chocolate and burnt black sort. And other grains – notably wheat, but also oats, rye and other cereals – can be malted for brewing too, as well as added in an unmalted state for a quite different effect. The corn added to a beer brings its own unmistakeable character to bear – not usually flatteringly.

It's not generally appreciated that the type and individual strain of yeast used in brewing is also a vital flavour factor. Breweries fiercely protect their yeast because its unique characteristics are vital to the continuation of their particular house style. Two beers brewed to be identical but using different yeasts will taste completely different. The exact character of the water used is also of enormous importance to the general flavour and texture of the range.

Nor does it end there. Alcohol, produced when yeasts consume the malt or other sugars, can be experienced as a flavour in its own right, especially in strong beers. When yeasts stop producing alcohol and instead release esters, heady fruity, acidic, even wine-like flavours can be created. Other ingredients, some of them traditional – like added sugars of one sort or another, or caramel (though caramel flavours can also be a naturally produced effect) – some of them not so traditional, all make their impact too. As of course does the brewing technique, the equipment used, the conditioning and handling of the finished beer, and what happens to it after it leaves the brewery but before you raise the glass to your lips.

Beers can taste of many things, some of them very surprising. But they can also taste absolutely simple (hoppy! malty! yeasty!), and at their very best and most inspiring, both the complex and the simple are of equal value.

This list is by no means definitive. It's a starting point. There are many crossing-over points between categories – nut flavours are as commonly dry in texture as they are sweet, for instance – but if they have to be divided up somehow, this is one way.

The Flavour List

Dryness

Dryness is a classic feature of well-hopped beers, but it is also created and enhanced by some malts. And some yeasts. Dryness might be straightforwardly astringent or bitter, or of the mouthpuckering, rasping sort. It might be both a texture and a flavour, perhaps salty or even briney; fragrant, perfumey, floral or drily acidic, like a fino sherry. Some beers have a geraniol quality. They might also taste surprisingly sappy, grassy, leafy, fresh mown or dried hay-like, herbal, piney, oily, resiny, even heathery. Their dryness could be earthy, peaty, woody in general or oaky in particular (oak-matured, perhaps?), have beechwood, tobacco or musky herbal notes. Or be tannic, medicinal, aspirin-like, flinty, minerally, quininey, (pleasantly, gently) sulphury. Perhaps drily savoury, sometimes identified as rind of Brie!

Sweetness

Sweetness in beer has many sources and its flavour takes many forms. Malts, added sugar (and other adjuncts) and yeast action all create sweet flavours. Fruit sweetness is dealt with in 'Fruit Flavours', below. Sweetness might otherwise be a ripe grain quality (barley is the sweetest grain of all), or take a subtle or pronouncedly nutty form, perhaps as hazelnut, cobnut, chestnut, walnut, almond or brazil. Sweetness might create impressions of vanilla, egg, toffee and butter, cream, custard, and malty biscuit flavours. More directly, it might taste of sherbet, fondant, boiled sweets, pineapple chunks, pear drops, Jelly Babies, pastilles, or the perfumey sweetness of Parma Violets. Or marshmallow. Or popcorn. There might be a straightforwardly sugar flavour (by no means necessarily indicating it's been added) of cane sugar, white, demerara or muscovado; golden syrup, butterscotch, caramel, Irn Bru, or sweet stewed tea.

Sourness

In moderation, the sourness created by yeast activity can be a positive factor in beer flavour – an aspect of freshness, a welcome soft tang, or a slight edge on a fruity flavour. Vinegariness is an off flavour, but positive sour flavours are usually merely tart, slightly sharp, perhaps slightly underripe and green, or plain citrussy and acidic. Sour boiled sweet flavours, and sour green apple, lead into:

Fruit Flavours

The fruitiness might be there because cherry, raspberry or peach juice has been added, in the case of certain (mostly Belgian) specialities. But it is also a quality characteristic of (but by no means mandatory in, or exclusive to) top-fermenting, warm-conditioned ale styles. All sorts of surprising fruit flavours turn up in beer, including green apple, red apple, cooked apple, cox apple, orange, tangerine, kumquat, grapefruit, marmalade, pomegranate, pear, lime, lemon, melon, apricot, peach, nectarine, ripe banana, green banana, plum, damson, blackcurrant, bramble, redcurrant, raspberry, tropical fruit, mango, pineapple and cherry.

Spice

Some beer styles are traditionally made with added spices, but this isn't usually true of the many and various beers in which the suggestion, often elusive, of spice aromas and flavours arises. Commonly experienced spice notes include: pepper, smokiness (smoked fish), ginger, clove, anise, coriander, cumin, cardamom, nutmeg, cinnamon, five spice, sandalwood, fresh leaf tea. As well as herbal flavours, commonly of mint, parsley, sage, bay leaf and rosemary.

Dark Beer Flavours

Rich dark beers, whether spicy or not, often demonstrate one or more of the following flavours: chocolate, cocoa, truffle, Ovaltine, liquorice, treacle toffee, tarriness, date, fig, burnt currants, burnt toast, coffee, espresso, cappuccino, coffee bean, raisin, sultana, Christmas cake/pudding.

Potency

Strong beers often acquire flavours more commonly associated with wines and spirits, as well as strong alcohol flavours in their own right. They might taste: red winey, oaky, port-like, sherryish (oloroso, manzanilla, cream, fino, whatever), brandyish, whisky-like, rummy (rum is particularly associated with the candy sugar used in some strong Belgian beers) or produce medicinal/cough linctus notes.

Vegetable Flavours

Some vegetal flavours are simply off flavours (see below), but others are part of the particular beer style, and this is most strikingly true of superstrength lagers and strong old ales. Commonly tasted vegetable flavours include: braising celery, cooking onions, fennel, turnip, pumpkin, parsnip, potato, green beans, mangetout, butter bean, and caramelized, scorched roasted vegetables.

Grains and Adjuncts

Barley, wheat, corn, rice, rye and oats are all used to make beers around the world. Each produces its own flavours, and might also be responsible for grain husk notes, though it's the unmalted cereals (corn, mostly, which can create sickly chicken-feed flavours) in some cheaply made beers that are to blame for the more forceful and unpleasant husky 'raw' grain taste. This might also reflect poor quality ingredients or a poor brewing technique in a beer that professes to be Pure. Other unwelcome adjunct flavours might include sweetcorn, popcorn and children's breakfast cereal flavours, brown flouriness, cooked or cold rice, and porridge, as well as a raw potato juice/skins flavour.

And finally (you might not want to read this bit):

Off Flavours

There are various reasons why off flavours develop. Brewing can be to blame, but so can poor packaging controls. Some beers have just gone stale by the time they emerge from the bottle or barrel. Others have been damaged by trivial problems like harsh supermarket lighting. Some of the off flavours (apart from the obvious vinegar) that are 'once smelled/drunk, never forgotten' are: wet cardboard, wet dog, tom-cat, skunk, urine (horse pee), manure, washing up liquid, soapiness, rotting fruit and vegetables, compost heap, bin bag (contents, summer), sulphury drains, cheesy, sweaty flavours, and pungent old vegetables. Plus industrial/chemical aromas and flavours, reminiscent of warm plastic, creosote, nail varnish remover, antiseptic, TCP or chlorine.

Beer With Food

. . . 'delicious with a wild boar sandwich' . . .

MANY PEOPLE'S EXPERIENCE of drinking beer with food goes only as far as a cold can of something, or a bottle of bitter with a pork pie. Because there are as yet no fixed conventions surrounding which beer should be drunk with which dishes, as there are in wine, it's a subject that's still wide open and ripe for experimentation. There are some beers, like some wines, that seem to partner most things fairly neutrally, and to this extent pilseners are the chardonnays of international beer. Other beer styles seem to cry out for certain pairings. Just as in wine-choosing, the most basic rule is to look for similar characteristics: robust, earthy beers are perfect for robust, earthy food; light, fruity beers with light, summery dishes or a fruity pudding. However, again as in wine-choosing, the second most basic rule is to pick something completely different: contrast can be as inspiring as similarity. Consider what characteristics you'd like to enhance in the dish: a mild and creamy chicken curry demands not a spicy beer, but a full-bodied, slightly sweet, slightly honeyed one with a lemon twist, to bring out the sweetness in the chicken and clean up the creamy sauce.

But as in most things, it's fundamentally down to personal taste. There are hundreds of beers listed in this guide that go well with food of one sort or another, and recommendations are often made in the individual listings. What follows here is just a brief bus tour round a country that demands serious travel.

The best place to start is with an aperitif. Beers of ravishing dryness fit the bill very well. Caledonian's Deuchars IPA, Maclays Export Ale and Fraoch Heather Ale are ideal Scots candidates, as is Anchor Steam's Liberty Ale from the USA, a beer that defines astringency. The drier, more elegant India Pale Ales, perhaps Ushers bottled IPA or Hanseatic's James Pryor's, are also good with salty appetizers and snacks, as, of course, are the ubiquitous pilseners – the drier the better. Try Jever. A gentler dryness, such as comes from the likes of South German pale lager beers (try Waitrose Bavarian), is a perfect foil for delicately flavoured dishes, like herrings in oatmeal, asparagus, butterfly prawns and potted shrimps, as well as spring rolls and garlicky food. So are the cleaner, more refreshing wheat beers.

Still on the trail of dry, clean flavours, a beer like Caledonian's Golden Pale is excellent with seafood, avocado dishes, taramasalata, fishcakes, dauphinois potatoes or a Caesar salad. It's also good with English farm cheeses, as are a host of other pale, hoppy gentle bitters, like Fuller's Chiswick or Young's Bitter and the classic IPAs. And pilseners, naturally. First-rate pilseners, which offer complex flavours with a firm backbone of floral, herbal hop dryness – beers like Pilsener Urquell, Bitburger, Gambrinus, and Sainsbury's Organic Pilsener – will happily withstand the onslaught of a stir-fry, onion tart, real sausages and pork satay, among many other spicy, creamy, sweet and salty dishes, from duck à l'orange to fish soup. But you will discover more unpredictable partnerships, too. Sam Smith's Oatmeal Stout is tremendous with a soft, creamy goat's cheese, and with Boursin. It just works. A really good, complex beer has so many aspects to its personality (so many more than the average wine) that it can be happily married with all sorts of foods.

The convention surrounding beer-drinking with (moderately) spicy and curried foods is to go for something exotic in itself, classically Tiger beer from Singapore, or Singha from Thailand. With their full, buttery richness and clean finish they are delicious with noodles, with mild curried dishes and with kulfi. But, surprisingly, so is Gold Fassl from the Czech Republic, and Zywiec, a Polish beer with mango fruit and floral dryness that make them ideal for accompanying spicy food. Full-flavoured, tasty, barley-sweet, perhaps slightly fruity beers such as Budweiser Budvar, Heineken Export, Pripps or Bohemia Regent are good with spicy chicken too, as well as fish in hollandaise sauce, garlicky and mayonnaisey food, mild creamy pâtés and aubergines. Filtered, golden 'Krystal' wheat beers are also worth listing here. A good unfiltered, cloudy wheat beer like Schneiderweissbier or Hoegaarden White, is splendid with spicy, even oily textures (good with German sausage), but also with canapés, and with puddings, especially those with a citrus accent. Some, like Erdinger Weissbier – sherbety, orangey and smooth – are a pudding in themselves. Pschorr-Bräu wheat beer is unmatchable with Somerset apple cake.

Crisp, fresh, but still tasty 'lager' beers – from Pete's Wicked Lager to Holsten Pils, Kronenbourg 1664 to Gold Bier – are ideal with fish and chips, crudités and dips, pilaf, pizza and pasta, grilled sardines and barbecue food. Slightly sweeter, fuller-flavoured beers – a Vienna-style amber lager, say, or a soft, buttery amber ale like Caledonian's 70/- – are even better with pizzas and tarts, and other savouries. The better ice beers are smooth and clean enough to flatter robustly flavoursome Mediterranean dishes, monkfish and croque monsieur. Ice beers seem even to cope with anchovies. A good oily smoked mackerel (and other rich but delicate, slightly oily food) is excellent with Sebourg Blonde, Caledonian's Golden Promise and Marston's Victoria Ale. Marston's bottled beers are good with just about anything. But if it's a kipper your heart yearns for (and whose doesn't) then there's a whole subculture of 'smoked' (and smoke-accented) beers queueing up for sampling: from the musky, clovey Aventinus, to the smoked cheesy Rauchenfels label beers, the more whiskyish and oaky Bières de Garde like Jenlain, and the very lightly smoky Broughton Merlins Ale, which is, incidentally, superb with smoked trout and salmon – as it ought to be, hailing from the Tweed valley. Some of the 'dunkel' (dark) wheat beers, with their clovey, gentle kipperishness, like Arcobräu Dunkel Weisse, are also good with smoked fish and meats.

The rival ubiquitous beer to a good pilsener, to choose to partner food, is a classic bitter ale, well balanced with fruit and hops. Black Sheep Ale, Fuller's ESB, and Caledonian 80/- go with most things. There's a huge range of variants on this essential style, all of them excellent with cold meats, lamb cutlets, game pie, even a humble ham and mustard sandwich. Try the initially fruity, but turning dry, strongish, amber-malt ales like King & Barnes Festive, Bishops Finger, Abbot Ale, even Golden Promise. Pale Ales proper, like Sam Smith's Old Brewery Strong Pale Ale, and Old Speckled Hen are also ideal here, as is the Dutch Budels Alt. Drier still, perhaps elect for Marston Pedigree, Tanglefoot or Batemans XXXB as a savoury form of liquid chutney to flatter cold cuts. Something drily, fruitily yeasty is ideal with herby things, and with lamb. All these ales are also excellent with wintry, warming vegetable dishes (Adnam's Champion Pale Ale is very good with potato bakes), as are bières de garde and other sibling Northern French beers. The 'artisanale' beers of this region are as one in spirit with the simple, rugged peasant food of the region. Lutèce bière de Paris is delicious with a wild boar sandwich. Try La Choulette Ambrée with duck à l'orange (in elegant wine glasses, naturally. The beer not the duck). Or a spicy, dense, complex British contender like Caledonian Edinburgh Strong Ale – perfect with game sausages/or venison burgers.

Best of all with game, with beef, goulash, oxtail and pot roast, and similarly densely flavoured dishes, are equally dense, dark and fruity, full-bodied Trappist and abbey beers, and their companion British strong old ales. Lighter-bodied dark beers with a dryish texture to counteract the strong flavours, and also clean up a dark meaty sauce are often even more suitable: try Thomas Hardy's Country Bitter, Nethergate's Old Growler and Old Nethergate's Special Bitter. Dark winter ales that topple over into succulent wineyness, like Ringwood's Old Thumper, The Bishop's Tipple, Theakston's Old Peculier and St Sebastiaan Dark, are potentially heavenly with the cheese course.

Having come full circle, we are now back at the aperitif list, and faced with a diverting alternative to a green and steely sauvignon, or an elegantly dry fino sherry. The better fruit beers, particularly a good (Belgian) lambic Kriek, offer a dry, sour-sweet champagne-style sense of occasion, and are perfect with light, creamy appetizers and starters, as well as with fruity, sweet or tart puddings. They're also glorious with cold chicken or salmon for a decadent summer picnic. You might follow this, for a lazy, heat-hazy lunch by the river, with a really fruity and light summery ale. What better than one from the land of the lobster lunch itself, Australia's Cooper's Sparkling Ale? Ch'ti bière de garde blonde from Northern France is another with summer in its genes; Enfant du Gayant's Bière du Desert is an elegant appley sparkler and an awful lot cheaper than champagne. All these are delicious with light, summery food like salads, avocadoes, white fish dishes, fruity puddings, and cut very competently through citrussy sauces and mayonnaise. Stout and oysters was a partnership that came about through historical accident, but one that has stood the test of time. Stouts are also surprisingly effective with all sorts of other fish and seafood dishes. The succulent Old Luxters Barn Ale is good with a warm salad of bacon and field mushrooms, and with cullen skink. Ridleys' Old Bob is a stronger summer beer for long, humid evenings on the verandah.

When the temperatures rise beyond British endurance, the super-clean and light refreshers of the Mediterranean, the USA and Australia come into their own. Peroni (Nastro Azzuro) and Moretti are two spritzy, thirst-quenching examples of the Italian style, and are as effortlessly good with pasta and pizza as a mineral water, with which they have much in common. Choose a more robust, acidic (even lambic) or yeasty beer if your summer eating involves anything seriously spicy, oily, rich or pickled. Pilseners are, of course, made for summer weather, but if something sweeter should be required, say for ratatouille, a strong, earthy pâté, or liver with caramelized onions (any sweet onion, or oily roast pepper dish) then the rich, slightly turnipy sweetness of Stella Artois, Elephant or Steinlager, or the delicious Sans Culottes from Northern France, or the tropical fruit palate of America's Michelob might fit the bill well. Whistle clean, but perhaps also slightly buttery, citric beers are good with white fish, but fuller-bodied, stronger-flavoured Export style lagers are better for tuna and monkfish. And when it comes to a cold lunch, one of the newer breed of dryish, clean, but full-flavoured dark beers can be, surprisingly, brilliant. Guinness Original isn't remotely new, but is nevertheless exceedingly versatile. Sam Smith's Oatmeal Stout and Broughton's version are both very successful. More savoury examples include Vassilenski's Black Russian and Maclay's Oat Malt Stout. Honey roast ham, beef in ale, steak and kidney pudding, shepherd's and cottage pies (pies of any kind), are all excellent foils for modern stouts and porters. The coffeeish ones can even make first rate pudding beers.

Bateman's Valiant, Black Regent and Budels Capucijn are all intriguing partners for coffeeish, toffeeish, vanilla puddings, and those of a syrupy, suety disposition. Try Belhaven St Andrews Ale or Kutscher Alt with sticky toffee pudding, Christmas and winter fruit puddings. Rodenbach Grand Cru is particularly fine with rhubarb, orange and marmalade puddings (and also *in* them, as an extra ingredient). Guinness Foreign Extra Stout is glorious with winter puddings too, particularly of the spicy, gingery sort; Trappist beers like La Trappe have an affinity with orangey, sultana, cakey desserts, and Cassovar is so good with chocolate mousse that it can take some time to discover that it's also a natural with summer pudding. Budels Parel from the Netherlands is sumptuous with creamy, custardy, vanilla puddings and biscuit-based summer desserts (and with trifles); Courage's Bulldog Strong Ale has an extraordinary gift for improving rum baba, and the egg-noggy Paasbier is, as you would expect from an Easter brew, ideal with simnel cake, as well as eggy, creamy dishes of all sorts. Appley, orangey wheat beers are, perhaps not surprisingly, delicious with appley, orangey puddings. Peru Gold enhances lemony-limey ones. Krieks and frambozens are almost sinfully wonderful with cherry and raspberry pies, ice-creams, brûlées, sorbets and fools.

But they also make ideal aperitifs . . .

The Microbrewery

Microbrewery just means small brewery, but a proper one, doing things properly, although on a miniature scale. Now that some of the original micros have become very successful and expanded their operations, they're not strictly speaking microbrewing any more. But the micro is difficult to define by size alone. It's more to do with the spirit of the company. A 'small is beautiful' approach. A handcraftedness behind its brewing machinery, techniques and ingredients.

One thing that is unquestionable is the international spread and energy of the micro movement. Little breweries are springing up all over the world, and they take many different forms. The huge scale of the micro revolution (for such it is) in America is creating a whole new beer culture there. Some have already become sizeable companies; some are exporting. In Germany, on the other hand, there is still a living village brewhouse tradition, and almost 200 new ones have sprung up in the last twenty years. Each country, each beer-drinking culture, expresses the global beer revival in its own language.

In Britain, our unique public house system and the beer wholesaling network have provided the conditions for the absolute explosion in small regional microbreweries, now gathering a quite unprecedented pace, with more and more new ventures starting up every year. To eke out a living, almost all of them are dependent on the (rather rare) genuine free house, which can take what beers it pleases, and the guest beer slot in the tied house (which can take what beers the *brewery-owner* pleases). For many it's a continual uphill struggle. Sure, if you can find 100 local pubs for sale and buy them up, a market is guaranteed. But few bank managers are that tolerant.

RETAILING AND CHOICE

Any keen world beer fans making the pilgrimage to Britain, and hoping to taste their way round the country, could probably, with a little elementary research, find a heartening proportion of our regional and microbreweries represented in the thriving real ale pub network. But if they were also hoping to amass a collection of our bottled beers to take home, they face serious disappointment; certainly if they had hopes of starting their collections in our high street off-licences and supermarkets.

When it comes to beer, whether from Britain or abroad, the major retailers are still surprisingly nervous. They play too safe and their ranges overlap dispiritingly often. Things may have improved a bit over the last five years, but not as much as they should have. One or two dare to strike out in a particular direction, but on the whole they stick in the by now very deep and well-travelled rut of the popular brands, and those best supported by the giant wheels of the drinks PR industry. Filling acres of shelf space with the mediocre products of nationals and multinationals, and leaving the individualists to the sidelines is something they wouldn't now dream of doing in their wine ranges. Racks and racks and racks of Blue Nun and Piat d'Or and the like, with just a few estate grown and bottled regional specialists pigeon-holed as Designer Wines, would let the side down shamefully.

And yet the change in our wine-buying habits, which in supermarket terms have turned right around and undergone a revolution in under ten years, has come about because the retailers have led the way. They rely on their fleets of wine-buyers to get out there and source out the best wines at the best prices: to travel the world, find the up-and-coming, do deals and bring back the contracts. Supermarkets, particularly, are now extremely confident about presenting the casual wine-shopper, looking for something to put in the trolley for the weekend, with stacks and stacks of complete unknowns. They know that people will choose an unknown – they don't need to have seen television advertising or drunk it in the pub. The customer will make a choice based on the label, the price, popular wine journalism, whatever – and if they like it, they'll be back. The next time, with a little help from in-store labelling (which Oddbins has made into an art form), and with informal and enthusiastic notes describing the wine's flavours and quality, they'll have a go at something similar or else have the confidence to try something completely different. If people steer their trolley straight past the beer aisle without pausing, it's probably because the impression given is of a commodity, stacked in tins in their thousands just like baked beans. This is as unfair and unrepresentative of the world beer culture, and as unlikely to attract serious browsers, as a wall of canned wine.

So why don't we see more of the hundreds of independent breweries in Britain in our retail outlets? Some of these regional and really small, so-called microbreweries are content just to make cask beer, and that's fine. But most are either producing bottled beers (albeit in a limited way) or else would do so at the drop of a hat, if it didn't entail: (a) expanding their brewery on a high-risk venture, and either (b) affording a bottling plant or (c) paying huge prices for contract bottling, and then (d) hiring an advertising agency to push the product so much that the retailers would feel they had to stock it. Because getting your beer into bottles is just the start. The biggest hurdle of all comes next: the natural scepticism and conservatism of the retail sector. For a small brewery to get its bottled beer onto a national listing in one of the big supermarkets demands not only that quality, supply and branding hoops be jumped through, but that a wee space also becomes vacant on the beer brands quota; there isn't usually much room left once the massed ranks of 'commodity' beer are assembled.

There is talk at present among certain of the microbreweries about getting together to establish a bottling co-op. This has often been mooted before, but if a whole network of such co-ops could be set up on a regional basis, with supporting regional outlets (or a bottling premises beer shop), in parallel to the wine-producing system that exists in France and gets small producers into the car boots of the public, then a whole new bottled beer culture could grow and flower in Britain. The locals and tourists would visit. And so too, before very long, would the supermarket and off-licence beer buyers.

Price

Prices aren't a feature of the main listings in this guide because (a) there's a remarkably small band of variation in beer pricing, thanks to our high expectations of low costs, and (b) it's a sweeping and possibly also inaccurate generalization, but in beer you get what you pay for. More than in the wine world, certainly, where a good bottle of red might cost £3.50 or £13.50, and price *can* be a factor in assessing star quality on the high street. The most expensive beer featured in this book costs £5.30, and comes in a stone bottle you can keep: it's Hoogstraten Poorter from Belgium, available from the Beer Cellar. The most expensive beer in the fairly familiar category is the strong Belgian Trappist ale, Chimay Premiere, which retails at around £3.75 for a boxed 75cl bottle. Most beers listed are under £1.50. It's even possible, though I haven't yet counted, that most are under £1. In these happy circumstances, price really pales into insignificance, and flavour and quality have confident top billing. Or should have. But we still have a bit of a problem with paying £1.50 for a good bottle of beer. Too many consumers expect supermarket beers (especially) to come in a tin like baked beans, and be as cheap, which just encourages the megabreweries of the world to keep churning out rubbish.

The following rough guide to beer pricing was based on a survey of supermarket and off-licence prices carried out in April 1995.

Canned ales

The great price divide in canned milds, bitters, stouts, pale ales, winter warmers and the like is caused by the dreaded widget. Widget-afflicted beers carry the promise of 'Real Draught Beer in a Can', using trademarked names like Draughtflow, Caskpour and Tapstream. They also bear a price-tag of around £1.15–£1.20 a shot. Best-known brands: John Smiths, Tetleys, Directors, Flowers, Pedigree, Boddingtons, Theakstons.

Ordinary (non-widgetized) canned bitters are typically 80–90p: John Smith's, Boddington's, Greene King IPA. And about £1-£1.20 in the premium/special bitter class: single cans of Ruddles County are about £1.25 a time. Milds can dip in price to as little as 69p, and hoppy but low alcohol bitters like the excellent Fuller's Chiswick about 75p (in a four-pack). Stouts range from around 88p a can (Guinness Original) to £1.17 (Murphy's). Stronger canned ales are typified by Abbot Ale at £1.35.

Canned lagers

At the bottom end of the market there are cheap British lagers. Mass market brands like Tennents and McEwans retail at about 80p. Less advertised lagers might be as little as 65p. The super-cheapies, low in alcohol and flavour, that almost nobody's ever heard of, can undercut this by far: Hector's lager (2.2% abv) is a piffling 29p for a 44cl can. But I don't recommend it.

Elsewhere in the mass market, familiar brands settle happily into the 75–85p bracket, like Carling Black Label, Carlsberg and Fosters. Own brands undercut them, of course: Tesco own brand 4% lager is about 60p a can in a four-pack, their Dutch lager 49p. 'Premium' canned lagers are often in the 99p category, like Stella Arois, Löwenbräu, Budweiser, Coors and Enigma. The trendier or stronger premiums can easily climb to the £1.30 level, though Grolsch, Holsten Pils and Kronenbourg 1664 are pitched a little lower. The superstrength league, like Carlsberg Special, pitches itself at about this price, too. At the other end of the scale, low (or no) alcohol products can cost as little as 33p (Swan Light in Tesco) or as much as 72p (Kaliber in Thresher), and average somewhere in the middle (in the way that averages do).

Bottled ales

Probably the average price for a bottled ale listed in this guide is £1.39. There are plenty at this price and slightly cheaper, one or two spectacular bargains, and a few daring brands that cross the £1.50 barrier. Quite often the price variation is simply down to size: 99p bottles tend to be of the 33cl size, £1.39 bottles at 50cl or more. Among ale brands under the £1 level there's Worthington White Shield, Guinness Original, The Bishop's Tipple, Royal Oak, Ushers IPA and Coopers Sparkling. At £1–£1.29: Abbot Ale, Caledonian brands like Golden Promise, 80/- and Merman, Black Sheep Ale from Yorkshire, Leffe Blonde, the mass-market Belgian abbey beer, Guinness Foreign Extra Stout, Sam Smith's Old Brewery Bitter, and Pete's Wicked Ale from the States. At £1.30–£1.50: Marston's bottled brands, Tesco Select Ales, McEwans bottled 80/- and 90/- Ales, Bateman's XXXB and Victory Ale, King & Barnes Festive, Old Speckled Hen, The Bishops Finger and Fullers ESB. At £1.50– £1.70: the Hanseatic brands, like James Pryors IPA, as well as Sam Smith's Oatmeal Stout, and Nethergate's delicious Old Growler.

Bottled lagers

Popular level for the mass market here is 99p: Oranjeboom, Rolling Rock, Bitburger, Peroni, Moosehead, Dos Equis, Kirin, Steinlager and Sol are all about this price. Michelob and Corona are just a little more, while Sapporo Draft takes its 'super-premium' status just a little too far at a whopping £1.59. Imports of solid reputation, usually from Germany and the Czech Republic, might cost as little as 90p for a 33cl bottle of Beck's Bier, or as much as £1.99 for a 66cl bottle of Pilsener Urquell. Amstel, Heineken Special Export, Tesco's Brandenburger Pilsner Neu, and Sainsbury's Bavarian Organic Pilsener are decent value. Stronger imports are typified by Elephant from Carlsberg

(£1.20), and a 65cl bottle of Fischer Traditional at £1.99. Ice beers are typified by Carlsberg Ice at around £1.15 for 33cl; ditto Dry Beers. Money can be saved by buying in quantity: at the Majestic warehouse chain, a 24-pack of Peroni Nastro Azzuro works out at just 79p a bottle. Ten-packs of dinky little French bottles, usually of Bières d'Alsace origin, vary widely according to strength and brewery, and can cost as little as £2.79 for Bière des Flandres at Sainsbury's, but are typified by Tesco's own brand packs at £4.79. A 48p bottle may seem like a bargain but 25cl doesn't go very far.

Specialist bottled imports

Krieks and frambozens from good labels like Timmermans or Lindemans are usually around £1.29 a bottle, though Belle Vue is £1.80 (37.5cl). Wheat beers are usually £1–£1.50, from the good value Hoegaarden White/Schofferhofer brands at 99p, to Pschorr-Bräu Weisse, Franziskaner and Erdinger Dunkel, all at £1.35, and Schneider Hefe Weisse at £1.49. Bières de Garde and other 'artisanale' beers from Northern France tend to be fairly expensive (in popular beer terms): Sebourg Blonde around £1.75 for 50cl, Jenlain £1.79, Ch'Ti Blonde £1.25 for 33cl, and Lutèce bière de Paris £2.39 – though for 75cl.

Unusual imports include Aventinus (50cl) at £1.69, Rodenbach at £1.69 (33cl), Duvel at £1.45, Chimay Red £1.65, and, at the Beer Cellar, plenty scraping (or even exceeding) the £2 a bottle mark, like Arcobrau Mooser Dunkel, Paulaner Salvator, Scherdel Pilsener and Rauchenfels Steinweizen. The Czech selection includes Bohemia Regent and Black Regent at £1.75, and the Dutch, Budels Alt and Parel at around £1.45. If they seem extravagantly priced in parts, consider for a moment that these are some of the very finest, most dedicatedly handcrafted beers the world can offer. Then compare the price to a decent claret. It won't seem expensive anymore.

THE LISTINGS

Africa

The very cradle of beer-making is probably in this continent. Fermented grain drinks of one sort or another have been made here for over 3000 years. In a perhaps uninterrupted line continuing from this ancient history, there are still fermented grain drinks of porridge-like consistency made in parts of Africa, but most brewing activity here is of a far more sophisticated order, though rarely purist and exclusive in approach. Heavy-handed use of adjuncts is the norm, and maturation times are often short in the cost-conscious quest for mass-market products.

As in most other large and overheated continents, lager reigns supreme in the beer league, though tropical stouts also have a huge following. There are well over 150 breweries, plus satellite brewing plants of the usual German and English (and other) giants. About 50 of these breweries are in Nigeria, famous otherwise for its extraordinary Guinness, which is finding its way back into Britain as a novelty import. Kenya has a temperate enough climate to enable the growing of hops on a small scale, and of barley for brewing. Often this is used unmalted. Tusker, from Kenya breweries, has been a very successful label for the home market. Incidentally, the choice of Tusker as a name has a rather grisly history: the brewery was founded in 1922 by a gold prospector and two British farmer brothers, one of whom met his demise under the big feet of a bad-tempered elephant. In South Africa, microbreweries have been appearing on the scene for the last ten years or so; indeed, they are also beginning to spring up all over the continent. South Africa Breweries, which was founded in 1895, is otherwise the country's biggest brewery, and widely exports its Castle and Freemans lagers. Freemans proved impossible to get hold of for these tastings, though it will probably be reimported before too long.

CASTLE **

South Africa. 33cl Bottled 5%

Golden, fizzy lager with a sweetly malty, moussey nose, slightly nougat-like, and sweet, clean-as-a-whistle barley grain flavours, subtle and light, with a moussey finish. Typical New World quaffing lager – of the same school as the Australian and American contingent. Though much nicer than many of their mass-market export brands: Castle verges on a three-star rating. One of the better international style lagers. *Serve:* fridge cold. *Avail:* Asda, BeerC, Wait.

TUSKER ***

Kenya Breweries, Nairobi, Kenya. 35.5cl Bottled 4.6%

Smartly repackaged Kenyan classic, now making very few references on its label to trampled brewers. Pale gold, sparkly lager with appetizingly flowery, fruity hop aromas and an unusual structure that brings dry, cleanly hoppy flavours to the very front and develops biscuity, creamy malt in the back and finish, before drying softly and persistently again on the aftertaste. Wholesome, genteel, moreish. *Serve:* light fridge chill. *Avail:* BeerC.

Australia

What we think of as Australian beer is, in truth, quite likely to be New Zealand owned. The New Zealand Lion Nathan brewing group owns Toohey's and Hahn (Sydney), Swan and its Emu brands (Perth) and South Australian Breweries (Adelaide) as well as Castlemaine (Brisbane): together these comprise almost 50% of Australian brewing, with most of what remains belonging to Foster's. Cooper's of Adelaide is the only old family brewery now left in action. There are a few microbreweries attached to the major cities, but many were squashed flat by the Great Australian Recession, the severity of which took this most optimistic of young countries rather by surprise.

Foster's, the best known of Australian brewing giants, was founded by the two Foster brothers of Victoria in 1888, and their Foster's beer was one of the pioneering lagers of the continent – kick-starting the whole ice-cold trend by providing ice from their own machine to the bars who took their beer. In more recent years, the company has had to find ways of expanding its market share to overcome the unique peculiarities of the country's geography: medium-sized to huge cities with thousands of miles of almost nothing in between. Historically, brewing companies (*all* companies) have tended to stick to their own patch – leap-frogging into someone else's can be extremely difficult. Foster's preserves its Victoria identity by producing Victoria Beer – which, incidentally, is now more popular in Australia than the ubiquitous Foster's Lager (mass-market novelty is hugely successful in such a conservative brewery climate) – but has also managed to get into New South Wales by buying up Tooth's, Sydney's old independent (Protestant) family brewery. Foster's also produce a Melbourne Bitter. Overseas, Foster's now owns Courage, one of Britain's big five, Beamish of Ireland, and Carling of Canada. Lion Nathan has moved into the United States, buying up Pittsburgh and Heileman. Back in Sydney, they own Toohey's, the old Catholic brewery, previously Irish and independent, now exporting to the world.

Australian brewing is pretty much run by two huge companies, and like all global giants, their products are more focused on sales and marketing than character and innovation. Of the two international brands, Castlemaine and Foster's, it's Castlemaine that has the slight edge in quality and flavour terms. They at least use whole Cluster hops, rather than the more common oil or extract, and their beers have a little more body and malt character. In general, the Australian mass-market favours pale, clean lagers with a sweetish edge:

70% barley malt, 30% liquid cane sugar is a typical brewing ratio, and 'lagering' is often only done for a pathetically brief 2 weeks (or less). The most famous Australian hop is Pride of Ringwood, used almost everywhere.

Tasmania has two medium-sized exporting breweries in Cascade – which was established in 1824 and is thus pretty much an antique by local standards – and Boag's. All their products are bottom-fermented, though each produces a 'Bitter', now becoming an increasingly common name for hoppy lagers. Tasmania produces good malting barley, and has the premier hop garden of the continent.

Cooper's of Adelaide is now enjoying a cult following – or rather a cult following so widespread that they have become virtually a national brand – but only a very few years ago Cooper's Sparkling Ale, their most famous beer, was considered a bit of a dinosaur. Top-fermented ales were the norm in early Australian brewing, and British settlers gamely tried to reproduce the bitters and milds of home in the harshest and most hostile of environments, until the heat and the lack of fresh ale ingredients overcame their efforts. But the old tradition of making bottle-conditioned beers, which started because very few outback hostelries had a proper cellar, has survived. Despite this and other colonial relics (there's still an old ale and a stout on Tooth's range), lager-making has been the natural brewing style of Australia since the Foster brothers started hawking their cold, refreshing beers round the pubs of Melbourne. And a tin of very cold, very bland lager in the fridge (in fact, quite a lot of tins) has become an essential, defining part of Australian life.

However, like the pie and peas reputation of Australian food culture, this is far from the whole story. There's now a growing realization abroad that Australia is an ideal holiday venue for serious food-lovers. There *is* a pie and peas culture, but there are also lobsters and Thai specialities. There is still a 'tinnie' or two in the fridge, but there might also be something more interesting. Probably the single biggest factor in the (slowly) changing attitudes to beer here has been the huge international success of the Australian wine industry. As cheap and delicious wines filter from the top of the social scale, beers are just beginning to filter up from the bottom. The huge success of Cooper's Sparkling Ale has blazed a trail, though there are few other native products ready to follow. The challenge of developing mass-market speciality beers is one that's currently concentrating the minds of the whole native industry.

Cooper's was founded by a Yorkshireman in 1862. It pottered along with a small, mostly local Adelaide following during the early mass-market lager years, but by the mid 1970s was in dire straits, down to just five batches a week. Although it's now a huge success, spawning at least two Adelaide competitors, Cooper's Sparkling Ale remains a traditional top-fermenting product, unpasteurized and bottle-conditioned with a little priming sugar. Its only ingredients are malt, hops, liquid cane sugar, yeast and water. Its famous sparkle ('sparkling' refers to its natural liveliness, and not clarity – this is a particularly cloudy beer and is still marketed under the 'cloudy but fine' copyline to reassure lager-drinkers) comes from a fairly heavy yeast sediment in action. The bottles are warm-conditioned for 4 to 6 weeks before being released. So extremely fashionable has this beer become, that the 1994 Australia Day Ball in New York toasted the home country, not with chardonnay, but with Cooper's Sparkling Ale.

Those microbreweries that have survived generally produce a fairly predictable range of draught products: perhaps a pilsener style lager, a dark beer like a bottom-fermenting porter, perhaps also a wheat beer, and an 'English-style' pale ale or bitter. Wheat beers are a natural for the Australian palate – not to mention the Australian climate – and with any luck we'll see one or two successful bottled wheat beer brands filtering into export in the next five years. Meanwhile, you'll have to go to Australia to enjoy its microbrewery products. Matilda Bay, in Perth, was the pioneering company, set up in 1984 by an ex-Swan brewer to make beers with better ingredients and longer lagering times than his old employers' products. For a while, its bottle-conditioned Redback wheat beer looked as if it might do a Cooper's. Unfortunately, as happens all over the world, success made it vulnerable to the attentions of the giants, and Matilda Bay is now owned by Foster's, with an additional brew pub in Melbourne.

Australia is only just beginning to develop its own microbrewery style. It's also only just starting out on its no doubt glorious future as a tourist destination. The two have begun to coincide, with brew pubs springing up in cafe and coffee cultural zones: in open squares, in beauty spots, and down on the converted docks. Many of the newest ventures are not brew pubs but brew restaurants, seeking to add a further novelty and gourmet individuality to Australia's burgeoning restaurant culture. Restaurants specializing in the new, native ingredients, seafood and Asian-influenced menus, particularly those in tourist or vineyard areas, are beginning to add their own little brewhouses to make beers that suit their dishes. This may point the road to the future of Australian microbrewing.

BLACK CROW**

Cooper's, Adelaide. 37.5cl Canned 3.6%: Despite the name, not a dark beer, but a paleish amber, filtered ale, with lightly fruity, mildly toffeeish aromas and flavours, drying softly in the finish. A refreshing alternative to other Australian canned beers, but very much in the marketplace to compete with the big, easy-drinking brands, rather than challenging anyone's taste buds or preconceptions. *Serve:* larder cool. *Avail:* specialists.

BOAGS EXPORT**

Tasmanian Breweries. 33cl Canned 4.8%: Imported Tasmanian lager with a fruity, appley, clean and soft malt sweetness, and a hay-like hop note, but no real dryness to speak of. A little toffee and honey add to the crisp, sweet flavour. *Serve:* light fridge chill. *Avail:* Odd.

BROKEN HILL*

Lager Beer South Australian Brewing. 75cl Bottled 4.9%:

Very keen for this beer to shine, as it might prove to be another Australian maverick. No such luck. But the one star rating might be partly down to storage and keeping problems: this example had a bit of a sicky nose, and a dry but not clean flavour, with cardboardy, acrid notes. Which is a pity, as this is apparently one of Australia's oldest genuine regional beers – acclaimed for its distinctive dryness and pronounced hop character –

from the famous mining town of Broken Hill (albeit now owned by the Adelaide brewing giant). *Serve:* light fridge chill. *Avail:* Somer.

CASTLEMAINE XXXX*
44cl Canned 4%:
Mild-mannered, softly malty, faintly hoppy, summer quaffer intended for thorough chilling and not too much scrutiny. But it's better than Foster's. *Serve:* fridge cold. *Avail:* widely.

COOPERS BEST EXTRA STOUT****
Cooper's, Adelaide. 37.5cl Bottled 6.8%:
A top-fermented, bottle-conditioned stout of world class. Gorgeous smells of fresh liquorice, cooked apple, orange and vanilla (with just a touch of that longed-for 'horse blanket' Brettanomyces character). Flavours are even better, with fruit, vanilla, coffee, dark and dry malted chocolate biscuit, and a creamy Ovaltine malt body. Rich and satisfying, but with just the right acidic yeast edge, and a soft, long hop dryness in the finish, partnered by lots of marmaladey, slightly brandyish alcohol. Complex, strong, delicious. Come on, Oddbins! *Serve:* room temp. *Avail:* specialists.

COOPERS SPARKLING ALE****
37.5cl Bottled 5.8%:
'I can't believe it's Australian' might be a slogan worth adopting in marketing this extremely surprising Australian-brewed classic, which tastes more like something Belgian than a beer from the land of ice-box tinnies. Top-fermented, bottle-conditioned ale, cloudy apricot gold in colour, with a rocky white head, and appetizing green banana/ tropical fruit aromas. There's more of these in the fresh and zingy flavour, too, with added passionfruit and peach, a tart citric note, and pale malty softness, drying gently at the finish. *Serve:* larder cool. *Avail:* Asda, BeerC, Odd, Sain, Tesco.

FOSTER'S EXPORT*
44cl Canned 5%:
Also Courage brewed. Doesn't taste remotely exported, either, though not entirely without merit. The nose is a bit nasty (wrong sort of fruit, wet cardboard), the flavour at first dry and bubbly, developing sugary grain flavours before (very gently) drying up again at the finish. Bland and mediocre rather than actually unpleasant. *Serve:* fridge cold. *Avail:* Asda, Sain, Thres.

FOSTER'S LAGER
44cl Canned 4%:
Made in England (actually) by Courage, who are now part of the Fosters empire. Remarkably disappointing, as amber nectar goes; it smells simply sweet, and tastes the same, barley sugary, but with less character than that implies. Also, strangely underfizzed, it turns limp and a bit sticky after a minute or two, making it unsuitable as a simple summer quaffer, either. Castlemaine is better. *Serve:* fridge cold. *Avail:* widely.

FOSTER'S ICE BEER**
33cl Bottled 5%:
Another Courage-brewed Fosters brand, smooth and golden with every angle knocked off and pared and honed, and in so doing, fulfilling every ice beer's ambition well. Smooth as smooth, creamy (almost Ovaltiney) with a buttery finish, and typically mouth-drying texture, almost like salts crystallizing in the mouth. As ice beers go, this is one of the best. *Serve:* fridge cold. *Avail:* widely.

SWAN LIGHT*
33cl Canned 1%:
Made in Britain (actually) by Carlsberg-Tetley, under licence. If you can't get hold of Clausthaler, Swan Light might be the next best thing, even though it's made of water, malt, sucrose, hops, yeast, carbon dioxide, E405, E224, antioxidant and papain (*reinheitsge* not). The finish is a bit synthetic, but it does otherwise have grain sweetness, and balancing dryness, albeit in half teaspoonfuls. Star awarded for tasting a lot better than many other low alcohol examples. *Serve:* fridge cold. *Avail:* Tesco, VicW.

TESCO GENUINE AUSTRALIAN LAGER**

37.5cl Canned 5.5%:

Brewed and canned by South Australian Breweries for Tesco, this pale beer has a pastille and nectarine nose, and a medium sweet, but creamily, fruitily sweet flavour, softer and moussier than the usual Australian brands (and stronger too at 5.5%). The overall effect is soft-bodied, malty and fresh, easy and smooth drinking, with a slightly drying, subtle finish. Like it. *Serve:* light fridge chill.

TOOHEYS EXPORT**

Tooheys Brewery, Sydney. 37.5cl Bottled 4.6%:

More substance than the better known Australian brands, but still a drink-very-cold, slips-down-easily uncomplicated quaffer made for a hot country. Very vaguely (*very* vaguely) a Vienna Lager, brownish gold with a malt accent, and sure enough there's a slightly buttery flavour with a gently drying malt and hop finish, all wrapped up in prickly fizz. Good for drinking with spicy food; best of all, a genuine import. *Serve:* fridge cold. *Avail:* Maj, Sains, Tesco.

TOOHEYS EXPORT

37.5cl Canned 4.6%:

Unmistakeable whiffs of tom cat, together with oddly pungent, sweaty socks and green banana flavours suggest this is either a beer with a major canning problem or just turns nasty in a tin. The jury is out. *Serve:* fridge cold. *Avail:* Maj, Sain, Tesco.

VICTORIA BEER**

33cl Canned 4.9%:

The Victoria Brewery, Melbourne, is now owned by Carlton & United, which is in turn owned by Fosters, who in their turn own Courage UK, who import this canned beer. It tastes like a classic big brewery approximation of a style: reasonably full-bodied, sweet and clean, but also two-dimensional, dull and formulaic. A sort of Australian Carling Black Label, in fact. *Serve:* fridge cold. *Avail:* Beer Paradise, Davies.

Austria

Like Britain, Austria was once the seat of a great empire. Just as the relics of the British Empire have included a scattering of pale ale and porter breweries across the world, the Austrian Empire has left lager breweries, some of them even making the amber coloured, subtly malty, sweetish and mildly spicy bottom-fermented beers the world knows as Vienna lager. The Vienna-style lagers produced across the world are made not to a Vienna recipe – the city itself makes very few beers in this style – but using the malt named after the style, vienna malt, which lends the characteristic flavours. Vienna malt is kilned to a specification which brings an amber blush to the barley grain, and, even more than our own pale ale malt, introduces a drying finish with a 'cured' spice element. Though before its drying finish, it also has an intriguing succulence.

There's the usual long tradition of monastic and Guild brewing in Austria, as tax records from the medieval period confirm. At the height of its Imperial glory, Austria exported beer, as well as brewers, all over the globe. Today Vienna is out-Vienna'd by Vienna style, but the amber lager was most certainly originally native to the city. It dates precisely from 1841, when Anton Dreher, one of the pioneers of modern lager brewing, taking his cue from recent scientific developments in Bavaria, launched his amber-coloured bottom-fermented beer into a marketplace thirsty for novelty. This style in turn influenced the production of the Märzen (and Oktoberfestbier) of Munich. Dreher, not just a pioneer but a brewery empire-builder, became a flying beer-maker in Bohemia, Hungary and Italy. His Italian brewery is now owned by Heineken, and still uses the Dreher brand name. The outposts of Empire have left a legacy of amber lagers as far away as Mexico. Other countries, never under the Austrian flag, also took up the style (just as they adopted the darker, browner Munich lager), and Vienna lagers are now found in Scandinavia, the USA, Canada and Australia.

At home, though, the Viennese brewing establishment has created an altogether different post-war Vienna style, of sweetish golden lagers, and has only very recently thought to produce and promote the amber lager style as its own. On the back of this development, brew pubs and a few micros have also sprung up. Beer bars are beginning to appear among the coffee houses, too. Aside from the rich golden style, the independents might make a Germanic range of specialities, perhaps a hoppy(ish) Pils, a malty Märzen, and, in ascending strength, a Spezial, a Bock and a Starkbier. Both altbiers and wheat beers are occasionally made, in a light-bodied version of the German style. Weak table beers, or Schankbiers, are widely available. There's a pure beer law of sorts: a natural beer law, which allows adjuncts to be used in up to 25% of the mash (usually it's rice), but nothing in the way of additives.

There are just over 50 breweries remaining in Austria, but all are dominated by the Big Two: Bräu AG and Styrian (Steirische). Brau AG (whose unabbreviated name is Osterreichische Bräu Aktiengesellschaft, or the Austrian Brewing Corporation), based in Linz, owns Anton Dreher's pioneer brewery, Schwechater, which today contains something of both the old and new worlds, with its use of hop pellets and extract, but at the same time following old traditions and continuing to kräusen its beers. Schwechater produces beers under the Kaiser brand name, as well as Hopfer, Steffl and Zipfer. Like Styrian, Bräu AG makes typically Austrian lagers in the full-bodied, grain-sweet and fruity style. The land of the Viennese pastry also applies its sweet tooth to its beer drinking preferences, it seems. Schwechater make the sweetest beers, followed by the fruit-sweeter Kaiser, and the slightly more restrained, hoppier Zipfer. Zipfer Urtyp is especially untypical of the Austrian lager model in being pale, zingy, dryish and refreshing.

Styrian (Steirische), the second largest brewing group, is based in Graz and its brewery there makes the rather cumbersomely named Reininghaus-Puntigam brands. Their other brewery, Gösser, makes a Spezial, Export and Gold under the Gösser brand name. Steirische beers are not so sweet as Bräu AG brands, but are still fruity in flavours, which is all the more surprising when you consider that they are based in the area famed for its Styrian hops.

Vienna has its own proudly independent brewery, Ottakringer, makers of Gold Fassl, a typical post-war golden-sweet lager now also being made in its newly acquired Czech brewery and imported into Britain from there (see Czech section). The other largeish, exporting independent is Eggenberg, which is located between Linz and Salzburg and makes one of at least two Austrian smoked malt beers, the wonderfully eccentric Nessie Scotch Whisky Malt Beer, as well as the very strong Austrian bock, Urbock 23.

MACQUEEN'S NESSIE***

Whisky Malt Red Beer Eggenberger Brewery. 33cl Bottled 7.5%:

Made with whisky malt imported from Scotland, and there's just a tantalizing hint of a mellow lowland Scotch on the nose of this pale, whisky gold beer. Flavours are similar to many other strong lagers: smooth, silky, and almost pungently alcoholic, with a textured, tasty, biscuity malt character and a distinctively whiskyish finish. Ridiculously easy to drink for a 7.5% beer. *Serve:* larder cool. *Avail:* BeerC.

URBOCK 23***

Eggenberger Brewery. 33cl Bottled 9.9%: An Austrian Bock beer, from a brewery that's beginning to specialize in strong European specialities. This sibling beer to the famous Nessie has a syrupy gold appearance, with physical weight and body, a faintly whiskyish flavour, but is also very creamy and pretty dry. Whisky butter, honey and alcohol are all evident, as are sour-sweet, slightly oaky, and biscuity creamy malt flavours, and a roast pumpkin sweetness on the finish. Extraordinarily delicate for a beer of this strength. *Serve:* room temp. *Avail:* BeerC.

Belgium

The sarcastic parlour game 'Name Ten Famous Belgians' is a ridiculously easy one to fulfil when it comes to world-class beers. Belgium may be laughed at, but never by people who know about brewing; for its range and individuality, for the sheer gastronomy of its flavours and textures, Belgian beer is unrivalled in the world.

It's often been written, but is none the less true, that Belgium treats its native beers with all the reverent seriousness we feel owing only to fine wine. You have only to visit a Belgian beer bar once to appreciate the depth of national respect: to see the long menu of available brands, to see an array of carefully tissue-paper-wrapped, dusty corked bottles among those waiting beneath the counter, and to see the racks of individually shaped and printed glasses, one for every chosen beer. The humbler street cafés might offer only four or six beers, but the better known may offer a menu running to hundreds, and there are also restaurants dedicated specifically to 'Cuisine de la Bière', in which each dish is partnered by a particularly appropriate Belgian style (and possibly also cooked using it). They have as many cafés in Belgium as we have pubs, serving a population only a fifth the size of ours. But they also have at the last official count, just 126 breweries left (there were over 3000 at the turn of the century), though there are tentative signs of a new microbrewery culture springing up.

On the one hand, fervent traditionalism; on the other, the fact that just two major multinational brewing groups control the Belgian market (Interbrew, owners of Stella Artois, have a whopping 63% of the cake alone), turning out increasingly popular mass-market products, many of them neutered versions of Belgian classics intended for export. At home, the best-selling beer brand is a bland pilsener-style quaffer, Jupiler, also an Interbrew product. Belgian pilsener beers are vastly inferior to Germany's, but then you can't be best at everything.

Back on the other hand, Belgium's traditional beer-making is still, to coin a phrase, probably the most wholeheartedly traditional in the world. Their native brewing styles have something in common with our own, in being (broadly) top-fermenting – in other words, they're properly *ales* and not 'lagers' (though they do make cold-conditioned, bottom-fermenting beers too). A tradition of strong, well-matured ales with good ingredients produces beers of astonishing, often fruity complexity. As a parallel to the cask-conditioned tradition of British ales, there's a thriving bottle-conditioning tradition here. Added to which, herbs, spices and fruit flavourings remain common ingredients in Belgian brewing, a welcome throwback to the hedgerow seasonings of pre-hop days. Along with the Netherlands (the two were of course once one country), this is the homeland of gin-making, and some breweries still put juniper in their beers. The ancient monastic brewery tradition survives here too, and Belgian Trappist beers are always worth sampling, though 'Abbey' beers, made by secular breweries, are much more hit and miss. Alcohol levels are often higher than we're used to, across the Belgian range; this in part derives from a ban on spirit sales in cafés earlier this century, when beer strength rose to take its place.

These high alcohol levels, and the accompanying cast of mind that treats strong beers more like a spirit – both in brewing them (with a spiritous potency, richness and strong, alcohol-influenced flavours) and in drinking them (these are beers that need to be treated more like cognacs) – can make many Belgian beers quite difficult to love, especially for those who hail from the land of quenching bitters. Belgian wheat beers are tremendously easy and delicious drinking; the lambics, once you've learned the language of their flavours, are also a treat, but many of the speciality beers, commonly of 8%–9% abv or more, can be over-sweetened or over-powered by estery flavours that take some getting used to. Some are superb, but many are not, a fact reflected in some of the judgements in the listings that follow. Another potential problem when tackling Belgian brewing on a project scale is what's called Label Beers – that is, the sale of the same beer under various different labels.

According to the Germans and Czechs, the King of Beers was a Belgian: the 13th-century Duke Jean I (or Jan Primus, transmogrified into Gambrinus in a well-known Czech lager), who supposedly invented the toast, and was one of the gloriously named Knights of the Mashing Fork. Their headquarters, the Maison des Brasseurs, is one of the most palatial in Brussels. That's how seriously Belgium takes its breweries. But the question facing the Belgian industry (and more crucially its drinking population) is, does it care enough to keep them? Besides the many little producers that survive in Belgium, there are two huge companies. The least enormous (only the third largest in Europe) is the French BSN, who control about 20% of the Belgian beer market under the Alken-Maes name. Cristal Alken, Mort Subite, Eylenbosch, Maes, Grimbergen and Judas are some of their brand names. The bigger giant is Interbrew, the second largest group in Europe (Heineken is the biggest), who have a staggering 63% of the home market. Their Stella Artois is the big international brand, closely followed by a portfolio that includes Bellevue, Hoegaarden, De Neve, Jupiler and Leffe.

BEER STYLES

Lambic

Lambic beers are Belgium's most famous. They are made by a process once the norm in beer making, but now unique to the Senne Valley, west of Brussels, an area also known as Payottenland. (Or, rather, unique except for two breweries now daringly making them in other areas.) Lambics are a real oddity in our industrialized world. Not only are they wheat beers, using unmalted wheat (30–40%), and not only do they use two- or three-year-old (even ten-year-old) hops (because it's primarily preservative, rather than flavour qualities that are wanted in this yeast-accented beer style), but they are also, most importantly, spontaneously fermented. The wild airborne yeasts (no brewers yeast is added) reach the infant beer (or 'wort') through purpose-built slats or vents in the brewhouse roof. This natural process is possible in spring, far too rampant by half in summer, and at its best in autumn.

Lindemans is typical, in using high doses of old hops and boiling for up to six hours. The spontaneous fermentation that follows is a slow business, reportedly only becoming visible 3–8 days after the wild yeasts have struck the cooling wort. At this point the young beer is run into 600-litre wooden casks, and the yeast foam is left in place for another month, after which the beer will remain in the casks for a year to two years. Maturation is a complex business, and flavour changes can be quite dramatically sudden, even months later. Lambics are considered youthfully 'green' until they're at least a year old; two summers is about right. Young lambics are sour-beery in character, and commonly have a russet appearance which is frequently described as 'vos' (foxy). Mature lambics generally grow pinker and more delicately translucent with age, and have a vineous lusciousness; the sherry and madeira flavours of a six-year-old are currently fashionable in Belgium. Not absolutely every lambic producer can be guaranteed to make his beers in this classic way, however.

Straight Lambic

Is the term used for unblended Lambics, which have the character of a super-dry, and slightly (or even extremely) sour farm cider, and like them have little fizz. Breweries are now coming up with ingenious new angles on what can be a very severe beer style: Timmermans Blanche Wit 'white lambic' combines an old lambic with a wheat beer and fruit essence, and may well be the start of a trend. The most traditional way of softening and sweetening a sour lambic is to add sugar. Ready sweetened, with dark sugar or caramel, these are marketed as Faro. Otherwise, in the Belgian café, sugar is quite commonly added and stirred in just before drinking. Faro isn't a bottle-conditioned product, because it is intended that the sweetness remains intact and doesn't just spark a further fermentation process. It's sterile-filtered, sweetened, and then zapped with carbon dioxide to add life in the bottle. Watch out, though: the label Faro is also misused in some quarters to denote any sweetened darkish beer. Faroes are quite commonly drunk 'long' chilled with ice. They're a popular television beer in Belgium.

Gueuze

(Pronounced gurzer, or curse, depending on who you talk to) is a lambic blend, typically of young and old beers, which has gone on to a secondary fermentation in the bottle, and so has a champagne-like natural sparkle all its own. Typically gueuzes blend many, many different lambic batches together, perhaps even as many as 40 (or more), in a process rather like making a good blended whisky. And like a good whisky, the better gueuzes feature much higher proportions of old lambic, and only a little of the youngest beers. A gueuze is corked if expected to age well: it develops a delectable fruitiness after the first two years or so, get more drily elegant and refined by the age of four, and (officially, at least) stops improving shortly thereafter. Youngish gueuzes have a still (as in flat) farm cidery palate, growing winey as they age, or like a dry vermouth. It's easy to drink them too young, particularly as many British retailers have no idea that they are intended for laying down. Filtered and pasteurized gueuze is getting more common in the export market; if the sugars in the younger lambic are protected from yeasts which would turn them into alcohol, the result is a sweeter beer. It's now commonplace to sweeten them up for 'modern' palates, a deplorable state of affairs.

Kriek

(Which is Flemish for cherry) is perhaps the most classic of all Belgian beers. It's traditionally achieved by macerating whole cherries in a lambic, though it's now commonplace to use a mixture of fruits and juices, or even just juice, for a sweeter, more aromatic effect. Traditionally, a sour, hardy Belgian cherry called the schaarbeek was used, but these are now very difficult to get hold of in volume. Many producers use a mixture of these and imported cherries from countries like Denmark. Liefmans (now part of Riva) use a lot of Danish cherries – which they find have the desired tartness – as well as Limburg fruits. Fruit lambic fermentation rooms are not for the faint of heart, being full of dust and grandiose spiders' webs; spiders are the fruit beer-maker's friend, catching the flies and insects that would otherwise be attracted to the fruity brew.

The fruit sugars spark off a natural secondary fermentation. Those breweries who opt for the cheaper, sweeter fruit syrups make almost undrinkably confected examples. Whole fruits impart a dry, almondy elegance because of the stones, creating a pink champagne-like effect. It's also traditional to use raspberries – most often the extract, as the pips can clog up the works – to make Frambozen (also Framboise or Framboos). Other fruit flavours originate in marketing departments. Mass-market krieks and frambozens are now commonly filtered and some also pasteurized; some show signs of the pressure to create sweet and undemanding fruit beers for a potentially huge world marketplace. On the other hand, some classic krieks are not actually based on a lambic beer at all: most famously, the superb Liefmans Kriek, which is a cherried version of its equally prestigious brown ale. One pound of whole fruit is added to each six-month-old gallon of Goudenband and left to macerate for 8 months, before being filtered and bottled. It's brewed just once a year, in July, at cherry-picking time. Those producers who still go through the laborious process of using whole cherries on a lambic base typically add the fruits to a 'one summer' lambic, veteran of three fermentation processes, to spark a fourth fermentation in oak barrels. They are bottled 6 to 12 months later. During bottling, cherry juice might be added, so sparking a fifth fermentation, this time in the bottle.

Wheat Beers

The best-known wheat beer brand in Britain, Hoegaarden (pronounced Hoo-garden), comes from eastern Brabant, where the style was once common-place: there were 35 breweries in Hoegaarden itself in 1880. By the 1950s, however, the popularity of the drink and the viability of its breweries had both fizzled out, before being revived again in the late 1960s, thanks to the pioneering De Kluis brewery. Its founder, Pierre Celis, left for America on the proceeds of its subsequent sale to Stella Artois, and set up a wheat beer brewery in Austin, Texas, which, with rather delicious irony, is now not only exporting to Belgium, but having its beers brewed in Belgium under licence. Since being bagged by Stella Artois/Interbrew, the beer is made in much more hi-tech style, using a legion of brand new 1400-litre fermenters. Special 'hot houses', maintained at a constant 28°C, have been created to improve secondary fermentation in the bottle. Brewery capacity has been increased to 800,000 litres a year.

Hoegaarden White is made from 45% unmalted wheat, 5% oats, and the rest barley malt, plus Kent and Styrian hops, and is spiced with curaçao orange peel and coriander. It's a top-fermented beer, re-dosed with yeast and sugar for more bottle conditioning. Older bottles have a smooth, honeyed character. Two dozen or so Belgian breweries are now also following where Pierre Celis has led. Though it goes against the grain, some companies are also producing filtered wheat beers.

Occasionally, wheat beers are made with bottom-fermenting yeasts (this is becoming pretty common for bottle-conditioning, particularly), but the tradition is for top-fermentation. The big difference between Belgian and German wheat beers is that Belgians use unmalted wheat (as well as barley), and Germans are bound by the *Reinheitsgebot* (pure beer law) to use only malted grains. This, together with the Belgian love of seasoning and spice (also *verboten*), is responsible for the major taste divide between the two. Some Belgian producers also utilize a lactic fermentation process (similar to that used by the makers of Berliner Weisse), that is empowered with the ability to transform sharp, green flavours into moussey, creamy ones. Which is, of course, why champagne makers also use it.

The use of unmalted wheat creates grainier, breadier wheat beers and also cloudier ones, thanks to the starches present in the unmalted grains. The tangerine flavours that accompany the malted wheat of the German style are echoed in the Belgian wheat beer by direct orange seasoning, from the widely used curaçao. A love of such spices is a direct hangover from the colonial past of the old Dutch Empire. Unmalted wheat also lends appley flavours.

Abbey Beers

There are Abbey Beers and there are Trappist Beers. Only Trappist monastery breweries can label their beers Trappist. Trappist beers tend to be rich and dark and potent (though there is also a blonde in the classic line-up), an authentic reference to the ancient purposes of abbey breweries, which made beers to act both as drink and nourishment, particularly during Lent. Abbey beers are not brewed at monasteries. They might be entirely secular-brewed beers simply referring to the Abbey style, or using the name of a defunct local monastery. Others have a licence to brew from surviving abbeys. Most use the Abbey Beer convention of using 'Dubbel' and 'Tripel' as label terms. In taking up the Abbey Habit they often make beers of almost unbearable potency and sweetness, though beers claiming to be of the Abbey style should always be strong, top-fermented and bottle-conditioned, as the Trappists are. The multinationals are certainly getting the Abbey Habit: Leffe is made by Artois (Interbrew) and Grimbergen by Alken Maes (Kronenbourg/BSN).

Trappist Ales

The Trappists settled in present day Netherlands and Belgium after fleeing persecution in France. They are Cistercians, and their policy of self-sufficiency has always included brewing. Five Trappist breweries survive in Belgium, and one in the Netherlands. The major Belgian brewery is Chimay (1850), the first to brew commercially, and still the most commercially-minded of the Belgian quintet. Its three ales, usually identified by the colour of their labels, are Red, White and Blue, in ascending order of strength. It's common in the Trappist (and Abbey) styles to use sugar, and specifically Belgian Candy Sugar, which often imparts a rummy richness (but just as often doesn't, when used with flair). The Trappists are characteristically better at handling these added fermentable sugars than just about any other brewery; typically, three fermentations, the final one in bottle, help smooth out such ingredients and add a delicate complexity. The second Trappist name is Orval (resumed 1931), who, unusually, produce just one beer, which has been widely imitated. Westmalle (1794), the third Trappist brewery, make both a Dubbel and a Tripel, beers that originated these now ubiquitous labels, and remain the classics of each style. The fourth, Westvleteren (1831), is the smallest of the five, and its beers are not exported to Britain. The fifth, Rochefort (1230), which resumed brewing only in 1899, makes three beers, also often identified simply by the colours of their bottle caps: Red, Green and Black. Despite their air of antiquity, the monastery breweries in fact ceased operations after the French Revolution, and didn't really get going again on a commercial footing until the 1920s.

Dark Ales, Pale Ales

There is a huge variety of both dark and pale ale styles in Belgium, and most independent breweries have their own versions. The dark ales include those inspired by British brewing, like the well-loved, heavily malted, lightly hopped Scotch style, which completely outranks our own beers of the same name. So-called Scotch Ales have been popular in Belgium since they were imported during the First World War. Douglas Scotch Ale, a fearsome 8.6% abv, is still made in Edinburgh by Scottish & Newcastle for the Belgian market, and has spawned a host of imitators. There's even a thistle-shaped glass to drink Scotch Ales from. The major force in this export trade has, since 1910, been the famous beer broking company John Martin of Antwerp. The original John Martin was born in Newmarket and went to live in Belgium at the turn of the century, from where, in 1912, his soft drinks company started importing Guinness. Guinness Dublin still make an 8% abv Guinness Special Export Stout for export to Belgium, which has to be reimported if we wish to drink it in Britain. A whole menu of other specially brewed, highly alcoholic Scotch and Irish Ales are made for Belgian drinkers.

There's also a home-produced Brown Ale style, epitomized by Liefmans' Goudenband, which is fermented for 7 days in open copper tanks, and matured in cool cellars for a minimum of 4 months, then bottled and matured again for several months before being released for sale.

The pale ales tend to be less pale, and more roasted in flavour than our own. Belgian breweries don't use the word 'ale' at all, other than to describe the pale ale style – amber in colour, mellow on the palate – that's epitomized by the classic De Koninck. It's warm-fermented with an ale yeast, and cool-conditioned, rather like a German altbier, to achieve this smoothness and subtlety. The brewery is famously closed every Friday for a thorough spring clean, leaving everything glittering; a fact, the brewery feels, which keeps their beer in such sparkling, fresh form. Originally a coaching inn, De Plaisante Hof, De Koninck is still family-owned and run, in a hands-on, only medium-sized operation. They are Antwerp's only brewery.

The very palest malts are used to make the flagship of the Strong Golden Ale style, Duvel (Devil), which is almost a style unto itself and one of the most dangerously quaffable strong ales in the world. The Moortgat brewery, who make Duvel, was founded in 1871 as a farm brewery, and started with a light ale. They tried to make a British ale just after the First World War, and Albert Moortgat was despatched to Scotland to bring home a yeast. He got it from a bottle-conditioned bottle of McEwans Ale (as was). The beer was to be christened Victory Ale, but Albert's pal the shoemaker exclaimed after tasting it that it was 'the very devil'. It's been Duvel since 1923. The beer is top-fermented (naturally) and cold-conditioned, filtered and reseeded with yeast and dextrose, then warm-conditioned in the bottle, and finally cool-cellared for at least a month. The whole process takes about 3 months. Just as unusually, it uses only Saaz hops. There are now plenty of breweries giving Duvel the sincerest form of flattery, some of them institutions in their own right. Belgians often drink the Strong Goldens slightly or thoroughly chilled.

Sour Red Beers

Apotheosis of the Belgian sour red style is Rodenbach from West Flanders, often called the 'Burgundy of Belgium'. Rodenbach is a family brand name, used only on their beers. Its distinctive rich but sour and refreshing character comes from the use of top-fermentation, unique and elderly yeast strains, rich Vienna malts, and vast barrel-like maturation vessels of uncoated oak. Brewers Gold, the classic hop variety of Belgian brewing, is used together with Kent Goldings. Uncomfortably for ingredients snobs, they also use a fair proportion of corn in the mash. Like a gueuze, Rodenbach is an age-blended beer; the oldest batches can mature for as long as two years, after which part of the beer is bottled straight, as Rodenbach Grand Cru. Alexander is made by adding cherry essence.

Seasonal Ales

The Saison is a survival of the old tradition of making strong, densely hopped, top-fermented ales in the spring, for drinking during the summer (when it was too hot for brewing). They were also made at other times of year. Saisons are native to southern Belgium and French Flanders; they're fundamentally a rustic beer style, with a country beer roughness, and both sharply refreshing and spicy, while retaining a certain creamy body. Classically they use pale malts, and frequently are also dry-hopped. There's always a degree of bottle-conditioning. In general this is a style in decline, though half a dozen good producers keep the tradition alive.

ABBAYE DE BONNE ESPERANCE***
Lefebvre. 75cl Bottled 7.5%:
Hope is rewarded! This cloudy, full golden ale is bottle-conditioned and cork-topped, making a delicious throaty pop when pulled. It has lovely fruity, pear and pineapple aromas with hop flower notes, a combination repeated in deliciously light and creamy style on the palate. The texture's perfect, creamy but lively, and the taste is light and summery, with banana and apple flavours, a sherbety sugar note in the back, and good floral hop character. Excellent with chicken and monkfish at a summer party. Unusually, it's better slightly chilled than at room temperature, with the aromas and flavours warming and flowering during drinking. Love these no-messing wine-sized bottles, too: perfect for sharing. *Serve:* light fridge chill. *Avail:* specialists.

ABBAYE DES ROCS***
75cl Bottled 9%:
Hope rewarded again, with this delicious, all-malt, bottle-conditioned ale. It doesn't taste remotely of its fearsome 9% alcohol, but is instead a very mature, soft, strawberryish beer with a liqueurish kick in the finish and a little oak age on the palate. Alcohol increases on the finish with drinking, but always knows its place, integrated into the mellow flavours, and not riding above them. *Serve:* room temp. *Avail:* Beer Paradise.

ARABIER***
De Dolle, Esen. 33cl Bottled 8%:
Light, bright amber, fizzy, bottle-conditioned ale, with a surprisingly hoppy, drily fruity, even

more drily nutty palate – dry all the way through, from first to last, and a spirity kick in the finish. There's also a high, sweet alcohol strain, teasing but not dominant on the tongue. Made by the 'mad brewers', but seems quite sanely judged. *Serve:* room temp. *Avail:* specialists.

Augustijn***
Van Steenberge. 33cl Bottled 8%:
An abbey beer, making plenty of references to its 1295 origins (though the brewery, of course, is much younger). Pale amber in colour, with sherbety Seville orange aromas, it's a refreshing, fruity and clean-edged, fairly fizzy ale, creamy with vanilla, elusive spice and oak notes and plenty of strong, sweet alcohol, going on to acquire orange, banana and sultana cake flavours as it warms, with a soft pang of dry hop in the finish. A classic Abbey Blonde, in short. *Serve:* room temp. *Avail:* specialists.

Augustijn Grand Cru***
33cl Bottled 9%:
A stronger, drier, fruitier version of the beer above, with more Abbey Tripel heady alcohol in evidence on the nose and in the mouth. But also more tropical fruit flavours in the middle, and a refreshing hop prickle at the end, with bitterness glowing on the aftertaste. *Serve:* room temp. *Avail:* specialists.

Barbar***
Lefebvre. 33cl Bottled 8%:
A bottle-conditioned bière blonde with a creamy, fruitily alcoholic flavour, dry and subtle, with a strong blonde alcoholic pang in the finish and an astringent, oaky note. One of the most drinkable Belgians in category. PS: name is short for Barbarian, and has no French elephant connections. *Serve:* larder cool. *Avail*: specialists.

Bellevue Framboise***
Raspbery Lambic Bellevue (Interbrew). 33cl Bottled 5.2%:
Not strictly the raspberry equivalent of the kriek (below), as the flavour is more alcoholic in style, with plenty of tinned raspberry and vanilla flavours, slightly oaky – irresistibly reminiscent of a potent raspberry trifle. Pretty sweet: have it instead of pudding, rather than with. *Serve:* light fridge chill. *Avail:* VicW.

Bellevue Kriek***
Cherry Beer 33cl Bottled 5.2%:
Absolutely scrumptious, if not exactly purist, mass-market cherry lambic, responsible for 75% of kriek sales in Belgium. Wonderful freshly-cooked cherry aromas and flavours, the flavour ripe and sweet but also with the sour, sappy note that comes off the really deeply purple fruits when lightly braised in a pan. Light, fresh and zingy, with a dry hop and elderflower finish and a summery, sparkling wine-like fizz. *Serve:* light fridge chill. *Avail:* Vic W.

Blanche de Namur***
Wheat Beer 25cl Bottled 4.5%:
Greenish yellow-gold, with an arrestingly floral aroma and a lively fizzy texture. Upfront but subtle lemon and clove, developing distinct lychee flavours. More tropical fruits follow, some of them a little odd (even sweaty), like the more exotic and peculiar-looking end of the supermarket fruits section - all very gentle and elusive, though. *Serve:* fridge cold, with an optional slice of lemon. *Avail:* BeerC.

Bokrijks Kruikenbier***
Sterkens 75cl Bottled 7.2%:
First of all there's the stone bottle, which is tall and very heavy and clad in a blue paper apron for a label, complete with hanky. Yet inside is no naff novelty, but a bottle-conditioned, golden amber spice beer with a strongly fruity, alcohol nose, and a ravishing orangey dryness, zest, juice, pith and all. Summery, refreshing, but also quietly austere, with a bitterness and sour oak notes that build with drinking, and clovey spices in the finish. We may wish all this wholesome freshness were available in a conventional glass bottle, but it's the stone that keeps it that way (light damage being the great curse of bottled beers). *Serve:* larder cool. *Avail:* BeerC.

BOON GUEUZE***
Boon. 75cl Bottled 6%:
Farm cidery, still, pleasantly sour gueuze with a little butterscotch note, a fresh yeasty tang, something vaguely sappy and apple woody. *Serve:* larder cool. *Avail:* Beer Paradise.

BOON KRIEK***
75cl Bottled 5%:
Sharp and cherry fruity with a little fondant sweetness, a hint of Parma Violet, and an echo of something faintly liquoricey at the back. *Serve:* larder cool. *Avail:* Beer Paradise.

BORNEM DUBBEL**
Van Steenberge. 33cl Bottled 8%:
Leaps out of the bottle like the genie out of the lamp. An auburn, slightly translucent ale with stinky overripe cheese on the nose, but a surprisingly reserved palate, with plum brandy, liqueurish character taking the lead, and a lively bottle-conditioned spritz. Pretty austerely dry, but oddly cereally and watery towards the back, and oddly absent in the finish, after a dry, bitter hop flourish. *Serve:* room temp. *Avail:* specialists.

BOURGOGNE DES FLANDRES**
Timmermans. 25cl Bottled 5%:
Dark coppery burnt orange in colour, with cocoa and Hunza apricots on the nose, and rich plummy fruit in the mouth, with a mild-style malt character beneath. But the finish is sweet, Coca-Colaesque, with lots of candy sugar in evidence, and dies away insubstantially quickly. *Serve:* room temp. *Avail:* specialists.

BRIGAND**
Van Honsebrouck. 33cl Bottled 9%:
Bright, barley sugar-coloured bottle-conditioned ale with wild, herbal, pungent esters on the nose and a huge foamy head. Initially seems sweet, but swiftly grows drily fruity and sour in the mouth, with a resiny, sappy finish, woody and herbal. *Serve:* larder cool. *Avail:* specialists.

BRUGES TARWEBIER***
Blanche de Bruges 25cl Bottled 5%:
Milky, pale apricot coloured bottle-conditioned wheat beer (*tarwebier* is Flemish for wheat beer) of remarkably delicious and elegant character. Cloudy, with sedimented yeast bits, it has fruity, peachy aromas, but is also unusually deeply hoppy and spicy on the nose. Flavours are dominated by tangerine and cox apple, and a little peanut buttery savoury sweetness (seasoned with nutmeg and coriander spice), followed by floral, herbal hop dry notes and a little soft clove on the finish. Close to the four-star border. *Serve:* light fridge chill. *Avail:* specialists.

BRUGSE TRIPEL***
33cl Bottled 9%:
Bottle-conditioned ale of pale, yellowish amber hue, with spicy, honeyed aromas and flavours, capped by a little nutmeg and lots of pepper on the finish. Silky and seductive, it develops soft alcohol richness and a distinctive rose water character after a little acquaintance, and leaves a compellingly honeyed aftertaste enlivened by a short, sharp hop bite. *Serve:* room temp. *Avail:* specialists.

BUSH BEER**
Dubuisson. 25cl Bottled 12%:
Clear pale amber, strong golden ale of phenomenal power. It's a blessing that there's hardly any nose. Flavours are smooth and mellow, whiskyish and oaky with a finish at once sherbety and tannic. Well done, no doubt, but overpowering. *Serve:* room temp. *Avail:* specialists.

CANTILLON KRIEK LAMBIC****
Cantillon. 37.5cl Bottled 5%:
Bottle-conditioned, cork-topped and authentic lambic kriek, with a strong fresh (shell-on) coconut aroma, and a light, softly sour, tangy, fruity flavour. Dry, citric, ripe, with yeasty bite, soft tart cherry fruit, almond flavours from the use of whole fruits (or rather, their infused stones) – this kriek's got it all. And this unusual suggestion of fresh coconut milk flavour, too. An excellent summer aperitif. *Serve:* larder cool. *Avail:* Beer Paradise.

Carolus D'or**

Het Anker. 33cl Bottled 7.5%:
Deep, gem-like russet-red, with spicy sweet malt on the nose, plus oaky plum and vanilla aromas. But it's incredibly sweet on the palate, with too much candy sugar in evidence, not balanced sufficiently by dry coriander and curaçao spice and oak notes, and the finish is oddly saccharin-like. There's also malt extract in the mouth, tons of brown sugar, and sweet Victoria plum and cold tea flavours. But all overwhelmed by sugar. This is the old Gouden Carolus, or rather replaces it in the new regime's menu. *Serve:* room temp. *Avail:* specialists.

Chimay Blue Cap***

33cl Bottled 9%:
Opaque chocolate brown, with smooth and mellow, malty, faintly sherbety, flavours and an oaky, tannic edge, mingled with a subdued cooked fruit character, and all reined in by a firm controlling dryness. One of the nicest 9%ers you'll ever taste. *Serve:* room temp. *Avail:* BeerC, Odd.

Chimay Red Cap***

Chimay. 33cl/75cl Bottled 7%:
Dark, sour, smooth, malty, fruity, acidic, mellow, blackcurranty. Delicious classic Trappist ale of reviving and comforting quality. *Serve:* room temp. *Avail:* Asda, BeerC, Sains, Tesco, Thres.

Chimay White Cap***

33cl Bottled 8%:
Translucent pale amber, with a sweet sandalwood nose, mingled with the sort of aromas that come off a delicious flavoured vodka. Flavours are austerely fruity and strongly resemble an apricot spirit, of the sort that's converted all the fruit character into pure alcohol. Otherwise, curiously low-key, hugely dry, with a smooth texture, orange water and panetone notes, and a layering, building astringency at the finish. *Serve:* larder cool. *Avail:* BeerC, Wait.

Corsendonk Agnus**

Oud Turnhout. 33cl Bottled 8%:
Bright, sparkly, slightly greenish gold bottle-conditioned beer with smoked cheese and scrumpy cider on the nose. Flavours are creamy-fruity, a little sour, with clove and coriander, and leathery, tobacco notes. Pronounced wheat beer textures and flavours, but with a pungent, strong alcohol accent, which can seem more than a little overwhelming. For sipping. *Serve:* larder cool. *Avail:* BeerC.

Corsendonk Pater**

33cl Bottled 8%:
Bottle-conditioned, chocolatey brown, opaque ale with smokey, dark malty flavours, smooth but also fairly subdued for its style and strength. Just a vaguely alcoholic note in the finish. *Serve:* room temp. *Avail:* BeerC.

De Koninck****

Antwerp. 33cl Bottled 5%:
Top-fermented, cold conditioned, De Koninck is a clear amber Belgian ale with nuts, fruit, zingy, sherbety pear drops and something faintly rhubarby crowding into the Saaz hop aromas. Flavours combine almond and chestnut notes with sherbety tang, fresh Cox apple, and a kumquat-like combination of sour-sweet orange flavours, all wrapped in a fat, yeasty richness. Flavours are integrated, mellow, subtle and mature, the texture soft and drinkable, but also persistently dry. There's a sour, yoghurty note in the otherwise impeccably clean, floral, sweetly herbal hop finish. A classic. *Serve:* room temp/larder cool. *Avail:* BeerC.

De Koninck Cuvee***

33cl Bottled 8%:
Special edition, anniversary beer, in a handsome, slender bottle. This top-fermented ale has home-made, hot brown bread and (shell-on) peanut aromas and, in the mouth a rich fruity character. Flavours are dominated by pastille and Jelly Baby sugars, with rich, plump yeasts, melon and nectarine juices, a Jaffa orange note, and lots of strong, sweet

alcohol. Much sweeter than the plain De Koninck classic, and much more potent. A sipping, contemplative beer. *Serve:* room temp. *Avail:* specialists.

DE TROCH GUEUZE CHAPEAU**

De Troch, Wambeek. 75cl Bottled 5.5%:

Filtered version of De Troch's classic 'traditional gueuze', a slightly milky pale orange, still (as opposed to fizzy) cider-like beer in a wine-sized bottle. Aromas are acidic and slightly farmhouse cheesey; flavours suggestive of sour plums and apples, with underripe greengage and apricot notes, and a pleasantly sour-sweet, acidic but toffeeish finish. A compelling aperitif beer, but tastes too buttoned up, green and lacking in body for a third star. *Serve:* larder cool. *Avail:* specialists.

DE TROCH TRADITIONAL KRIEK****

75cl Bottled 5.5%:

Stunningly yummy lambic kriek, with sweet pear drop aromas and a dense rosy-puce colour. Flavours are delectable, starting out sweet with fondant cherry, growing sherbety, acidic, and finishing triumphantly sour-sweet, with masses of almond dryness and a distinctive lemon tang. Moreish, lovable kriek from one of the very best producers. *Serve:* larder cool. *Avail:* specialists.

DENTERGEMS**

Wit Biere Riva. 25cl Bottled 5%:

Bottle-conditioned wheat beer. Ghostly pale and cloudy, with an appetizing butter and lemon nose, and a delicate wheaten flavour with a lemon and clove finish. A little lacking in life and texture perhaps, with an ever so slightly cardboardy stale note at the close. But don't be put off. *Serve:* light fridge chill. *Avail:* BeerC.

DOUBLE ENGHIEN**

Brune Silly. 25cl Bottled 8%:

Light amber sibling to Scotch de Silly. Smooth, creamy and walnutty, with a mildly whiskyish kick in the finish, and nutskin dryness following on. *Serve:* room temp. *Avail:* BeerC.

DUVEL****

Moortgat. 33cl Bottled 8.5%:

This particular 'devil' (the original and best) is a shiny yellow-gold with a downy white head, and looks innocent enough. Taste it, though, and there's masses of straight, sweet alcohol among the heathery, pine resiny notes, the almost eggy sweet cream, the tart lemon and green banana flavours, and a dry, dry, mouthdrying hop background that creeps in after a minute or two, and stays and grows, with floral, bitter hop and more pungent alcohol in the finish. *Serve:* room temp/larder cool. *Avail:* BeerC, Odd, Tesco, Thres, Wait.

FACON SCOTCH CHRISTMAS**

25cl Bottled 6.1%:

Pond-dark Scotch Belgian ale with an estery nose, and a really nutty, Christmas cakey, slightly rummy, sweet and spicy, faintly sappy and resiny flavour, with no finish to speak of. Actually it smells compellingly of meths. *Serve:* room temp. *Avail:* specialists, Selfridges.

FLOREFFE DOUBLE**

Quenast. 33cl Bottled 7% (Floreffe Red Label):

Top-fermented, bottle-conditioned abbey ale with a fizzy, sour brown start, and growing merely fizzy and mild-mannered on the palate, with just the subtlest touch of ripe banana and a little soft alcohol flavour. Competent, but dull. *Serve:* room temp. *Avail:* BeerC.

FLOREFFE MEILLEURE***

33cl Bottled 8% (Floreffe Blue Label):

Reddish brown abbey brune, bottle-conditioned and with spicy, sour-sweet aromas. Gassy in the mouth, with malty, raisin, strawberry and cherry flavours, it also has pungent, musky alcohol and spice in the finish, followed by the faintest hop note. *Serve:* room temp. *Avail:* BeerC.

FLOREFFE TRIPLE**

33cl Bottled 7.5% (Floreffe Yellow Label):

The middle beer has classic Triple character, in so far as it's top-fermented, bottle-conditioned, and pale amber in colour. Flavours are typical of a creamy abbey blonde, too, with biscuity pale malt and lots of alcohol, a little pear and apple fruit, and spice in the finish: a hint of clove, coriander, and masses of pepper. But all subtle and low key in final delivery. Perhaps *too* subtle? Not quite a three-star beer. *Serve:* room temp. *Avail:* BeerC.

La Gauloise**

Brune Du Bocq. 33cl Bottled 9%:
Bottle-conditioned, foxy red ale with a candy sugar, fruity nose, and a candy sugar fruity palate, spiced with a suggestion of rum baba, muscovado and a sweet egg-nogginess. *Serve:* room temp. *Avail:* BeerC.

Grimbergen Dubbel**

Alken Maes. 33cl Bottled 6.5%:
The abbey from which these recipes supposedly come was founded in 1128, but these are notably sweet, commercial modern versions of the old abbey style, made by a Belgian mega-brewery. Translucent russet, with a candy sugar, rummy, spicy fruit nose, and sweet, fruity, cold sweet tea on the palate, which give way to a remarkably literal toffee apple flavour: the red apple and the sweet crispy toffee working together. Cloying and sticky in the finish. *Serve:* room temp. *Avail:* specialists.

Grimbergen Tripel*

33cl Bottled 9%:
An Ambrée of pale barley sugar colour, with a big rocky head, and lots of alcohol on the palate, sweet, winey and spiritous, with caramelized turnip notes, drying for just a moment before turning wholeheartedly sweet in the finish. Overdone, confected, without sufficient structure or contrast. Strength is the watchword here. *Serve:* room temp. *Avail:* specialists.

La Guillotine*

Huyghe, Gent. 33cl Bottled 9.3%:
Triple-fermented, fizzy, pale strong golden ale from a painted stone-effect bottle. Aromas and flavours are violently alcoholic and overwhelmed by estery potency. Flavours, such as they are, feature whisky and wine together, with lots of overripe alcoholic fruit (like bad, fermenting pineapple). Verging on plain unpleasant to drink. *Serve:* room temp. *Avail:* specialists, Selfridges.

Gulden Draak**

Van Steenberge. 33cl Bottled 10.5%:
Their flagship ale, densely auburn-coloured, bottle-conditioned and with an alcoholically jammy nose. Pleasanter than expected for the strength: it's slightly smokey (smoked cheesey), smooth and spritzy, with a vaguely brandyish finish, but otherwise brimming with sweet maltiness. *Serve:* room temp. *Avail:* specialists

Hanssens Gueuze****

Hanssens. 37.5cl Bottled 5.5%:
Corked-topped gueuze with the loudest, most confident of pops when opened. Deep cloudy amber, with an estery nose, it produces seductively velvety, but also sharp, and dry, but also fruity flavours, with peachy, leathery, oaky tannins at the back. Rich and complex, but also spritzy and with quaffable lightness of touch. *Serve:* larder cool. *Avail:* Beer Paradise.

Hanssens Kriek****

37.5cl Bottled 5.5%:
Just the right balance of sweet cherry fruit and yeasty lambic sourness in this really exceptional cork-topped Hanssens Kriek. Deep, lingering cherry flavour, elegant elderflower champagne balance, the softest tart lambic tang, and just a hint of blood orange juice character. Depth and roundness, length and complexity, and just plain scrumptious. *Serve:* larder cool. *Avail:* Beer Paradise.

Hoegaarden****

White De Kluis. 33cl Bottled 5%:
Opaque lemony gold bottle-conditioned wheat beer, with a delicious nose of cooked

puréed apples and lemon zest. Classic Belgian wheat beer flavours follow, a delicate wheaten breadiness, sweet and sharp citrus notes, gentle hints of clove, cinnamon and coriander (the beer is seasoned with coriander and curaçao), with a lingering apple strudel and honey finish. A lovely dry prickly-bubbly texture helps create a light, fresh summery drink of real elegance. *Serve:* larder cool/light fridge chill. *Avail:* Asda, BeerC, Odd, Safe, Tesco, Thres.

Hoegaarden Forbidden Fruit***
33cl Bottled 8.8%:
Bottle-conditioned orangey brown, slightly cloudy. Flavours are of orange and vanilla with an oloroso sherry, dark sweetness, complex and fruity with a hint of toffee, and a pleasantly musky alcohol pungency. The finish is spicy, with coriander and pepper, perfumey cumin, and a sticky-date sweet note. Rich and dangerously drinkable. *Serve:* room temp. *Avail:* BeerC.

Hoegaarden Grand Cru***
33cl Bottled 8.7%:
Bottle-conditioned 'Tripel' of unmistakeably Belgian character, fruity, malty, whiskyish and saddle soapy on the nose. A strong golden ale with a lively texture and elusive flavours of whisky, cream, spice, peat-smokey malt, orange and coriander (though this isn't a wheat beer), drying and drying and drying some more on the palate. But at the same time fruity, like peaches steeped in alcohol, and exotic, alcoholic mango. Austere but exciting. *Serve:* room temp. *Avail:* BeerC, Odd.

Hoegaarden Julius**
33cl Bottled 8.5%:
A spice bier blonde of nectarine flesh hue, bottle-conditioned and translucent. Alcohol, whisky, peach and marmalade aromas give way to a spritzy-textured beer with a strong whiskyish kick, orange liqueur notes, and vanilla oak maturity. Its potency really oozes through on the finish and glows on the aftertaste: very much a sipping beer. *Serve:* room temp. *Avail:* specialists.

Hommel Bier***
Van Eecke, Watou. 25cl Bottled 7.5%:
Ochre beige, cloudy, spritzy hop ale, full of life and extremely refreshing. It's the hoppiest beer in this section, but also has sherbet-fruity yeast tang, a little resinous bite, and a floral edge. But mostly it's just irresistibly hoppy. Dangerously quaffable for a 7.5% abv beer. *Serve:* larder cool. *Avail:* specialists.

Hoogstraten Poorter***
Sterkens. 75cl Bottled 6.5%:
Sibling beer to Bokrijks Kruikenbier, also in a stone bottle, and this time clad in a British Rail-style napkin. The beer, however, which was first brewed in 1985, is far from vulgar. Top-fermented, garnet-red, it has a lovely tannic winey fruity nose, almost rioja-like. On the palate, there's Merlot wine strawberry softness, plum sweetness and grapefruit sourness and a resiny hop flourish. It dries in the mouth with an almost fruit lambic elegance, with dry strawberry, oaky tannins and great finesse. Extraordinarily delicious beer that should be served in elegant wine glasses and will completely fox even those guests who can be relied on to know everything (but hide that bottle). A whisker off four stars. *Serve:* room temp/larder cool. *Avail*: BeerC.

John Martin's***
John Martin's, Antwerp. 33cl Bottled 5.8%:
Brewed by the Palm brewery for the famous John Martin's, beer broker to Europe. An extremely delicious and complex beer, approximating in flavours a happy hybrid of West Country bitter and a particularly light, fruity Trappiste. Fruit, toffee and hop aromas and flavours, with a dry, moreish, floral bitterness, succulent buttery raisin and orange, and a cakey, creamy malt character, finished with a very Belgian sweet pang of brewing sugar right at the back. Excellent drinking. *Serve:* larder cool. *Avail:* specialists.

JUPILER*

Interbrew, Brussels. 25cl Bottled 5.2%:
Pale, soft-bodied, with a textured maltiness, and a creamy, almost moussey (almost strawberry?) finish. Too subtle, and too dilute in character to merit more than one star; there's also something sticky and unclean in the finish which robs Jupiler of its simplicity. *Serve:* light fridge chill. *Avail:* Asda, Co-op.

KWAK**

33cl Bottled 8%:
Clear amber top-fermented ale with alcohol, sour fruit and something vaguely cheesy on the nose. Flavours are similar, but with scented pear, orange notes and masses of marzipan. *Serve:* larder cool. *Avail:* specialists.

LEFFE BLONDE***

Abbey Beer Brewery St Guibert (Interbrew). 33cl Bottled 6.6%:
The fathers of the Abbey of Notre-Dame de Leffe were apparently brewing in 1240, but sadly do so no longer; Leffe Blonde comes from a more secular tradition. Robust amber in colour, with banana aromas and a bittersweet edge. Green banana and pineapple juice flavours, with a little refreshing orange, and lots of yeasty character. There's a slight sourness, almost camphorwoody; the dry, prickly texture makes this strong beer dangerously drinkable. So, no reason why it should fall in its ambition to become the first truly mass-market abbey beer. *Serve:* larder cool. *Avail*: Asda, Odd, Tesco, Wait.

LEFFE BRUIN**

33cl Bottled 6.5%:
Top-fermented abbey ale of the dark brownish-red sort, with a malty, fruity flavour and a firm hop finish. Just awfully dull, and fairly heavy going. *Serve:* room temp. *Avail:* Beer Paradise.

LIEFMANS FRAMBOISE***

Riva, Dentergem. 37.5cl Bottled 5.1%:
White-tissue-wrapped pudding in a glass, and a star among the raspberry lambics. The nose is glorious, a mixture of oozingly ripe and paler, sharper fruits, with creamy cocoa and hop flower aromas besides. Not remotely sticky or oversweet, it's delicate and fresh, intensely raspberryish but also with lemon, vanilla, a little sourness, a floral hop note, and a gently drying, perfumed finish. Ideal after fishcakes. *Serve:* larder cool/light fridge chill. *Avail:* BeerC.

LIEFMANS GLUHKRIEK***

25cl Bottled 6.5%:
People used to add sugar and spice to a kriek for a winter toddy. This innovation does it for them. Heated in a pan, this ruby-red lambic acquires lovely, warm spicy cherry aromas and flavours, with a mulled wine richness. *Serve:* Hot! for once. *Avail:* specialists.

LIEFMANS GOUDENBAND****

Riva. 37.5cl Bottled 8%:
Out of this handsome tissue-clad bottle comes an opaque chocolate-brown ale with a slender beige head. Bottle-conditioned, it has musky, malty, sherbety fruit smells, rather like alcoholic strawberry. This prepares you for the most wonderful winey, plummy, Merlot softness on the palate, with more jammy strawberry, and faintly spicy malt richness, giving way to a dark sweet note, before finishing with delicious lemony, tart flavours. Complex, mellow, delicious: a beer of rare quality. *Serve:* room temp/larder cool. *Avail:* specialists.

LIEFMANS KRIEK****

37.5cl Bottled 6%:
Maybe it's true that since the sale to Dentergem, Liefmans classic kriek is not what it was (and then again maybe it's better than ever), but this is not only the definitive Belgian cherry beer, it's also the only one made on a brown ale base – whole cherries are macerated in the brewery's famous Goudenband. The sense of occasion begins with the pink tissue paper, and a dark, unlabelled bottle topped with a wire-caged cork. Taste it, and there's all the cherry succulence and sharpness, almond and

elderflower delicacy, and a citrus zestiness that comes from a good cherry lambic, but also, in this case, a rich, plummy wine-like (Merlot) backdrop, from the Flemish brown ale. *Serve:* larder cool/light fridge chill. *Avail:* BeerC.

LINDEMANS KRIEK***

Lindemans. 37.5cl Bottled 4%:
Deep berry red with a pinkish head, with good almond paste smells and fondant cherry fruit aromas, perfumy and appetizing. Tastes like a sweet cherry and almond champagne, very sweet indeed, but with a redeeming dry, slightly citric edge. Rich and delicious but hardly beer-like. It may not be absolutely traditional, it's certainly not refined, dry and elegant, but it's incredibly yummy. Seventy per cent is exported. *Serve:* larder cool. *Avail*: Odd.

LINDEMANS PECHERESSE**

Peach Lambic. 25cl Bottled 2.5%:
Strictly speaking, to be disapproved of as a bit of an upstart, but the sweet peachy flavour (actually more like apricot) and sharp, tropical fruit, sour-sweet notes make this peach lambic easy to love. Not remotely beer-like, but a more successful peach wine than any peach wine on the market: unlike sparkling wine, lambic ales are a perfect foil for fruit flavours. Should perhaps get a third star for providing an aperitif beer at such a pifflingly low alcohol level. Love the decadent art nouveau nude on the label, too. *Serve:* light fridge chill. *Avail*: Odd.

LUCIFER**

Riva. 33cl Bottled 8%:
One of Duvel's better known imitators, I mean flatterers. It's the requisite yellowy apricot in colour, with fruity alcohol of the banana and pineapple sort, soft vanilla notes and a whiskyish, creamy finish. Just a little on the heavy side, perhaps, and lacking the balance and assurance of the original. *Serve:* room temp/larder cool. *Avail*: specialists.

MAREDSOUS 8*

Moortgat. 33cl Bottled 8%:
Top-fermented, bottle-conditioned abbey beer which smells a bit like Stilton, and tastes of surprisingly little, just oddly blunted and keggy, with the mildest of malt palates. Where has all the strength (and flavour) gone? *Serve:* room temp. *Avail*: specialists.

MAREDSOUS 10

33cl Bottled 10%:
The blonde of the pair, pale, bright and lively, with aromas reminiscent of a sweaty Tupperware box, and sharp, sour, fruity, but also slightly cheesy flavours. *Serve:* room temp. *Avail*: specialists.

MECHELSCHEN BRUYNEN**

Het Anker. 33cl Bottled 6%:
Top-fermented Brune de Malines, of foxy auburn colouring, with esters and cheesey pungency joining the fruity malt nose. Lots of spice on the palate, of the you-love-it-or-hate-it sort, with fino sherryish notes, clove and masses of anise combining to create a musky, perfumy character, with a pungency that takes over the show, rather. Very much a spice ale; an ale for spice ale fans. Others might be irresistibly reminded of Fisherman's Friend lozenges. *Serve:* room temp. *Avail:* specialists.

MORT SUBITE CASSIS

Alken Maes. 25cl Bottled 4%:
What have they done to these beers? Tasted together, in a row, they were among the very toughest assignments of this whole *Guide* (which is saying something). It's as if you had foolishly neglected to add water or fizz to a concentrated juice or syrup, and the shock is of similar proportions. The blackcurrant version is particularly afflicted with a sugary, confected aroma, and a strawberry and blackcurrant boiled sweet character on the palate, with an intensity so great that it's actively unpleasant. The mineral, industrial finish doesn't help much, either. *Serve:* light fridge chill. *Avail:* BeerC.

MORT SUBITE FRAMBOISE
25cl Bottled 4%:
Candy-floss, cheap boiled raspberry flavoured sweets, Cremola, the syrup on the ice-cream from an ice-cream van. Yes, you might secretly be a fan of ice-cream topping, but you wouldn't want to drink 25cl of it. Believe me. A nasty industrial finish again, too. *Serve:* light fridge chill. *Avail:* BeerC.

MORT SUBITE GUEUZE**
25cl Bottled 4.5%:
Gueuze lambic of toffeeish colour and aroma, but with an appetizing sherbety sourness too. Flavours follow in butter toffee, barley sugar mode, with a gentle lambic sourness to balance. Too gentle: in typical, highly commercialized Mort Subite style, this is a confected, fondanty, formulaic version of a Belgian classic, intended for lazy foreign palates like ours. But not as appallingly bad as the Mort Subite fruit beers. *Serve:* larder cool/light fridge chill. *Avail:* BeerC.

MORT SUBITE KRIEK
25cl Bottled 4%:
Fuschia pink, with cherryade aromas, and a cremola, children's cherry sweets (chewitts!) flavour; sweet, fondanty, pink marshmallowy. Not even a very subtle sour note can redeem matters. No finish. No star rating. *Serve:* larder cool/light fridge chill. *Avail:* BeerC.

MORT SUBITE PECHE
25cl Bottled 4%:
Pineapple ice-lolly aromas, melted and warm, and thin, icky pineapple-ade on the palate, with a pineapple-chunk sweetie sour edge. *Serve:* light fridge chill. *Avail:* BeerC.

OERBIER***
De Dolle. 33cl Bottled 7.5%:
De Dolle, the 'mad brewers', are an architect and a doctor who rescued this brewery from closure and brew at weekends. Oerbier uses six different malts and three hop varieties. This, the brune to Arabier's blonde, is bottle-conditioned with a lively fizz, fresh fruity aromas, and sherbety, zingy, fruity lemon and orange flavours. Doesn't taste remotely alcohol-potent, just fresh and zippy from first to last, with a lovely soft, dry hop aftertaste. A real pick me up. *Serve:* larder cool. *Avail:* specialists.

ORVAL****
Orval Trappist Monastery. 33cl Bottled 6.2%:
Golden amber ale in a voluptuous little bottle, perhaps a reference to the average monastic girth? There's alcohol, wild estery smells, fruit and oak maturity on the nose, and there's plenty of time for sniffing, while the huge, rocky head is ever so slowly subsiding. Flavours are dry and elegantly austere, with alcoholic potency successfully ambushed by seville orange, vanilla, a notable oaky, woody character, and a penetrating, persistent astringency that dries up all before it. Smooth, mellow, silky, but strong, with a faintly malt whiskyish finish. The most 1990s of all Trappist ales: already a bit of a cult in the States. *Serve:* room temp. *Avail:* BeerC.

PALM SPECIALE**
33cl Bottled 5%:
Bright amber, top-fermenting ale with a slender head, and pale ale flavours in a near-English idiom. Slightly grain husky in the mouth, but otherwise gently dry, softly malty, mildly nutty, with a spritzy, lively texture and peppery finish. Kind, subtle, drinkable. Slightly *too* subtle? *Serve:* larder cool. *Avail:* specialists.

PETRUS OUD BRUIN***
Bavik. 25cl Bottled 5.5%:
Top-fermented, auburn brown ale with plum and orange aromas, and sharp, sherbety fruit flavours. It's really zingy (gassy) and fresh, but also rich and puddingy, with lemon mousse and home-made plum jam notes, and a little creme caramel combined with a soft hop flavour in the finish. Matured for 20 months. *Serve:* room temp. *Avail:* specialists, Selfridges.

PIRAAT**
Van Steenberge, Ertvelde. 33cl Bottled 10.5%:

Very bright, and very strong pale lemon gold beer with alcoholic and overripe fruits on the nose, and a drily fruity flavour, growing astringent and developing floral hop excess in the finish, together with pungent alcohol. Smooth and deadly. *Serve:* room temp. *Avail:* specialists.

ROCHEFORT TRAPPISTES 8**
Rochefort Trappist Monastery Brewery. 33cl Bottled 9.2%:
Mineral dry, overwhelmingly alcoholic bottle-conditioned Trappist ale, translucent amber red in colour, with pear drops, potency, sour oak, and strong, sour fruit on the nose, and overripe banana, estery fruits and overweening alcohols on the palate. As one of the six remaining Trappist monastery breweries, Rochefort (like the rest of them) is accorded enormous, and sometimes uncritical status. Doubtless this beer is made laboriously well, but the fact remains that when the top is off the bottle, and the glass is in the hand, this is a beer that tastes mostly of its own strength. *Serve:* room temp. *Avail:* BeerC.

ROCHEFORT TRAPPISTES 10***
33cl Bottled 11.3%:
Russet-brown ale with drier and subtler aromas than the number 8, sherryish and porty. Silky alcohol-driven flavours suggest the blackest, most overripe banana, both sweet and musky, with rum butter and Coca Cola notes and a pronouncedly sour finish. Rather like a spirit, yet only of wine strength. Still tastes mostly of that potency, and takes some getting used to, but flavours are more integrated and a little kinder than previously. *Serve:* room temp. *Avail:* BeerC.

RODENBACH****
Rodenbach. 25cl Bottled 5%:
The famous Belgian sour red beer in its blended, accessible form. Dark, rich auburn in colour, with a soft, dry malt nose, and flavours that blend champagne sherbet with malty, raisiny fruit. Tart, refreshing and satisfying beer ideal for the weary in spirit. *Serve:* room temp. *Avail:* BeerC.

RODENBACH ALEXANDER***
33cl Bottled 6.5%:
Top-fermented, matured in oak, this cherry Rodenbach has a cherry brandyish nose, and a flavour combining a particularly sappy, oaky kriek with a sherryish (manzanilla) richness that is also slightly pointed and briney. Flavour-spotters might also detect a little vanilla, a little orange, and a sundried fruit succulence, all preserved in alcohol. Excellent for sipping before Sunday lunch. *Serve:* larder cool. *Avail:* BeerC, Wait.

RODENBACH GRAND CRU****
25cl Bottled 6.5%:
Rubbery accented, strong alcohol fruit on the nose, and on tasting (wowee!) a sharp, vivid, sour-sweet bolt from the blue: lemon, sweet and then sour, and lots of savoury, pomegranate fruit flavour, a deep oaky dryness, and, as it warms in the glass, marmalade orange, plum, tart unripe blackcurrant and rhubarb fruits. Delicious. But shocking. Wakes up the taste buds. An ideal aperitif beer. *Serve:* room temp/larder cool. *Avail:* BeerC.

ROSE DE GAMBRINUS****
Frambozen Lambic Cantillon. 37.5cl Bottled 5%:
A classic raspberry (and cherry) lambic, with a wonderful translucent bloody orange colour, and appetizingly sour yeast, oaky fruit aromas when the cork is popped. On the palate – wowee! – amazingly tart, lemon and unripe raspberry bite, tantalizingly sour, but just fruit sweet enough to compensate; further redeemed by the softest texture and a rose floral delicacy. There's a little oak-aged complexity hovering in the background, too. But mostly it's tart, with the texture (and more than a hint of the character) of a really good still farm cider. Tart and authentic and moreish. *Serve:* larder cool. *Avail:* specialists, Beer Paradise.

SAINSBURY'S BELGIAN ALE***
Traditional Gueuze 75cl Bottled 6%:
Perhaps not so traditional as it might be, and

certainly sanitized and smoothed out for British palates, but none the less a delicious beer in an impressive, wine-sized, cork and wire cage topped bottle. In fact it's from a very good producer, Boon, although it's also been sweetened up. Very slightly translucent amber brown, with robust sweet and sour flavours – a little citrussy pineapple, a little banana, a little butterscotch and spice – with a sherberty, moussey texture, creamy yet refreshing, and a gentle, oaky tannic dryness. Excellent with a cold lunch (as a kind of liquid chutney?).*Serve:* light fridge chill/larder cool.

ST BENOIT BLONDE**

Bière d'Abbaye Du Bocq. 33cl Bottled 6.5%: Bottle-conditioned, and a pretty yellow amber, with an amber milky cloudiness, and a fruity, overripe pineapple, almost cheesey nose. Wheaten, grain flavours, honeyed apples, a little alcohol and clove on the palate, but with something cardboardy and grain husky on the finish, and a dry, fizzing hop kick, that grows astringent with drinking. *Serve:* larder cool. *Avail:* BeerC.

ST BENOIT BRUNE**

Biere d'Abbaye 33cl Bottled 6.5%: Bottle-conditioned, amberish-brown, with a sour-sweet, oaky nose and when tasted, a soft, soft water texture and mellow flavours. It's fresh and lemony, with prickly bubbles, but also gently sour-oaky and malty, as well as wheaty, with spicy, smokey grain, and coriander and nutmeg notes, and an occasionally piercingly dry woody hop flavour in the finish. But there's also a keggy, over-processed quality about it that lets the side down rather. *Serve:* larder cool. *Avail:* BeerC.

ST BERNARDUS PATER***

St Bernardus, Watou. 33cl Bottled 6%: Dense chocolate brown, with pear drops and solventy alcohol aromas and a lively fizziness. Flavours are creamy, with smooth chocolate malt, a hint of something liqueurish, sherberty tart notes on the finish, but then a bitter, dry aftertaste with a persistent sourness. *Serve:* room temp/larder cool. *Avail:* BeerC.

ST BERNARDUS PRIOR

33cl Bottled 8%: .
Harshly alcoholic on the nose, estery and wild, with distinctly Stilton like fumes. Flavours are also pungent, wild and a bit blue cheesey. Rocquefort, anyone? *Serve:* room temp. *Avail:* BeerC.

ST BERNARDUS ABT

33cl Bottled 10%:
Also horribly over-brewed, over-ambitious, over-thin, and plain harsh. Virtually undrinkable. *Serve:* room temp. *Avail:* BeerC.

ST LOUIS GUEUZE*

Brewery van Honsebrouck, Ingelmunster. 25cl Bottled 5%:
A lambic blend which tastes sweetened up for export, made by one of the two daringly non-Senne Valley lambic producers. Bright brassy gold (filtered, too), with a barley-sugar nose and flavour, redeemed a little by tart fruit and vanilla notes. Oddly confected in character, only occasionally displaying good sour-sweet musky lambic qualities. *Serve:* larder cool. *Avail:* Maj.

ST LOUIS KRIEK*

25cl Bottled 5%:
Confected, syrupy, concentrated cherry flavours, strongly fondanty, as if cherryade has unwisely been blended with cherry brandy, and a few perfumey Parma Violets thrown in for good measure. Only for the seriously sweet-toothed. *Serve:* light fridge chill. *Avail:* Maj.

ST PAUL DOUBLE**

Sterkens. 50cl Bottled 6.9%:
St Paul Double and Triple are paired with St Sebastiaan Dark and Grand Cru, which are variants on the same beers. St Paul Double is very like Seb dark, but is a lighter garnet-red, and tastes like a dry-hopped version. It has more upfront fruit, Merlot like, less of a nose, and more resiny floral dryness in the flavours and finish. Strawberry is the dominant flavour here, coating the mouth and coming to a dead halt where the finish should be. Less structure, too sweet, but still delicious. *Serve:* room temp. *Avail:* BeerC.

ST PAUL TRIPLE***
Blonde 50cl Bottled 7.6%:
Bottle-conditioned golden beer in a glass bottle painted to look like the traditional stone. Tastes like a dry-hopped version of St Sebastiaan Grand Cru, with a resiny, dry, floral hop finish to add to that tasting note (below). Firm and fruitily dry, delicious beer. *Serve:* room temp/larder cool. *Avail:* BeerC.

ST SEBASTIAAN DARK**
Sterkens. 50cl Bottled 6.9%:
Stone-bottled, bottle-conditioned garnet brown beer with a damson, vanilla and date nose, and a pleasing spritzy texture. Flavours are dominated by yeasty fruit and sweetness, with mellow pear drop, summer fruit, plum jam and sour-sweet malt notes – a bit sweet all round, but with a redeeming bitter backbone, drying up nicely at the finish. *Serve:* room temp/larder cool. *Avail:* BeerC.

ST SEBASTIAAN GRAND CRU***
50cl Bottled 7.6%:
Flip-top stone-bottled golden ale with nail polish, yeast and banana aromas and yeasty fruity flavours, with a spicy character suggestive of ginger cake, nutmeg, all-spice and cinnamon. Spritzy and lively in texture, with a gently drying, prickly, warm spice cake finish in the mouth, and some distinctive, but not too intrusive, strong alcohol flavours, sweet and sour pungent, caramelized vegetable notes. Rather delicious. *Serve:* room temp/larder cool. *Avail:* BeerC.

SAISON DE SILLY***
Silly Brewery. 25cl Bottled 5%:
Dark amber, with a spirity nose which suggests both Cointreau and cognac, and a light, spritzy texture, transforming its sherryish, Jaffa orange, buttery sultana flavours into something clean and refreshing. Oak and vanilla lurk in the finish. An elusive, complex, satisfying little beer, which occasionally seems exactly like oloroso piggy-backing a cheap champagne. *Serve:* light fridge chill. *Avail:* BeerC.

SAISON DE PIPAIX***
Vapeur, Pipaix. 75cl Bottled 6.5%:
Unfiltered, unpasteurized, top-fermented, bottle-conditioned classic Saison ale made from barley malt, hops, yeast and water only. The great heavy bottle with its period label is nice too. It has almost gueuze-like qualities, combining tart apple and pear fruit, a toffeeish note, a fat yeasty tang, and something honeyish in the finish. An extremely quenching, light and summery, pleasantly sour beer of real delicacy. *Serve:* larder cool. *Avail:* specialists, Beer Paradise.

SAISON REGAL**
Purnode. 25cl Bottled 6%:
A traditional Ardennes beer from a large farmhouse brewery. The colour is a deep, luscious amber; the nose sweetly, faintly carroty, with sour and citrus notes, the texture clean and spritzy. Dry malt and fresh yeasty acids dominate flavours, which are slightly smoky, with a little buttery toffee and orange, but which trail off a bit in the finish. *Serve:* larder cool. *Avail:* C.

SAISON 1900***
Lefebvre. 25cl Bottled 5.2%:
Cloudy amber, bottle-conditioned beer with spicy tropical fruit, nutmeg and lemon on the nose and palate. Flavours are soft, fruity and gently drying, with gentle spice (ginger) warmth in the finish and a little floral, herbal hop flavour. Mouth-filling, with creamy wheat texture. *Serve:* larder cool. *Avail:* specialists.

SCOTCH DE SILLY**
Silly. 25cl Bottled 8%:
Bright dark amber with nutty alcohol on the nose, and smooth, nuttily alcoholic, softly sour, but also thin and refreshing flavours. But, Scotch fans note: it does also have a rich creamy head. *Serve:* larder cool. *Avail:* BeerC.

STELLA ARTOIS**
Leuven. 33cl Bottled 5.2%:
Made in England (actually) by Whitbread, under licence from Belgium's biggest

brewery. It describes itself as 'strong', and despite being only 5.2% alcohol has a typically strong lager, slightly turnipy nose (sweet and caramelized turnip), and is initially sweet on the tongue, before hop dryness chips in, giving way to sugar syrup at the finish. Swinging back a final time, the aftertaste turns dry and salty. *Serve:* light fridge chill. *Avail:* widely.

STELLA ARTOIS*
50cl Canned 5.2%:
Bright yellowish gold with a pungent strong alcohol flavour and a dry, strong, but finally bittersweet kick at the finish. Tastes stronger than a 5.2% lager. *Serve:* fridge cold. *Avail:* widely.

STELLA ARTOIS DRY*
27.5cl Bottled 5.5%:
Imported genuine Belgian product. Its much vaunted 'crisp dry taste' is in truth a bit of a conundrum, as this is actually a rather sweet beer, with a slightly vegetal, strong lager nose and taste. The dryness is all in the texture, which is mouth-coatingly, tongue-claspingly drying, but gives way to a synthetic-tasting sweet finish that's hard to shake off. Very gassy, too. Only just scrapes a star. *Serve:* fridge cold. *Avail:* Asda, Wait.

STRAFFE HENDRICK***
25cl Bottled 6%:
The only product of a small independent, from the town of Brugge. Harvest gold-coloured, with a slender white head and candy sugar, fruity, banana and alcohol estery aromas. Flavours offer many of the same, but also come up with a scented, fresh, ripe and juicy French pear note in the middle, before drying almost ferociously florally in the finish. A complex, fruity, dry, gently sour-sweet beer: deliciously drinkable, interesting but very accessible. A good one for the larder. *Serve:* room temp/larder cool. *Avail:* specialists.

STUDENT**
Wit Bier Lefebvre. 33cl Bottled 4.5%:
Wheat beer with a collegiate theme and the admirable motto: '*carpe diem; in birra veritas*'. Pale and cloudy, with tangerine on the nose, and a fresh, zingy flavour, mildly bready and remarkably tangerine juicey, with sherbet and pepper on the finish and gentle spice. Summery, undemanding, sweet and easy, with a (sweetened-up?) candyish, bubblegum finish. *Serve:* light fridge chill. *Avail:* specialists.

TIMMERMANS BLANCHE WIT***
Timmermans, Itterbeek. 25cl Bottled 3.5%:
A Belgian wheat beer/lambic blend of modest alcohol and good flavour that is spawning a host of imitators. In the glass, it produces a huge great foamy white head, and lightly estery, baked apple, bready aromas. Flavours produce a gentle, but delicious marriage of soft lambic sourness and appley, Opal Fruity wheat beer sweetness. Easy, summery drinking. *Serve:* light fridge chill. *Avail:* specialists.

TIMMERMANS FRAMBOZEN**
Raspberry Lambic. 25cl Bottled 4%:
Serve it *as* pudding, rather than with it, or as an ingenious kind of liquid sorbet between courses. Intensely raspberryish, with sweet strawberry and jammy flavours, but saved from stickiness by a compelling almondy, dry, sour-sweet edge. *Serve:* fridge cold. *Avail:* Thres.

TIMMERMANS GUEUZE CAVEAU***
33cl Bottled 5%:
Golden gueuze which smells of fresh-baked brandy snaps. Flavours are sour-sweet (sourer than sweet, as a gueuze should be), with a soft, winey tartness, underripe Cox apple notes, creamy and kind rather than lemony and eye-watering. Unfiltered, matured for several years in oak, bottle-conditioned, Timmermans Caveau will now go on to improve, grow more complex, and achieve more honeyed moussey character with cellaring. *Serve:* larder cool. *Avail:* specialists.

TIMMERMANS KRIEK***
Cherry Lambic. 25cl Bottled 4%:
A beer that cries out for a summer wedding.

Deeply red, effervescent as champagne, with a lovely winey, fruity nose, and delicious cherry, almond and elderflower flavours. Not remotely sticky, though; tart citrus notes and a dry, moreish texture balance the rich fruit beautifully. *Serve:* fridge cold. *Avail:* Thres.

TITJE***

Bière Blanche Silly Brewery. 25cl Bottled 5%:
Cloudy pale gold with the most alluring fresh tangerine juice (plus a little grapefuit) nose. To taste, melon, pear and orange join an almost savoury wheaten huskiness, leading into a tangerine pithy, fruity finish with a little cumin and coriander spice lingering in the mouth. A moreish, tasty, summery beer with a delightful home-made lemonade quality. *Serve:* light fridge chill. *Avail:* BeerC.

TOISON D'OR**

Het Anker. 33cl Bottled 7%:
Clear amber Triple with a fruity, slightly spirity nose, suggesting a sort of banana brandy. It's more reticent on the palate, though, sweetish and whiskyish certainly, but with a finish at once overpoweringly sugary and spiked by bittersweet, kumquat-like fruit. Followed by lots of earthy spirit alcohol on the aftertaste. *Serve:* room temp. *Avail:* specialists.

TRIPLE MOINE**

Du Bocq. 33cl Bottled 8%:
Delicate pale gold beer with a quietly alcoholic nose, and spritzy, delicately star-fruity, savoury fruit flavours, resinous with a cigar box and herbal finish. *Serve:* room temp. *Avail:* BeerC.

VIEUX BRUGES KRIEK**

Van Honsebrouck, Ingelmunster. 37.5cl Bottled 5%:
Soft and gluggable cherry gueuze for beginners, at first fondanty with cherry sweetie flavour, before growing a little drier with a short acquaintance. Uncomplicated, easy drinking with strawberry juice notes in the finish. *Serve:* larder cool. *Avail:* specialists.

WALKABOUT

Belgian Lager 44cl Canned 3%:
Weak, disappointing, grainy and watery mass-market table lager from the Walkabout Beers of the World pack, which features four canned beers, also from Britain, Bavaria and Italy. *Serve:* fridge cold. *Avail:* Wait.

WATOU WIT BIER**

Van Eecke. 25cl Bottled 5%:
Bottle-conditioned wheat beer with densely ochre-beige colouring, and remarkably spicy (rather than fruity or sweet) flavours, with lots of nutmeg among its bready, wheaten textures. Short, soft, flavoursome, but a little unrelenting on the spice front. *Serve:* larder cool. *Avail:* specialists, Selfridges.

WESTMALLE DUBBEL****

Westmalle. 33cl Bottled 6.5%:
Auburn red, bottle-conditioned Trappist ale with soft, creamy yeast fruit aromas, and lots of lively bubbles. Flavours are of cherry and plum, oaky sour and dry, a little vanilla, and remarkably yeasty, but overlain by a serious, spiritous character, elegantly dry and very grown up. The classic of the style. *Serve:* room temp. *Avail:* BeerC.

WESTMALLE TRIPEL****

33cl Bottled 9%:
A blonde of translucent apricot colour, bottle-conditioned, and with yeasty, pineapple chunk and orange rind fruit, and a grapefruit pithy, very bitter finish. Flavours are also profoundly whiskyish, peaty, almost briney, with sour oak finesse. An intriguing Scotch alternative in the drinks cabinet, and the undisputed classic of the style. *Serve:* room temp. *Avail:* BeerC.

YERSEKES MOSSELBIER**

25cl Bottled 4.5%:
Made to drink with mussels, in honour of the prime mussel-fishing port of the north coast. Bottle-conditioned, translucent, and mildly fruity, with sweet-sour notes and mild malt and spice flavours. Firm, with a hint of sweetness, and a gentle hop backbone. A modest quaffer, but good with seafood and fish. *Serve:* light fridge chill. *Avail:* specialists, Selfridges.

Britain

Uniquely in the world, British beer culture is still very much pub-centred, and our native beer styles consist entirely of top-fermented ales. The pub system supports the draught ale culture; the draught ale culture supports the pub system – the two in an imperfect but lovable symbiosis. But in addition to this ying and yang, a thriving marketplace for interesting bottled (and to a lesser extent, canned) 'take home' products has evolved in the last ten years. The only real problem, apart from the difficulties of getting your bottled ales into the marketplace at all, is that, unlike the other great ale-making nation, Belgium, we have not (yet) developed a bottled beer culture that truly reflects our strengths.

The post-war 'rationalization' of both brewery companies and individual beers, and the attempt to force upon us lamentably dire mass-market keg beers, typified by the infamous Watney's Red Barrel, are market forces which have effectively been turned around in the last 20 years – a situation almost entirely achieved by the work of CAMRA, the Campaign for Real Ale. Widely cited as the most effective of any consumer pressure group in Britain, they have helped create the present optimistic climate in which microbreweries are opening at a rate of about one every ten days. Almost without exception these little companies are dedicated to the production of good cask ale. And there's no doubt that, on draught in the pub, real ale is a far superior product to keg beer (to put it mildly). Why? Simple. Because it hasn't been pasteurized and filtered. It contains active yeast, which mellows and improves its flavours and textures. It's naturally spritzy and fresh-tasting. Keg beer is a pasteurized and filtered (otherwise known as brewery conditioned). It has been processed at the brewery for better keeping qualities. The benefits are similar to those which have also brought the world processed cheese and UHT milk. Nor does the comparison end there, in many cases.

But few bottled beers are real ales. Only those which are bottle-conditioned, with active yeast improving and conditioning the beer in situ, are truly 'real'. So perhaps it's time to stop narrowly concentrating on what's real and what's not, and concentrate instead on what's *good* and what's *bad*. In the pub, a simple matter: you're unlikely to ever taste a keg beer on draught that is as good as even the worst real ale. But in bottle, judgements are nothing like as simple, a fact reflected in the listings that follow. The best bottled beer range in Britain, from Caledonian Brewery in Edinburgh, is entirely keg beer. If we were to insist only on real ale, we would also be dismissing many of the great beers of the world, only a minority of which are bottle-conditioned.

But why should keg beers in a bottle be so much better than keg beers on draught? Bottling is kinder to beer character than kegging, and incomparably superior to canning, widget or no widget. It's also partly the fact that beers given the higher status that bottling entails have been more carefully produced, and are issued with great pride by the brewery in question, occasionally even outranking their cask products.

Twenty-five years ago we hardly drank any lager in Britain. Today we make a depressing amount of dire, tasteless rubbish, and almost as dire a selection of foreign names made here under licence. There are one or two glowing exceptions, like the very decent lager made by Belhaven, but bottom-fermented beers have never, and will never be part of the native beer culture of Britain. Lagers of quality, which have Bavarian and Czech traditions and not low-cost keg beer as their model –like the fresh, wholesome pilsener made by the Freedom Brewery in Fulham, London – might, however, become very welcome visitors. There are other visiting beer styles which may take up residency. Wheat beers are now widely made by British real ale breweries.

For more detailed information on individual breweries and their products, see the British Breweries Directory, on page 246.

THE BEER REGIONS

The thriving microbrewery network – blessedly free of the burden of tradition, and set up by enthusiasts who know what they like and, more importantly, know what their *customers* would like – are making the ales they want to make wherever they are. Established breweries, too, are beginning to act in a more consumer-conscious way, and adjust their beers accordingly. But underneath all that, it's still broadly true that particular styles are associated with particular regions, though these traditional models are widely flouted.

The North West

The North West is well known among cask beer fans for producing some of the most straightforwardly fresh and honest (and good value) draught beer in Britain. At their best, north-west-produced milds and bitters have bagfuls of malt and hop character, and enviable balance. The worst that can be said is that they are perhaps a little old-fashioned.

Yorkshire

Yorkshire produces its own distinctive beer style, thanks to the Yorkshire Square system of fermentation vessels, which create beers of characteristic creamy, fragrantly bitter, yeasty nuttiness. Black Sheep, Sam Smith and Tetley use them (Tetley's are stainless steel). John Smith doesn't.

Midlands

Midlands beers are still dominated by the looming presence of Burton-on-Trent, which remains the capital of British brewing, thanks to the great export enterprise based on its naturally calcium-sulphate-rich waters. The soft, mineral-water flavour and body that this imparts is recognized across the globe as the foundation stone of India Pale Ale. Burton beers are best characterized by this full-bodied, dry and refreshing brewing style. The Burton Union system of fermentation, still responsible for the pungently yeasty individualism of Marston Pedigree, has now been dropped by its old chief exponent, Bass. Straddling the Midlands and the West, Hereford and Worcester is the second hop-growing centre of England, famous for its aromatic Goldings.

East Anglia

East Anglia is the traditional and modern heartland of English barley farming. Beers are, however, concerned to express a balance of malt with hop dryness, and often have a rich 'bloom' of yeasty fruit character, full-bodied and satisfying. East Anglia is also, following the decimation of the old brewing heritage by the bullying mega-breweries in the 1960s and 1970s, now producing a rich crop of independently-minded small breweries.

South East England

South East England (more specifically, Kent) is the hop garden of England, and its quaint old oast houses still pepper the countryside. Not surprisingly, beers here tend to make the most of this, and the ravishingly dry, perfumed, well-hopped style is common, often with a dryish malt element to enhance the effect.

West Country

West Country beers have more or less reinvented themselves in the last 20 years. Devon's oldest surviving brewery is Blackawton, founded in 1977; and a rash of now classic breweries followed, starting with Butcombe in 1978, which was followed by Cotleigh in 1979, and Exmoor (Golden Hill) in 1980. This is a region teeming with brewing enterprise, and some of our most exciting microbreweries are here. One of the most distinctive modern West Country beer styles is the pale, golden, elegantly dry, yet barley-sweet ale of modest alcohol, but which tastes of western sunshine.

Wales

Wales has a long tradition of sweetly malty, dense and creamy ales, originating from a similar historical situation to Scotland's, and continuing still. Some of the sweetest, maltiest beers in Britain are to be found here, traditionally rounding off with a drying malt finish. Micros and modernity now provide other styles and flavours, of course.

Scotland

Critics of modern Scottish brewing are likely to point out that its most successful independent breweries, like Caledonian, Belhaven and Maclay, have deserted the traditional Scots beer style, which is distinctively malty, for English Bitter. There are two sound objections to this rant. First, better that than the extraordinarily, mind-bogglingly bad 'Scotch' beers of the two major players in Scots brewing, Tennents and McEwans, who make canned so-called ales of quite stunning mediocrity and badge them with the 'traditionalist' 60, 70, 80 and 90 shilling labels. (They then compound this misery by controlling some 80% of the so-called free-trade market.) Secondly, that modern Scottish independents are developing their own beer styles, which have one foot in the past, but also look to the modern palate. The malty, sweet beers of Scots history were made as a response to the deprivations of the climate and economy. Hops couldn't be grown up here, and barley was freely available. Malting was something of a local speciality, done for both brewing and whisky distilling. And rich, sweet beers were also of nutritional value in difficult days, and in an unforgiving climate. Given a choice, many Scottish breweries would have leapt at the chance of a regular and affordable hop supply.

Modern Scots independents make beers that are both robustly malty and vigorously hoppy, and with their own distinctive house style. Their beers often have rich, satisfying texture, thanks to the Scottish tradition of not fermenting out so much malt sugar as the English, and leaving a good malty body behind. The Scotch Ale which has developed as a sort of pastiche of the traditional, dense sweet style, and has been taken up by the whole world, is no longer made in Scotland itself (if, indeed, it ever was), although a more refreshing malty variant on the theme continues to be popular with the old English allies in Tyneside. At least in name, if not in authenticity. Traquair House, using its 18th-century brewhouse and old recipes, makes ales closer to the real old Scots style than any other brewery. Additionally, a delicious modern twist has been given to the malt tradition by the Oatmalt Stout and Oatmeal Stout of Maclay and Broughton respectively.

The 'shilling' system is still widely used to denote strength, a hangover from the days when these were the actual prices per barrel for a brewery's range. 60/-, the weakest, is usually a mild-equivalent beer, but in independent hands, specifically those of Caledonian, 60/- it is a succulently flavoursome, hoppy amber ale of more character than any other beer so labelled. 90/- is traditionally a strong, dark, dense beer, but in big brewery hands scarcely reaches 5% abv. In the traditional shilling language, 60/- is also known as a Light, 70/- a Heavy or Special, 80/- an Export, and 90/- a Strong.

BRITSH BEER STYLES

Mild

The mildest alcoholically, but not necessarily in flavour. The name might even mislead: milds were of the strength of a strongish modern bitter at the turn of the century. A survivor from the Victorian era, Sarah Hughes Original Dark Ruby Mild has an original gravity of 1058 and would therefore burst out of the top of the strong bitter class were classifications made purely on grounds of potency. Modern milds generally come in two varieties: the malty, dark (sometimes very dark) fruity sort, and the light, tangy, perhaps even slightly hoppy, thirst quenching sort.

Milds are usually dark in colour, at their best with a finely poised balance between the rich and nutritious comfort of dark, perhaps fruity malts, and the light drinkability of a modest-in-alcohol, made-for-quaffing ale with a discreet, but crucial, yeast and hop presence cutting through the malt richness. It's this combination which made milds the natural after-work drink in the industrial heartlands of Britain earlier this century. This is still a beer style with a rather self-conscious blue-collar image problem, which is a pity, because good milds have the potential to experience a great revival; low alcohol and good flavours make them natural 1990s beers. Realizing this, some breweries are renaming their milds. Fuller's, for example, have reintroduced the old word for a mild, Hock.

Many producers, all over Britain, still produce milds, though they don't always call them that. The heartland of the mild is still the Midlands and Wales, though the north-west is also mild-friendly, and a mild equivalent has also survived in Scotland. Welsh milds tend to be the darkest and sweetest of all. Midlands milds tend to be the most interesting and complex: there are two Midlands classics, Highgate Mild and Banks's Mild, now rechristened plain Banks's. Highgate uses six different malts.

Bitter

This is the word most foreigners and many ex-pats abroad use to describe British beer. Microbreweries across the world, but especially in America, are striving to recreate the perfect balance of a good English bitter, and refashion it in their own image. Bitter is by no means the only beer style made in Britain, but it is the one known internationally, and the style of beer many Brits themselves think of as interchangeable with the word 'beer'.

Bitter is often referred to, colloquially, at the bar counter as 'ordinary', to distinguish it from special or strong bitters. A good 'ordinary' is the pinnacle of the brewer's art, in achieving a flavour and texture that's both refreshing and complex. Bitters take many forms, and have a surprisingly diverse character when all grouped and tasted together: some might have a hop-accented dry palate, made more complicated and interesting with yeasty fruits and acids, and the richness and body of good malts; some might be yeast-accented, with a rich, fat bloom of fruit complexity; others may take their lead from the nutty, woody dryness, and buttery succulence of cured and amber malts. Put all these variables together and you have a beer style of endless and fascinating variety. There is no more rewarding an area of study in the whole field of world beers.

It is, of course, top-fermentation which is the secret of this extraordinary variety. Bottom-fermented lager beers have in common a reined-in conformity of flavour and texture. Naturally, they too vary enormously (bottom-fermented ales are made, after all), but with nothing like the degree of flamboyance and unpredictability, the scope and breadth of the top-fermented ales of the world. And particularly of Britain. Top-fermentation allows the yeast to work in contact with the air, and this is the crucial factor in developing the fat, yeasty tang and rich fruits of many classic bitters. Yeast, not in any bready, baking sense, but in these various acidic, rich, fruity, sharp, sweet and sour guises, makes itself felt as a third flavour (along with malt and hops) in the British ale style, and thus creates a roundness and depth of flavour and texture that's unrivalled anywhere. Yeast is particularly felt in the character of beers made using traditional fermentation methods, notably the Open Squares of Yorkshire and the Burton Union method still used by Marston. Burton Union allows the rising, fermenting yeast to be trapped in an open trough, placed above the main fermentation vessels and connected to them by feeder pipes. Not only is the overflow contained, but the top, clean yeast is preserved and used again. Not only does the resulting beer drop very 'bright', but the yeast used in this system has naturally evolved its own powdery structure; the beers look bright, but actually contain the finest yeast suspension, which produces their characteristic yeast 'bite' and moreish dryness.

Bitters vary more than any other beer style the world over, but common to all of them is the hop dryness from which they get their name. Many brewers talked to in researching the British Breweries Directory use only pale malt in their bitters, though others use crystal and perhaps even a pinch of darker, more flavoured malts. Pale malts contribute to the moreish dryness of the classic bitter style. Classically, the hops used are Fuggles and Goldings, for aroma and flavour, though many other varieties are also used these days. Late hopping and dry hopping in the cask lend a resinous, almost oily freshness to the hop character of many bigger, beefier bitters.

Stronger bitters are known as Best Bitters, or Specials. They are usually stronger flavoured than 'ordinaries', and are more often of the fruity but hoppy sort.

Pale Ales and India Pale Ales

Pale Ales aren't usually particularly pale in themselves. Their pale label is a historical one, a name that reflected their comparative paleness to the standard brown beers of the day. Pale ales are classically amber in colour, and characteristically of a lovely gem-like clarity. Their flavours are more malt-accented than hop-accented, but often still with a ravishing dryness, which comes from the nutty dry, oaky, slightly spicy character of the malt itself. Hop and yeast flavours are there, but in a supporting rather than leading role. Often they are stronger than the bitter in a modern brewery line-up.

Sam Smith of Tadcaster is the classic British pale ale producer, and it's their Old Brewery Strong Pale Ale that's been so hugely influential in developing the style in the USA. Their Yorkshire Square Fermentation System, like the Burton Union one, is a two-storey affair that allows the expanding yeasty beer to rise into the upper square, and leave a yeast deposit behind when it sinks back again. Like that of Burton, the Yorkshire yeast has developed its own character, in response to this assault course.

India Pale Ales date from the transporting of Pale Ales to colonial outposts of Empire, or rather to its thirsty officials. India Pale Ales are hoppy beers, far hoppier than plain Pales, and are often even paler, thanks to their hop-accented recipes. They should also have more single-minded hop dryness than bitters. Hops are not only valuable in beer for their flavours, but for their preservative role, and high hop rates in the India-bound pales were essential to keep them fresh on the long voyage. The importance of good keeping qualities also meant that the original IPAs were pretty high in alcohol. Some of them still are. India pale ales can vary from a modern interpretation – which makes them pale, delicate, astringent, with hops well to the fore – to a more Victorian approach, which creates fruity, malty complexity behind a breathtaking astringency. Ushers IPA is one of the first sort. Caledonian's Merman is of the second kind.

Brown Ales

Brown ales basically fall into two camps: the brown and the amber. The brown ales of the north of England are really pale ale hybrids, with Newcastle Brown the clear, amber flagship beer. Northern browns are more likely to have a soft, fruity malt character chiming in with the drier, nuttier malt character of the pale. The brown ales of legend have more or less died out, but war babies would probably define them as similar to the surviving classic Manns Brown Ale, a sweet, densely coffeeish, rather mild, malty beer of pond-like brownness. These days, better brown ales, of more interesting and complex character, are being made in the USA than in London, the historic home of the style, where chloride-rich water made brown ale a natural product, and India Pale Ale incredibly difficult (if not impossible) to make. Pete's Wicked Ale is a bottom-fermented American Brown, of smooth, chocolatey malt richness, crystal malt succulence, and with firm but gentle hop character. How unlike the sticky brown beers that pass for brown ales in Britain now.

Porter and Stout

Porter came first. We think of stout as an Irish style, and certainly Ireland has made it its own, with a bitter, roast barley interpretation that's associated with Guinness right across the world. But porters, London porters, came first, in the 18th century, and it was their huge popularity in Dublin that caused Arthur Guinness to take up, first London-style porter-brewing, and then launch his own Extra Stout Porter to recoup his Irish drinking audience. A strategy that worked.

As is also mentioned in the Irish introduction, porters originated (so apocryphal brewing history has it, at least) with the market porters of London's Covent Garden. Modern porters take either the historical route or follow the 1990s model: porter-brewing has enjoyed a huge revival here in the last few years, and its continuing success will probably be built on the modern style. This is hugely varied in itself, but, to generalize, is a distinctively softer, more coffeeish and chocolatey, perhaps also fruity interpretation. To this end, lots of chocolate malt typically appears in the ingredients list. Some don't even feature the roast unmalted barley that is present in the classic stouts, though others keep this to a minimal showing. Stouts are stouter, as the name suggests, with bigger body, more burnt black malt bitter dryness, and much higher hopping than the modern porter (though quite stout porters are also made in Britain, especially when following 19th century recipes). Plenty of stout porters, both top- and bottom-fermented, are also made overseas, but almost none of them (bar a Sri Lankan and a couple of others) use the word stout, which is why imported porters are often more stout-like in character. Probably this is down to the fact that the outposts of Empire tended to pass on the English porter style and not the Irish dry stout.

Many good stouts and porters feature not just scorched malts and barleys of various sorts, not just a degree of hop dryness, not just a fat yeasty tang (and not, perhaps, just a tangible water character), but also the elusively warm, leathery, woody, slightly sweaty aroma and character widely referred to as 'horse blanket'. You know it when you taste it, but it's difficult to define. What is certain is that it comes from Brettanomyces, a friendly organism particularly to be found lurking in old oak.

Imperial stouts are relics of an export trade that once sent strong, highly-hopped porter beers to the Russian Empire. So popular did they become that Russia developed its own, extremely strong, complex, densely flavoured variant. Courage's Imperial Russian Stout is in this vein; Sam Smith's, which dates only from the 1980s, a more modern, softer example. The Russians also liked stouts (they're invariably called Russian Stouts, although quite often they are porterish in character) made with the roasted 'brown' barley of the day, which gives a savoury, Pontefract-cake-like liquorice character. Vassilenski's Black Russian, also made in England, is an old-recipe-based porter of this sort.

Sweet stouts are made so very sweet by either pasteurizing the beer to within an inch of its life before adding the final dose of sugar, or simply adding a variety of unfermentable sugar. If it weren't unfermentable, the yeast would attack and gobble it up, leaving something thin and high in alcohol. Milk and cream stouts originate in one ideal solution to this problem: using lactose, an unfermentable milk sugar, to sweeten the beer.

Strong Old Ales

Strong ales and old ales are not interchangeable terms, but are often used to mean the same thing. There are strong ales that achieve high alcohol levels without ever quite cultivating old ale character, or, for that matter, intending to. And there are, occasionally, convincing old ales that turn out to be only of fairly moderate strength. Strong ale is a term used with scientific accuracy – it's either high in alcohol or it isn't, after all – whereas, Old Ale tends only to be used in a complimentary way, when the characteristics of the style have clearly been achieved.

An old ale is a strong ale with a richness of flavour and texture, often, but not always, with added sugar to increase both alcohol and sweetness levels. Often old ales are darkest brown in colour, though they might also be red, or even tawny in hue. But they *always* have a rich weight of body, achieved by starting with a pretty high original gravity, and not letting the yeast attenuate as far as it would like. This is where added sugars of various sorts come in handy. A pretty hefty original gravity, particularly in an all-malt beer, means not just malt body, but lots of malt flavour, typically rich and dark, though some examples also have a robust hop dryness. It's usual to include 'coloured' malts of various specifications, crystal and chocolate mostly, black and burnt malt only by the pinch. Though at least one English example, which also happens to be the undisputed classic, Thomas Hardy's Ale, achieves its succulent dark richness by using only pale malt and boiling for much longer than usual, so as to caramelize it. The final flavour factor is typically a huge, generous yeasty character, with an acidic kick that cuts through the sweet dark malts. Bottle-conditioned examples improve with cellaring for five, ten, even 20 years.

The dark old ales, winter ales, Christmas ales and the like that have become so fashionable have also spawned a new interest in the spiced ales of the past. Coriander, cinnamon bark, nutmeg and cloves, orange peel, juniper and honey are all being experimented with.

Barley wine is the terrible and misleading term often awarded to the strongest kind of bitter, once it's got beyond Special, Extra and the like. At high alcohol levels, and after a long maturation (perhaps even reseeded with a fresh yeast in the conditioning vessels) these ales no longer resemble bitters in their proper sense, but they have followed the bitter line of descent, rather than the dark and sweet old ale line. Often, at high or extreme alcoholic strength, barley wines do acquire a vaguely vineous smooth, winey character, though it's more often spiritous and sherryish, or whiskyish (or brandyish) on the palate. They tend to be paler than old ales, and crystal-malt rather than dark-malt accented. In well-made examples a rich succulence results, often punctuated by pungent alcohol flavours in their own right.

ABBOT ALE**

Greene King, Suffolk. 33cl Bottled 5%: Nine out of ten marks for packaging, with its miniaturized strong-ale shouldered bottle and renaissance abbot label. The nose is pleasing, too, aromatic and tobacco-like.

There's just enough malty fruit on the tongue, with a camphor and sandalwood finish, in which classic hop dryness builds slowly and layers in the mouth. Points are lost for a keggy, over-fizzy texture, which blunts the beer's natural generosity. *Serve:* larder cool. *Avail:* BeerC, Safe, Thres, Wait.

ABBOT ALE*

44cl Canned 5%:
'Premium conditioned', one of the newer methods for supposedly reproducing cask ale quality without recourse to the dreaded widget. Remarkably different to the bottled Abbot Ale, the fruitiness almost gone, replaced by a strong-alcohol, slightly turnipy, sweet winey backnote, and vivid dryness pushed to the front. The finish gets horribly clingy once the dryness subsides. *Serve:* larder cool. *Avail:* widely.

ABINGTON BITTER

Abington Brewery (Wells). 44cl Canned 3%:
Pale bright amber, very fizzy, mildly malty, sweet-nosed commodity bitter with a super-fizzed, watery, very slightly nutty flavour. Also sold in a PET. *Serve:* larder cool. *Avail:* Sains, Wait.

ACE LAGER*

Federation, Tyne & Wear. 50cl Canned 3%:
Supposedly a pilsner lager, and it has a promisingly mango fruit and grainstore nose, but the flavour and texture is thin and disappointing, wet cardboardy, and almost acrid in the finish, though a buttery barley and gently hoppy alternative finish struggles through in some samples tasted. *Serve:* fridge cold. *Avail:* Safe, Somer.

ADNAMS BROADSIDE**

Strong Pale Ale Adnams, Suffolk. 27.5cl Bottled 6.3%:
Very Adnams aromas, of celery and walnut, from this deep-reddish amber beer, and more of the same on the palate, but with a little orange, and lots of strong sweet alcohol chiming in before the finish. A bit cloying and over the top, lacking balancing dryness and hop flavours: it comes to a dead stop just where the lingering astringency should be. A beer for sipping. *Serve:* room temp. *Avail:* specialists, BeerC.

ADNAMS CHAMPION PALE ALE***

27.5cl Bottled 3.1%:
Bright amber, lively beer with a fresh and appetizing walnut and green celery nose, and nutty, refreshing flavours: nuts, celery, hops – a veritable salad of a pale ale. A delicious bitterness creeps in after a while and then begins to dominate. Arrestingly clean and zingy, and admirably full- flavoured for a mere 3.1%. *Serve:* larder cool. *Avail:* specialists, BeerC.

ADNAMS SUFFOLK STRONG ALE*

44cl Canned 4.5%:
Not particularly strong at 4.5%. High marks for packaging: 1920s railway poster style. Low marks for texture: dramatically over-fizzed, with an oddly lemonadey backdrop to the flavour, though a real beer, with decent malt and hop balance, lurks uneasily underneath. But the finish is deliciously hoppy, with a bitterness that builds slowly and persists. The middle, at first a little sweet (even orange squashy), gradually becomes completely dominated by an astringent dryness, almost anaesthetizing the back of the mouth, though the aftertaste is a little cloying and sugary. *Serve:* larder cool. *Avail:* Asda, Safe, Sains, Somer, Tesco, VicW, Wait.

AKA

Extra Strong Lager Courage. 33cl Bottled 7.5%:
Brewed with champagne yeast, and as weird in its way as the Bass 'champagne' beer, Zeiss. The fancy slim bottle and vaguely imported, quasi-Mexican look, plus the unusual strength and pretensions of this beer, all add up to a fresh attempt at creating a new designer lager. Aromas are off-puttingly soapy and petrol-like, and flavours are sweet yet tannic, overbrewed and industrial. Seriously strange, unbeer like and frankly unpleasant. Perhaps give up the champagne yeast plan, chaps? *Serve:* fridge cold. *Avail:* Davies.

ALBION PORTER***

Marston, Burton-on-Trent. 50cl Bottled 4.8%: The subtlest fruity, malty, slightly spicy aromas and flavours may not at first appear to be natural three-star material, but this Marston bottled beer, like all their others, has the unmistakable stamp of quality. It's elegant rather than bland, very gently coffeeish, very gently bitter, with a faintly fruity aftertaste. *Serve:* room temp. *Avail:* Tesco, VicW.

ALLOA EXPORT 80/- ALE*

Carlsberg-Tetley. 50cl Canned 4.2%: Vanilla nosed, with surprisingly unconventional vanilla and rum butter flavours, a little hop character, and traces of malty fruit, though the finish is suffused with sticky brewing sugar flavours and adjuncts. *Serve:* larder cool. *Avail:* Co-op, Safe, Sains, Somer, Tesco, VicW.

ALLOA SPECIAL 70/- ALE

50cl Canned 3.5%: Fizzy pop-like, thin beer with masses of adjunct flavours, unmalted cereally, caramelly, vaguely roasty. Watery and a touch acrid in the finish. *Serve:* larder cool. *Avail:* Co-op, Sains, Somer, Tesco.

ALTENDORF

Courage. 44cl Canned 2.2%: Pale in colour, pale in flavour, low in alcohol. The finish is the best part, though even that grows adjuncty dry after a minute or two. Cheap 'foreign' quaffing beer for the financially challenged. *Serve:* fridge cold. *Avail:* Asda.

ALTENDORF SUPER STRENGTH

44cl Canned 8%: The least objectionable of all the British 'Supers', but even this is so crude a product, and so naturally belonging to the park bench school of brewing, that I can't bear to give it a star rating. It's sweetish (but not too sweet), unmistakably alcoholic, mildly fizzy, with a vaguely whiskyish kick. But still difficult to drink. *Serve:* fridge cold. *Avail:* Saf.

ANSELLS DRAUGHT BITTER

Carlsberg-Tetley. 44cl Canned 3.5%: Cask-flow system draught beer, to be fridge chilled for three hours, after which it's widget super-creamy, shaving foamy stuff, with a seriously bland flavour: faintly hoppy, oaky malty, nutty sweet, but only very slightly. Unsatisfying and unrefreshing. *Serve:* fridge cold, as instructed. *Avail:* Asda, Somer, Tesco, VicW.

ASDA BEST BITTER*

50cl Canned 3%: Light amber, unusually clear and bright, with spent fireworks and spoilt fruit on the nose. Watery to drink, with a faintly fruity flavour, and a fat, buttered note at the back, let down by the general blandness of the whole, and the distinctly tinny finish, though the texture is appealingly spritzy. (*Stop Press*: this product has been replaced by Asda Draught Bitter, or will be by the time you read this. There's also to be a new Asda Draught Stout.) *Serve:* larder cool.

ASDA CHESTER'S DRAUGHT ALE*

44cl Canned 3.8%: Brewed for Asda by Whitbread, a pale amber widget beer with a slender cream head but very little flavour, beyond a fruit juicey, bubble-gummy sweetness, mandarin on the finish, and the faintest malt and hop notes. Otherwise, sugary and bland. *Serve:* fridge cold.

ASDA LAGER

50cl Canned 3.2%: Brewed for Asda in the UK, this must be a 'value' product because it tastes of virtually nothing. Clean and fizzy, with the subtlest of lager flavours, a little corn sweetness, and a tinny finish that grows actively unpleasant after a few minutes. *Serve:* fridge cold.

ASDA ORIGINAL LIGHT ALE

50cl Canned 3.1%: Bright, barley-sugar gold stuff, which smells disconcertingly like warm luncheon meat, and tastes (no! not of meat) but of something dilute and creamy. A bit nutty, a bit eggy, slightly biscuity, but mostly dispiriting blandness. *Serve:* larder cool.

ASDA PORTLAND BITTER*
50cl Canned 4.5%:
Fruity nosed, reasonably refreshing 'nitrogen-flush', creamy bitter, surprisingly dry, but which contrives to have a sweet, slightly sticky texture at the same time. *Serve:* larder cool.

ASDA SUPER STRONG
44cl Canned 8.5%:
Tastes like Courage's Altendorf 'Super', but perhaps a shade less sweet. Strong, certainly. Super, 'fraid not. *Serve:* fridge cold.

BADGER COUNTRY BITTER
Hall & Woodhouse, Dorset. 44cl Canned 4%:
Thin, sugar-syrupy, lemonadey stuff with sticky sugar at the back, and only weakly malty at the front. Fizzy, caramelly, a little woody, very sweet. *Serve:* larder cool. *Avail:* Sains, Somer, Tesco.

BALLARD'S OFF THE WALL*
Ballard's, Hampshire. 27.5cl Bottled 9.6%:
Their annual harvest ale, bottle-conditioned, and a deep auburn brown. The sample tasted was obviously not yet ready to drink; who knows what it will have turned into in another two years? It had a silky texture, good natural liveliness, and an intensely sherbet, spiritous, pungent, burnt jam, muscovado, unripe plum, estery alcohol flavour. Like a dense fruit gravy. *Serve:* room temp. *Avail:* specialists, BeerC.

BALLARD'S WASSAIL*
50cl Bottled 6%:
Bottle-conditioned, russet-amber beer with promising cherry and rose aromas, but odd-tasting, emphatically sweet and sour flavours, tart and smokey, sour and fruity: old apples, sour plums and smelly cheese. Also a bit sickly and flat, and of syrupy intensity. Has the bottle-conditioning failed to ignite? Possibly another beer that needs more time. Pretty sure it's not meant to taste like this. *Serve:* room temp/larder cool. *Avail:* specialists, BeerC.

BANKS'S***
Banks's, Wolverhampton. 55cl Bottled 3.5%:
The old Banks's Mild is thus rechristened, or rather abbreviated, thanks to the insurmountable image problem Mild presents in the 1990s. Deliciously garnet-red in colour, gassy but not bubbly in the mouth, with mild, soft-watered, faintly strawberryish maltiness, and just a touch of woody sourness. Very tenuously reminiscent of a kriek. Nice lingering finish, too. (Also sold in cans.) *Serve:* larder cool. *Avail:* Asda, Odd, Safe, Sains, Tesco, VicW, Wait.

BANKS'S BITTER
50cl Canned 3.8%:
Unspoilt by progress, perhaps, but also ruined by canning. Chilling is required, and rapid pouring, to make the 'in-can system' work. No nose, other than something mildly sweet. A super-micro bubble texture foams in the mouth, but is not widget-dense. Modest flavours, sweet and malty, elusively hoppy, with the tiniest hint of oak and orange. Very keggy, pretty sweet, with an icky finish, at once sugary and drying. *Serve:* light fridge chill. *Avail:* Co-Op, Safe, Sain, Somer, Tesco, VicW.

DRAUGHT BASS**
Bass. 50cl Canned 4.4%:
Really not at all bad canned version of a draught classic, mercifully free of widget fluffiness and foam. Sparkling, rich amber in colour, with fresh bathhouse aromas, spa water-like and appetizing. Very gently malty with a persistent, soft dryness, that grows more mineral-rich in flavour and moreish with acquaintance, but with a sudden sweet note in the finish. Surprisingly light and quenching, but more likely to make you drop everything and rush off in search of the real thing, hand-pulled at the pub, than anything. *Serve:* larder cool. *Avail:* widely.

BASS DISTINCTION ALE*

33cl Bottled 5.1%:
Not very distinctive ale, sadly. An imaginative palate can detect caramelly malt and hop dryness, a little red apple, and strong ale richness, but the finish is cloying and sweet, and the general texture flaccid and wilted. Bottle-conditioned version, please! *Serve:* room temp/larder cool. *Avail:* Thres.

BATEMANS VALIANT****

Batemans, Lincolnshire. 50cl Bottled 4.3%:
Deep amber nectar with very yeasty, ripe banana, coconut and pineapple sweetie aromas, and an unmistakably Batemans flavour, but with a surprise in the finish. It starts out yeasty, crisp, crystal malty, with assertive hop and yeast bite and masses of black pepper, but . . . just when you're expecting it to turn austerely astringent, it instead mellows and softens into something golden, buttery, honeyed and toffee sweet, and a complex, satisfying finish embraces all these flavours. Clean-edged, moreish, irresistible, and all for a mere 4.3% alcohol! A modern classic. *Serve:* room temp/larder cool. *Avail:* Asda, BeerC.

BATEMANS VICTORY ALE***

50cl Bottled 6%:
Green banana, pear drops, cinnamon spice, lemon and Seville orange all crowd onto the palate of this strong, Union Jack-adorned, handsomely bottled beer. The fruits and spices are wrapped in a buttery, even slightly honeyed silkiness, the finish very dry, with a fruity alcoholic kick. Heady stuff, and with an alcoholic pungency that sticks to the roof of the mouth and climbs up the sinuses (not altogether unpleasantly). *Serve:* room temp. *Avail:* Asda, BeerC, Odd.

BATEMANS XXXB***

50cl Bottled 4.8%:
Many similarities to Sainsbury's Premium, also by Batemans, also 4.8%, but also distinctively different. With more pear drops on the nose (and something farm-yardy), and flavours that are drier, woodier, more sandalwood than banana, it's still a ravishingly dry beer, with yeasty, hop resin 'bite', and an astringency at the finish that builds into something almost briney in character. Also sold as part of the excellent Brewer's Heritage pack. *Serve:* larder cool. *Avail:* Asda, BeerC, Safe, Sains, Wait.

BEANO STOUT***

Tolly Cobbold, Suffolk. 27.5cl Bottled 4.1%:
Tolly's 1994 Beer of the Year, their fourth annual such bottling. A recreation of a 1950s stout, using English malt and hops. Dark blackest brown, no head, and a faintly ripe banana-fruity, yeasty, estery nose. Chocolate malt, roast barley, bitter black malt all crowd onto the palate; the final effect is of a remarkably succulent, fruit-sweet stout, but with an unusual delicacy at the same time. A tremendous hop dryness, rushing in from the back, makes the texture refreshing rather than cloying. *Serve:* larder cool. *Avail:* specialists, BeerC.

BELHAVEN BEST*

Draught Belhaven, Dunbar. 44cl Canned 3.5%:
Draught-flow-widgetized canned draught style bitter, honey brown, with a small cream head. Not as whipped up into a frenzy as some widget beers, and some robust flavours survive the process: hazelnut, caramel, gentle woody notes, and some buttery yeast richness. No real finish, though it dries just a smidgeon at the end. Widget chilling is the real problem. *Serve:* fridge cold. *Avail:* Asda, Safe, Somer, Tesco, VicW. Available widely in Scotland.

BELHAVEN EXPORT**

55cl Bottled 3.9%:
Vanilla, hops and butterscotch on the nose; creamy smooth malt on the palate, soft, soft water and a hop finish that begins gently but builds, growing oakier as it dries. There's an ingenious herbal hop twist waiting in the wings, too. Verging on a three-star beer. Also appears as Belhaven Premium in the excellent Brewer's Heritage pack. Stores all list it for

Scotland. *Serve:* larder cool. *Avail:* Asda, Co-op, Safe, Sains, Somer, Tesco, VicW.

BELHAVEN LAGER***
55cl Bottled 4.1%:
A surprisingly tasty, moreish beer from a lamentably dowdy, anonymous-looking bottle. An appetizing, peppery hop nose leads into a clean, sweet buttery barley flavour, with pronounced fresh roasted grain, flowering into delicious hop dryness. Wake up Belhaven! And take a lesson from Caledonian, 30 miles upriver: if this were attractively bottled, and called something like Golden Promise, it would get a lot more attention. Stores all list it for Scotland. *Serve:* light fridge chill. *Avail:* Asda, Co-op, Safe, Sains, Somer, Tesco, VicW.

BELHAVEN PALE ALE**
55cl Bottled 2.6%:
More of a mild than a pale ale, with dark, auburn-brown colouring, a sweet hazelnut nose, and a mild, sweetish malt character, of the nutty (rather than fruity) sort, enlivened slightly by a dash of demerara and tea, and finishing with a gentle dryness. The flavours, though, are all as low-key as the low-alcohol levels suggest. *Serve:* larder cool. *Avail:* Safe.

BYB
Bentley's Yorkshire Bitter Whitbread. 44cl Canned 3%:
Adjunct city, sickly with carrot soup and nutty flavours, dish-watery in the mouth. *Serve:* larder cool. *Avail:* Co-op, Somer, Thres, Wait.

BISHOPS FINGER***
Kentish Strong Ale Shepherd Neame, Kent. 50cl Bottled 5.4%:
Strikingly bottled, in brandy style, and brewed from barley malt, Kentish hops, yeast and water only. Russety-brown, with a powerfully malty, arrestingly hoppy nose. Flavours start out with great chewy mouthfuls of strong ale malty fruit and a little buttery raisin, followed by huge waves of tremendous hop dryness, and a powerfully dry, lingering finish. *Serve:* larder cool. *Avail:* Asda, BeerC, Odd, Safe, Tesco, VicW, Wait.

BISHOPS FINGER*
Kentish Strong Ale 44cl Canned 5.4%:
'Serve chilled; pour quickly', they say, but the fridge is the sworn enemy of a beer like this. Smokey, oaky, fruit-and-nut nose; warm, deep nutty, fruity character on the palate – both blunted by canning and chilling to the level of a banana sandwich on granary – dry prickly fizz, and an austere hop finish. But a bit thin, a bit keggy, and far too cold. *Serve:* fridge cold. *Avail:* widely.

THE BISHOP'S TIPPLE**
Gibbs Mew, Wiltshire. 33cl Bottled 6.5%:
Strong alcohol, vineous flavours produce an almost sickly, slightly cloying texture in this otherwise admirably complex ale (perhaps the spritzy vigour of bottle-conditioning is the answer?). There's a lot going on in here, though: woodsmoke, oak, bittersweet fruit, even a touch of fennel on the nose; a darkly, densely fruity, plumminess in the flavour, with a Coca Cola-sweets note. It's also smooth and super-silky in texture. The Bishop probably serves it as a wee tot, rather than in pints. *Serve:* room temp/larder cool. *Avail:* Safe, Somer, Thres.

BLACK SHEEP ALE***
Black Sheep, Yorkshire. 50cl Bottled 4.4%:
From Paul Theakston's own Yorkshire brewery, 'and nowhere else', a wry reference to the fate of the beers of his family's brewery (now owned by S&N). Stylishly packaged, lovely bright amber orange beer, with a walnut and braised-celery nose, pale ale mineral softness, a gentle fruit sweetness, a medium-roasted creaminess, and a delicious toasted walnut finish. The walnut is joined by floral hop dryness and yeasty astringency, which builds and layers in the mouth. A refined and complex beer, but just a little overfizzy; a bottle-conditioned version would probably elevate it to four-star status. *Serve:* larder cool. *Avail:* Odd, Safe, Sain, Tesco, Thres, Wait.

BODDINGTONS BITTER
Whitbread. 44cl Canned 3.8%:

Amber-coloured, tinny and sweet, caramelly and cloying, with a lemonadey nose and a slight dryness at the very finish. All criticism of the dreaded widget is temporarily halted. *Serve:* larder cool. *Avail:* widely.

Boddingtons Draught*

44cl Canned 3.8%:

Widget, nitrogen-bubbly version with a shaving-foam head, and super-creamy texture that at least works better with a gently hoppy bitter (such as this) than a sweeter, malty one. But still pretty dismal stuff. *Serve:* far too cold. *Avail:* widely.

Boddingtons Export***

33cl Bottled 4.8%:

Whitbread's new widget in a bottle Boddingtons manages to be lively but not remotely foamy. It still has to be chilled, and this is far too cold, but even so makes it into three-star territory. This Boddingtons, more than any yet tasted in your own sitting room, has a sharp, slightly sour yeasty character and a good robust hop bitterness, which grows drier and more astringent with drinking, developing, as it breathes and warms, a pleasantly hop floral, barley-husky note in the finish. But look what Caledonian beers achieve without all this messing about with bottle widgets. *Serve:* light fridge chill. *Avail:* Sains, Wait.

Bombardier**

Charles Wells. 50cl Bottled 4.3%:

Beautifully packaged, but flavours are not much in advance of the canned version, despite the merciful absence of widget foam. Again, a mildly oaky, smokey, decidedly malty, faintly fruity beer with vague hop balance, but not enough. Lacks balance and bite. And texture. *Serve:* larder cool. *Avail:* Asda, BeerC, Thres.

Bombardier*

44cl Canned 4.3%:

Too cold, after the prescribed two hours in the fridge, and the 'new draught in-can system' is still responsible for a thick micro-fizz cream texture, but there's also a slightly smokey sweetness, a little oak, lots of malt and a touch of fruit here. Underneath. *Serve:* fridge cold. *Avail:* Safe, Sains, Somer.

Brains Bitter

Brains, Cardiff. 44cl Canned 3.5%:

Very fizzy, big fat bubbly (they actually crackle as they disperse), thin and sweetly malty beer that tastes very like an old-fashioned shandy. This is not a compliment. *Serve:* larder cool. *Avail:* Asda, Safe, Sains, Somer, Tesco, Thres.

Brains Draught Dark

44cl Canned 3.5%:

Sweet, alcoholic, chestnut aromas rise from this dark-ruby black beer, and expectations rise a little too. Flavours, however, are dominated by a thin, dishwatery note, despite the mildly malty, very faintly coffeeish character, that clings a little as it warms. *Serve:* larder cool. *Avail:* Safe, Somer, VicW.

Brains Ipa**

27.5cl Bottled 4.5%:

Bright dark amber, with a braising-celery nose, and sweet, malty, smooth and creamy flavours, finishing in a gently drying hop note. But this is a beer dominated by sweetness, of the demerara sugar and vanilla sort, and consequently is a little soupy. Remarkably unhoppy for a supposed India Pale Ale, but rather comforting none the less. *Serve:* room temp/larder cool. *Avail:* specialists, BeerC.

Brains Sa*

Draught 44cl Canned 4.2%:

Widget 'draughtflow' bitter with a dense marshmallowy head, a soft woody nose, and a super-widgetized whipped-up texture, beyond which it's hard to taste anything much, but there's a little woodsmokey, medium sweet, saddle soap and tobacco character beyond the industrial foam. A resolutely keggy comedown for a Welsh classic. *Serve:* light fridge chill. *Avail:* Asda, Safe, Sains, Tesco, Thres.

BRAKSPEAR'S (HENLEY) STRONG ALE ***

Brakspear, Oxon. 33cl Bottled 5%:
Deep shiny copper, medium fizzy ale with appetizing smokey malt, banana, orange and alcohol aromas, and a lively, quite refreshing texture. Flavours are soft, working against the fizz, with oaky malt, orange liqueur notes, a pleasantly serious background dryness, and hop resins in the finish, which also develops a dark, sweet Coopers marmalade flavour. Likeable, if a little muffled by bottling. *Serve:* room temp. *Avail:* Sains, Thres, VicW, Wait.

BRAKSPEAR'S (HENLEY) STRONG ALE**

44cl Canned 5%:
Creamy, slightly foaming as it's poured, and although there's no widget in evidence this reddish-auburn bitter produces a sleek little head. Fruity, malty, bitter flavours, with a touch of oak and of dark sherryish marmalade, but also a bit thin, and a little sugary beneath the well-balanced top flavours; the finish lets it down. Certainly one of the better canned beers, though. *Serve:* room temp/larder cool. *Avail:* Sain, Thres, VicW, Wait.

BREAKER LAGER

Bass. 50cl Canned 5%:
Syrupy malt sweetness, with a dessicated coconut edge. Otherwise, bland, cereally, tastes cheaply-made. Dipping its pinkie in the pool of positive unpleasantness. *Serve:* fridge cold. *Avail:* Asda, Sains, Somer, Tesco, Thres, VicW.

BREWER JAMES CRYSTAL ALE**

Hanseatic. 50cl Bottled 4.5%:
Brewed for Hanseatic Trading Company by McMullen. Bottle-conditioned orangey-brown ale with a strong, sweet caramel aroma and flavour, and a drying crystal malt finish with mineral dryness. Oddly two-dimensional, considering it's supposed to have further conditioned in the bottle, and costs £1.50 a time. Metallic and thin at the finish too. Barely scraped a two-star rating. *Serve:* larder cool. *Avail:* Thres, Wait.

BROUGHTON SCOTTISH OATMEAL STOUT***

Broughton, Borders. 50cl Bottled 3.8%:
A black beer from an unassuming brown bottle, with a beige foamy head, and a creamy, mellow character, perhaps just a little muffled and overprocessed in the mouth. Still, a delicious and comforting beer, developing, as it warms and relaxes in the glass, flavours of chocolate, mocha, a little liquorice dryness and toasted grain, just a touch of cold tea, and an alluring creaminess reminiscent of warm, melted chocolate hazelnut ice-cream, all tidied up with green apple and green banana freshness in the finish. Do *not* chill, despite the bottle's advice. *Serve:* larder cool. *Avail:* BeerC, Tesco.

BULLDOG STRONG ALE***

Courage. 33cl Bottled 6.3%:
Imported from England, it reads on the neck label, and this was originally a Courage beer destined entirely for export (since 1947). Which may explain why it's more interesting than most home-based Courage brands. Dark amber in colour, with a strongly buttery alcohol, sweet and sour nose, and a profoundly malty, fruity flavour, with soft but vocal hop notes in the background, developing a rum butter pungency, a little oaky and tannic. Good flavours, and good texture too: soft water in evidence, but with a delicate, micro-bubble spritzy character playing against the smoothness. *Serve:* room temp. *Avail:* Wait.

BURTON ALE**

Ind Coope, Burton-upon-Trent (Bass). 44cl Canned 4.8%:
A 'chill briefly, pour quickly job' (no widget) which turns into an unappealing stagnant pool if this isn't done with the proper gusto. Delicious dry-hopped aromas, sandalwood, pot pourri and herbal, and a lovely full amber colour. Expectations are high. To taste: an oaky, gentle sourness is balanced with rich buttery malt, and silky, slightly pungent hop resins. Has the potential to be a great canned beer if they can get the gas process right: at

the moment, it's either spritzy but cold and muffled, or pond-like and delicious. *Serve:* light fridge chill. *Avail:* Asda, Sains, VicW.

Burton Porter***

Burton Bridge Brewery, Burton-upon-Trent. 55cl Bottled 4.5%:
Bravely packaged with a vivid sulphur-yellow slash of paint across its black bottle: a nice historical/artisanal touch. The beer is densest brown-black, with straightforwardly yeasty, doughy aromas. On the palate there's black coffee, bitter chocolate, burnt toast, and a hint of sweet fruit. Powerfully dry and firm, with an astringency that threatens to envelop the whole structure. Can seem severe, even unlovable, unless the taster is in an equally serious and uncompromising mood. *Serve:* room temp. *Avail:* specialists, BeerC.

Burton Strong Pale Ale***

Marston, Burton-upon-Trent. 50cl Bottled 6.2%:
This delicious beer smells like crisp, cold bacon, or perhaps just florally nutty. There's something lightly smoked in the flavours, too, which are drily nutty, good and hoppy, with lots of zizz and spritz, and sweet malt and red apple notes to balance the nut-skin dryness. The finish is elusively briny, and the aftertaste lingeringly hoppy. A sleek, elegant aperitif beer of underestimable strength. *Serve:* larder cool. *Avail:* VicW

Burtonwood Bitter*

Burtonwood, Warrington. 44cl Canned 3.8%:
A 'serve chilled and pour quickly' job, but the texture still emerged thin and tinny, of the old school. Flavours are dry, woodsmokey, reminiscent of a chestnut-wood fire, and verge on the austere, though a sweet note emerges as the cold bitter warms in the glass. *Serve:* light fridge chill. *Avail:* only regionally at present.

Cain's Best Bitter*

Robert Cain, Liverpool. 50cl Canned 4%:
Bright amber bitter with an initially good robust nose that peters out too quickly. Dry, woody, malty and hoppy, yes, but also dreadfully dull, rather too gassy, and with a slightly icky finish. Like an insensitively kegged version of a decent cask ale (which, of course, it is). *Serve:* room temp/larder. *Avail:* Safe, Somer, Tesco, VicW.

Cain's Dark Mild**

50cl Canned 3.2%:
Widget-free, faintly smokey, mildly liquoricey, soft and porterish dark mild with a gently bitter, burnt toast edge, and malt that lingers in the mouth. Bubbly, refreshing, and a bit can-muffled, but okay. *Serve:* larder cool. *Avail:* specialists.

Cain's Formidable Ale**

27.5cl Bottled 5%:
Barley sugar-coloured beer from the old Higsons brewery. Sweet, lightly fruity aromas, like waxy old cooking apples, but a disappointingly monotonous flavour for a 'strong' bottled ale, spritzy and sour at the front, then mild and sweetly nutty. Soft water, soft bodied, with no finish to speak of. Just scraped into the second division. Part of the Brewer's Heritage pack. *Serve:* larder cool. *Avail:* Sains, Tesco.

Cain's Superior Stout**

50cl Bottled 4.8%:
The original Robert Cain, founder of the old Higsons brewery, advertised his ales as superior, a tradition now revived. The bottle's nice, ridgey and handsome, but the stout disappoints a little. It's soft, very gently chocolatey, very mildly coffeeish, with an unmistakably keggy texture. There's just a hint of warm liquorice and hop dryness in the finish. But otherwise, too nervous and too processed. New, so no national retail listings as we go to press. *Serve:* room temp. *Avail:* specialists.

Caledonian 70/- Amber Ale***

Caledonian, Edinburgh. 50cl Bottled 3.35%:
Delicious, accessible, easy ale with a soft amber malt sweetness, which is swept away with the usual Caledonian hop flourish. Its nose is sultana buttery with a little orange; the

flavour similar, rich, round and mouth-filling, but also soft and gently hoppy, with a distinctly herbal (rosemary?), seductive finish. *Serve:* larder cool. *Avail:* Asda, BeerC, Safe, Sains, VicW, Tesco.

CALEDONIAN 80/- EXPORT***

50cl Bottled 4.1%:
You'd know it was a Caledonian beer even if tasting it blindly: the freshness, honesty and good ingredients shine through. Deep burnt-orange in colour, it has spice and pungent 'red malt' flavours, but also clean, dry floral hop notes; the finish is gently drying, with a touch of succulent buttery ripeness. Superbly balanced on all three fronts: fragrant soft malt, dry aromatic hop, and a delicious fruity yeastiness. *Serve:* larder cool. *Avail:* Asda, BeerC, Odd, Sains, Tesco, VicW.

CAMERONS DRAUGHT BITTER*

Camerons, Cleveland. 50cl Canned 3.6%:
A new-draught-system, non-widget beer, bright orangey-tan in colour, with toffee apple and dry malt on the nose. The flavour – at first dry but not especially clean – swiftly grows much drier, initially of the cured malt sort, but quickly develops a remarkably old-fashioned bitterness – not floral, not hoppy particularly, just bitter. The texture is typically keggy and fizzed up, but this is nothing like the worst canned bitter in its class. *Serve:* room temp/ larder cool. *Avail:* Asda.

CAMERONS STRONGARM

44cl Canned 4%:
The 'Ruby Red' contains what's quaintly described as a 'beer engine' (widget), and requires a two-hour chilling. The head may last all the way down the glass, as advertised, once this is done, but the flavour suffers ritual sacrifice. The nose is sweet and vaguely woody, and the flavour – as far as it's detectable at all through such dense, unforgiving cream (Gaelic coffees are refreshing compared to this) – is blandly nutty and sweet, with a little chestnut and dry malt. *Serve:* fridge cold. *Avail:* Asda, Somer.

CAMPBELLS 70/- HEAVY

Whitbread. 44cl Canned 3.4%:
Dark amber, with rubbery, petrolly aromas, but after this initial excitement, remarkably fizzy and bland. Flavours are hinted at rather than openly expressed, with more disconcertingly industrial character than anything. Pretty undrinkably vile, in short. A score of minus one. *Serve:* room temp. *Avail:* Somer, Tesco, Thres.

CAPSTAN

Abington (Wells). 44cl Canned 2.2%:
Yeoman-like commodity bitter, weak and fizzy and barely tasting of anything, bar a very vague dryness in the finish. *Serve:* larder cool. *Avail:* Safe.

CARLING BLACK LABEL*

Bass, Burton-on-Trent. 50cl Canned 4.1%:
Granddad would probably greatly enjoy this with his Sunday lunch. It's as smooth as they come, rounded and fairly sweet with a buttery finish. A bit over-gassy, but has a not unreasonable body and flavour for a 4% lager. It might also be amusing to present one of your yuppier friends with this (can unseen, of course); the brand is so deeply beyond unfashionability that serious social embarrassment could result if they liked it. *Serve:* fridge cold. *Avail:* widely.

CARLING PREMIER*

44cl Canned 4.7%:
A widget lager from Bass that could easily be mistaken for the far more high-profile, and far more pretentious (and expensive) Enigma, were it not for its slightly sweeter finish, which is followed by a single pang of bitterness. It is smooth, and surprising, as advertised, but these are not necessarily compliments. An inappropriate, dense widget creaminess leaves it cloying in the finish. *Serve:* fridge cold. *Avail:* widely.

CASTILLE LAGER

Abington Brewery, Bedford. 44cl Canned 2.2%:
Extremely weak lager made by Charles Wells,

who do a lot of contract brewing of this kind. Tastes of nothing other than a seriously dilute lager-ade, with a cheap dry finish. *Serve:* fridge cold. *Avail:* Sains.

Castle Eden Ale

Whitbread. 44cl Canned 4%:
Fiercely widgetized ale that takes an age to settle itself, whereupon it turns photogenically amber, with a pretty little head. Sweet and malty, with faint hop echoes, but foamy and fruity, with a sappy, leathery edge, and very processed in the mouth. *Serve:* fridge cold. *Avail:* widely.

Chelmer Gold***

Ridleys, Essex. 27.5cl Bottled 5%:
A delicious newcomer to the ranks of bottle-conditioned English ales, in a too small and too self-effacing little bottle. The conditioning certainly has confidence, though; the beer springs out of the bottle with explosive enthusiasm. Deep gold in colour, with fresh hoppy aromas, it has good, rich buttery yeast, nicely poised malt and hop balance of the creamy blonde sort, and a resiny, dry finish. Good texture, too. But, for heaven's sake get a packaging and marketing budget. *Serve:* room temp. *Avail:* Tesco, Thres.

Chiswick Bitter**

Fuller's, London. 50cl Canned 3.5%:
A canned version of a classic cask ale, of moderate strength but, for a canned bitter of such subtlety, so good as to be verging on three-star status. Lively, widget-free, gently and distinctively floral-hoppy, drily malty, faintly wood-smokey, with good gentle mineral water character. Soft, refreshing, delicate. *Serve:* larder cool. *Avail:* Safe, Sains, Somer.

Clan Lager

44cl Canned 3%:
Bland, pale stuff of the usual commodity sort. *Serve:* fridge cold. *Avail:* Co-op.

Coach House Bitter

Abington (Wells). 44cl Canned 2.2%:
Same old thing in a different can. See Capstan. *Serve:* larder cool. *Avail:* Tesco.

Co-op Premium Export Lager*

44cl Canned 4.3%:
Peach juice, and a little spice on the nose; soft-bodied in texture, with a dry prickly backbone, and a mildly malty flavour, finished with a hint of nectarine. Modest, but likeable. A whisker off two-star status. *Serve:* fridge cold.

Co-op Strong Export Ale

44cl Canned 5%
Sweet-nosed, sweet-toothed, shandy-like and caramelly, but with the additional burden of strong beer pungency, vegetal and unpleasant, in the middle. The finish develops a slightly redeeming hop dryness after half a glass or so. *Serve:* larder cool.

Coronet Bitter

Bass. 44cl Canned 2.3%:
Coron-Niet. A cheap commodity bitter, and the same old thing, Bass-style. See Yeoman's. *Serve:* larder cool. *Avail:* Co-op.

Coronet Lager

44cl Canned 2.3%:
Smells very cheap and a bit medicated. Tastes of nothing at all, other than a mild sweetness. *Serve:* fridge cold. *Avail:* Co-op.

Courage Light Ale

Courage. 33cl Canned 3.2%:
Pale amber, watery and adjuncty stuff with only the faintest dry, nutty note on the otherwise sticky, icky finish. *Serve:* larder cool. *Avail:* widely.

Crest Export**

Premium Lager Abington (Charles Wells). 25cl Bottled 5%:
Orange lager with barley sugar, dry malt and hazelnut aromas, and a prickly, bubbly texture with bitter (rather than hoppy) citrus pith flavours in the finish, as well as a slightly sticky, brewing sugar note. *Serve:* fridge cold. *Avail:* Sains.

CREST LAGER
44cl Canned 3%:
Mediocre, bland, clean, though the colour is impressively golden. Unfortunately, a distinctly cereal/adjunct flavour and an oddly formulaic bitterness in the finish gets in the way of its even being a useful lunchtime quaffer. *Serve:* fridge cold. *Avail*: Wait.

DEUCHARS IPA***
Caledonian, Edinburgh. 50cl Bottled 4.4%:
Bright amber ale with a velvety texture. Radical, ravishing dryness quickly takes over, mouth-filling and mouth-coatingly super-hoppy. The overall effect is quite severe, and would be more so if not for a compelling malt fruit richness just before the finish. But you can taste the quality and (at the risk of sounding like a dog food commercial) the prime ingredients. In this case it's Golden Promise barley malt, crystal malt, and whole Fuggles and Golding hops. Excellent aperitif material. *Serve:* light fridge chill. *Avail:* Asda, BeerC, Odd, Safe.

DIRECTORS DRAUGHT**
Courage. 44cl Canned 4.8%:
There's a tight, beige creamy head astride this widget-assisted 'draught' beer, but the aromas are promisingly sherryish and fragrant. Unfortunately, the shaving-foam barrier created by the nitrogen and the fact that it has to be served fridge cold almost destroy the flavour. But signalling through the fog there's a sweetish, slightly plummy (or is it porty?) fruit, a little oaky wood character, a reasonable malt and hop balance, and a dryish finish. Leave it to warm for ten minutes after pouring, and it's the most drinkable canned widget bitter in Britain. *Serve:* fridge cold. *Avail:* widely.

DOUBLE MAXIM*
Vaux. 50cl Canned 4.2%:
Amber, widget-free bitter of fruity character, but the fruit has tipped over into sweaty, slightly eggy flavours, and the texture is on the flaccid side. *Serve:* larder cool. *Avail:* Safe, Somer, Tesco.

DRAYMAN'S BITTER
Mansfield, Notts. PET 3%:
Sweet butter icing on the nose, and a mildly buttery flavour, but overwhelmed by thin and watery texture. *Serve:* larder cool. *Avail:* Co-op, Somer.

DRAYMAN'S DARK MILD
PET 3%:
As expected, after the bitter (above). *Serve:* larder cool. *Avail*: Somer, Tesco.

EAGLE BITTER**
Charles Wells, Bedford PET 3.5%:
Suprisingly drinkable, dark amber, fizzy bitter, with sweet malty aromas and similar flavours, seasoned by a slow-building dryness but giving way to a sweetish finish. Good and malty, drinkable PET version of a good cask ale, though. Also available canned (Safeway). *Serve:* larder cool. *Avail*: Wait.

EDINBURGH STRONG ALE***
Caledonian, Edinburgh. 50cl Bottled 6.4%:
A Scots 'wee heavy', brewed on these premises since 1869, and made from Scottish barley malt, Fuggles and Goldings whole hops, water and yeast only. Deep amber-brown in colour, it has an enticingly fragrant, buttery malt, pungently spicy, raw fruit-cake nose, and all these things and more in the mouth, with plenty of raisin, vanilla, honey, a little oaky sourness, and resiny, oily fresh hop flavours. Complex and delicious, but also a little flaccid. A teensy bit cloying? Perhaps, but still a terrific beer for high days and holidays. *Serve:* room temp/ larder cool. *Avail*: specialists, BeerC.

EVERARDS TIGER***
Best Bitter Everards, Leicestershire. 27.5cl Bottled 4.2%:
Bright amber-coloured, with a typically dry-hopped, hop-resiny pungency, herbal and floral; some caramel sweetness, a little nuttiness, and grain-husky, hop-flower flavours. Quite thin-bodied, but the big hop finish, lingering and warming, helps create roundness. Tasty and easy to drink. Part of the excellent Brewer's

Heritage pack, and also available canned (Asda). *Serve:* room temp/larder cool. *Avail*: Sains.

FALCON

Carlsberg-Tetley. 50cl Canned 3.3%:
Hot contender for worst-tasting lager in the British section, certainly with the biggest (toad-eye) bubbles, and a soapy, sweet, flabby but gassy, tinny flavour – almost *without* flavour until the finish, when a dry hop turns up for duty, terribly late and lazy. *Serve:* fridge cold. *Avail*: VicW.

FARGO**

Charles Wells, Bedfordshire. 50cl Bottled 5%:
Their flagship ale, handsomely bottled but disappointing in both flavour and texture. Roasty and amber malty on the nose and palate, it has a soft floral hop finish and a savoury nutty edge. But a bit thin and obvious, and a bit flabby in the mouth. *Serve:* larder cool. *Avail*: Asda.

FEDERATION EXPORT IPA**

Federation, Tyne & Wear. 27.5cl Bottled 4.4%:
Dingily labelled, deep bright-amber beer with nutty, grain-husky aromas, and a distinctive whiff of braising celery. The flavour is similar, with some chestnut, but dies away a little in the middle, before coming back with a strongly nutty finish. A bit keggy, but smooth and drinkable. Part of the Brewer's Heritage pack. *Serve:* room temp/larder cool. *Avail*: Sains, Tesco.

FEDERATION SPECIAL

50cl Canned 4%:
No widget, no gadget, just a barley sugar-coloured bitter with a geraniol and herbal hop nose, and a peculiar flavour, dry-hopped and flabby, with a sweet note among the sandalwood and sweaty cheese, plus fruity flavour – something exotic and not very sweet: sharron fruit or pomegranate? *Serve:* room temp/larder cool. *Avail*: Safe, Somer.

FELINFOEL DOUBLE DRAGON*

Felinfoel, Llanelli. .50cl Canned 4.2%:
Auburn-brown 'national ale of Wales' with an off-putting old banana and plum nose, but a much nicer flavour, despite its undoubtedly keggy failings. In its draught cask-conditioned form this is a terrific beer, and just a little of that quality gets through the tinning process. Initially quite dry, with a sweetish malty balance, some stewed-tea flavour and an oily nut finish. *Serve:* larder cool. *Avail*: Safe, Tesco, Thres, VicW.

FLOWERS IPA

Draught 44cl Canned 3.6%:
Copper-coloured beer with a typically widgetized super-creamy texture, semi-sweet, mildly malty, with a drying, woodsmokey finish. The brewing recipe is exactly as per Flower's Original, only 80% srandard white malt replaces the pale malt of the other. *Serve:* fridge cold. *Avail*: widely.

FLOWERS ORIGINAL*

Draught 44cl Canned 4.4%:
Earns a star because, while not exactly nice, it is one of the least objectionable widget beers, despite the fact that the draughtflow system strikes again, with its confectedly whipped-up texture. There is a degree of malt and hop balance beyond the foam, however, though the finish is tinny and tannic. *Serve:* far too cold. *Avail*: widely.

FRAOCH HEATHER ALE***

Maclays, Alloa. 50cl Bottled 5%:
Made by Maclays under contract to a non-brewing wholesaler, and obviously a natural for export, with its label's ancient Scots symbols (pict-ograms?) and storyline about legendary Pictish ale made from heather and the like. Actually, yes, they did use heather to season ales, but not like this. Deep amber-gold beer with a good spritzy texture, a Parmesan cheesy nose, lots of smokey dry malt and bagfuls of dry-hopped, resiny (and, yes, faintly heathery, floral) bitterness, that builds and dries and grows quite austere. An excellent aperitif beer. *Serve:* larder cool. *Avail*: specialists.

FREEDOM PILSENER***
Freedom, London. 33cl Bottled 5.4%:
Exciting, fresh and yeasty pilsener made in Fulham, and only bottled in a small quantity at present. At the time of writing, Young's are packaging the beer and insist on sterile-filtering it, but the Freedom chaps are planning their own bottling line for later in 1995. Clean and wholesome but decently weighty flavours, with just a little toffee and apricot preceding the long, dry, hop floral finish. Maris Otter malt, Bavarian yeast, and Liberty hops from Washington state are used. *Serve:* light fridge cool. *Avail:* Odd (London).

FULLER'S ESB****
Fuller's, London. 55cl Bottled 5.9%:
Proof, if ever proof were needed, that a bottled beer doesn't need to be bottle-conditioned to be great. Like Caledonian, this has all the finer qualities: generous handfuls of good ingredients and a brilliant partnership of textures and flavours. The fruity malt nose has a good leaf-tea aroma, and the flavour offers delicious dry, fresh hop and drily aromatic malt, balanced with full, almost lush fruit sweetness, and a finish which achieves both a dry delicacy and a buttery vanilla softness. Altogether very satisfying and wholesome, but tastes slightly under-strength – beware! *Serve:* room temp/ larder cool. *Avail*: widely.

FULLER'S LONDON PRIDE*
4x50cl Canned 4.7%:
More afflicted by canning than sibling Chiswick Bitter, and didn't quite scrape a two-star rating. Auburny amber, with refreshing, caramelized fruit sweetness and a touch of woodsmoke: perhaps the caramel fruitness is too persistent and too thin, with not enough balancing dryness, but there is no tinny taint to the flavours, at least (and, to its credit, it's made from hops, water, malt and yeast only). *Serve:* larder cool. *Avail*: Thres.

FULLER'S PALE ALE**
27.5cl Bottled 3.2%:
Modest, but tasty little beer, mildly hazelnutty, with a faint yeasty richness, before developing a pleasantly forthright, long and dry finish. Refreshing, straightforward, wholesome stuff, but a little over-gassy. *Serve:* larder cool. *Avail*: specialists.

FULLER'S 1845***
55cl Bottled 6.3%:
Complex and rewarding, but easy drinking bottle-conditioned ale, handsomely packaged for the brewery's 150th anniversary. Sparkly, foxy-auburn in the glass, bright and lively, with buttery malt, sultana, oak and spice on the nose. Flavours are dominated by dryness from the first, with bitter notes right at the front, followed by malty orangey fruit, light and cakey, and a seductively contrasted lingering dry finish, arrestingly fresh and vigorous. Amber malt succulence, followed by dry-hopped astringent elegance. Delicious. *Serve:* room temp. *Avail:* Asda.

GALES HSB*
Strong Bitter Gales, Hampshire. 44cl Canned 4.6%:
Orangey-brown, bursting with fizz, with a sweetly malty, chestnut-woody flavour, that develops toffeeish notes and just a touch of orange and spice. Robust enough flavours but it's too gassy, too sweet, too thin. *Serve:* larder cool. *Avail:* Asda, Safe, Sains, Somer, VicW.

GALES PRIZE OLD ALE**
27.5cl Bottled 9%:
Two stars only for a fine, well-made beer, but this tasting sample was too raw and young to contemplate drinking, like unwisely taking a swig from a newly-made port. Dark and sticky, with treacle toffee, molasses, Oxo stock cube and cough mixture all much in evidence, and just the faintest hint of the sherryish, Madeira-wine-mellow richness to come (in about five years). Don't drink Prize Old Ale too young, for heavens sake, or it will taste like something dug up from a Roman villa. *Serve:* room temp. *Avail:* specialists, BeerC.

GILLESPIES DRAUGHT MALT STOUT
Scottish & Newcastle. 44cl Canned 4%:
According to the blurb on the can, Gillespies

takes its character from the Scottish stouts popular at the turn of the century. If this is the case, heaven help them. I found it almost undrinkable, possessed of the unique characteristics of being whipped and creamy (thanks, Tapstream widget system) and desperately thin at the same time. Flavours are dominated by demerara sugar and cold tea, with no real stout character to report, and the finish is cloying. Sugar and unmalted ingredients, no doubt. *Serve:* light fridge chill, according to instructions. *Avail:* widely.

GOLD BIER***

Tennents, Glasgow (Bass). 33cl Bottled 5%:
Scottish barley malt, continental hops, pure Highland water and no additives, the label says, and you can taste the good ingredients in this modest but wholesome and tasty little lager. Golden, certainly, and fizzy, with lots of apple-juicey freshness, ripe barley flavours, and a clean, gently hoppy finish, when a pineapple-chunk-sweetie, slightly sour, citric note also makes for refreshment. A simple, clean-edged beer, ideal for lunchtime with a sandwich. *Serve:* light fridge chill. *Avail:* Thres.

GOLD LABEL

Whitbread. 27.5cl Canned 10.9%:
Big butch beer in a wee gold tin. Aromas suggest Flash floor cleaner. Superstrength brewing translates into flavours that are harsh, hard-edged, soapy and solventy. *Serve:* larder cool. *Avail:* Asda, Safe, Sains, Thres, VicW, Wait.

GOLDEN PALE***

Organic Pale Ale Caledonian Brewery, Edinburgh. 50cl Bottled 4%:
Organic Scots barley and organic Kent hop flowers create a pale-amber, aromatically hoppy new stablemate to Golden Promise. Good lively texture; the flavour sharp, cleansing and astringent, with a dry salt note, but also rich, with just enough butter and orange to balance. Moreish. Almost a four-star beer. *Serve:* larder cool. *Avail:* Asda, BeerC, Odd, Safe.

GOLDEN PRIDE*

Fuller's, London. 27.5cl Bottled 9.2%:
Not a Caledonian beer, but a disappointingly thin and harsh Fullers super strong ale. Gassy, with plenty of fruit and malt, but overwhelmed by pungently sweet alcohol, this beer manages to be both thin and cloying. *Serve:* room temp. *Avail:* specialists, Selfridges.

GOLDEN PROMISE****

Organic Ale Caledonian, Edinburgh. 50cl Bottled 5%:
One of the great bottled beers of the world. More organic barley malt and hop flowers, yeast and water create a fragrant amber-coloured beer of inspiring deliciousness and finesse. Sherbety pineapple chunks on the nose introduce a unique blend of flavours: banana oil, musky malt, toffee and butter, a little orange-water, and a perfumed, floral hop character, leading into a clean dry finish (which itself builds and layers into a moreish astringency). *Serve:* larder cool. *Avail:* Asda, BeerC, Sains, Thres.

GREENE KING IPA*

Greene King, Suffolk. 44cl Canned 3.6%:
Widget-free, draught-effect canned beer just a whisker off a two-star ranking. The nose is appetizingly malty, and slightly oaky, joined on the palate by a little sweet orange, sour yeast and tannins, and by a gently hoppy backdrop which rises on cue at the finish. A bit keggy, a bit fizzy, but tastes fairly wholesome, at least. *Serve:* larder cool. *Avail:* Safe, Somer, Tesco, VicW.

GREENMANTLE ALE**

Broughton, Borders. 50cl Bottled 3.9%:
'Greenmantle had appeared at last to an awaiting people', according to John Buchan's novel of the same name. Let's hope they thought it was worth it. The bottled version of this classic cask beer is rather afflicted with a keggy, overprocessed quality, and has a curiously thin, almost absent middle, with good Scots water where the beer should be. On the plus side, it has good bourbon cask aromas,

and some slightly smokey malt fruit. *Serve:* room temp/larder cool. *Avail:* BeerC, Co-op, Safe, Sains, Somer, Tesco.

Hampden Lager

44cl Canned 2.8%:
Glasgow-aimed (Hampden Park loyalists), Glasgow-based wholesaler-commissioned commodity lager; cheap and orange-coloured, raw-grainy and fizzy. *Serve:* fridge cold. *Avail:* Co-op.

Headcracker***

Woodforde's, Norfolk. 33cl Bottled 7%:
A very strong pale Norfolk ale. The nose is alluring, with cured malt aromas, smoked and woody, and overlain with bags of sweet, ripe and overripe fruit, and estery alcohol. Delicious drinking, too, dry but full-bodied, yeasty but also very hoppy, at once fruity and astringent, floral yet malty, with a herbal, leathery, orangey complexity that's irresistibly moreish, and a lingering bittersweet finish. Great beer, terrible name. *Serve:* room temp. *Avail:* specialists, BeerC.

Hector's Lager

Hall & Woodhouse, Dorset. 44cl Canned 2.2%:
Wherein lies the market for 2.2% lagers? Scrooges at Christmas laying in super-cheap supplies for palming off on visitors? Unfortunately, Hector's is even more unpleasant to drink than it strictly needs to be. *Serve:* fridge cold. *Avail:* Tesco.

Heldenbräu*

Whitbread. 50cl Canned 3.2%:
Slightly greenish yellow-gold cheap lager with Germanic pretensions (earning a naff can award for the Gothick Germanick eagle design?). Slightly sweet – some Cox apple at a stretch – grainy and bland, sparkly and weak, but grain chimes in cleanly at the finish, with a touch of hop too. Refreshing at least. *Serve:* fridge cold. *Avail:* specialists.

Heldenbräu Super

44cl Canned 8.9%:
Driest of the 'Supers', drily alcoholic and pungent, with lots of crude brandyish spirit in the finish. Can't imagine anyone not on a park bench enjoying this. *Serve:* fridge cold. *Avail:* Somer.

Hemeling*

Bass. 50cl Canned 3.5%:
Reasonably edible cheap quencher with mildly malty, sweetish flavours, and a savoury, cereally edge. The finish is a bit adjunct-sticky. *Serve:* fridge cold. *Avail:* Asda, Tesco.

Herald Lager

Courage. 44cl Canned 2.2%:
There are two sorts of very weak, cheap, crudely packaged 'commodity' lager. The (mercifully) almost tasteless, and the other kind. This is the other kind, which decides to try and taste of something, and succeeds only in tasting horrible: sugary, sticky, adjuncty, with a nasty lingering aftertaste. *Serve:* fridge cold. *Avail:* Wait.

Heritage Draught Bitter

44cl Canned 3.9%:
Widget bitter that smells of damp. Attractively pale amber in colour, it's sweet to the point of tasting remarkably like fluffy white marshmallow, with a little tannin in the finish. *Serve:* fridge cold. *Avail:* Spar.

Hofmeister*

Courage. 50cl Canned 3.4%:
Brewed under licence from Henninger-Brau of Frankfurt. Mild, sweet nose and flavour, very gently fizzy, a drying, slightly tinny finish. Exceedingly bland, but could be far, far worse. *Serve:* fridge cold. *Avail:* widely.

Hofmeister Special

44cl Canned 9%:
Strongest of the off licence 'supers', and one of the sweetest, pungent with wild and wilful alcohol, and a root vegetable finish. Tastes mostly of its own potency. Horrid. But not as horrid as LCL Super. *Serve:* fridge cold. *Avail:* specialists.

Hooper's Ginger Brew**
33cl Bottled 4.7%:
We feared some newfangled novelty horror, but this is nostalgic stuff, with a decent lager backdrop, a fresh, tangy ginger-root flavour at the front, and ending with a spicy, floral dryness. Simple and clean ginger beer (and not really 'strong in alcohol', despite the label's boast). *Serve:* light fridge chill. *Avail:* Sains, Thres, VicW.

Imperial Russian Stout***
Courage. 27.5cl Bottled 10%:
Bottle-conditioned 'Russian' stout of Victorian intensity and body, deep and luscious, fruity and complex. Perhaps just a little overwhelmingly rich; not as well balanced to a modern palate as the Sam Smith's 1980s version. Nonetheless, a tradition worth preserving; it's a pity that the brewery now make so little of this, and so patchily. *Serve:* room temp. *Avail:* specialists.

Imperial Stout****
Sam Smith, Tadcaster. 33cl Bottled 7%:
Glorious slim bottle, with Victorian design, despite only being ten years old as a Sam Smith brand. Espresso, dark sweet sherry and Madeira on the nose are powerfully repeated on the palate, along with bitter chocolate, rich black coffee, Seville marmalade orange, vanilla and oak. Good black malt and hop dryness tidy up the richness in a finish that is lingering and coffeeish. An excellent digestif. *Serve:* larder cool. *Avail:* BeerC, Odd.

Independence Scottish Lager**
Belhaven. 35.5cl Bottled 5%:
Made by Belhaven for a Scots wholesaler, and presumably aimed at export markets. A golden lager of robust flavour, roughly in the Export style, with creamy malt sweetness and spiritous alcohol character, strong-flavoured but still fairly refreshing, if over-gassy, and a bit dull. *Serve:* light fridge chill. *Avail:* Tesco.

Jaguar*
Bass. 44cl Canned 2.3%:
The pleasanter sort of commodity lager (*see* Herald), quaffable, bland and spritzy stuff without any real claims to flavour and texture. *Serve:* fridge cold. *Avail:* Somer.

James Pryor's Special IPA***
Hanseatic. 55cl Bottled 4.5%:
McMullen-brewed, bottle-conditioned sibling beer to Brewer James Crystal Ale and Vassilenski's Black Russian. Copper in colour, with robust, bittersweet malt aromas and flavours, a slightly buttered but also fresh and appley sweetness, and a woody, slightly sour note. Made mostly for export, presumably, with the 'British in India' approach of the label copy, and the prominent Union Jacks? *Serve:* larder cool. *Avail:* Odd.

John Smith's Bitter
Courage. 44cl Canned 4%:
Thin, sweet, with a little vanilla, a bit sticky, with not enough balancing hop dryness (to say the least). A little of the perfumey quality that takes hold in the draught canned version (below). Pop-like. *Serve:* larder cool. *Avail:* widely.

John Smith's Draught Bitter
44cl Canned 4%:
Dark-amber with a tight little creamy head and a sweet nose. Sweet malty beers and widgets don't perform well together; the problem is worsened by a curiously perfumed note, which gives the head an oddly soapy taste. The caramelly sweetness and slight grain-husk woodiness can only exacerbate the cloyingly creamy, deeply over-whipped texture. Its only natural advantage is Jack Dee. *Serve:* fridge cold. *Avail:* widely.

John Smith's Strong Ale**
50cl Canned 5%:
Surprisingly palatable, dark reddish-brown beer, with decent texture and flavour for a non-draught-process, old-fashioned can. Fruity, tea-baggy, gently hoppy at the front, with nice nutty, toasted grain at the back and a little resiny hop oiliness and ripe banana yeast. The whole structure is only slightly let

down by an unsubtle brewing-sugary note. *Serve:* larder cool. *Avail:* specialists.

JORVIK LAGER

Mansfield, Notts
PET 3%:
Very pale gold, with extremely pale flavours, like something that's been over-diluted. Virtually tasteless. *Serve:* fridge cold. *Avail:* Co-op.

JOSEPH JONES STRONG ALE*

Robert Cain, Liverpool. 50cl Canned 5%:
On the positive side, there's a dry-hopped, subtle perfumey, pine-resiny flavour, and something toffeeish in the finish. On the negative, enormous fizzy bubbles, nail polish aromas and sweet, thin (brewing sugar) flavours at the back. Needs tinkering with. *Serve:* larder cool. *Avail:* specialists.

KALTENBERG PILS*

Whitbread. 44cl Canned 6%:
Licensed by the Bavarian brewery of the same name. The nose is slightly vegetal, the flavour inverted in the all too common strong lager manner – that is, super clean and curiously absent. Gentle dryness chimes in at the middle, followed by a slightly quininey hop finish. *Serve:* light fridge chill. *Avail:* Somer.

KESTREL PILSENER*

Younger's (Scottish & Newcastle). 50cl Canned 3.4%:
Makes much of the fact that it's brewed using Saaz hops, and there is certainly a little (just the faintest) Saaz flavour/aroma, but otherwise this is a light, thin lager with a bit of a sticky finish. Formulaic, bland, cheaply made. *Serve:* fridge cold. *Avail:* widely.

KESTREL SUPER

50cl Canned 9%:
One of a whole sub-culture of 'superstrength' canned lagers, almost all of them as dire as this one. Very sweet, overwhelmingly candied, sugar-syrupy flavours, mercifully low on turnips (a common strong lager characteristic) but high in the taste of alcohol, here with a distinctly whiskyish accent, as befits a Scottish 'super'. Now number three seller in a very lucrative UK marketplace. *Serve:* light fridge chill. *Avail:* specialists.

KING & BARNES CHRISTMAS ALE***

King & Barnes, Sussex. 33cl Bottled 8%:
The 1994 bottle (to drink before Xmas '95, but there will be another for next year), bottle-conditioned, and a cheeringly seasonal opaque reddish-auburn. It achieves a convincingly draught-like, real ale texture, and creamy smooth flavours, with bags of malt and deep, dark Christmassy notes (a liquid mince pie), dry and delicious floral hop flavours and just enough softly sour oak to tidy up the richness. Mellow and delicious sipping beer: good for private celebrations. *Serve:* room temp. *Avail:* Odd.

KING & BARNES FESTIVE ***

King & Barnes, Sussex. 55cl Bottled 5.3%:
Bottle-conditioned translucent amber-red ale, which should be served at room temperature (though I like it larder cool) and allowed to settle and clear before serving. English makers of bottle-conditioned ales don't generally advocate swirling and adding the sediment to the glass, in the Belgian manner! A deliciously fruity beer, with buttery, caramelized fruit and summery cherry aromas, and a herbal, hay-like hop smell, too. To taste, dry malt fruits with orange, spice, pepper and vanilla – big and bold, but also dry, verging on refreshing, the gentle astringency building slowly in the mouth. *Serve:* room temp/larder cool. *Avail:* Odd, Safe, Wait.

KING & BARNES OLD PORTER****

King & Barnes, Sussex. 55cl Bottled 5.5%:
A new porter from this excellent producer, and head and shoulders above the competition, hence the four-star classic status. All natural, unpasteurized, it's densely black in the glass, with yeasty, warm, horse blanket and slightly floral aromas. Flavours encompass both dark, bitter chocolate, and the creamy, malted kind, also gently fruity,

with a persistent soft dryness that grows long and deep, and an aftertaste that's faintly leathery, woody and liquorice spicy. Complex and delicious. *Serve:* room temp. *Avail:* Odd.

Lamot Pils

Lager Bière Bass. 50cl Canned 5%:
Pretentious nonsense, that 'lager biere' tag, and it's not exactly 'seriously smooth' either: just a rather wet, golden, fizzy lager, with a touch of sweet malt at the front, and a distinctly hard, tinny finish. Presumably this is a leftover brand from some rather silly 1980s Gothic-Germanic marketing that nobody at Bass can quite bear to knock on the head. *Serve:* fridge cold. *Avail:* widely.

Landlord Strong Pale Ale*

Taylor, Yorkshire. 27.5cl Bottled 4.1%:
Terribly disappointing bottled beer that doesn't deserve the Landlord tag. Amber-coloured, buttery stuff lacking in body, texture or finish, though there is a roast grain note on the aftertaste. Just rather flaccid and dull. *Serve:* larder cool. *Avail:* specialists.

LCL Pils*

Federation, Newcastle. 27.5cl Bottled 5%:
It's the darnedest thing: this lager makes many of the right moves, with a sweet, smooth, fairly full-bodied grain flavour, and clean, dryish finish, but its oily consistency strikes an almost fatty note, irresistibly reminiscent of, well, margarine, and it's this that gets in the way of liking it a lot more. *Serve:* fridge cold. *Avail:* Co-op, Safe, Sains, Tesco, VicW.

LCL Pils*

50cl Canned 5%:
Much as above, only the margarine is now more of a low-fat-spread flavour. Despite this slight peculiarity in both LCL beers, they are perfectly acceptable in other departments . . . just too sweet and oily to be described as pilseners. *Serve:* fridge cold. *Avail:* Co-op, Safe, Sains, Tesco, VicW.

LCL Super

50cl Canned 8.5%:
Easily the worst so-called 'super' in these tastings, with lots of sugar syrup and carrot soup-like flavours besides the pungent lager alcohol; extremely crude and sickly. *Serve:* fridge cold. *Avail:* Somer, Tesco.

Lees Harvest Ale**

Lees, Manchester. 27.5cl Bottled 11.5%:
Nutty and baker's-yeast sweetness on the nose of this perilously strong annual bottling, the 1994 one tasted. Tawny and clear in the glass, it still tastes young and raw, but with a toffeeish note, yeasty bloom and Madeira richness preceding a promising hop finish. Will almost certainly be very fine once its had some cellar age. *Serve:* room temp. *Avail:* specialists.

London Pride***

Fuller's, London. 55cl Bottled 4.7%:
Foxy-red, dry-hopped and succulent, with buttery, toffee richness just about holding its own beneath the dominating hand of the drying malt and herbal hop astringency, and vigorous oaky tannins. There's plenty of yeast bite, and a cured, slightly pungent maltiness: the wood and spice playing against a honeyed, sweet note. Irresistible stuff, if just a little heavy-handed with the hop sack. *Serve:* room temp/larder cool. *Avail:* Asda, Maj, Safe, Sains, Somer, Tesco, Thres, VicW.

Long Life*

Ind Coope, Carlsberg Tetley. 50cl Canned 4.2%:
Cheap-looking 'beer' in a gold and blue can (they call it a beer, but it's a lager really). More deeply coloured and fuller bodied than many cheap lagers, it's sweet and fairly clean, with no adjunct or tinning flavours at least. Two-dimensional perhaps, but fine with a sandwich. Why don't they do this beer a favour and give it a better name? Almost a two-star rating. *Serve:* light fridge chill. *Avail:* Thres.

Mackeson Stout*

27.5cl Canned 3%:

The star is more for nostalgia than for quality. Just as blackish auburn, dark sugary, fruitily liquoricey as it ever was. Deliciously icky in the finish. Perversely. *Serve:* room temp. *Avail:* widely.

McEWAN'S BEST SCOTCH
Scottish & Newcastle. 50cl Canned 3.6%:
Bright auburn with a thin little white head, smoky chestnut-skin aromas, and more of the same, in dilute form, in the thin, sweet flavours, and a grain husky, unmalted adjuncts taste, all unanimously supporting the fact that this is a beer brewed to be cheap rather than interesting. At least there's no widget to add to its problems. *Serve:* larder cool. *Avail:* Asda, Safe, Tesco.

McEWAN'S EXPORT
50cl Canned 4.5%:
Not as dreadful as the so-called Pale Ale, but still pretty dreadful. Roast barley, sugar and corn, a sweet and cloying adjunct festival. *Serve:* larder cool. *Avail:* Asda, Safe, Somer, Tesco.

McEWAN'S LAGER
50cl Canned 4.1%:
If speaking strictly comparatively, the Scotch (above) ought probably to get a star rating, in the company of this really outstandingly mediocre lager. Husky cereal flavours, cardboardy and a little acrid, with a sticky brewing sugar finish. Thin and gassy stuff. *Serve:* fridge cold. *Avail:* widely.

McEWAN'S PALE ALE
44cl Canned 3.2%:
Must be a joke. Dark, plummy-brown beer with a caramel, roast-barley nose, and a sugar syrup, corny, vaguely roasted, sweet and sticky palate. One of the crudest and most unpleasant of British beers, and certainly not a pale ale, by even the most imaginative definition. *Serve:* larder cool. *Avail:* Asda, Safe, Sains, Somer, Tesco.

McEWAN'S 70/-
44cl Canned 3.7%:
Mahogany-coloured beer with a dense white head. Easily as horrible as the Pale Ale, with flavours that suggest straight dark sugar, and something unpleasantly fruity and fondanty. Like a badly-made Scots Heavy dunked with a pineapple ice-lolly. No, no, it's worse than that. *Serve:* larder cool. *Avail:* Safe, Somer, Tesco.

McEWAN'S 80/- ALE**
55cl Bottled 4.5%:
Uncomplicated, reasonably quaffable beer, 'made with classic roast barley', and there's a characteristic toasted brown-loaf flavour in the finish. The nose is lightly malt-sweet, slightly spicy; the texture smooth, verging on creamy, and fairly sweet, in the traditional Scots style, but with enough hop dryness (as it warms and improves) to clean up the edges. A bit gassy and two-dimensional, not really worthy of its handsome bottle. *Serve:* room temp/larder cool. *Avail:* Asda, Safe, Sains, Tesco.

McEWAN'S 90/- ALE**
55cl Bottled 5.5%:
Even more classic roasted barley gives the 90/- a deep reddish hue, and a toasted grain, woodsmokey nose enlivened by fruit and sherbet sharpness. The flavours also, follow two quite distinct ambitions, with a bitter (rather than hoppy) backdrop, a dark smokeyness, as well as yeasty toffee sweetness and overripe fruit notes; this roasted but sweet character forms a rather unwilling arranged marriage that doesn't quite deliver. It's also rather depressingly thin, probably down to corn adjuncts and brewing sugar. *Serve:* room temp/larder cool. *Avail:* Asda, Safe, Sains, Somer, Tesco, Wait.

MACLAYS EXPORT ALE***
Maclays, Alloa. 50cl Bottled 4%:
Golden russety-brown, with an invitingly hoppy, herbal, pot-pourri nose, and an almost overpoweringly assertive, dry, dry hop (and drying, tongue-furring malt) character. Hop resiny, piney flavours, herbal and geraniol notes are slightly offset by a touch of

caramelly sweetness (but not much) and the finish has a slightly peaty, whiskyish character. Easier to admire than to love, perhaps. *Serve:* larder cool. *Avail:* Asda, BeerC, Safe, Sains, Tesco.

Maclays Oat Malt Stout***
50cl Bottled 4.5%:
It's a pity there isn't more information on the label (there's none besides that which is required by law); it's possible to take a dislike of marketing just a little too far. The beer itself has good stouty colouring, dark coffee and treacle aromas, and a dry, semi-spritzy texture which works well against the creaminess of the malted oats, and the bitter, dark, burnt currant, liquorice (Pontefract cakes!), slightly tarry and medicinal flavours. The overall effect is savoury, rather than sweet or fruity, and moreishly drinkable. *Serve:* larder cool. *Avail:* Asda, Safe, Sains, Somer.

Maclays Scotch Ale**
50cl Bottled 5%:
Paler than the Export, with Dundee whisky marmalade on the nose, and a sweeter, banana-accented fruitiness, perhaps rather caramelly, with hazelnut notes. Mild, soft-bodied, slightly disappointing. *Serve:* larder cool. *Avail:* Asda, BeerC, Safe, Sains, Somer, Tesco.

Malthouse Bitter
Hall & Woodhouse, Dorset. 44cl Canned 3%:
Mildly nutty, fizzy water stuff. A high nought though. *Serve:* larder cool. *Avail:* Somer.

Manns Brown Ale*
Ushers. 50cl Bottled 2.8%:
The bottle's nice: tall and brown, and preserving its old-fashioned red and white livery. For a famous classic, Manns is remarkably low in alcohol, and alcohol is barely the point. Instead, this is a beer for chocoholics and breast-feeders, with its dense, dark sugar, and mild, sweet coffee, and sticky sweet finish relieved only by a momentary note of orange. For keeping at the back of the cupboard, just in case. *Serve:* room temp. *Avail:* Somer, Tesco.

Mansfield Bitter*
Mansfield, Nottingham. 44cl Canned 3.9%:
Nitrogen-flush rather than widget bitter, refreshing if a little sweet, with a spritzy texture, and rudimentary hop and malt balance. Could certainly be better. But could also be much, much worse. *Serve:* larder cool. *Avail:* Asda, Safe, Sains, Tesco.

Marks & Spencer Best Bitter
Whitbread. 44cl Canned 4.4%:
Ingredients: malt, wheat, sugar, hops, yeast and water. Flavour: cheap beer for the masses style: fizzy, sweet alcohol fruit sugary, with a cloying finish, and some bitterness following. Marks & Spencer can do better than this. *Serve:* larder cool.

Marks & Spencer Caledonian 80/- Export***
see Caledonian 80/-

Marks & Spencer Schonbrau*
Pilsner Lager Whitbread. 50cl Canned 3.5%:
A Whitbread lager (brewed exclusively for M&S) made from malt, hops, yeast and water only, for which heroic effort they earn a brownie point. Weak and slightly watery flavour with a gently tinny finish. *Serve:* fridge cold (and don't expect much).

Marks & Spencer Traditional Yorkshire Bitter***
Black Sheep, Yorkshire. 50cl Bottled 4.4%:
Slightly different reformulation of Black Sheep Ale, with more citrus on the nose, less mineral water softness and more clean-edged bitterness on the palate from start to finish (though less at the end), and less sweet banana malt in the middle. A less complex version, but still delectable. Love the folk art sheep label, too. *Serve:* larder cool.

Marks & Spencer Wethereds Draught Bitter
Whitbread. 44cl Canned 3.8%:
Sweet marshmallow and cheap, warm vanilla ice-cream aromas and flavours, with a pot

pourri, husky hop finish, all whipped up into a frenzy of creaminess with the Whitbread widget. A bit sickly and difficult to drink. *Serve:* fridge cold.

MARKSMAN LAGER**

Mansfield. 44cl Canned 4.1%:
The packaging is basic, in a plain silver can, and this is no great billboard marketing star but, especially considering its anonymity, this is a tasty little number, with fresh aromas, and pale malt textures on the tongue, joined by a little apple and vanilla butter. The finish is decently dry, too. Modest, certainly, but useful for the store cupboard. *Serve:* light fridge chill. *Avail:* Asda, Somer, Tesco.

MARSTON INDIA EXPORT PALE ALE***

Marston, Burton-upon-Trent. 50cl Bottled 5.5%:
One of four very smartly and soberly packaged classic beers in dark, period bottles, very much a set (called Head Brewer's Choice), and well worth buying and drinking as one. This is a delicious, subtle, comforting IPA of nutty, amber colours and flavours, with a lovely Burton mineral water presence in the mouth, a Burton Union yeasty tang of the gently sulphurous, bath house sort, and hazelnut semi-sweetness. Complex, nutty and hoppy, but gentle and quaffable. *Serve:* larder cool. *Avail:* Tesco, Thres, VicW.

MARSTON LOW C*

27.5cl Bottled 4.2%:
Twice-fermented to convert all the sugar to alcohol, apparently (though this doesn't account for the low calorie count, as alcohol is horribly fattening). Barley sugar coloured, with a chestnut wood nose and a hint of vegetable in the nutty, caramelly, mildly vienna style flavour, it also has an oddly synthetic quality. But it *is* only 72 calories a bottle. *Serve:* light fridge chill. *Avail:* Asda, Tesco, VicW.

MASTER BREW BITTER*

Shepherd Neame, Kent. 50cl Bottled 4%:
Disappointing beer in an extravagant brandy-style bottle, a house trademark. Bright caramel orange, it smells like a jar of instant coffee, and tastes thin and hoppy, with a sweet, glucose syrup overlay, and a sourly fruity, orange malt note. Curiously tasteless, blunted by bottling, it has more texture than flavour, and a lingering dry finish. It also tastes even weaker than it really is. *Serve:* room temp/larder cool. *Avail:* Odd, Safe, Sains, Somer, Tesco.

MASTER BREW PREMIUM*

44cl Canned 4%:
The absence of a widget is on its side, and a successful new technology canning method which produces a perhaps slightly flabby (but not overgassy, at least) bitter from a tin. Smokey, oaky, caramel sweet, chestnut woody, but also thin and with an almost raw, dry-hopped floral punch in the finish that's a tad overdone. *Serve:* room temp/larder cool. *Avail:* Safe, Sains, Somer, Tesco.

MERLIN'S ALE***

Broughton, Borders. 50cl Bottled 4.2%:
Merlin lived in the Tweed Valley, apparently (or possibly just had a holiday cottage here?). Creamy amber, with appetizing but elusive aromas, and a creamy, but lively blend of hops and malt, a nice sourly woody note, and a combination of smoke and vanilla that's unique. Just a little fruit, too, before the hoppy, dry finish, which builds with drinking. Unusual and moreish, if just a tad keggy-tasting. *Serve:* larder cool. *Avail:* Co-op, Safe, Tesco.

MERMAN XXX***

East India Pale Ale Caledonian, Edinburgh. 50cl Bottled 4.8%:
A delicious recreation of Edinburgh's own IPA style, based on a recipe of 1890. Pungently malty and fruity on the nose and in the mouth, with added muscovado, marmalade and rich dark malt notes, it's just about to cling to the roof of the mouth, when along comes a positive tidal wave of dry, floral hop flavours to clean up the finish. Heady but refreshing, classic stuff. Teetering on the brink of four-

star status. *Serve:* larder cool. *Avail:* Asda, BeerC, Tesco.

MISTRAL

Charles Wells, Bedford. 44cl Canned 2.3%:
Low-alcohol lager which tastes even weaker than it is. Sugary grain fizz with very little flavour and no finish. Bland, boring, cold and wet. *Serve:* fridge cold. *Avail:* Safe.

NETHERGATE OLD GROWLER***

Special Porter Ale Nethergate, Suffolk. 50cl Bottled 5.5%:
Naffly labelled but delicous porter, dark ruby-black with a creamy downy head, and a dry, very clean, astringently spritzy texture. Bags of espresso, bitter chocolate, a little raisin and liquorice in the finish. Contains whole Goldings hops, crystal and chocolate malts, yeast and water. *Serve:* larder cool. *Avail:* BeerC, Safe, Sains, Tesco, Thres, Wait.

NEWCASTLE AMBER*

Scottish & Newcastle. 55cl Bottled 3.3%:
The rarely seen Amber was introduced in 1931 as a light ale version of the Brown, below. Light, quenching, with a rich amber note, but also brewing sugar very much in evidence in the slightly sticky finish, and adjunct character in the main body. *Serve:* larder cool. *Avail:* specialists.

NEWCASTLE BROWN**

Scottish & Newcastle. 55cl Bottled 4.7%:
As the back label blurb says, 'in 1927 Colonel Jim Porter created a premium bottled beer with its own unique colour, taste and strength'. Unfortunately this isn't it (presumably the original had more character). Nice aromas: woody, caramel sweet, a touch of toasted walnut, but alas the flavour is nothing like so intriguing, being thin, sweet and caramelly, with just a little nuttiness. The finish is thin and sugary. *Serve:* larder cool. *Avail:* widely.

NEWCASTLE BROWN

50cl Canned 4.7%:
Infinitely worse than the bottled version, thin and caramelly, with slight roastiness, but watery and unpleasant. Tastes more like a 2.7%er. *Serve:* larder cool. *Avail:* widely.

NEWCASTLE EXHIBITION*

Draught Ale 44cl Canned 4.3%:
Tapstream widget-ized, and should thus be fridge chilled, but it actually improved when sampled at larder temperature. Bright, shiny amber in colour; creamy and sweet on the palate, with a dry, nutty edge and an apple juice note. Otherwise, thin, insubstantial, structureless and dull. *Serve:* larder cool/light fridge chill. *Avail:* Sains, Tesco.

NEWQUAY STEAM BITTER

Whitbread 44cl Canned 4%:
Brown sugar aromas are far from a promising start. Thin textured and bland, with a drying (though not really hoppy) finish. Overgassy, but there is a little malt character underneath the identikit canned fizzy beer flavour. Unfortunately the aftertaste is tainted and metallic, so it's difficult to warm to. *Serve:* larder cool. *Avail:* Tesco, Thres.

NEWQUAY STEAM LAGER*

44cl Canned 5.3%:
Widget lager with a rather over-zealous foaming instinct. Sweet cereal nose, giving up pineapple fruit notes when provoked. Cereally flavour too, with a drying finish, which builds as you drink. Strong in alcohol, but modest in character. Just scraped a star. *Serve:* fridge cold. *Avail:* Asda, Thres, Tesco, VicW.

OAST HOUSE BITTER

Hall & Woodhouse, Dorset. 44cl Canned 2.2%:
Pale bright amber with a mildly nutty, but also oddly estery nose and palate. Better than most 2.2% beers, but this isn't saying much. *Serve:* larder cool. *Avail*: specialists.

OLD BOB***

Ridleys, Essex. 27.5cl Bottled 5.1%:
Dark amber ale with a cooked fruit, citrussy, banana sherbet nose, and flavours that begin as butter and fat, with strong, soft vanilla, and

acquire delicate fruity flavours of the plum, orange and blackcurrant sort. Luscious but with a green, sharp note to freshen. Dry and quenching, but also silky in texture. Very easy drinking. Moreish. Part of the Brewer's Heritage pack. *Serve:* room temp. *Avail:* Sains, Tesco.

OLD HOOKY**

Strong Ale Hook Norton, Oxon. 50cl Bottled 4.6%:
Fans of honeyed, toffee-nosed beers will probably love this full amber-coloured, fresh smelling, mild mannered, butter-sweet example, pale malty, with a touch of orange and a little hop dryness at the finish. Not really a strong ale at all, at 4.6% (less than most standard lagers), it's nonetheless awfully pleasant, if unexciting, drinking. Just a tad flabby perhaps. *Serve:* larder cool. *Avail*: BeerC, Tesco.

OLD JOCK**

Strong Ale Broughton, Borders. 27.5cl Bottled 6.7%:
Two tasting samples of Old Jock, and neither as complex as on previous occasions, when this would have been a natural three-star beer. Still, the classic yeasty Broughton nose when first poured remains intact, as does its darkest ruby glow. Flavours are sweetish, with hedgerow fruits, creamy, malty and mellow, and with just a touch of sour oak. Very, very soft-bodied, but (this is where the trouble lies) to the point of tasting distinctly over-processed and keggy, almost 'cooked', which also leaves it tasting under its considerable strength. *Serve:* room temp. *Avail:* BeerC, Sains, Tesco.

OLD LUXTERS BARN ALE***

Old Luxters, Oxon. 50cl Bottled 5.4%:
Bottle-conditioned, reddish-amber ale with buttery caramelized cooked fruit, and just very slightly warm rubber aromas. Flavours are succulently buttery, toffeeish, with more dark cooked fruits, robustly smoky malt, and just enough sour oaky tannins, although fairly light bodied at the same time. A dry, dry backdrop builds and moves into the middle with drinking, and a drying maltiness conspires with herbal hop flower notes in the finish. Delicious, if just a little flabby and lacking in zizz on occasion. *Serve:* room temp/larder cool. *Avail:* BeerC.

OLD MANOR BITTER

Mansfield, Notts. PET 3%:
Red apples on the nose, but very watery and virtually tasteless stuff of quite appalling mediocrity. *Serve:* larder cool. *Avail:* Safe.

OLD NETHERGATE SPECIAL BITTER***

Nethergate, Suffolk. 50cl Bottled 4%:
A delicious beer in a dismal bottle, complete with 1970s styling (someone else who should look at Caledonian's packaging). Auburn-red, with a rocky head and promisingly sherbety, almost kriek-like aromas. Tasting brings vivid malt fruit beautifully balanced by floral hop flavours, apparently drying at the finish, but then blossoming out into soft banana, pineapple, and a little chocolate. The dry, almost spritzy texture means it's refreshing, too. A great achievement for a mere 4% alcohol, verging on four stars. Brilliant with avocado salad. *Serve:* larder cool. *Avail:* BeerC, Thres.

OLD NICK***

Barley Wine Young's, London. 27.5cl Bottled 6.8%:
Gentle malt and alcohol on the nose of this dark russet-brown strong ale don't prepare you for the sweet and buttery, slightly rummy (or is it manzanilla sherry?), pungent alcohol and seville orange flavours to follow, drying and woody with perfumey hop notes in the finish. Such particular flavours, teased out from a strong and complex beer, can appear a little sickly on the page, but all is mellowly integrated and delicious, I promise. Old Nick grows drier (even from the very front) and more compelling with knowing. *Serve:* room temp. *Avail:* BeerC.

OLD SPECKLED HEN***

Strong Pale Ale Morlands, Oxfordshire. 50cl

Bottled 5.2%:
Named after a vintage MG sports car, and rather stylishly packaged itself in an elegant tall-necked bottle. Aromas, too, are appetizing, with vivid banana and tropical fruit, and the flavour achieves a fine malt and hop balance, in which buttery toffee and floral dry hops are much in evidence, along with a deliciously dry yeast 'bite'. *Serve:* larder cool. *Avail:* widely.

OLD SPECKLED HEN*

48cl Canned 5.2%:
This robustly flavoured ale should have had two stars, but after following the can's instructions to 'chill for at least six hours' (to make the new in-can draught system work), much of the flavour has been ice-boxed out. Deep golden-orange, fizzy, with appetizing yeasty, roast grain and coffee on the nose and palate, and good nutty flavour (especially those bitter brown skins), it then sweetens, and dries at the finish with a yeasty flourish. Or it would if it weren't so damn cold. *Avail:* widely.

ORIGINAL FLAG PORTER**

Elgoods, Cambridgeshire. 33cl Bottled 5%:
Made by Elgoods for Vinceramos, mostly for export, but occasionally seen here. Pure beer, made from malt, hops, yeast and water only, using a yeast culture revived from an 1825 parent found in a bottle of beer in an English Channel shipwreck. And then using a period porter recipe, which may explain why it's slightly unsatisfying to a modern palate. There appears to be no roasted unmalted grain, for a start (perhaps they are hoping to export to Germany, and abiding by the Reinheitsgebot). Nice to drink, though it goes a bit flabby in the glass: aromas and flavours are coffeeish, with a little bitter chocolate and a fruity tang. The initially soft hop finish grows drier and acquires a faintly cough mixtureish note. *Serve:* room temp. *Avail*: specialists.

OYSTER STOUT**

Marston, Burton-upon-trent. 50cl Bottled 4.5%:
Bottle-conditioned stout made for drinking with shellfish, and perhaps it shines in the presence of crustaceans, but on its own a bit of a limpid pool, not quite of three-star merit. Only subtly portery, and with a faintly seaweedy, oyster juicey note, soft-textured and a bit keggy and muffled. Least exciting of the four Head Brewer's Choice bottled beers. *Serve:* room temp. *Avail*: Odd, Sains.

PEDIGREE***

Marston, Burton-upon-Trent, Staffs. 56.8cl (an imperial pint) Bottled 4.5%:
A not altogether flattering bottled version of a world classic robs it of a fourth star. Coppery, slightly sparkling, with drily malty, banana toffee aromas, and a tongue-drying textured malt and astringent hop flavour, taking in a little tobacco-woody chestnut and vanilla, and a touch of nutmeg, and all wrapped in a super-soft mineral rich Burton water. Blunted by bottling, but nonetheless admirable, though perhaps difficult to love. *Serve:* larder cool. *Avail:* Asda, Odd, Safe, Sains, Tesco, Thres, Wait.

PEDIGREE*

Draught Bitter 44cl Canned 4.5%:
A travesty of a great beer, not least because the widget demands radical over-chilling and thus effortlessly ruins it. Creamy, whipped-up, with the texture of thin foamy cream, and once this barrier is breached, a tremendously dry and bitter, slightly pot-pourri floral flavour develops. The finish is decidedly mineral and a bit tinny. *Serve:* far too cold by half. *Avail:* widely.

REDRUTH BREWERY MILD

Redruth, Cornwall. 44cl Canned 2.3%:
Dark auburn-brown with roast barley, corn and sugar syrup on the thin, roasty palate. Icky, sticky stuff. *Serve:* larder cool. *Avail:* Asda.

RIDING TRADITIONAL DRAUGHT BITTER*

Mansfield, Nottingham. 44cl Canned 3.8%:
Amber-red bitter with an initially foamy head, that dissipates quickly, leaving mild brown bread aromas. No nitrogen flavours and

textures here, instead something a bit watery, with a toffeeish sweetness, and a little hop flavour in the background. Bland and gassy and fairly sweet. Prefer the Mansfield Bitter. *Serve:* larder cool. *Avail*: Asda, Safe, Sains, Tesco.

RINGWOOD OLD THUMPER***

Ringwood Brewery, Hampshire. 27.5cl Bottled 5.8%:
Deep orange-coloured strong ale, with lovely warm, sweet and woody aromas, and a fresh-ground coffee note. Flavours are of the ravishingly dry-fruity kind: dried banana and pineapple chips of the health store sort, pear, a little plumminess; only just enough fruit sweetness to save it from the complete austerity that threatens in the hop flower and dry malt finish. An excellent digestif. *Serve:* room temp. *Avail*: Thres.

ROBINSONS PALE ALE**

Robinsons, Liverpool. 27.5cl Bottled 4%:
Bright amber-coloured, initially fizzy, with a sweet and sour acid-drop nose and a little banana. At the first sip, it's dry and prickly, almost salty, developing sour-sweet fruit, with touches of oak and honey. Smooth but zingy; good for a mere 4%:. Almost a three-star beer. Part of the Brewer's Heritage Pack. *Serve:* larder cool. *Avail*: Sains, Tesco.

ROYAL OAK***

Traditional English Ale Eldridge Pope, Dorset. 33cl Bottled 4.8%:
There's no doubt about which oak: Charles II is pictured on the label. A pretty auburn ale, with an appealing malty-fruity, sour-sweet nose and a good lively texture. Flavours are apple and banana fruity, with toffeeish sweetness and a confectioner's custard, vanilla note at the back, followed by a very clean, very gentle but firm hop dryness. Just a little thin, perhaps: fairly low in the three-star rankings. *Serve:* room temp. *Avail*: BeerC, Sains, Tesco.

RUDDLES BEST BITTER*

Ruddles, Rutland. 50cl Canned 3.7%:
Not a widget job, but one of the newer breed of no-nitrogen 'draught can systems' that are thankfully not so intrusive. The opening flavour is disappointing, being thin and caramelly sugary, but things improve in the finish, with woody, herbaceous, oaky notes. *Serve:* larder cool. *Avail*: widely.

RUDDLES COUNTY*

50cl Canned 4.9%:
Non-widget again, with quite a good nose for a tinned bitter, and much like the 'Best' except the dryness chimes in sooner, and there's more direct malty fruit in the middle. A more robustly flavoured beer altogether, but made cloying in texture because of the same sweetish, thin caramelly flavours that bedevil the 'ordinary'. *Serve:* room temp/larder cool. *Avail*: widely.

RUDDLES COUNTY**

27.5cl Bottled 4.9%:
Unpromisingly packaged in a short fat bottle with a foil ringpull top, and sold in multipacks, but this is an enjoyable, if modest, bottled version of a decent cask ale. It's still a little caramelly and push-button in its assembly of strong flavours, but this is also a fresh and perky beer, good with a lunchtime sandwich. It has fresh malt and hop flavours, a little buttery, a little toasted-sugary, with cooked fruit notes. Much more successful than the canned version. *Serve:* larder cool. *Avail*: widely.

SADDLERS BITTER

Ashby Beer Company (Courage). 44cl Canned 2.2%:
Smells of peanuts, and tastes of unmalted cereals, but otherwise of nothing in particular. Thin and unpleasant to drink. *Serve:* larder cool. *Avail*: Asda.

SAFEWAY BEST BITTER

44cl Canned 3.5%:
Supposedly brewed using only the finest ingredients. Joke! (presumably). Dark amber stuff with a sweet nutty nose; fizzy beer with a sticky character, that comes to an even

stickier end. Watery and actively unpleasant. *Serve:* larder cool.

Safeway Bitter*

50cl Canned 3.5%:

Golden amber, and fairly bland, but with sweet and bitter notes, a little nut here, caramel and vanilla there, cold tea flavours and more than a little earthy. But better than the 'Best'. *Serve:* larder cool.

Safeway Bottle Conditioned Ale**

55cl Bottled 5.3%:

Rich, cloudy, russet-coloured ale, brewed in England for Safeway (by King & Barnes?). Delicate malty fruit flavours, with plum and summer fruit notes, a little oaky vanilla, and a delicious dry, hoppy backbone and finish. Just a little light-bodied, but spritzy and quenching. As it warms, it develops a dintinctive rose aroma. Verging on three stars. *Serve:* room temp/larder cool.

Safeway County Festive Ale***

50cl Bottled 5%:

Smooth and delicious, with a mildly nutty, fruity nose, and a veritable nut festival on the palate – sweet, musky, bitter skins and all – but also deeply fruity, with plum and banana, orange zest and sultana, before giving way to a resiny, tannic hop finish. Lively, but also creamy in texture. Sounds like a King & Barnes beer, but drinks like a Bateman ale? Almost four-star quality, whatever its origins. *Serve:* larder cool.

Safeway Export Strength Lager

see under Netherlands.

Safeway Lager

50cl Canned 3.6%:

Brewed and canned in the UK, but has a curiously American accent: a pale 'lite' beer with a fizzy, cereally, rice-and-unmalted grain style character, and a tannic, cereal husky finish. Not even clean tasting. *Serve:* fridge cold.

Safeway Strong Bitter*

50cl Canned 4.5%:

Pungent sour-sweet malt aromas, typical of a coppery, orange coloured beer: sweetish, malty, light-bodied in the mouth, keggy and overfizzy but with a little oaky wood and a touch of marmalade orange on the finish. *Serve*: larder cool.

Sainsbury's Blackfriars Porter**

50cl Bottled 5.5%:

Coffee and orange aromas; flavours of bitter black coffee with a touch of sugar, a little chocolate, and a roasted grain note. But the beer is unbalanced for the style, with too much caramel and muscovado on the palate, and a slightly cloying finish. More hops please! *Serve:* larder cool.

Sainsbury's Bottle Conditioned Ale*

50cl Bottled 4.5%:

Tastes distinctly Brewer James-like to me, but this could be a coincidence. Coppery in colour, with tinned peach aromas, a soft-bodied, oddly tasteless beer with a hard prickly edge, a few more tinned peach notes and an oddly metallic finish. No real evidence of bottle conditioning in the flavours and textures, which are as crude as the Brewer James example. *Serve*: larder cool.

Sainsbury's Blue Riband Export Lager

27.5cl Canned 4%:

British brewed, and odd-smelling lager (birdseed!), with a weak-tasting, oddly birdseedy, slightly honeyish flavour. A bit flat and unrefreshing, too. *Serve:* fridge cool.

Sainsbury's Green Riband Export Lager

44cl Canned 3%:

British brewed, clean and dilute-tasting, watery and supremely inoffensive 'lite' lager. Pale but not interesting. *Serve:* fridge cold.

SAINSBURY'S MIDLAND MILD
44cl Canned 2.7%:
Chocolate dark, thin and fizzy stuff, sweet and two-dimensional, like a sort of coke with a kick. The odd, slightly industrial odour doesn't help matters, either. *Serve:* larder cool.

SAINSBURY'S PARKIN'S BITTER
44cl Canned 3%:
Shandyish, lemonadey, enthusiastically over-fizzed. 'A traditional bitter brewed in Burton on Trent' it says on the can. Some mistake surely? No nose. No finish. Not drinkable, frankly. *Serve*: larder cool.

SAINSBURY'S PARKIN'S SPECIAL BITTER
50cl Canned 4%:
A bit browner than the beer mentioned above, and smells a bit more like beer, but still remarkably fizzy and shandy-like. *Serve:* larder cool.

SAINSBURY'S PREMIUM ALE***
50cl Bottled 4.8%:
Delicious and succulent Bateman's-brewed beer. The nose suggests dried banana chips; the flavour, very drily nutty and aromatically banana fruity, has mouthfilling dry floral hop character, prickly dry bubbles (tiny, not gassy), and a superclean, bitter grapefruit finish, so grapefruit-pith dry that it almost cures the tongue, with balancing rounded yeast 'bite' coming to the rescue. Undeniably austere, but moreish and compelling nonetheless. Tastes about two degrees stronger than 4.8%. *Serve:* larder cool.

SAINSBURY'S RUTLAND BITTER*
PET 3.4%:
Nicer than usual PET bitter from Ruddles, a decent source at least. Nutty nosed, bright, deep amber in colour, it has sweetish walnut cake flavours, celery notes, and a dryish nutty finish. *Serve:* larder cool.

SAINSBURY'S SUPER STRENGTH LAGER
44cl Canned 8.5%:
Sweet, roast turnipy, with a decidedly earthy finish, and too much brown sugar on the palate, as well as masses of crude 'super' alcohol. *Serve:* fridge cold.

SAINSBURY'S TRADITIONAL BITTER
44cl Canned 3.4%:
Brewed in Lancashire, apparently. Industrial, wet wood shavings and mouldy pear aromas aren't the best of starts. Remarkably bland, sweetish beer with a slightly soapy texture and faintly bitter background. And crudely fizzed up. *Serve:* larder cool.

ST ANDREWS ALE***
Belhaven, Dunbar. 55cl Bottled 4.6%:
Rich brown coloured, with even richer, malty-fruity, butterscotch aromas. A good, dry, prickly hop character, introducing a wonderfully soft, buttery (rich dark toffee), fruity sweetness, with a little baked apple and the tiniest hint of prune. Dark malts, succulent yeast fruits, vividly hoppy: this is an admirably well-made ale, at once deeply mellow and arrestingly clean-edged. Tremendous stuff for a mere 4.6% alcohol, and the illustrative label's nice too, but such a stodgy, historical-academic name rather lets down a delicious modern beer. *Serve:* room temp/larder cool. *Avail*: Asda, Co-op, Odd, Safe, Tesco, VicW.

SAM SMITH OATMEAL STOUT***
55cl Bottled 5%:
Period-labelled and in the distinctive Sam Smith tall clear bottle; densely dark with no head to speak of, but pretty Brussels lace down the side of the glass. A surprisingly clean, summery quality emanates from this dark brew, with banana oil, fruit essences, orange and bramble flavours, a little chocolate and raisin, and a delicious mandarin 'lift' at the finish. Not remotely cloying, but dry and spritzy in texture. Good with garlicky salad. *Serve:* larder cool. *Avail*: Asda, Maj, Safe, Tesco, Wait.

SAM SMITH OLD BREWERY BITTER*
Draught 44cl Canned 4%:
Canned with a 'Tapstream system' widget, which produces a bright dark amber keg

bitter, with a small tight head. Sweet malt aromas, and an emphatically nutty sweetness on the palate, with a little caramel and vanilla. Very smooth, softly drying, creamy, but not as whipped-up by excessive nitrogen as the Whitbread beers. And it's nice to know there's only malted barley, hops, yeast and water in its brewing. *Serve:* far too cold (two hours, by instruction). *Avail:* Asda, Maj, Safe, Tesco.

Sam Smith Old Brewery Strong Pale Ale ***

55cl Bottled 5%:

Stridently orange beer in a tall clear glass bottle. An appetizing tropical and banana fruit nose, and two distinct strands of flavour: the first caramel, crystalline, slightly cloying; the second dry, hoppy and insistent until at the finish it's joined by a soft, buttery malt loaf note. The two strands only just meet and integrate. Nevertheless, a modern classic, and a cult beer in the USA, where it's been incredibly influential in the microbrewery movement. Wholesome stuff, too, brewed purely from malt, hops, yeast and water. *Serve:* larder cool. *Avail:* widely.

Sam Smith Pure Brewed Lager*

50cl Canned 5%:

The brand that's replaced the original 'Natural Lager', and the weak link in the Sam Smith chain, especially disappointing after tasting the rest of the range. Golden lager, with grain and barley sugar sweetness on the nose, more of the same on the palate, but also distinctively tinny, and losing its life and condition far too quickly in the glass. Flabby, bland and under par. (NB: there appears to be a bottled version coming out, which will no doubt be better.) *Serve:* fridge cold. *Avail:* Asda, Co-op, Maj, Sains.

Sam Smith Taddy Porter***

55cl Bottled 5%:

An almost-black beer in a clear glass bottle, with fresh, chocolate-malty aromas, a little cooked banana fruitiness, and a spritzy, dry texture which lends a light, refreshing quality to its dark flavours. One of the most straightforward of porters, with a creamily sweet, vanilla fruits finish and a gentle bitter note which lingers in the mouth. Very good with hot cross buns. *Serve:* larder cool. *Avail:* Asda, BeerC, Safe, VicW, Wait.

Scorpion Dry**

Strong Premium Lager Scorpion Island, Sunderland. 44cl Canned 5%:

Vaux-brewed, and presented Indiana Jones style in a crude gold can. Supposedly dry and refreshing, Scorpion is actually notably sweet, but still fairly refreshing, and reasonably full-bodied. The advertised clean finish is spot on: it just comes to a dead halt. The unintended sweetness, meanwhile, develops a gentle but persistent pumpkin flavour. Intriguing and slightly odd. *Serve:* fridge cold. *Avail:* Asda, Co-op, Safe, Somer.

Shepherd Neame Original Porter**

50cl Bottled 5.2%:

Quite a puritanical little number this, with armfuls of Kentish hops evident in the assertive, savoury dry opening, though malt-loaf-style buttery fruit notes appear in the middle, and the finishing hop character is more gentle and slower-building than expected. Should probably be a three-star beer but, for me at least, it never quite makes it from plainsong to Haydn opera. *Serve:* larder cool. *Avail:* Safe.

Shire Bitter

44cl Canned 3%:

A Spar/Landmark brand, and one of the least attractive supermarket own brand bitters tasted this year. Brown sugary on the nose, and slightly, weakly, feebly tea-baggy and sugary on the palate. Thin and sticky. Must be very very cheap. *Serve:* larder cool. *Avail:* Spar.

Shire Mild

44cl Canned 3%:

Almost black, with an off-putting vegetable nose, and dishwatery flavours, laced with chocolate malt. Thin and a bit sickly. *Serve:* larder cool. *Avail:* Spar.

SKOL

Ind Coope, Carlsberg Tetley. 50cl Canned 3.4%:
As the terrible old joke has it, Skol is a Scandinavian drinking toast, and this beer tastes . . . just like drinking toast. In fact, toast would be an improvement to this bland, thin, sugar syrupy, glucose and grain lager. The finish is adjuncty (rice? maize?) and sticky. Can't think who's still buying this dire 1970s stuff. *Serve:* fridge cold. *Avail:* specialists.

SKULLSPLITTER***

Orkney Brewery, Orkney. 27.5cl Bottled 8.5%:
Not a promising start: the label is exceedingly naff, complete with out-of-work actor (not even Jessie Rae) dressed up as Thorfinn, otherwise known as the Skullsplitter or, at his day job, seventh earl of Orkney. But this is distraction. The beer itself is rather delicious, and ideal for autumn sipping: a smooth and silky, dark-amber concoction, initially with a great fluffy head which fizzles away. Its flavours are of a super-strong pale ale, with celery, walnut, a sweet nuttiness, and lots of slightly orange-juicey, fruity alcohol, with a mellow malt-whiskyish, peat and vanilla finish. Extremely good and complex beer. But please, the name and the label! *Serve:* room temp. *Avail:* Safe.

SOMERFIELD BEST BITTER

44cl Canned 4%:
Brewed in Yorkshire, probably by Wards, though (like most other own brands in this guide) nobody's telling. Aromas are slightly sulphurous and eggy, and the flavour also has a bit of that, with spritzy fizz and malty sweetness, as well as just a hint of banana. Undistinguished, gassy, old-fashioned bitter in a can. Crude, in other words. *Serve:* larder cool.

SOMERFIELD BITTER

44cl Canned 3%:
Fizzy shandy-style so-called 'bitter', bright orange and gassy, with a cooked-greens nose, and a sugary, slightly fruity flavour. Remarkably unpleasant, despite the can's assertions that it's brewed with spring water. *Serve:* larder cool.

SOMERFIELD LAGER

44cl Canned 3%:
Brewed using spring water for a clean refreshing taste, according to the can. Bland, fizzy and wet, according to the *Guide*. In fact worse than bland: there's an undeniably adjunct-laden, and hard metallic edge in the finish (such as it is) as well. *Serve:* fridge cold.

SOMERFIELD (DRAUGHT) PREMIUM BITTER *

44cl Canned 4.2%:
Distinctly Boddington's-like, bright pale gold bitter with a sweet nose, and a creamy (widget-assisted) texture, with the persistently hoppy, bitter dryness and background fruity complexity of the Boddingtons brand. But chilling for two hours does it no favours. *Serve:* light fridge chill.

SPAR PREMIUM BITTER*

44cl Canned 4%:
Brewed for Spar by Cains of Liverpool. A bright, dark amber beer with a vaguely rhubarby nose, creamy roast barley and husky grain in the mouth, and sweet fruity notes in the finish, which also introduces a brief creamy malt and hop dry finish. Having said all that, it's terribly dull. *Serve:* larder cool.

SPAR TRADITIONAL BITTER*

44cl Canned 3%:
Also from Cains, and a softer, blander, weaker version of the Premium, with creamy, very mildly malty and hoppy flavours and a soft bitterness in the finish. Extremely wishy-washy. *Serve:* larder cool.

SPITFIRE**

Bottle-Conditioned Beer Shepherd Neame, Kent. 50cl Bottled 4.7%:
Orangey-amber beer, with a lovely sweet, orange-fruity, yeasty nose. Initial flavours are rather too gentle and disappointingly thin, with mild, soft echoes of Vienna malt, chestnut notes, a little smokeyness, but with this

perfumed dryness in the finish (it's dry-hopped with Goldings), which builds and layers and becomes rather too assertive, unbalancing the whole effect. *Serve:* larder cool. *Avail:* Asda, BeerC, Safe, Tesco.

STANFORD BITTER

Abington (Charles Wells). 44cl Canned 3%: Another incarnation for Abington Bitter. *Serve:* larder cool. *Avail:* Co-op.

STONES BITTER*

Bass. 50cl Canned 3.9%:
Pale amber, with a little white head. Pale in character, too: slightly malty, slightly hoppy, slightly sweet. It's on the way to being interpreted as subtle rather than bland, but then reveals itself as too fizzy, a bit eggy, and with more than a hint of demerara sugar flavour. *Serve:* larder cool. *Avail:* specialists.

SWEETHEART STOUT

Tennents (Bass). 50cl Canned 2%:
Shandyish, sweet and fruity, yes. Stout, no. *Serve:* larder cool. *Avail:* specialists.

TANGLEFOOT**

Hall & Woodhouse, Dorset. 50cl Bottled 5%: Brightest amber, with a barley sugar, root vegetable, sour-sweet nose. Flavours are dominated by strong sweet alcohol of the roasted pumpkin sort, joined by a little glucose (Lucozade!), and bags of typically dry-hopped, herbal hop character. A little viscous, as if hop resins and sweet alcohol have emulsified, salad dressing style. Better than the tinned version, but still a little flabby. *Serve:* larder cool. *Avail:* Safe, Sains, Somer, Tesco, VicW, Wait.

TANGLEFOOT*

44cl Canned 5%:
Tinned chick peas on the nose, followed by bittersweet aromas; mouth-drying malt, at once astringent and fruity on the palate, and a hop resin kick at the end, which lingers on. Oddly pungent and a wee bit sickly; canning is presumably responsible for a slightly soapy, flaccid quality, thankfully absent in the more successful bottled version. *Serve:* larder cool. *Avail*: widely.

TAYLOR'S SPECIAL PALE ALE*

Taylor, Yorkshire. 27.5cl Bottled 3.3%
Very similar to the equally disappointing Landlord Pale; a disappointing beer out of a nice period bottle. It's amber-gold, with vaguely buttery, caramel flavours and a hint of spice, but all rather dilute, and flabby in texture. *Serve:* larder cool. *Avail*: specialists.

TENNENTS EXTRA*

Premium Lager Scottish & Newcastle. 50cl Canned 4.8%:
Uninspiring international-style lager which earns its star by being a lot better than many other UK brewed examples. Hardly any nose. The flavour offers grain sweetness, of the thin and sugary kind, with the requisite dryness chiming in at the close. *Serve:* fridge cold. *Avail:* specialists.

TENNENTS LAGER*

50cl Canned 4%:
As an experiment, I tried drinking this out of a wine glass to see if it vastly improved it. And – oddly enough – it didn't. But this is nonetheless a fairly clean, decently thirst-quenching example of cheap mass-market canned lagers, with only a very slightly grainy, tinny edge. I would rather drink this than McEwans. I would also rather drink this than American Budweiser. (But the question is, would millions of Americans find Tennents too hoppy?) An ideal budget beer to keep very cold and swig restlessly while idly roaming the kitchen in search of distractions. *Serve:* fridge cold. *Avail*: widely.

TENNENTS PILSNER**

50cl Canned 3.4%:
Why bother to use Czech yeast and only brew such a low-alcohol lager? At 5% this would probably have been quite interesting. Briney, mineral aromas; flavours express a little of the famed yeast, a little barley butter, a slight Czech dryness (but with grain notes) at the finish, which is also just a little tinny. Not a pilsner by any means, but the structure is

almost there, though it's possibly only a bungalow. *Serve:* fridge cold. *Avail:* widely.

TENNENTS SPECIAL 70/- ALE

50cl Canned 3.5%:
Slightly sherbety, mildly eggy, faintly fruity beer-type-stuff, rather unsettlingly diverted from proper ale flavour and strucure. Not nice. *Serve:* larder cool. *Avail:* widely.

TENNENTS SUPER

50cl Canned 9%:
Fuller barley sugar colour than its Kestrel Super Scots rival, but otherwise similar in character, though there's less whisky and more golden syrup in this one, and a little sugary fruit of the banana fritters and tinned pineapple sort (complete with the syrup and lashings of evaporated milk). *Serve:* light fridge chill. *Avail:* widely.

TENNENTS 80/-

44cl Canned 2%:
Enthusiastic widget beer: you get a four-second warning before it erupts all over your shoes. Deep coppery-amber in colour, it's sweet and vaguely malty, though it is also plain sugary, and full of all too visible adjunct flavours, with a sticky cloying finish. But better than McEwans. *Serve:* fridge cold. *Avail:* widely.

TESCO BEST BITTER*

44cl Canned 3.9%:
Brewed by Vaux, and the star is awarded for Tesco having taken the trouble to source out a canned supermarket 'value' bitter that stands head and shoulders above the rest. Vigorously hoppy, with a touch of malt balance, and a finish that slowly dries with drinking, growing almost astringent by the end. There's a lemonadey, sweet note, and it's very fizzy. Keggy, certainly, but not tinny. The ingredients are listed: malted barley, starch, wheat, hops, yeast, caramel, carbon dioxide and preservative. Nothing unusual there. *Serve:* larder cool.

TESCO EXTRA STRENGTH LAGER*

50cl Canned 5%:
Not particularly strong, at 5%, and a pale gold, light, bright, clean and quaffable beer which doesn't taste of anything in particular. No dryness, no hop, no malt, no yeast character: just a sort of beerade, with some grain sweetness, and no finish whatever. *Serve:* fridge cold.

TESCO INDIA PALE ALE**

Select Ales Marston, Burton-upon-Trent. 50cl Bottled 5%:
Bottle-conditioned IPA brewed exclusively for Tesco by Marston. Ingredients: water, malted barley, hops, glucose syrup, yeast, caramel and carbon dioxide. Nothing surprising there, but what does surprise is how mild-mannered and inoffensive this beer is. Its soft texture has some initial hop and yeast bite, but this trails off leaving more structure than flavour; the finish builds slowly, becoming good and hoppy, and developing good tannic, oily resins, but what's left in the middle is akin to a sweetish mineral water. *Serve:* larder cool.

TESCO LAGER**

50cl Canned 4%:
Sweetish, buttery lager, easy, clean and inoffensive. Fairly fresh-tasting, and with no unmalted adjuncts or unwanted tinny flavours, it's a perfectly acceptable, if underwhelming table lager, which is exactly what it sets out to be. Tastes quite like Carling Black Label. *Serve:* light fridge chill.

TESCO MILD***

Select Ales Marston, Burton-upon-Trent. 50cl Bottled 3.8%:
Delicious, mildly porterish mild with lots of ruby-coloured, roasted barley, and a dark malt, coffeeish note, before growing faintly fruity in the finish, which grows gently drying. Otherwise, just a little thin, but refreshing in texture. *Serve:* larder cool.

TESCO ORGANIC BEER***

Caledonian, Edinburgh. 50cl Bottled 5%:
A reformulated version of Golden Promise,

with all the same components but a slightly different emphasis. Lemon and hop flowers on the nose; soft water texture on the palate, with barley, butter, new-mown hay, a little sappiness, a little spice, and good citrus freshness, followed by a dry, dry finish, floral with rose and herb garden character, and plenty of crystal malt bite. *Serve:* larder cool.

Tesco Porter***

Select Ales Marston, Burton-upon-Trent. 50cl Bottled 5%:
Traditionally brewed, with a little roasted (as well as malted) barley, plus wheat malt, caramel and glucose syrup. Nice liquorice and coffee aromas, light and fresh, set the tone for a soft and very drinkable porter of almost quaffable texture. It has more toffee character than is usually found in porters, too, balancing the black coffee, dried fruit, vanilla, and plummy fruit, and a distinctively grapey flavour. Not at all severe, only very gently dry, it's a porter for Easter rather than Christmas. *Serve:* room temp/larder cool.

Tesco Premium Ale***

Caledonian, Edinburgh. 50cl Bottled 4.1%:
Tesco's own version of Caley 80/- isn't quite so exciting as the original, with a more even-tempered soft maltiness and a big dry finish (as opposed to the initially astringent, mellowing Caledonian 80/- proper), but is still a delicious beer, full of good honest ingredients. *Serve:* larder cool.

Tesco Stout***

Select Ales 50cl Bottled 4.2%:
Another of the Marston-brewed Select Ales range. Dark browny-black, headless and sparkly stuff, with roast coffee bean and green banana aromas. A good spritzy texture, and light, very gentle stout flavours, poised on the borderline between subtlety and wishy-washy; the three-star rating opts for the former verdict, but it's a close call. Certainly good with food, though: stood up well to egg and roast aubergine salad. *Serve:* larder cool. *Avail*: Tesco.

Tesco Strong Yorkshire Bitter

50cl Canned 5%:
Wheat and propylene glycol alginate join the ingredients list this time, but it's heavy-handed use of the caramel that's resulted in the overbearingly sweet and sugary flavours here, made worse by pronounced strong alcohol (vegetal) flavours, with more than a hint of swede in evidence. Stick to the Best. *Serve:* larder cool. *Avail*: Tesco.

Tetley Bitter*

Draught Carlsberg-Tetley. 44cl Canned 3.6%:
One of the better widget beers, less foaming than others, a bright copper colour and with a firm Yorkshire head. Sweet, nutty aromas and flavours, mild mannered, almost innocuous, but a nice dry hop note is struggling through the nitrogen cream. Pity it has to be served so over-chilled to make the widget work. *Serve:* far too cold. *Avail*: widely.

Tetley Mild*

Draught 44cl Canned 3.2%:
The can instructs chilling for three hours, but as with most other widget beers, this one actually improves if you only larder chill it. Treated this way, it's auburny-orange body achieves a soft white head, a sweet, mildly malty nose, and more of the same on the palate. There's also something a bit icky, an icing-sugar sweetness creeping in, and something fruit juicey, but just enough soft oak and dryness to make it tolerable. Otherwise, as with most other widget beers, it makes you long to dump it in the sink and rush off for a freshly-pulled cask-conditioned pint instead. *Serve:* larder cool/fridge cold. *Avail:* widely.

Theakston Best Bitter*

Scottish & Newcastle. 55cl Bottled 3.8%:
'Brewery conditioned', as it says on the label, and this is a keg beer displaying many keg beer failings (of course, many bottled beers are strictly speaking keg, but some are far keggier than others). It has no nose to speak of, is a bright sparkly-gold, with a bubbly soft

water texture (perhaps even a little soapy), and a mild, sweet and hazelnutty flavour with a little unmalted cereal and even less hoppiness. *Serve:* larder cool. *Avail:* Safe, Sains, Thres.

THEAKSTON BEST BITTER

44cl Canned 3.8%:

A highly successful widget beer, in that it makes a very pretty picture in the glass. Chilling for the two hours instructed also makes it taste very mass-produced Scottish, with adjuncts and thin sweetness very much to the fore: such a disappointment, following on from the delicious nutty, sweet and oaky aromas that emanate as it thaws. Buy the bottled one. And if you want a canned bitter, buy Draught Bass instead. *Serve:* light fridge chill. *Avail:* Safe, Sains, Tesco, VicW.

THEAKSTON OLD PECULIER**

27.5cl Bottled 5.6%:

Densely ruby-coloured, with a soft, buttery plum pie and custard nose, and some of the same in the gentle, dry flavour, which also has prickly bubbles, a little creaminess, and a little chocolate. The finish, though short and lacking in hop character, has all these, and is warm and subtle. But not the triumph of complex flavours that it might be; keggy and blunted in character, especially for a 5.6% beer. *Serve:* larder cool. *Avail:* widely.

THOMAS HARDY COUNTRY BITTER***

Eldridge Pope, Dorset. 55cl Bottled 4.2%:

Bottle-conditioned, glorious reddish-amber beer with a lovely refermented sparkle. Alluring warm banana and red summer fruit sherbety aromas; warm malt flavours with a summery, fruit punchy quality, and a decidely floral hop dryness with a quinine-like spiky, mineral edge, leading into a toasted nut finish. Rich and refreshing at the same time, and lower in alcohol than many standard Euro lagers. *Serve:* larder cool (too cold and you'll squash the flavours). *Avail:* BeerC, Odd, Safe, Tesco, Thres.

THOMAS HARDY'S ALE**

33cl Bottled 12%:

The 1994 bottling of this bottle-conditioned beer was all that could be offered by the retailers for tasting, and it's difficult to judge the vintage's worth in 20 years, when it will probably reach its peak. Though my guess would be, tremendous. Aromas suggest plum chutney, deeply caramelized, dark marmalade and balsamic vinegar. Flavours are (naturally) raw and unripe, but the texture is very silky, and cognac-like notes mingle with fresh mandarin, sweet grapefruit, sour damsons, dark rich malt and a touch of oak, all blended with masses of still rather crude spiritous alcohol. Lay it down for New Year's Eve, 1999, when it will probably emerge as a four-star classic. *Serve:* room temp. *Avail:* BeerC.

THWAITES BEST BITTER**

Thwaites, Lancs. 44cl Canned 3.4%:

One of the very nicest canned English bitters, respectable enough for socializing, and worth stocking up with. No widget here, but a robustly malty, refreshingly bitter ale with a moreish hop-resiny finish. Not tinny either; it works as well as it probably could within the limitations of beer canning, with good strong flavours, wholesome ingredients, and not a bad texture either. A surprise hit, in canned beer terms. Almost three stars. *Serve:* larder cool. *Avail:* Asda, Safe, Sains, Tesco.

TOLLY'S STRONG ALE**

Tolly Cobbold, Suffolk. 33cl Bottled 4.6%:

Hardly a strong beer, but displaying plenty of strong ale character nonetheless. Reddish coral in colour, it has a fruity nose, a decent lively but not gassy texture, and a frankly modest (even a bit keggy) mild-mannered flavour, with a little sour-oak malt, creamy sweetness, alcohol notes, and a gently drying finish. Probably intended mostly for American export, where the Suffolk Punch label would also go down very well. *Serve:* room temp/ larder cool. *Avail:* BeerC.

TOURNAMENT BITTER
Ashby (Courage). 44cl Canned 2.2%:
Tastes exactly like all the other 2.2% commodity bitters. Of nothing much, in other words. *Serve:* larder cool. *Avail:* Wait.

TRAQUAIR HOUSE ALE****
Traquair, Borders. 33cl Bottled 7.2%:
A dark, strong Scots classic which, despite coming from a tiny 18th-century brewhouse, has been hugely influential in export markets, particularly in the USA, where all beer buffs seem to know it. Serious alcohol and fruity malt on the nose, and delicious plum pie and vanilla flavours, with a little oak and amontillado sherry character. Soft and drinkable with a sherryish dryness that stops it cloying, and a sweet note reminiscent of the sticky skins of supermarket dates in a box. Excellent with hard farm cheeses, particularly those with an acidic or goaty accent. Also unrivalled as a Christmas Eve sipping beer, with candles and log fires and a glittery tree. *Serve:* room temp. *Avail:* specialists.

TRENT BITTER
Bass. 50cl Canned 2.8%:
Of very modest strength, and just as bland as the Mild, but without its mildness; the mild is, a style much more at ease with low alcohol levels. *Serve:* larder cool. *Avail:* Co-op, Safe, Tesco, VicW.

TRENT MILD*
44cl Canned 2.7%:
A budget mild from Burton-upon-Trent. Fairly fizzy, mildly sweet and malty, faintly coffeeish, very modest, but it could be worse (and frequently is: *see* McEwans). *Serve:* larder cool. *Avail:* Co-op, Safe, Somer, Tesco, VicW.

USHERS DARK HORSE PORTER***
Ushers, Wiltshire. 33cl Bottled 5%:
Good porterish smells, and rich flavours, cut through by a lively fizz. Sweet black coffee, dry fruit (raisin and apple), a soft yeasty tang and gently bitter in the finish, with mild spice and liquorice on the aftertaste. But a bit too fizzy. *Serve:* larder cool. *Avail:* Tesco.

USHERS FOUNDERS ALE*
44cl Canned 4.5%:
Serve cool and pour quickly, for a fizzy, reddish amber beer with bubblegum and banana and peach bath oil aromas. Flavours are even more compellingly odd, sweetish in effect, but with a slightly redeeming dry hop backbone. But still too sweet and extremely fizzed up. *Serve:* larder cool. *Avail:* Somer, Tesco.

USHERS INDIA PALE ALE***
Ushers, Wiltshire. 33cl Bottled 5%:
Like many other IPAs, this superb Ushers one is better larder cool than at room temperature. Aromas of toffee and vanilla introduce a zingy, spritzy, fresh and wholesome beer with yeasty fullness and bloom, and robust dry hop flavours, almost of raw hop flower, perfumed, floral, husky, oily authenticity, building and growing astringent with aquaintance. Added to which, its lively, prickly texture creates a beer of elegance and ideal aperitif material. *Serve:* larder cool. *Avail:* Odd, Tesco.

USHERS 1824 PARTICULAR ***
33cl Bottled 6%:
In the King & Barnes and Batemans league: a big, bold, fruity bitter with hearty hop resins in the finish and a rich, fat yeasty floom, with lots of soft, strong banana, filling the mouth with flavours. Rich, but ultimately drying, so clean and refreshing to drink. *Serve:* larder cool. *Avail:* Tesco, Wait.

VASSILENSKI'S BLACK RUSSIAN**
brewed for Hanseatic Trading, Leicester, by McMullen. 50cl Bottled 4.8%:
Best known of the 'Hanseatics', this liquorice and Pontefract cake-flavoured beer, with its stewed-tea finish, is nevertheless oddly thin-textured and unsatifying. It has good robust flavours, but like the famous Pontefract cake sweets, a savoury, rather than sweet liquorice quality which leaves a craving for something else to take the taste away. Still, supposedly a remarkably good recreation of a 19th-century Russian Empire stout. *Serve:* larder cool. *Avail:* Safe, Tesco, Thres, Wait.

VAUX DOUBLE MAXIM*
Vaux, Sunderland. 50cl Canned 4.2%:
Amber coloured, widget-free ale of fruity character. Unfortunately, the fruit tips over into sweaty, slight egginess, and there's a brewing sugar suggestive sweetness. As well as something oddly butterbeany. *Serve:* larder cool. *Avail:* widely.

VAUX EXPORT BITTER**
50cl Canned 4.2%:
We are instructed to serve it chilled. Bright light-amber in colour, with an initially firm little head, this is a slightly sour and oak-woody bitter, with a little earthiness and something vaguely fruity and yeast-fatty. Also identifiably tinny, which spoils things a bit, but there's plenty more to recommend it. Joins the ranks of the not-too-bad canned bitters. *Serve:* light fridge chill. *Avail*: Asda, Safe, Somer.

VAUX LIGHT ALE
44cl Canned 3.3%:
Watery, cereally, pale amber stuff, vaguely sweet and malty. *Serve:* larder cool *Avail*: Somer, Tesco.

VAUX SAMSON*
44cl Canned 4.2%:
Draughtflow-afflicted, which means the super-creamy, foamy and whippy texture is far too dominant, but otherwise, a typically northern bitter, dry and malty, woody and a bit grain-husky, with a soft, fragrant hop background. Tastes keggy, but has flavours, at least, to break through the cream. *Serve:* light fridge chill. *Avail*: Asda, Safe, Somer, Tesco, Thres.

VICTORIA ALE***
Marston, Staffordshire. 50cl Bottled 4.8%:
Brewed exclusively for Victoria Wine by Marston, and a beer of such exceptional quality that it almost earned four stars. Here's Marston in a Caledonian mood; they should be making this for supermarkets, too. A lovely, deep gleaming amber colour, with a ripe, dry-hopped, spicy nose, and delicious and delicate flavours: softly malty and buttery with orange notes and a restrained yeasty fullness, there's also a firm, floral hop background and nutty notes in the finish. Refreshing, tasty, complex, clean. Fill those trolleys! *Serve:* room temp. *Avail:* VicW.

WADWORTH OLD TIMER**
Traditional Strong Ale Wadworth, Wiltshire. 27.5cl Bottled 5.5%:
Garnet-red, with a strong ale fruit nose, and smokey, fennel and cheesey notes. In the mouth, there's blackly overripe banana among other fruits, more smokey cheese, pungent malt and yeast character, and a bourbon-like spirit quality; all in all it tastes more like a 7.5% than a 5.5%. Silky in texture, but still a little cloying and a teensy bit sickly if not treated with caution. Part of the Brewers Heritage pack. *Serve:* room temp. *Avail:* Sains, Tesco.

WADWORTH 6X
Traditional Draught Bitter 50cl Canned 4.3%:
A non-widget draught-style tinned beer, with an unpleasant spoilt-fruit nose, and even worse-off flavours of the over-sulphury, cabbagey sort. Could have been a rogue can. *Serve:* larder cool. *Avail:* widely

WADWORTH 6X EXPORT **
Bottled 5%:
Wadworth's newest product was still at the test-marketing stage when this tasting was done. Amber in colour, with a smokey malt nose, and a sultana, buttery, lush fruit flavour, bags of sour oak and caramel sweetness (but not enough hop balance), it's also a little flabby in texture, though semi-spritzy in style, and grows rapidly flabbier after a few minutes in the glass. *Serve:* room temp/larder cool. *Avail*: Asda.

WAITROSE LAGER
44cl Canned 3.9%:
Despite appearances (heraldic and folk imagery), an English lager, bright yellow-gold with toad's eye bubbles, and sugary cereal nose. Lots of cereal and sugar on the palate too, sweet and grainy, a bit sticky, with cloying pumpkin flavours, and a glucose finish. Not very

nice. (In fact difficult to drink even when it's a free sample, and you're thirsty and it's just after 6pm, and it's been a cow of a day. So it must be pretty dire.) *Serve:* fridge cold.

WAITROSE MIDLAND BITTER

44cl Canned 3.4%:
Toad's-eyes bubbles and obnoxious smells are not a tremendous start. Flavours are slightly phenolic, thin and bland, fairly bitter, but not enduringly so, woody and a tiny bit herbal at the edges. Otherwise harsh, crude and metallic. *Serve:* larder cool.

WAITROSE STRONG LAGER*

44cl Canned 4.6%:
Brewed in England, and not very strong, actually. Tropical fruit on the nose, a little pear and butter on the palate, leading into a flabby finish. Not a clean lager, with oddly inappropriate fruit, but there are at least no off-flavours. *Serve:* light fridge chill.

WAITROSE TRADITIONAL PALE ALE*

44cl Canned 3%:
Bright orangey-gold beer brewed and canned in England. At first refreshing and clean, with at least a hint of the promised pale ale character, a little fragrant malt and hop dryness, but this gives way to a dishwatery finish, unfortunately. *Serve:* larder cool.

WAITROSE WESSEX BITTER

44cl Canned 4%:
Stridently fruity pear drop and boiled sweetie aromas, and there's fruit on the palate too, but also caramel and sherbety sweetness, and brown sugary, stewed tea. It's also on the flat and flaccid side. *Serve:* larder cool.

WALKABOUT PACK: TRADITIONAL ENGLISH DRAUGHT ALE**

44cl Canned 4%:
Best of the 'walkabout' package of four canned ales from around the world (the others are Bavarian, Belgian, Italian), a deep bright amber bitter with a hop and walnut nose, and a dry-hopped, slightly resiny, refreshing palate, of the Young's/Adnam's/Taylor's sort. Good bitter not quite completely ruined by canning, in other words, getting drier as it's drunk, with a robust, bitter-herbal aftertaste. *Serve:* larder cool. *Avail*: Wait.

WARDS BEST BITTER*

Wards, Sheffield. 44cl Canned 4%:
Bright pale-amber ale with a cardboardy nose, and modest but competent canned bitter flavour, overlain by an unfortunate slight egginess just before its decent bitter finish kicks in. Thwaites is much nicer. *Serve:* larder cool. *Avail*: Safe, Somer, VicW.

WATNEYS BROWN ALE

Carlsberg-Tetley. 33cl Canned 2.7%:
Have no nostalgic cravings for this product. Caramelly, sweet, crudely made, thin and watery. *Serve:* larder cool. *Avail*: Sains.

WEBSTER'S DRAUGHT BITTER

Carlsberg-Tetley. 44cl Canned 3.5%:
Walnut-brown beer with a very enthusiastic widget, even after several days in the fridge. Flavours are sweet and caramelly, watery and sugary, with a nasty, dirty earthiness. Revolting. *Serve:* fridge cold. *Avail:* widely.

WEBSTER'S YORKSHIRE BITTER

44cl Canned 3.5%:
Dark amber, very fizzy, sweet-nosed, bland and sugary, with an acrid note in the finish that lingers unpleasantly. *Serve:* larder cool. *Avail:* widely.

WHITBREAD BEST BITTER

44cl Canned 3.5%:
Non-widget, new draught-system beer, supposedly aerated as it's poured. Dark orange, caramelly, thin and fizzy, brown sugary, teabaggy, with a touch of fruit and a tinny finish. *Serve:* larder cool. *Avail:* widely.

WHITBREAD BEST MILD*

44cl Canned 2.6%:
Very low in alcohol for a regular beer (even a mild), soft and malty and sweet, with a stewed tea and Coca-Cola-going-flat finish. *Serve:* larder cool. *Avail:* widely.

WHITBREAD FOREST BROWN ALE
27.5cl Canned 2.7%:
Vimto-like, fizzy, caramel-sugary, with a stewed tea, cola and cherryade finish. Is this really beer? *Serve:* larder cool. *Avail:* widely.

WHITBREAD LIGHT ALE
44cl Canned 3.1%:
Almost lager-like, but of the watery, sugary kind. Very gently hoppy, with a wet cardboardy finish. Tastes rather like it's been made in a sodastream machine. *Serve:* larder cool. *Avail:* widely.

WHITBREAD PALE ALE
44cl Canned 3.4%:
Barley sugar gold, barley sugar aromas, and barley sugar flavour too, by jingo! Lucozadey, sweet and fizzy, orange: where's the pale ale? *Serve:* light fridge chill. *Avail:* widely.

WHITBREAD WHITE LABEL
44cl Canned 1%:
Ingredients: water, barley malt, hydrolyzed starch, carbon dioxide, yeast, hops, caramel, preservative E224 and stabilizer E405. Which is probably why it tastes like this. *Serve:* larder cool. *Avail:* Wait.

WORTHINGTON DRAUGHT
Best Bitter Bass. 44cl Canned 3.6%:
Easily the sweetest 'best bitter' to emerge from a can in these tastings: creamy, malty with a little nut, vanilla and oak, but brown sugary at the close, and growing horribly cloying after a few mouthfuls (in an almost saccharine style). Probably good for breastfeeders. *Serve:* larder cool ('no need to fridge it with Worthingtons widget', thankfully). *Avail:* Wait.

WORTHINGTON WHITE SHIELD***
Bass. 27.5cl Bottled 5.6%:
This famous old bottle-conditioned ale was equally famously 'cleaned-up' by Bass a few years ago, and now lacks all of the bits and some of the character of its former incarnation. But it's still delicious. Amber gold, suspiciously clean and sparkling stuff, with a sulphurous fruit nose, and smooth, polished flavours that roll effortlessly to the back of the tongue. Prickly dryness, lush fullness, serious alcohol and sweet fruit, all in mellow and elegant mood. *Serve:* room temp/larder cool. *Avail:* Sains, Tesco, Thres.

WREXHAM LAGER*
Wrexham Lager Co (Carlsberg-Tetley). 50cl Canned 3.4%:
Sweet grapefruit on the nose, and clean(ish) savoury, husky grain flavours, with citric, crusty old tangerine notes in the finish. *Serve:* fridge cold. *Avail:* Sains, Somer, Tesco, Thres, VicW.

YEOMAN'S BITTER
Bass. 44cl Canned 2.3%:
Bright-amber beer with a sweet nose and no flavour, beyonds adjuncts and sugar. Only beer in the most technical sense. *Serve:* larder cool. *Avail:* Somer.

YOUNGER'S DRAUGHT BEST BITTER
Scottish & Newcastle. 44cl Canned 3.7%:
Can reads: traditionally brewed ale with a full, smooth, hoppy flavour. Tasting note reads: cheaply-made beer for the masses with an inappropriately creamy, sweet flavour and an adjunct-laden, corn and sugar finish that's unpleasantly persistent. *Serve:* light fridge chill (tapstream widget). *Avail:* widely.

YOUNGER'S HEAVY 70/-
Quality Ale 50cl Canned 3.5%:
Light, bright-amber beer, watery, but with a vaguely fruity, malty yeasty tang, and a very blunted, mildly hoppy finish. Bland and mediocre stuff. *Serve:* larder cool. *Avail:* Sains, Tesco.

YOUNGER'S NO 3*
Traditional Ale Scottish & Newcastle. 55cl Bottled 4.5%:
Port-wine coloured, with only the subtlest, mildest nose, but offering a little sweet chocolate and fennel if swirled in the glass. Soft-bodied, bland and sweetish to taste, with a little redeeming chocolate malt and roasted grain, but a watery cereal note, and a

disappointing, almost absent finish. Keggy but not overfizzed, at least. *Serve:* larder cool. *Avail:* Asda, Safe, Sains, Tesco.

YOUNGER'S TARTAN SPECIAL

50cl Canned 3.7%:
Bright dark-amber, fizzy, thin and pop-like stuff, with caramel sweet notes, some fruity banana, and the mildest reminder that this is beer, in the all-too brief hop note at the finish. *Serve:* larder cool. *Avail:* widely.

YOUNG'S BITTER**

Young's, London. 44cl Canned 3.7%:
Widget-free, traditional canned bitter, a little over-fizzy but with a moreishly refreshing character. Barley-sugar gold in colour, with a subtle, fresh hop nose, and a perhaps over-delicate, but discernible balance of dry and floral hop notes with drying and sweeter, slightly fruity malts. A slightly austere, herbal hop note appears and builds in drinking. Quite an achievement for a canned bitter of such modest strength: one of the canned beer choices of the year. *Serve:* larder cool. *Avail:* Somer.

YOUNG'S STRONG EXPORT**

27.5cl Bottled 6.4%:
Bright deep-gold ale with an extraordinarily literal, buttery braised-celery nose, and flavours that are dominated by strong alcohol itself, as well as celery, walnut and sour oaky, chestnut wood, sandalwood and herbal notes. As the astringently dry hop finish deepens and lengthens, these herbal, spice notes acquire an almost antiseptic quality that lingers long in the mouth. A knock-out. But knock-outs are not always a pleasant experience. *Serve:* room temp/larder cool. *Avail:* BeerC.

ZEISS

Deluxe Lager brewed for Premium Beer Co, London by Bass. 27.5cl Bottled 8%:
Brewed using a champagne yeast (which is supposed to impress us), so even more of a barley wine than usual. Unfortunately an overpowering cat's pee smell makes tasting difficult, though I can report the flavour as mostly pungent alcohol. Presumably aimed at daredevil youths, as at over £1 for a small bottle it's too costly for park bench oblivion-seekers. *Avail:* Tesco, VicW.

Bulgaria

Astika**

Astika, Haskovo. 33cl Bottled 4.5%: Brewed under classical technology with natural products, according to the label, supposedly resulting in 'veritable taste'. Anyway, ugly bottle, but simple and clean little lager: mildly malty, creamy and refreshing, soft and easy, with no adjunct flavours or hard edges. *Serve:* fridge cold. *Avail:* specialists.

Canada

Now that Marlboro is no longer the Big Country, the title can revert to the great expanses of wild landscape that we associate with Canada. Canadian beer marketing makes the most of these associations, all mountains, forests, fresh air and sparkling mountain water. Ice Beer, which in its present incarnation, at least, was a Canadian invention, is a gift for this kind of Big Country marketing. And yet Canadian exporters are city-based. Very urban, very large.

The largest of them all is Labatt, a huge company with international properties, notably Moretti in Italy, and Rolling Rock nearer home in the USA. Like Molson, Labatt gets around the problem of supplying mass-market lagers to its huge home country by spreading its series of brewing plants, like pearls on a string, across the southern border country from eastern seaboard to west coast. This is also a handy position for exporting to the US. Labatt makes a series of fairly bland lagers in various strengths. At home it also produces a couple of ales, (an English and an Irish Red) and a porter. But the true foundations of its modern fortune is the Ice Beer, an invention Labatt gave the world. Well, not an invention as such, as Eiswein and Eisbock work on a similar principle, but in its brewery-adapted lager-making technique, with refrigeration coils and the like (*see* New Zealand), certainly. The product was launched in 1993, and after a slowish, niche-market start has quite suddenly bolted into true mass-market status. Having at first been apparently content to watch the rest of the world take up this technique, and use the term Ice Beer for the resulting super-smooth lager, Labatt is now growing positively litigious. As far as they are concerned, they own the Ice Beer name, and intend to protect it. It's a smallish market, with just four brands in it, two of them Canadian, Labatt and Molson, and a third made by Labatt for Carlsberg. The fourth is Foster's (or in Britain, Courage).

Molson, the other huge Canadian brewer, was founded by a migrating Englishman, John Molson, who left the home country in 1782 and started up the brewery in 1786. It's the oldest surviving brewery in the whole continent. Molson own the third big name, Carling. Foster's have a piece of the Molson action, as do Miller, the American brewer. Recently Molson have developed an all-malt lager range called Molson Signature, but these beers are only seen in the home market. At the moment. They also make the largest range of non-lager products of any of the Canadian giants, all characteristically smooth and thin.

The final well-known Canadian name is Moosehead, the largest independent in the country, and confined, in its brewing plant at least, to the eastern seaboard. Its focus, for that reason, is very much the export market. There's also a thriving microbrewery culture, dating from 1982, which is forcing the hand of the giants and putting them in think-tank mode, as is also happening over the border in America. The 'craft breweries' of the States are frequently referred to as 'cottage breweries' here, even though some of them are large by other countries' standards. Brewpubs are a particular success. The little independents might make a proper, Saaz-influenced, unpasteurized lager to show Canadians what the style should really be like. They also produce Germanic classics of the Märzen and Bock sort, as well as more English influenced Pale Ales and Bitters (as well as the occasional Old Ale), and more Scots-influenced (but micro-style) Scotch Ales and Oatmeal Stouts, red American style Irish Ales, northern French Blondes and Brunes (particularly in Quebec), as well as vaguely Belgian dark strong ales, modern porters and stouts, and perhaps a wheat beer. In fact, the first modern Canadian Ice Beer, Niagara Eisbock, was a wheat beer, made by a microbrewery in 1989. They were inspired by the Eiswein that's made by local hoteliers at Niagara Falls. It's a younger, smaller scale micro network than that of the United States, but feels as free as it's neighbour to borrow freely from the world's classic beer styles, and mix them all together on a worldwide beer menu.

AROUND ONTARIO**

Lakeport Brewing, Hamilton. 34cl Bottled 5%:
Golden beer, with gentle orange fruit, malt and wet cardboard on the nose, and flavours as clean as Canada itself: mountains, lakes, moose (no, no moose) and all. Tastes like a Dry Beer in that its dry malt, creamy flavours are finished with an oddly tongue-curing dry beer style texture that coats and clings and generally outstays its welcome. Would have been three stars but for this, and an acrid note that creeps in, suggesting (like the cardboard aromas) a beer past its best. *Serve:* light fridge chill. *Avail:* BeerC.

LABATTS*

Canadian Lager 44cl Canned 3.8%:
Made in England (actually) under licence. As cheapish, UK-brewed tinned lagers go, this is as good as most for quaffing with a tuna sandwich. Clean, mild, soft-bodied, with some pleasant textured pale malt drying on the tongue, and no hop flavour to speak of. *Serve:* fridge cold. *Avail:* Asda, Somer, Tesco.

LABATTS BLUE*

33cl Bottled 5%:
Grainy, slightly vegetal nose; the flavour clean to the point of absence. There's a prickle of dryness at the end, dissipating all too quickly and leaving a not very clean finish in its wake. *Serve:* fridge cold. *Avail:* Odd, Tesco, Wait.

LABATTS ICE BEER*

33cl Bottled 5.6%:
Made in England (actually). The nose is oddly manure-like, the flavour more straightforwardly popcorny, with a little pineapple syrup perhaps, and a husky cereal finish with some dryness. As the bottle itself boasts, it's 'mightily easy to drink', or rather, fiendishly strong for something that doesn't taste of much, but then that's almost a working definition of the ice-beer style. Smooth and unobjectionable is the charitable view. *Serve:* at 42 degrees, apparently. *Avail:* Maj, Odd, Somer, Tesco, Thres, Wait.

MOLSON SPECIAL DRY**

33cl Bottled 5.5%:
Two stars for wackiness in the dreary world of the superclean: at first sip it seems innocuous enough, but swallows as a woody, herbal, lemony thing, developing tons of dusty white pepper on the strongly spiced finish. No stars at all for the brewery, if they really were aiming for a clean finish that leaves no lingering aftertaste. Nothing like as tongue-curing as the Japanese dry beers, just weird. *Serve:* fridge cold. *Avail:* Odd, Sains, Somer, Tesco, Thres.

MOOSEHEAD**

Canadian Lager Beer Moosehead Breweries. 35.5cl Bottled 5%:
Imported bottled lager, apparently made from 'Canadian barley, a secret blend of hops and a yeast selected years ago to produce fine lager'. Mild, pleasantly pale-malt character, with delicate apricot flavours and a floral hop finish. Its qualities are much more subtle than this description suggests, but they are there, and the overall effect is of wholesomeness. *Serve:* fridge cold. *Avail:* Thres.

The Caribbean

The Caribbean is not a part of the world many people would associate with brewing, but there are something like 20 breweries on these islands, and at least five of their beers are available in Britain. In addition to this home-grown industry, Heineken and Guinness are also still very active. Guinness has been exporting here, and brewing here, for over 150 years, and its original beer, West Indies Porter, has now transmogrified into Foreign Extra Stout. The Caribbean in general has a tremendous liking for stout, particularly of the dense, rich, fruity and fairly sweet sort. There may partly be old colonial reasons for this, although the stout market stretches beyond colonial borders. Tropical stouts, as they are often described, are generally bottom-fermented, and often of a strength we usually only see emanating from Belgium.

Aside from dark, porter and stout-style beers, the region is more or less dedicated to the production of light and refreshing pale lagers made for hot weather, tourists and seafood. Red Stripe lager from Jamaica is the best known of the Caribbean exports, although the British sort is made under licence by Charles Wells in the rather less exotic location of Bedfordshire. They also make a stronger Red Stripe lager, of the Carlsberg Special sort, called Crucial Brew, which was launched in 1989 and is marketed at Britain's black population. Like Australian (and many other) lagers, Caribbean beers are typically brewed using 70% malt, 30% adjunct, in this case corn. The Red Stripe brewery also produce Dragon Stout, which is imported into Britain and has been getting good notices.

Other imports into Britain include Banks' Lager from Barbados, which appears here as Bajan, as we already have a Banks brewery. It's brewed here under licence, and now also imported. Carib Lager from Trinidad (the brewery also brews Foreign Extra Stout) is also available here in specialist outlets. Unfortunately, samples of both these proved impossible to get hold of.

DRAGON STOUT***
Desnoes & Geddes, Jamaica. 28.4cl Bottled 7.5%:
Dark ruby-brown tropical stout, very sweet and lacking in zizz and vitality, and only just earning its three stars. Bottles vary. Cold tea, cold coffee, and strong sweet alcohol on the nose; a soft, faintly Coca-Cola-ish body, with some dark sweet fruit, a hint of burnt strawberry jam, and liquorice toffee notes.

Good flavours, but the flabby texture lets it down. *Serve:* room temp/larder cool. *Avail:* BeerC, Safe, Tesco, VicW.

RED STRIPE

Jamaica Strong Lager 33cl Bottled 4.7%: Made in England (actually) by Charles Wells of Bedford, and not really that strong, when the standard Euro lager now weighs in at 5% alcohol. Two bottles tasted both produced odd, soapy flavours with thyme and geraniol notes, though the finish was discernably hoppy. *Serve:* fridge cold. *Avail*: Co-op, Somer, VicW.

RED STRIPE*

Strong Lager 44cl Canned 4.7%: Better than the bottle (in our tastings at least), bland and watery perhaps but with some malt and fruit flavours and a drier, more refreshing texture. *Serve:* fridge cold. *Avail*: Co-op, Somer, VicW.

China

China is a fledgling brewing country, and as its relationships with the rest of the world soften and shift, there may yet be grounds for predicting the arrival of Chinese beer into the world marketplace on a major basis. Certainly the process has begun, albeit on a miniature scale: demand for western products has led to a queue of multinationals at the border, and plans to create brands for export has led to a stream of Chinese prototypes in the American market. Japan is looking hard at the Chinese market, too; this would be an ideal target for many of Japan's westernized lager-beers, complete with (high-status) English labels, if their own power-base at home is threatened by the dawning of the Japanese microbrewery, and the craze for European imports.

China is not entirely a novice brewing country. Far from it. China grows its own hops, and malts its own barley. Plenty of little local breweries already operate, and there are also some enormous great modern plants, too, which are presently geared to producing local beers for their own provinces. Not surprisingly, considering the scale of the country, there is no national brewery. But there is Tsingtao. Tsingtao is a late Victorian brewery. At the time, German traders had actually leased Tsingtao port as a base from which to export Chinese goods, and import others. The brewery the Germans established here is now a major exporter, even though China's beer production, despite rising by about 20% a year, still can't keep up with demand for beer at home. Brewery advisers are flooding in from all over the world, but particularly Germany, Britain and the USA, to offer solutions to the production crisis.

CHINESE GINSENG BEER*
33cl Bottled 4.1%:
Brewed in Britain (actually) under licence, from natural ingredients only, including some ginseng herb seasoning. It looks and smells like a very ordinary lager, and disappointingly also tastes like one, presumably using corn or rice (or both) for this light-bodied thinness. There's just the faintest ginseng, herbal echo on the aftertaste. But possibly it's deserving of three stars for homeopathic value?. *Serve:* fridge cold. *Avail:* Beer Paradise.

SHANGHAI BEER**
Shanghai Brewery. 35cl Bottled 4.5%:
Packed by the China National Cereals, Oils and Foodstuffs Import and Export Corporation, Shanghai, and made of purest water, barley malt, hops and yeast. Pale metallic gold in colour, it has biscuity, fruity (lychee! – or else this is shameful national

stereotyping), peachy, lemon aromas. Flavours are initially clean, barley sweet and grain savoury, but (oh dear!) the finish turns just cardboardy and faintly acrid enough to spoil the clean, clear flavours, growing more mineral and aspirin-like with gulping. It also goes flabby very fast in the glass. *Serve:* light fridge chill. *Avail:* BeerC.

TSINGTAO BEER

Qindao, Shandong. 33cl Bottled 4.5%: The problems that half-haunt the finish of Shanghai Beer are all too evident from the very first whiff of this. Basically it's unjudgeable, as two samples have both been decidedly awry: metallic and hollow, but also acidic; and also stuffed with overcooked cabbage flavours. *Serve:* light fridge chill. *Avail:* specialists.

Cyprus

Keo**

Keo, Limassol. 33.5cl Bottled 4.5%: 'Brewed from the finest malt and choicest hops . . . long matured, bottled fresh and unpasteurized' according to the label, and this is an encouraging preamble to any beer. Dryish malt-bodied, with a hint of grapefruit, sweeter, butter and honey notes in the middle, and a little hop at the finish, which builds in drinking and also develops a vanilla sweetness. Verging on three stars. *Serve:* light fridge chill/fridge cold. *Avail:* BeerC.

Czech Republic

and Slovakia

The Czech Republic shares the honour with Germany in developing the modern face of world beer. Germany claims the invention of the lager, but the clear, golden beer that most of the world now makes and drinks traces its root back to Bohemia, and specifically the town of Pilsen. In recognition of that fact, the word pilsener, or pilsner, or just pils, is today the world's most widely-used beer term. Though more often than not it's used inaccurately, pretentiously, grandiosely, to misdescribe modest lagers with not the remotest Czech character.

Until 1842 beer was brown, or at least russet, or another variant on the brown theme. The Bavarians had been making lager-style beers, dark and cloudy (and no doubt delicious), probably for centuries, having discovered that storing (or 'lagering') their beer in the Alpine caves to the south kept them in good, drinkable condition during the spoiling heat of summer. But also discovering that this process changed their flavour and texture utterly. This knowledge was more empirically touchy-feely than really understood. Much more recently, in the 1830s, the (brown) lager-making process had been scientifically investigated and perfected in Bavaria. At the time, Bohemia was a German-speaking part of the Austrian Empire, and in 1840 Anton Dreher, the Austrian father of lager brewing, had launched his amber lager in Vienna, in a rush to capitalize on Bavarian expertize, so it was perfectly natural that brewers in the town of Pilsen should rush to attempt the bottom-fermenting style themselves. In fact it was Josef Grolle, a German brewer from just over the present-day border, who was contracted, more or less by the whole town, to produce a lager beer in Pilsen, at a new brewery to be built specifically to develop this new style. The brewery is still operational, and its beer is known the world over as Pilsner Urquell, which is german for ' the original pilsener'. Which it is.

Quite why the Bohemians came up with a bright, golden lager is nothing like so clear as the beer. There are no surviving minutes of a stormy brewers' committee meeting in Pilsen, where one faction demanded they make brown Bavarian lagers like their German rivals, and another made a presentation in favour of launching a whole new style of beer that would always be associated with Pilsen and make it famous. Some have rashly concluded that Grolle must have made his beer clear and pale by some kind of happy accident, but brewing doesn't work that way. What you put in, certainly in terms of the malt type and colour used, is what you get out (unless you're prepared to boil for an awfully long time, but in any case this process is only used to make pale malts act like dark ones, and not the other way round). The barley malt still used in the world's best lagers is known as Pilsener Malt because it's only lightly (or fairly lightly) toasted. It wasn't accidental that this malt was used, and the brown malt left out. Similarly, the clarity of the new beer would have been achieved by arriving at a yeast strain and a methodology that produced a clear beer through patient trial and error. With the business contacts and marketing power of the Austrian Empire at his disposal, a population hungry for further novelties, and the newly-emerging clear-glass industry, the clear golden beer of Pilsen was an immediate hit.

Bohemia, one of the two provinces of the modern Czech Republic (the other being Moravia, to the east; Slovakia, to Moravia's south east now being independent) is the heart of the Czech state – including Prague within its borders – and the heart of the regions's brewing heritage. Budweis, otherwise known as Ceske Budejovice, is also here. Bohemia also has a long and noble history of hop growing, indeed is the pre-eminent hop garden of Europe. The promise of authentic Czech hops, or more specifically, the use of authentic Saaz hops, is still the proudest boast of the world's pilsener makers. Hops have been grown in Bohemia since at least the 9th century, and though the region is now also an important malting barley grower, it was then more interested in wheat, both for baking and brewing. By the 16th century, Budweis was supplying (brown) beer to the royal court, which became known as the Beer of Kings.

Adolphus Busch, originator of the mass-market beer brand, toured Europe in search of brewing inspiration before returning to America to found what is now the world's biggest brewery (est. 1860), making the world's number one lager, Budweiser. He used the name Budweiser rather than Pilsener because pilsener had already become a generic part of the brewing and drinking language, widely used all over Europe and beyond. Budweiser, however, he could trademark. Hence the continuing unseemly scuffles that break out from time to time between Anheuser Busch and the Budweis-based Budvar brewery, makers of Budweiser Budvar. Budweiser Budvar should not, of course, have to drop its own town name from its beer labels, the idea is absurd, but the fact remains that of the two rival Budweisers, the American one was actually brewed first. And thus can use the word 'Original' in its advertising. And does. It also uses 'King of Beers', a reference to the town of Budweis being the home of the royal court brewery, which doesn't endear them to the Czechs either. Adolphus Busch went on to use another Bohemian town, Michalovce, as the inspiration for his Michelob brand. His favoured practice of using beechwood to condition and clarify his lagers isn't a Bohemian one, however. He picked up that in Bavaria.

Only the most willing hostage to fortune would claim with confidence that the Czech Republic has probably the most traditional and least spoilt brewing culture in the world. Already, Westernization has brought change. It's one of those sad ironies that it was the backward-looking, conservative and stagnant society of the old Czechoslovakia that also preserved the old traditions more or less intact. The demands of the new world, of privatization and market share in export markets is gradually threatening the old order, and at present it's impossible to confirm that the new order understands what it was that made Czechoslovakian beer so pre-eminent in the world. Already breweries are dumping their old equipment in favour of modern, high-tech installations. Stainless steel maturation tanks are replacing the old wooden vessels. Ingredients, long a sacred cow in Czech brewing, may be rationalized next, who knows? But there are still plenty of small (and small-thinking) breweries about, producing mostly local beer for a keen local population, despite the advent of national brands and imports. The Czechs love their beer and are now at the top of the world consumption league table having toppled the Germans. As long as they continue to be prepared to support the old quality standard, and export markets continue to be prepared to pay for it, there should be a clearly-labelled stopping point for this little industrial revolution in brewing.

As in Bavaria, brewing in the Czech Republic still continues at village level, despite the big companies' factory operations. Just about every little hamlet either has its own brewhouse or knows someone who does. Local beers are still offered in the regions, and the beer taverns are being preserved (though in some cases also enlarged and commercialized beyond recognition) by the new Czech industry, tourism. Prague alone has 20 surviving beer taverns, with more opening to cope with the sudden desire of the whole planet to trundle through the city. When millions of visitors invade a legendarily unspoilt place, it doesn't stay famously trapped in time for very much longer.

Real Czech pilseners aren't always very hoppy beers. This often puzzles those who've been primed with descriptions of the classic pilsener style, and perhaps tasted German (and most particularly, North German) examples, which tend to be more textbook in structure and flavour than the Czech originals. The Classic Pilsener Style (no beer style is surely more deserving of capital letters than this) of the sort we look for when tasting lagers labelled Pilsener, is a drier, firmer beer than usually comes from Bohemia itself. North German pilseners, in particular, classically exhibit a floral, hay-like dryness on the nose, a delicate blend of pale, creamy malt body and hop dryness on the palate, and a lingering, assertive hop finish, perhaps floral, herbal, grassy or hay-like again. These are the characteristics that make us raise our happy glasses and cry 'Good Pilsener'. Bitburger is the mass-market German classic of this sort.

Czech Pilseners, however, are often much more elusive in flavour and texture than this. They might make a great feature of the famously soft water of the region, and particularly of Pilsen itself. They will probably make more of the extraordinarily good local barley than many German examples. Traditionally, its natural sweetness is deepened and accentuated by a malting specification that's a little fuller in colour (and flavour) than the traditional German Pilsener Malt. Starting with a reasonably high original gravity (a measure of the amount of fermentable sugar present in the liquid, before the yeast is added), and not letting the yeast attenuate very far, means beers are made with fairly moderate alcohol levels, but lots of satisfying, creamy body (from the malt sugars that remain, ungobbled by yeast).

Gambrinus is typically Czech in being at once rich and refreshing. It has a vividly barley sweet, buttery palate, cleaned up in the finish by a lemony, floral dryness, courtesy of the equally extraordinarily good local hops. Budweiser Budvar is also typically Czech, with its gentle, soft fruitiness in the middle, soft water body and big flowery finish. Czech pilseners tend to have more yeast character than their North German counterparts. Pilsner Urquell, the classic Czech beer, is especially notable for its exquisite balance, with barley and toffee sweet notes, floral and herbal dryness, and a soft, easy drinkability. It's easily the most subtle of the world's classic lagers. (And let's hope it stays that way; rumours about production problems, following the recent modernization of the brewery, have dogged the beer in the last year or so).

Thing are changing fast, but the traditional line-up of the Czech brewery might contain four to seven beers from a fairly standardized range. Firstly, a modest-in-alcohol (perhaps even as little as 3% abv), light and quaffable lager designed for quenching the thirst of factory workers (and others). These beers are nothing like so boring as they sound, having good ingredients to compensate for moderate strength, and at their best, an appealing yeasty, pale malt freshness. The 'session beer' of the taverns, classically with even more of this appetizing freshness, is usually about 4% abv. The third beer, the 'premium', which includes Pilsner Urquell and Budweiser Budvar, generally falls into the 4.5–5.5% category (though P.U. is only 4.2%). Fourthly come the 'specials' of over 5.5% abv, which don't usually go beyond 6.5% abv. The three typical additional specialities are unfiltered beers, wheat beers and dark lagers. Many brewers still make the black (or brown) lager common to most brewing cultures in Eastern Europe. Slovakia has an excellent example in the delicious Cassovar. The tasty Bohemia Regent 'green label' pilsener-style lager comes with a twin, the Black Regent. It's characteristic of these Czech/Slovak black lagers that they, like their cousin Köstritzer Schwarzbier, over in the former East Germany, have a soft, quenching lightness about them that's irresistible in combination with their rich, creamy dark malt flavours.

As a general rule, the minimum lagering period is about a month, with premiums and specials (officially) getting the classic three-month maturation, though eight weeks is now more common. Saaz hops (called Zatec locally) are always used, either in combination with other varieties, or on their own, such as in Pilsner Urquell. Saaz gives a pilsener aroma that's unmistakable, and also unsubstitutable. They are added (as whole flowers naturally), in three additions in the making of Pilsner Urquell, and the first of these is followed by an unusually long boil, roughly twice as long as the traditional 90 minutes. Other aspects of the Pilsner Urquell brewery are not as unspoilt by progress. The brewery no longer has its own maltings, for instance. And the antique brewing and maturing vessels have been usurped by stainless steel. Once all their brewing was done in great underground halls, a complex labyrinth of over 1000 open oak fermenting vessels, and an astonishing six miles of tunnels (mimicking the conditions of an alpine cave), containing some 3,500 maturation vessels, of pitch-lined oak.

You will not find the designation 'pilsener' on many beers that come out of the Czech Republic. Here, at least, the term is taken to be exclusively applicable to the breweries of Pilsen (Plzen) itself. Only Pilsner Urquell and its near neighbour Gambrinus are entitled to describe themselves thus, although, oddly, Gambrinus doesn't make much of this opportunity in its labels and marketing.

Asda Czech Pivo Lager**

Lieberec, Bohemia. 33cl Bottled 5%:
Asda's new own-brand Czech lager needs to be drunk fairly cold, or its perfumey peach and mango fruit character grows a little sticky. There's not much in the way of finish, or structure come to that, and its floral, musky edge could be unpopular with quaff-seekers, but it's a pleasant enough beer, acquiring a gentle, lingering dryness after a little while. *Serve:* fridge cold.

Black Regent***

Black Lager Trebon. 50cl Bottled 4.5%:
The brewery was established in 1379, and the black lager (so they say) originally brewed by monks. It uses four kinds of malt, and is lagered for 60 days. The most delicious beer, with buttery, ripe and toffee sweet aromas and flavours, and a dark, coffee note with just a hint of treacle toffee. The 'black' soubriquet shouldn't mislead you: this is not something dense and rich and pond-like, but a refreshing, ripely sweet and clean beer with the softest background hop flavour and just a touch of orange zest. Its only drawback is that it can go a little flat in the glass. *Serve:* larder cool/ light fridge chill. *Avail*: BeerC.

Bohemia Regent***

Lager Beer Trebon. 50cl Bottled 4.8%:
Bohemia Green Label, as it's also known, is clean, sparkly and easy to drink, with a ripe barley, honey and, particularly, toffee palate, and a very gently drying hop finish, floral with a hint of spice. Moreish. *Serve:* light fridge chill. *Avail*: BeerC.

Budweiser Budvar***

Ceske Budejovice. 50cl Bottled 5%:
Not to be confused with a rather less exciting American beer of a similar name. Finest Saaz aroma hops, Moravian malt and soft well-water are used to make a classic beer, sweeter and rounder than Pilsner Urquell. Bright gold in colour, with appealing citrus (sweet pink grapefruit) and yeasty aromas. Rich smooth barley sweetness combines with subtle hop dryness and a little spice, before a big flowery finish. If we're going to nitpick, just a little over-gassy. *Serve:* fridge cold. *Avail*: widely.

Cassovar***

Slovak Dark Beer Kosice, Slovakia. 50cl Bottled 5.25%:
A dark beer – a lovely dark ruby-black, in fact – that's more for spring than winter. Delicious aromas of damson, strawberry, cocoa, a little port wine. In the mouth, creamy chocolate malt, milky truffle, cranberry and damson and other summer fruits, and a coating, textured dryness at the finish (more of a texture than a flavour). Perhaps a little light-bodied? a little over-gassy? *Serve:* larder cool. *Avail*: BeerC, Wait.

Eisbrau Czech**

Traditional Beer Chebski Starovar. 50cl Bottled 4.5%:
Part of the Pilsener Breweries Group, this brewery has been making beer in the royal town of Cheb since the 13th century. This is almost a textbook Czech pilsener, which does all the right things, with clean and medium-weight barley body, followed by a good soft hop and pepper finish. But it's just a bit too

textbook. *Serve:* light fridge chill. *Avail*: Beer Paradise.

GAMBRINUS***

Pilsen. 33cl Bottled 4.9%:
Named after the secular patron saint of brewing, Duke Jean I of Brabant (or Jan Primus). Unmistakably a premium Czech pilsener, rich but refreshing, full-bodied but clean. Rounded, barley sweet and buttery, with a twist of lemon, and a fresh hop floral dryness: these characteristics are all identifiable, but subtly. This is a quenching pilsener beer first and last, made with a double decoction system (as opposed to Pilsner Urquell's more thoroughly malt-squeezing triple), and of a slightly lighter, fresher, hoppy but less dry character than its local rival. Delicious. *Serve:* light fridge chill. *Avail*: BeerC.

GOLD FASSL***

Pivovar/Ottokringer. 25cl Bottled 5.2%:
One of the very nicest of beers to emerge from a 25cl bottle. Orange and mango aromas, and on the palate, delicious full-bodied sweet barley and pulpy exotic fruit flavours, mango included, followed by gentle hop flowery notes in the finish. Three stars might be a wee bit on the generous side, but they are deserved for services-to-beer-from-little-bottles, at the very least. From a fairly new outpost of an Austrian brewing company, renewing old Empire links, perhaps. *Serve:* light fridge chill. *Avail*: Odd.

PILSNER URQUELL****

Pilsen. 30/75cl Bottled 4.2%:
King of the bottled beers (all right, all right, there are many great bottled beers in the world), or if not the king, certainly in the royal family. Let's not be hasty, but simply say that among the classic beers of the globe, Pilsner Urquell deserves special mention for its less-is-more, pared-down subtlety, and moderate alcohol levels. Triple decoction mashing, using barley malted to their own specifications, superb spring water, local Saaz hops, and a good long lagering all contribute to its quality. Both full-flavoured and clean, with fat, ripe buttery barley, but also restrained with firm hop dryness, this is altogether the most refined and elegant of pilseners. A lingering herbal dryness in the throat leaves you wanting more. *Serve:* fridge cold. *Avail*: widely.

STAROPRAMEN**

Prague Breweries. 33cl Bottled 4.2%:
Bass have acquired a stake in this brewery, snapped up the import rights and now look set to make Staropramen a familiar Czech brand. It's a pleasant beer, reportedly Prague's favourite quaffer (in terms of volume drunk), but only modest in scope. Golden and spritzy, with a lively fizz, it's very, very clean-edged indeed, and only retrieved from complete dullness by a buttery note, with just a hint of orange zest. But it is a bit dull nonetheless; the Carling Black Label of the Czech Republic. *Serve:* light fridge. *Avail*: Safe, Sains, VicW, Wait.

TESCO VRATISLAV LAGER*

50cl Bottled 5%:
Hopes were high for this own-brand Czech, but its richness is oddly smokey, a little fatty even (like one of those little processed Austrian cheeses), the texture is a little over-fizzy, and the finish has a husky, savoury aspect, building only into a dry hop character by the end of the bottle. Strangely bland, depite all this. *Serve:* light fridge chill.

WAITROSE CZECH LAGER**

Vratislavice. 50cl Bottled 5%:
Bright-gold beer with fresh, hoppy, delicately fruity aromas and a refreshingly clean flavour. It perhaps suffers in going straight from a gently barley-butter prologue into a dry hop finish, without much else going on in the middle. Good value, though. *Serve:* fridge cold.

ZAMEK**

Pilsener Budvar Brewery. 33cl Bottled 4.5%:
Truly the last word in pilsener, as they say on the label. Was expecting great things from the

Budweiser sibling, but it's just a little over-sweet and over-ripe in the middle. The nose is barley sugarish, with some butterscotch notes; the palate offers more of the same, with ripe barley oozing butter, a touch of golden syrup, a little honey, and a soft, drying pale malt texture. The dry hop finish, initially white peppery, appears and builds in drinking. (Zamek postscript! A second tasting, some weeks later, found this beer in a completely different mood, with dryness balancing the butter all the way through. On this form, a three-star beer.) *Serve:* light fridge chill. *Avail:* Co-op.

ZISKA CZECH PILSENER**

Pivovar Numburk. 25cl Bottled 4.5%
Zamek now appears to be only the second-last word in pilsener, which has probably mucked up their advertising a bit. Named after the great 15th-century Czech hero, Ziska is sweet and grainy on the nose, with rich buttery flavours, a soft water texture and a lingering, though perhaps over-gentle hop note in the finish. Nice, but modest lager not really of the pilsener sort. *Serve:* light fridge chill. *Avail:* Thres.

Denmark

Denmark has a reputation as a formidable brewing nation. Certainly it has a formidable brewery, in the shape of Carlsberg. But aside from that, the Danish influence is more rooted in history than it is of contemporary importance. There are only something like 20 breweries left, many of them small and local in scope.

The Carlsberg story is a mini-series-like drama, unfolding over several generations of family politics. The brewery was founded in the 18th century by the Jacobsens, a Jutland farming family. Christian Jacobsen broke the farming tradition by opting instead for the big city of Copenhagen and a brewing career. His son, Jacob Christian Jacobsen, took over his father's top-fermented wheat beer brewery just at the same time that the fame of the new Bavarian 'lagered' beers was erupting all over Europe. He went to Bavaria to learn how it was done in 1845, and brought home some actual Bavarian yeast, from the famous originator of the scientifically based lager-making method, the Spaten Brewery. The story has it that he got the yeast back to Denmark by stagecoach, and kept it in a fit state to use by keeping it under his hat and chilling it in cool water at every stop, over a journey of some 600 miles. (Yes, I know what you're thinking, but let's not pick a fight with a legend).

Jacob then went on to make Denmark's first bottom-fermenting beer, under the city ramparts, with specially granted royal permission. In 1847, he built a new brewery, on a hill (or berg), and named it after his son, Carl. Carl went on to build his own new brewery, an architectural jewel known as New Carlsberg. The scientific orientation of the brewery and its Jacobsen owners led to a sheaf of important discoveries in the Carlsberg laboratories, not just about the way yeast cultures work; it also formed the basis of a hundred other pieces of scientific advancement. Yeast science was crucial, though: it was Carlsberg who, in 1883, was the first to isolate a single-cell yeast culture. In 1876 the Carlsberg Foundation was formed, which today holds the controlling interest in the brewery and uses its huge trust fund to donate a vast amount of money every year to the arts and sciences, both in Denmark and abroad. When Jacob died in 1887, he left the whole empire to the Foundation. Carl, his son, was an expansive and cultured man who collected the great art treasures that still grace the city, built the Elephant Gates to his new brewery, and was responsible for donating the Little Mermaid to Copenhagen.

Carlsberg today is in control of the vast proportion of Danish brewing.

Only half a dozen of the remaining breweries are truly independent, the rest are Carlsberg companies in one way or another. Tuborg, the second-best known Danish brewery, was absorbed in 1970. Carlsberg has subsequently invested in Albani, Denmark's next biggest brewery and its largest independent, plus Faxe, Ceres and Thor. Albani, founded in 1859, is based in Odense, and enjoys 50% of its local market. It owns two other breweries. Its export lager, Giraf, was originally devised as a way of sponsoring the purchase of (yes, you guessed it) giraffes for Odense zoo, after their old one died in 1961. Albani use a two-yeast fermentation system unique in Denmark, which means its beers are unusually highly attenuated. They are pasteurized for export.

Denmark is best known for its mildly malty lagers, a style that has influenced many other lager breweries all over the world. But a range of other beers are made for the home market, many of them following the strong Danish sense of the seasons and their celebrations and festivals. Many breweries still make a Paske Bryg (Easter beer). Huidtøl (white beer), originally but no longer made with wheat, and originally but now rarely a top-fermenter, is sometimes seen. Bottom-fermented stouts and porters are also made, as well as dark lagers approximating to the Munich and Vienna styles. But it is pale, mildly flavoured lagers that still dominate volume brewing here, as well as the typically Danish strong lagers, of 6% or 7% abv, which contrive to be clean as well as packed with estery alcohol flavours. The strong lager trend which, as in Switzerland at Hurlimann brewery, grew out of applications for yeast science advances, climbs at Carlsberg to the dizzy heights of 9% abv, with Carlsberg Special Brew. Though, tellingly, this beer is made for export markets, and not marketed at home. Too much tax, for starters. All the breweries specialize in their own versions of the traditional low-alcohol table beers, which are not taxed, and so are much cheaper than regular and strong lagers.

Surprisingly, there is no pure beer law at work in Denmark, a factor probably heavily influenced by Carlsberg's extreme ambition in export markets. The brewery licenses its name all over the world. Some Danish beers are all malt, but most use at least a proportion of corn.

BEAR BEER**

Harboe Brewery. 33cl Bottled 4.4%:
As they say on the label, this light, spritzy lager is best served icy cold. But then they also say polar bears are cuddly. There's water, malt, hops, yeast, carbon dioxide and antioxidant in here, but what's really apparent on tasting Bear is its incredibly zingy, mountain-fresh, spring water character. There's also a very subtle apple note, and a faintly barley-husk flavour. So clean you want to wash your hair in it. *Serve:* fridge cold. *Avail:* specialists, Selfridges.

CARLSBERG ICE BEER**

33cl Bottled 5.6%:
Made by Labatt of Canada (actually), who have trademarked their own ice brewing process; radical chilling freezes the water, which is then removed, concentrating alcohol levels (and justifying a price tag of over £1 for a small bottle). The result: a strong lager that tastes super-smooth, sweet and clean and easy, until the slightly liquorice finish, which is oddly warming and lingers long. *Serve:* fridge cold. *Avail:* Somer, Tesco, VicW.

CARLSBERG LAGER

44cl Canned 3.4%:
Made in England (actually) and bland, bland, bland. Huge toad's-eye bubbles are an unpromising start. Sugar-syrupy sweet grain and a dry-textured malt follow, though heavily diluted by cold watery fizz. The finish is sugary and tainted. Probably the worst 'foreign' lager on the high street. *Serve:* fridge cold. *Avail:* widely.

CARLSBERG SPECIAL BREW*

48cl Canned 9%:
The classic Made For Britain Carlsberg product. Nicer than all the other canned superstrength lagers combined, but this isn't really saying much, as they're all vile and undrinkable. There's none of the habitual 'super' whisky or banana fritter in the flavours here, but lots of caramelized sweet turnip, slightly redeemed by a (rather token) show of hop dryness and pepper in the finish. It still tastes more of alcohol than anything. *Serve:* light fridge chill. *Avail:* Tesco.

CERES STOUT**

Ceres, Aarhus. 33cl Bottled 7.7%:
Contains caramel (E150). Dryish, spritzy stout with coffee, cold tea, raisin and bags of alcohol in evidence on the palate. And a slightly cloying muscovado, tea-baggy finish. *Serve:* room temp/larder cool. *Avail:* BeerC.

CERES STRONG BREW***

33cl Bottled 7.7%:
Pure beer, made from malt, hops, yeast and water only. Very pale gold, and with the classic strong Danish lager nose, mildly malty and estery. Flavours start in the same vein, but there's a surprise in the finish, which grows quite suddenly creamy, with barley richness. *Serve:* light fridge chill. *Avail:* BeerC.

ELEPHANT**

Carlsberg. 33cl Bottled 7.2%:
A veritable feast of sweet roasted vegetables crowd onto the palate of this extra strong lager, which has pronounced caramelized pumpkin, parsnip and sweet potato flavours, and lots of pleasantly pungent alcohol. A wee bit syrupy, and slightly cloying. *Serve:* light fridge chill. *Avail:* Asda, Thres, VicW, Wait.

FAXE***

Premium 33cl Bottled 5%:
Made from good ingredients and using Faxe's own spring water. A malty, fruity, pale and citrussy nose leads into a velvety textured, yet refreshing flavour, with a little buttery barley in the middle, and a slightly spiky, astringent finish. Surprisingly dry for a Danish lager, and an excellent aperitif. *Serve:* light fridge chill. *Avail:* Asda, BeerC, Tesco.

FAXE**

Premium Litre Can 5%:
Very decent party quaffer in a rather startling litre-sized can. Once chilled, it's light (the beer, not the can) and clean with a softly malty finish, showing a little honey and barley sugar sweetness, and a growing gentle bitterness. *Serve:* fridge cold. *Avail:* Asda, Co-op, Somer, Tesco, VicW.

GIRAF GOLD**

Albani, Odense. 33cl Bottled 5.6%:
Groovy bottle, in its giraffe print livery. Pleasant but slightly odd lager, clean up front, strong in the middle, and with a nectarine fruity, lemon acidic, cigar box and slightly sweaty finish. Tastes stronger than it is. A lager intended for contemplative sipping, perhaps. *Serve:* fridge cold. *Avail:* Asda.

GIRAF STRONG**

33cl Bottled 7.9%:
This Giraf, on the other hand, doesn't taste of its almost 8% alcohol. It's clean, strong, but just a little dull: full-bodied, with a sweetish, alcoholic edge, and a touch of whiskyish honey in the finish. This beer falls naturally into the 'Danish Bock' category, but it's Giraf Gold that tastes more like one. *Serve:* fridge cold. *Avail:* specialists.

LIMFJORDS PORTER***

Thysted Bryghus. 33cl Bottled 7.9%:
Confusingly, this beer also describes itself on the label as a Double Brown Stout. It's dense black,

headless, with liquorice and black coffee aromas. In the mouth, there's immense body, and almost as much bitterness. Flavours combine vanilla sweetness with a robust, concentrated liquorice, black malt, figgy and slightly tarry character. A must for porter-heads everywhere. *Serve:* room temp. *Avail:* Beer Paradise.

Odin Pils

44cl Canned 5.5%:
Brewed in the UK (actually) for Danish Interbrew. Ridiculously strong for a cheap tinned lager. Ridiculously bland for a strong tinned lager. *Serve:* fridge cold. *Avail:* Spar.

Porse Guld*

Export Beer Thysted Bryghus. 33cl Bottled 5.8%:
Subtle – too subtle for its strength – but it does have a slightly creamy, slightly fruity, mildly alcoholic palate. Loses its condition in the glass rather quickly, and when it does, the finish tastes rather cereally. *Serve:* fridge cold. *Avail:* Beer Paradise.

Scandia Gold Bier

44cl Canned 5%:
Brewed in the UK (actually) for Danish Interbrew. The sweet one of the conventional strength trio, with a roasted parsnip nose, and sweet fruity flavours that grow sweeter and more like tinned fruit syrup with each sip. The finish is icky sticky too. *Serve:* fridge cold. *Avail:* Spar.

Scandia Lager

44cl Canned 3%:
Also brewed in the UK. Popcorn aromas, followed by an initially promising slight creamy sweetness, but this is swiftly banished by a finish that's persistently grain husky, mineral and aspirin dry, with a cardboardy flavour. Tastes very cheap and a bit nasty, to be perfectly frank. *Serve:* fridge cold. *Avail:* Spar.

Scandia Pils*

44cl Canned 5.5%:
Also brewed in the UK. The label on the tin says 'strong in alcohol', and while it's not outlandishly strong, flavours do hammer home every percentage point. It's sweet and fairly clean at the front, with an unusual dryness following on, which hits the roof of the mouth from the middle, and coats it with an astringency that persists for hours. It gets drier and fiercer with knowing, the dryness acquiring a slightly TCP aspect, and growing citrus fruit pithy in the finish. The single star could entirely have dissolved away by the time you read this. *Serve:* fridge cold. *Avail:* Spar.

Scandia Super

44cl Canned 8%:
Also brewed in the UK. Less sugar sweet than some 'supers', but with a roast pumpkin flavoured alcoholic intensity that's rather sickly. The finish grows tannic. *Serve:* fridge cold. *Avail:* Spar.

Viborg

Lager 44cl Canned 2.3%:
Brewed in the UK (actually) for Danish Interbrew. Low in alcohol, low in colour, low in flavour. Watery and bland. It must be very cheap. *Serve:* fridge cold. *Avail:* Spar.

Viborg Pils**

Strong Lager 44cl Canned 4.5%:
Also brewed in the UK for Danish Interbrew. Not very strong lager, as it happens, but full golden in colour, with sweet, barley sugary aromas and flavours, partly redeemed by a just very slightly creamy pale malt, biscuity flavour, drying up with recognizable malt and hop flavours in the finish. It goes flat far too quickly, but is far nicer to drink than the Scandia range, and better than the strident yellow tin and silly Viking Cyborg name suggest. *Serve:* fridge cold. *Avail:* Spar.

Waitrose Danish Lager

Odense. 33cl Bottled 4.6%:
Made by Albani, presumably. Sweet phenolic corn on the nose; mildly malty, semi-sweet, corn-rich flavours on the palate, its bitter drying finish distinctly cardboardy in emphasis. Pretty duff stuff to be honest. *Serve:* fridge cold.

Finland

When modern Finland was a part of the Russian Empire, in the 19th century, it had a rather distinguished brewing culture. The oldest surviving brewery was founded by a Russian in 1819: beers sold under the Koff brandname are a shortening of Sinebrychoff, the second biggest brewery in the country. The biggest is Hartwall, who also own Lapin Kulta, the only Finnish beer currently imported here. The third largest is called Olvi. There are also a clutch of little independents, some of them now owned by the ambitious Hartwall.

Finland has its own unique beer style, a rye beer called Sahti. Traditionally, as is the case elsewhere in the northern Scandinavian lands, this was a home-brewery-based beer culture, and sahti was traditionally made at home, from a 50/50 rye and barley mash, and flavoured with juniper. In the old days it was frequently to be found in the home sauna, a good brewing environment! Often it had a pronounced wild yeast character: the lambic of the north. Sahti is still made in thousands of homes and farms, but it's now also made on a commercial basis by five companies, and doesn't always contain much rye. A yellow version is made with oats, and the stronger versions can go rather instantly to the brain: the scrumpy of the north.

There's a strong tradition of using other berries beside juniper in home brewing, and also in spirits: berries are also used to flavour vodkas and liqueurs. Finland once grew its own hops, though it does so no longer. But a huge amount of barley for malting is still grown, much of it exported, and some of that export ends up in whisky maltings in both Scotland and Japan. Finland's own version of a Brewing Ingredients Law dictates that all beers contain a minimum of 80% malt. The most commonly used adjunct is unmalted barley itself, rather than corn or rice, though wheat and sugar are also used. Koff produce the strongest beer in Finland, Koff Porter (7% abv), a Finnish Russian Empire classic which, the brewery claims, got its original yeast from a bottle of Guinness. They also make an Extra Strong Export in roughly the Carlsberg Elephant style. The estery, full-bodied style of these strong Scandinavians is sharply in contrast with the workaday lager style, which might be malt-sweet, or simply clean and light. Advertising in Finland is only permitted for the weakest, table lagers, so all the breweries make a beer of this strength. Moderate strength beers, in particular, are served at even lower temperatures than the weather outside, so clean flavours are more important in the mass-market than character and structure. But more interesting beers are also made, notably the Vienna lager, of amber, malty succulence, often made as a Christmas beer.

LAPIN KULTA**

Hartwall Brewery, Tornio. 33cl Bottled 4.5%: The only beer exported from Finland comes from the only brewery in the world to be staffed entirely by women (a recent Christmas card featured a tree covered in baubles and the legend 'the only balls to be found in our brewery'). Lots of credit for Lapin Kulta's flavour is given to the fresh sparkling waters of Lapland's fjeld streams. Pale gold, with a sweet malt, slightly hoppy nose, and good initial texture, though it subsequently goes a bit flat a bit too quickly. Flavours are grainy, sweet and fairly clean, developing a dry hop finish that grows dominant with drinking. Aftertastes are a tad mineral husky, but this is otherwise a blameless, if slightly dull, drinkable little beer. *Serve:* fridge cold. *Avail*: specialists, BeerC.

France

Few people asked to name the great brewing nations of the world would even mention France. (The very word is almost interchangeable with the word wine in many minds.) Asked to think further and come up with other traditional French drinks, there would be a long list of spirits, perhaps calvados and the ciders of Brittany and Normandy. But probably not beer, unless the respondent was one of those people whose idea of a fun day out is to take a boat to Boulogne with a large empty van. Partly this is because British visitors tend to swoop out of the channel tunnel or the ferry terminal at 80 miles an hour, not pausing for breath until they hit the Loire Valley, and the margins of French wine tourism. But the north has a different texture. Beyond those vast D-Day Landing beaches is a gentle landscape, gently rolling in the central belt, and with orchards that enhance its similarities to the English west country (not to mention cheese, cider and cream), before flattening out into great plains to the east, as French Flanders gives way to Belgian Flanders. It's this north-eastern section, together with the area surrounding Strasbourg, further south along the German border, which are the great brewing areas of France.

Beer-making is very much a northern French tradition. Too cool and wet even for the sharp, green wines of Muscadet and Champagne, the Pas de Calais and Departement Nord have instead fostered an artisanal brewing tradition: Biere Artisanale is, indeed, its proudest boast. Further south in Alsace, where there is also plenty of wine-making going on, brewing is much more of an industry, churning out vast quantities of Biere d'Alsace, most of it mass-market, a little of it more interesting, and properly exploiting Strasbourg's fine trading location, by trucking cheap and cheerful beer to the whole of Europe.

There are also just two brewing multinationals. There's Heineken, actually a Dutch company of course, but who also own Pelforth (in Lille) and 33, and then there's France's very own big player, BSN. BSN, who control so much of mass-market Belgian brewing, are in fact a French company, based in Strasbourg, and owners of the Kronenbourg and Kanterbrau brands. So close to the German border, it's perhaps not surprising that Alsatian brewing should focus very much on producing lagers, and stronger, export-style brands, but there's less positive German influence than there once was, and the lagers have grown more international in style (thinner and blander in other words), in the last 20 years. Close to Strasbourg, there's also a scattering of independent companies, led by the Fischer Brewery (also called Pecheur, which is 'fisher' in French) based in Schiltigheim since 1827. Fischer also brew under the Adelshoffen name, and produce a Bière au Malt Whisky, Adelscott, reflecting the French love affair with all things Scottish. Unfortunately, this product has been deleted from all its 1995 national retail listings in Britain. Meteor, another independent in this area, is still family-owned, and proud of the fact that their Meteor Pils was given permission to use the pilsener name by the Czechs, back in 1927. It's unpasteurized, and has had good notices from French critics. They also make Mortimer (8% abv and their flagship brand), Ackerland Blonde and Brune, as well as the pils and a (pasteurized) lager under the Meteor name, and produce around 400,000 hectolitres a year.

In general French lager aims squarely at the budget end of the import market, and ten-packs of dinky little 'stubbies' have become its trademark. They're not usually 100% malt (20-30% adjuncts is a depressingly common figure) and are not usually lagered in any meaningful sense, either. Like most of their British equivalents, French lagers are frequently only given three or four days to 'mature'! Compare and contrast this with the three months traditional in Germany and the Czech Republic. Light, clean flavours are the aim of mass-market French lager brewing, often with a faint sweetness, and a very gentle hop dry note in the finish. But cheap French lager all too often tastes of the high adjunct levels used in its making. French lager breweries get around this to some extent by placing great emphasis on the hi-tech, state of the art state of their brewery plant. The French are in general completely in love with modernism, and breweries of the larger, more industrial sort are often breathtaking temples of stainless steel. Typically, French lager brewery literature not only features hundreds of loving full-colour close-ups of the equipment itself, but a continual emphasis on the hygiene of the whole operation, and the subsequent consistency of the product. These, rather than flavours, are its main concern. This factory-friendly, forward-looking, confidently modern approach probably helps to explain why it was that the president of Fischer raised objections to the *Reinheitsgebot*, Germany's Bavarian Pure Beer Law of 1516, and engineered its humiliating defeat in the European Court. Perhaps it was not only a matter of free trade (Germany had previously been able to regulate not only its own beers, but those of importers on a purity basis) but also stemmed from a serious irritation with the idea of such silly and outmoded ingredient restrictions.

The northern tip of France is much more interesting as a beer region, with many of the speciality producers in Pas de Calais, Artois and Picardy, and especially congregating around Lille. Over in Strasbourg, Bière d'Alsace as a style may have just about been watered down to a level of complete meaninglessness, but here it's quite a different story. The Bières Artisanale of the very north take their cue much more from neighbouring Belgium than from Germany (almost all bière de garde producers are located very close to the Belgian border) and are still very much a living tradition, with the Biere de Garde at its forefront.

The 'beer to keep' or 'beer to put by' was originally a rustic, farm-based style, and is classically a medium-strong (6.5–7.5% abv), top-fermenting, bottle-conditioned ale of reddish-brownish hue and a distinctive sour-oaky, spicy malt character. Vienna malts are often used, for a richly buttery but spicy effect, or else paler malts are given the Very Long Boil treatment, caramelizing them in situ. Because the desired flavours are very much malt-accented, the hops chosen are usually of only a mildly bitter (but perhaps also slightly pepper-spicy) sort. Sugar is often used, and some breweries soften up their water for a soft, minerally body. Cold maturation is common, which increases the impression of a smooth, mellow altbier-style texture. But despite the sour-oaky palate of many classic bières de garde, it's now the norm to mature the beer in metal, rather than wood.

Often there is the added excitement of a corked and wire caged bottle, and bottles are often of a good hefty 75cl size; both of which lend the style a distinctive French look. Jenlain, from the Flemish-named Duyck Brewery, near Valenciennes, is the recognized classic of the style. Some bières de garde are still top-fermented, but few are bottle-conditioned any longer: look out for the appellation 'sur lie' on the bottle. It's now also common to find bottom-fermented examples, of smoother, mellower, more predictable character, though 'lager' yeasts are often used at 'ale' temperatures for added fruitiness. Bières de garde can also be of a more amber, golden hue, (the Ambrée) with a correspondingly sweeter flavour, as well as pale gold, as a Biere de Garde Blonde.

Duyck makes a very fine Blonde called Sebourg (6% abv), actually made in the next village to Jenlain, but also top-fermented (at the moment) and unpasteurized, with creamy malt, sweet alcoholic fruit, and a floral, musky finish: the hayfields, lush pastures, and forest fruits of this quaintly titled Little Switzerland area are all intended to be reflected in its flavours. They use Champagne barley, Alsatian hops and a soupçon of wheat. But the classic Duyck product, and the classic bière de garde, is Jenlain, named after their village. Then farmers, the Duyck family started making it in 1922; they still run the brewery, though they're no longer farming. At the time there were about 2000 breweries in the area, almost as many as there are churches. Jenlain was originally brewed in winter ready for drinking in the spring, in the traditional bière de garde way, and this was the first bière de garde to be bottled for sale to non-local markets; originally people would visit the farm breweries with their own containers. The beer is made with barley malt from the Beauce, Gatinais and Brie regions, northern French hops, and artesian well water, is fermented for five days and matured for a month before filtering, after which it's matured again. Originally, only top-fermenting yeasts were used here, but bottom-fermenters have been used in recent years, although top-fermenting is now being tried out again. The brewery are at some pains to point out that it's roasted malts that give the beer its rich colouring, not caramel or other adjuncts, and the classic bière de garde earthiness, what the brewery describe as 'a tang of the soil' is retained and cultivated as an authentic flavour of the true, dark, country beer. They sell 12 million bottles a year. There's also a Jenlain Blonde.

The three most exciting artisanale breweries of the north, besides Duyck, are Castelaine, La Choulette and Enfants de Gayant. Castelaine, of Benifontaine, are responsible for the Ch'Ti (local patois for a northerner) trio of bottom-fermented, filtered bières de garde; the blonde is of 6.4% abv and clean but complex fruitiness. La Choulette, in Hordain, produces three bottle-conditioned classic beers, all at 7.5%: La Choulette Ambrée, with lots of vanilla butter and spice; the equally potent Robespierre, of honey and whiskyish strength and sweetness, and the brandy-snappy, strong and smooth Sans Coulottes. All three are top-fermented, but also made with a little specially adapted bottom-fermenting yeast, and thus manage to be both fruitily various and smoothly mellow in character. They are lightly filtered, but not too much: lots of life and vigour remains.

Enfants de Gayant, of Douai is a little more various in its range: Lutèce Bière du Paris (6.4% abv) is a kinder, softer but still sour-oaky and vanilla flavoured bière de garde with a huge export market. Bière du Demon (12% abv) is a radically strong lager following in the general direction of the Belgian 'devil beer' classic, Duvel, of dry, whiskyish character. Bière du Desert (7% abv), a Bière Blonde Speciale, has a creamy, moussey light fruitiness that makes it an excellent celebration beer. The company also own the Abbaye de Saint Landelin range of three abbey-style beers, Ambrée, Blonde and Brune (a classic French trio).

Also near Lille, in Ronchin, is the less well known Jeanne d'Arc brewery, whose products include Ambre des Flandres, and the Orpal beers, all in the artisanale tradition, as well as a more conventional French lager, Cristalor, and a famous (in France at least) succulent and spicy top-fermenting Ambrée called Grain d'Orge (grain of barley), a 'produit de terroir' (country beer) that so inspired the French chef Bernard Broux that he has named his restaurant after it. Gold Triumph and Scotch Triumph, both at 6% abv, are also well-known in France: Gold Triumph uses Vienna malt and lagers for six weeks. Scotch Triumph is an award-winning brown ale, long matured, but, like Gold Triumph, in fact bottom-fermented. The 'Scotch' is an occasionally seen homage to the Scottish dark and malty beer style, also beloved of Belgians, but in both countries far richer, maltier, stronger and more interesting than any beers now produced in Britain under that name. Another relic of the British presence in this region is a love of porter beers: Pelforth make a decent one in their Lille brewery.

Like many other breweries of this region, Jeanne d'Arc uses good ingredients, and makes its beers in a small-batch, hands-on, old-fashioned way that would probably horrify the stainless steel merchants. Many of these artisanale breweries of the north are successful expansions from old farm breweries, and a few, like La Choulette, still reflect this in their endearingly low-tech premises. Success is putting pressure on this old world, however: bières de garde have been a huge hit in export markets and the demand for more and more varied products is becoming almost burdensome. Because bière de garde is now made year round, a new seasonal product is being adopted by many companies: the bière de mars, or March beer, a satisfying beer of good malty body, which takes its cue from the traditional German Märzen style.

Grande Brasserie Moderne (which also calls itself Terken), though only about 15 km from Lille, and established in 1892, is quite a different sort of operation to the traditional farm brewery of the area. Its 1920s brewery is gleamingly, proudly modern, but the brewing itself takes the trouble to use Czech yeast, and lager for a minimum of six weeks for its stronger, flagship brands. Best known of these is their delicious bière de garde, Septante 5 (7.5% abv), now poised for serious export across (or rather under) the channel. Breug, Noordheim and Upstaal are three of the better known budget brands GBM makes for packaging in ten-packs of 25cl bottles. All in all, they sell two million cases of beer a year to the UK.

It's Kronenbourg we know best in Britain, partly because it's brewed here under licence and so gets a big marketing push; after Kronenbourg, probably the almost ubiquitous Fischer. It at least is an independent: the trend in French brewing this century has been very much to centralize, simplify, and less euphemistically, close down a lot of other independents, though things are showing a slight improvement. There are now over 30 independent companies, and about 20 brew pubs, most famously the Frog & Rosbif in Paris. In developing its embryonic microbrewery culture, France is looking to the British (or rosbif) model. Other established breweries, thriving in France, but yet to make an impact here, include: Annoeuillin (Pastor Ale bière de garde, and a wheat beer), St Sylvestre (Trois Monts and Bières des Templiers) near the Belgian border, and the Strasbourg-based Schutzenberger (independent) lager brewery, makers of Jubilator (7% abv).

ACKERLAND***

Biere Speciale Meteor, Hochfelden. 25cl Bottled 5.9%:

A stubby six-pack of strong lager that looks like nothing very interesting: just the usual Strasbourg style, you might think. But this is something different: a good Meteor beer in an over-modest little bottle. Amber in colour, it has ripe banana and tropical fruit aromas as it warms, and mellow, smooth, malty, gently alcoholic flavours, with a touch of Vienna malt spice and subtly peaty, whiskyish notes combined with a very gentle sweetness. A rather elegant Export style lager from an inelegant container. *Serve:* light fridge chill. *Avail:* Tesco.

ADELSHOFFEN

Fischer, Schiltigheim. 25cl Bottled 3%:

On the basis of two sample bottles, even worse than the Export version, below. Warm, sweaty plastic on the nose, acrid and flabby in the mouth, phenolic at the finish. It can only improve. *Serve:* fridge cold. *Avail:* Asda, Co-op, Tesco.

ADELSHOFFEN EXPORT

25cl Bottled 4.5%:

Bière d'Alsace of no great interest even when it's on form, but also tends to be a bit cabbage-nosed and sweaty flavoured. Cereally sweet and dull, dull, dull. *Serve:* fridge cold. *Avail:* Co-op, Wait.

ALSADOR**

Bière d'Alsace Fischer, Schiltigheim. 25cl Bottled 5%:

Packaged for Victoria Wine by the ubiquitous Strasbourg (large) independent. If you were bracing yourself for Adelshoffen boredom, you'd be greatly cheered up by this buttery nosed, softly malty, potable little beer, which, like the Safeway own brand, has a dry malt front, and a soft, sweetly buttery barley finish. Unambitious perhaps, but pleasant drinking. *Serve:* fridge cold. *Avail:* VicW.

AMBRE DES FLANDRES***

Jeanne d'Arc, Ronchin. 25cl Bottled 6.4%: A bière de garde under the Orpal brandname, with gently sour, brown malt hues and aromas, and similar flavours, oaky, dry and fairly austere, but redeemed by a balancing tea-like sweetness. Rather splendid, smooth and mellow bottom-fermented Flemish ale of distinctive character. *Serve:* room temp. *Avail:* specialists.

L'ANGELUS***

Biere de Froment Annoeullin. 75cl Bottled 7%: Delicious French wheat beer, guaranteed 30% minimum wheat in the mash, packaged in a grandiose champagne-style bottle complete with gold foil, cork and wire cage. Soft, lemon moussey flavours, with a little melon and peach, and faintly perfumey: a creamy treat for high summer in the garden. *Serve:* larder cool/ light fridge chill. *Avail:* Beer Paradise.

ASDA BIERE DE LUXE*

25cl Bottled 4.8%:
Produced for Asda by the Terken (GBM) brewery, a Breug-like, fine but unexciting, clean and light-bodied lager. A little pale malt is evident at the front, then an apple-juicey note, and just the faintest hop echo in the finish. But it's too modest, and too dull, even to qualify for a two star Dull rating. *Serve:* fridge cold.

BIÈRE DU DEMON***

Enfants de Gayant, Douai. 33cl Bottled 12%: A show-offy strong beer with a proudly alcohol-rich copyline, and a recipe that involves water, malt, hops and yeast only. Surprisingly dry, whiskyish flavours, tempered with a little roast swede and parsnip sweetness, and lots of strong, strong alcohol in evidence (and no wonder at 12%). Actually, I find it quite difficult to drink: there is more machismo at work here than is expressed in its infinitely softer and mellower mentor, Duvel (Belgium). 'Le Plaisir Diabolique' certainly. *Serve:* room temp/larder cool. *Avail:* BeerC.

BIÈRE DU DESERT***

Bière Blonde Speciale 33cl Bottled 7%: Sibling beer to the Demon. Pale yellow gold beer with an appetizing hay barn and apricot nose, and wonderfully creamy (almost coconutty), moussey and toasted champagne-like, sparkling flavours and textures. This biscuity creaminess is followed by a refreshing gooseberry sharpness and peppery hop in the finish. Truly delicious and very easy to drink for a beer of this strength. Wholesome too: only malt, hops, yeast and water are used. *Serve:* larder cool/light fridge chill. *Avail:* BeerC.

BRANDEBURG*

Bière Blonde St Omer. 25cl Bottled 2.8%: Light, quaffable, low in alcohol, with a gentle, soft malty dryness, and very little else to report. *Serve:* fridge cold. *Avail:* Wait.

BREUG*

Terken (GBM), Roubaix. 25cl Bottled 4.5%: Sherbety, slightly orangey, clean and spritzy, thin and bland quaffer from a brewery that knows more about hygiene than it knows about beer making. A case of Kills All Known Flavours Dead, perhaps. *Serve:* fridge cold. *Avail:* Wait.

LA CHOULETTE***

Ambrée La Choulette, Hordain. 75cl Bottled 7.5%:
A bière artisanale of classic pedigree, with a caramel, vanilla, slightly sherryish nose, and flavours to match, but with added spice, sandalwood and oak to temper the luscious buttery toffee, and all wrapped in a refreshing fizz of excellent texture. The finish is warmly spicy, with nutmeg, ginger cake and orange flavours. Thoroughly scrumptious stuff, soft and comforting, and perilously easy to quaff for a 7.5% beer. Good with chicken. *Serve:* larder cool. *Avail:* BeerC.

CH'TI***
Bière de Garde Blonde Castelain, Benifontaine. 33cl Bottled 6.4%:
Ch'ti gets its name from the local patois for 'northerner', in this old mining region. It's a delicious beer, with deeply fruity and toastily malty aromas and flavours; high citric, apple and banana character (plus pineapple chunks) just before the finish, following on from a middle that's beautifully balanced, mellow, fruit and malt accented, clean and refreshing, complete with a gently dry kick. Notably fruity, particularly tasty; at the top of the three-star league. *Serve:* larder cool. *Avail:* Safe, Wait.

CRISTALOR**
Bière Blonde de Luxe Jeanne D'Arc, Ronchin, Lille. 25cl Bottled 4.7%:
Butterkist! Or at least, a profoundly butter popcorn nose, with a toffee accent. The flavour is similar, on a soft, pale-malt body, and the finish a little sticky. Should be popular with steamed-pudding lovers. *Serve:* fridge cold. *Avail:* Maj.

CROIX DORÉE*
Bière des Flandres 25cl Bottled 5%:
Slight, undemanding, biscuity lager, pale and not very interesting. *Serve:* fridge cold. *Avail:* Asda, Somer, Tesco, Wait.

FISCHER BIÈRE D'ALSACE*
Fischer, Schiltigheim. 25cl Bottled 5%:
The classic little French stubby, clean (on a good day), light and quaffable, though not burdened with too much in the way of character. See also supermarket own label bières d'Alsace. *Serve:* fridge cold. *Avail:* Asda, Somer, Thres.

FISCHER STRONG LAGER*
66cl Bottled 5%:
Flip-top bottled, spritzy strong lager with discernibly root vegetable, caramelized swede sweetness, and an oddly metallic finish, rather mineral, a little cardboardy. Disappointing. *Serve:* light fridge chill. *Avail:* Safe, Somer, Tesco.

FISCHER TRADITION***
Bière Blonde Speciale 65cl Bottled 6.5%:
Flip-top bottled, and once the flip has flopped, pungently buttery, sweet alcohol aromas prepare the way for a turnip festival. There is a touch of that in the flavour, but also lots of fruit and freshness and a good lively fizz. The finish is a bit samey, and risks stickiness, so it only just scrapes that third star rating. Dangerously quaffable stuff, though. *Serve:* light fridge chill. *Avail:* Asda, Tesco.

GOLD TRIUMPH**
Bière Blonde Jeanne d'Arc, Ronchin. 25cl Bottled 6%:
Also frequently listed under its Orpal brandname. Sweetish, slightly toffeeish, mildly honeyish, faintly spicy, strong and smooth, with a salty note. Just a bit thin and lacking in structure, perhaps? *Serve:* room temp/larder cool. *Avail:* specialists.

GRAIN D'ORGE***
Jeanne d'Arc, Ronchin. 75cl Bottled 8%:
Handsomely packaged top-fermented Bière Blonde des Flandres, with a cork and wire cage, and a satisfying pop on opening. Amber gold in colour, with appetizing sour-oak aromas, and buttery amber flavours seasoned with spice and oak, finishing in a warm, rich, spicy and whiskyish glow. Sweetness builds in drinking, with caramelized pumpkin sugars coming through, just as the texture falters and turns a little flabby in the glass. These let it down a little. *Serve:* room temp/larder cool. *Avail:* specialists.

JADE***
Bière Biologique Castelain, Benifontaine. 75cl Bottled 4.6%:
Not a washing powder, but an organic French lager, unpasteurized and very handsomely packaged in a large and heavy bottle, complete with cork and wire cage. Inside, there's a fresh, dry, hoppy lager on a good soft-water body, flowering into fat, rich buttery barley and finishing with firm, bitter (almost minty) hop astringency. Probably the best

French lager you'll ever taste. Excellent for socializing: a very drinkable, accessible beer in a dinner party bottle. *Serve:* light fridge chill. *Avail:* Beer Paradise.

Jenlain***

Bière de Garde Ambrée Duyck, Jenlain. 50cl Bottled 6.5%:
Corked and wire-caged country ale (there's also a metal-cap version) made from artesian well water, champagne malt and Flemish hops, and cold-conditioned for 40 days. Spiritous, slightly whisky nose; oaky, slightly sour and whiskyish flavour, with cardomom and other spice, and pronounced malt character, all wrapped in a clean and spritzy texture. The finish is strongly suggestive of anise, and a little liquorice. *Serve:* larder cool. *Avail:* BeerC, Odd, Tesco.

Korersbier**

Bière d'Alsace 25cl Bottled 4.4%:
Lemon and banana on the nose, vanilla and buttersweet notes on the tongue, but also fizzy and very clean in texture, with just a hint of hop flavour in the super-clean finish. Spritzy and extremely refreshing, but with a satisfying tasty fullness at the front: altogether one of the very nicest 25cl 'stubbies' to come across the channel. *Serve:* fridge cold. *Avail:* Odd.

Kronenbourg Red & White

Kronenbourg, Strasbourg. 44cl Canned 4%:
Made in England (actually) by Courage. Semi-sweet, almost rubbery nose; grainy, cereal sweetness in the mouth, and a finish absent but for an adjuncty slight dryness. Dull and flabby. *Serve:* fridge cold. *Avail:* widely.

Kronenbourg 1664**

Bottled 33cl 5%:
A surprisingly drinkable lunchtime lager from France's national brewers. Smooth and clean, but not without flavour either; there's decent (if subtle) dryish hop and sweet barley malt balance in there. Fine with pizza. *Serve:* light fridge chill. *Avail:* widely.

Kronenbourg 1664*

Strasbourg. Canned 50cl 5%:
Also made by Courage under licence. Surprisingly fruity, banana and pineapple aromas emerge when the glass is swirled. Not at all bad for a mass market tinned lager; clean, smooth, with some of the bottled beer's character, and no metallic taint, at least. *Serve:* fridge cold. *Avail:* widely.

Lutèce Bière de Paris***

Enfants de Gayant, Douai. 75cl Bottled 6.4%:
Grandly corked and packaged, and obviously a big hit in Italy and Canada; Italian language information abounds on the label, and you can get a 5 cent refund on the bottle in Quebec. Pure malt brewed, it has a delightful Vienna malt colouring, with an appropriately sour oaky nose, growing warm and ripe banana-like. A lively fizz and a clean, dry texture introduce sour-woody, spicy, vanilla, slightly whiskyish flavours, and a powerful, lingering finish. *Serve:* larder cool. *Avail:* Odd.

Marks & Spencer Alsace Gold***

Fischer, Schiltigheim. 33cl Bottled 6.5%:
Bière d'Alsace produced and bottled by the ubiquitous Fischer brewery. Spritzy in texture, with tropical fruit aromas. To taste, pleasing malt fruit is hotly pursued by hints of butter and toffee, and a little honey at the finish, where there is also plenty of strong alcohol bite. Over-ripe pineapple flavours, unbalance the final effect a little. *Serve:* light fridge chill.

Marks & Spencer Biere D'Alsace**

Fischer, Schiltigheim. 25cl Bottled 5%:
Creamy grain-sweet lager with a distinctive soft-bodied fruitiness; Body Shop style strawberry notes on the nose and (more subtly) on the palate. The creamy, almost moussey texture prevents the finish turning clean, however. A light summer quaffer which tastes under strength. *Serve:* fridge cold.

Meteor**

Bière d'Alsace Meteor, Hochfelden. 33cl Bottled 4.6%:
Initially not very impressive, but it improves as

it breathes and warms a little. Post-breather, flavours are modestly creamy, slightly fruity, light and quaffable. Good for the store cupboard. *Serve:* light fridge chill. *Avail:* specialists.

MORTIMER ***

Bière Forte Meteor. 25cl Bottled 7.6%: Wittily packaged orange-amber strong beer in a third-sized whisky bottle, complete with whiskyish label and the italicized inscription 'Pure Malt' adding to the visual pun. There's also something faintly whiskyish – a mellow but also slightly briney example – in the flavours, which are smooth, drily nutty, sweetly alcoholic, with a touch of cinnamon stick and a gently potent kick. *Serve:* larder cool. *Avail:* specialists.

NOORDHEIM**

Terken (GBM), Roubaix. 25cl Bottled 4.7%: Nicest of the three Terken imports (though still very modest), with just enough creamy pale malt body to keep it out of the single-star doldrums where its siblings reside, and a dryish hop note in the brief, businesslike finish too. Repackage it as Flanders Gold in 50cl bottles and it would jump off the shelves. But 'Noordheim'? Non. *Serve:* light fridge chill. *Avail:* specialists.

PELFORTH BLONDE**

Pelforth. 33cl Bottled 5.8%:
Heineken-owned brewery, drinkable beer, but it tastes more like a 4.8% lager than a 5.8% blonde. Slightly creamy, but clean, with mildly alcoholic flavours, and apple and banana cake notes in the finish, which is also gently drying. The texture is quite diat pils-like, crisp and dry. Watch out for the strength: a quaffable wolf in sheep's clothing. *Serve:* light fridge chill. *Avail:* Maj.

PELFORTH BRUNE**

33cl Bottled 6.5%:
An even stronger Pelforth beer, with warm, plummy and malty aromas, and less fruity, but also rather sweeter, caramel and toffee, dark sugary brune flavours. An undemanding pick-me-up; prefer the blonde. *Serve:* light fridge chill. *Avail:* Maj.

PILSOR**

Bière de Luxe Jeanne d'Arc, Ronchin. 25cl Bottled 4%:
Extremely fruity, summery lager with a strong melon flavour at the front (of the orange-fleshed, Charantais sort), and lots of passionfruit at the back. No structure, no malt or hop flavours, no finish: just a friendly, vaguely beery fruity fizz. But oddly likeable. *Serve:* fridge cold. *Avail:* Kwik Save.

RHINBERG**

Bière d'Alsace 25cl Bottled 4.5%:
Lemony, peppery, soft-bodied, prickly with tiny bubbles on the roof of the mouth. More refreshing and drier, but less tasty and soothing than the Tesco own brand, though it does have some of that lovely mild, sweet maltiness. *Serve:* light fridge chill. *Avail:* Tesco.

ROBESPIERRE***

Sans Culottes La Choulette, Hordain. 75cl Bottled 7.5%: Another strong, bottle-conditioned, big and beefy ale in the Northern French 'artisanale' tradition. Strong alcohol aromas, a little swedey, brown sugary, with a spiritous potency, and this character crowds into the finish, a touch overpoweringly. There's also some honey and golden syrup, and a whiskyish kick to this densely flavoured, pale-gold beer. *Serve:* larder cool. *Avail:* BeerC.

SAFEWAY BIÈRE D'ALSACE**

25cl Bottled 5%:
Good example of an own-brand bière d'Alsace, golden in colour with an upfront dry hop character leading into slight sweetness and toffee-accented, pale-malty finish. Tasty, light and refreshing: a good barbecue beer. *Serve:* fridge cold.

SAINSBURY'S BIÈRE D'ALSACE*

25cl Bottled 4.9%:
'Cereally sweet with a bad wet cardboardy

finish; thin, watery and refreshing' reads one tasting note for this beer. The second sample seemed less afflicted, with at least hints of a fragrant dry malt and gentle hop flavour. The finish in both seemed tainted, though. Hope you catch it on a good day. *Serve:* fridge cold.

SAINSBURY'S BIÈRE DE GARDE**
Castelain, Benifontaine. 75cl Bottled 6%:
Resplendently jewel-like, glowing reddish amber top-fermented beer, pleasant, but not exciting in style. Hints of sour oak and red malt pungency and fruit, but with a demerara sweet, soft-bodied interpretation, finished with a slender malt dryness. Tastes like a neutered supermarket version of a French classic. *Serve:* larder cool.

SAINSBURY'S BIÈRE DE PRESTIGE**
Fischer, Schiltigheim. 65cl Bottled 6.5%:
Sweetie-nosed, bright-golden strong lager in a Fischer flip-top bottle. Dense, slightly syrupy, barley-sweet lager, almost overwhelmed by its own potency. Pineapple chunks marry with caramelized pumpkin flavours; seems sweeter and more unrelenting than the Fischer branded version. *Serve:* light fridge chill.

SAINSBURY'S BIÈRE DES FLANDRES*
25cl Bottled 3%:
Almost a low-alcohol beer from French Flanders; the bad grammar is intentional. Pronounced butter and vanilla aromas, with a splash of ginger, but the flavour isn't quite so delicious, thinnish and dilute, a bit woody, with a gingerish note (a ginger ale style finish, too). Not exactly beery, but a pleasant enough drink. *Serve:* fridge cold.

SAINT LANDELIN AMBRÉE**
Enfants de Gayant. 33cl Bottled 6.8%:
Secular brewed 'abbey beer', harking back to the long defunct Abbey of Crespin (est. 1032). Reddish-brownish pink, with corresponding (yeasty) aromas of plums, peaches and raspberries. A bit fizzier than the near perfect 'Blond' (below), and a bit more muffled in its flavours, but still delicious, with tinned chestnut purée sweetness, and biscuity vanilla malt flavours. Unfortunately comes to a bit of a dead halt where the finish should be. Surprisingly gentle, sweet and unassuming pudding of a beer for a hefty 6.8%er. *Serve:* larder cool. *Avail:* BeerC.

SAINT LANDELIN BLOND***
33cl Bottled 5.9%:
A top-fermented ale made of strictly pure ingredients, and rich golden in colour. Aromas are of sweet, creamy, fruity alcohol, with a little barley sugar, and, lo and behold, all these crowd wonderfully generously onto the palate. Flavours are notably creamy, easy and delicious, with apple and banana offset by apricot, an irresistibly biscuity malt texture on the tongue, and pots of honey in the finish. Undemanding but a real treat. *Serve:* larder cool. *Avail*: BeerC.

SAINT LANDELIN BRUNE**
33cl Bottled 6.2%:
Dark and pondy beer with a peculiarly flat Coca Cola flavour, bucked up by roast grain and a slightly cough mixtureish, but also banana fruity finish. It grows a little more coffeeish as it warms, and improves in texture if you swirl it about to get the bubbles going. The finish grows intriguingly minty and chocolately, though sadly more After Eight than Bendicks. *Serve:* room temp. *Avail*: BeerC.

SANS COULOTTES***
Bière Blonde Artisanale La Choulette, Hordain. 75cl Bottled 7%:
Initially might fool you into thinking it's something Bavarian, with its rich gold colouring and deep, rocky head. Strong beer aromas come off this vision: slightly root vegetable, the famous caramelized swede, a little honey. These are present on the palate, where there's also brandy snap, a rum butter note, a sweeter (roasted parsnip and sweet potato) vegetable character, and richly yeasty, strong alcohol flavours. *Serve:* room temp/larder cool. *Avail*: BeerC.

SCOTCH TRIUMPH**

Brune Jeanne d'Arc, Ronchin. 25cl Bottled 6%:
Dark, dark ruby-red with a little strawberry on the nose, and sweet, malty flavours, but growing distinctly more sweet than malty. Tastes more Welsh than Scottish, in effect. But there are more strawberry jam and summery fruity malt notes among the overt sugar syrup flavours. Incredibly smooth and gloopy. *Serve:* room temp. *Avail*: specialists.

SEBOURG***

Bière de Garde Blonde Jenlain. 25cl Bottled 6%:
Creamy pale gold with an appetizing sour fruits nose, and initially a big frothy head. Robust but clean and refreshing; flavours balance floral dryness and ripe barley sweetness with a hint of orange water. Perfumed, slightly musky, lingering finish. Excellent with oily fish. *Serve:* light fridge chill. *Avail*: Odd.

SOMERFIELD FRENCH PREMIUM LAGER

Bière d'Alsace. 25cl Bottled 5%:
Disappointing beer with sharp, even slightly tart flavours and a cereally, creamy texture, turning dry and just a bit acrid at the finish. Cardboardy on the nose too; possibly stale. *Serve:* light fridge chill.

LA STRASBOURGEOIS

Bière d'Alsace Fischer, Schiltigheim. 25cl Bottled 4.9%:
Typically lager gold, with lots of fizz and sparkle, a soft malty front, a dryish pale-malty middle, and a grapefruity citrus tang at the close, when peppery dry hops also chime in and build with drinking. *Serve:* fridge cold. *Avail*: Safe.

TESCO FRENCH LAGER**

Bière d'Alsace. 25cl Bottled 5%:
Fresh, appley and pale, fragrant malt aromas; creamy, almost Ovaltiney malt sweetness, barley grain ripeness, and a slightly peppery finish. Not much in the way of hoppiness, but it doesn't seem to matter. Creamy, soothing, an ideal nightcap. Almost in the three-star league, for its freshness and simplicity and good, tasty ingredients in the often hit-or-miss bière d'Alsace category. *Serve:* light fridge chill.

'33'

Export Premium Lager. 33 Brewery 25cl Bottled 4.8%:
Eggy nose, grain and unmalted cereal flavours, although flabby and mediocre. *Serve:* fridge cold. *Avail*: Asda, Maj, Safe, Sains, Wait.

UPSTALL*

Terken (GBM), Roubaix. 25cl Bottled 3%
Mildly sweet and cereally, bland and fizzy, pale lager with a vaguely apple-juicey note. Clean, at least, but monstrously dull. *Serve:* fridge cold. *Avail:* specialists.

WAITROSE FRENCH LAGER*

25cl Bottled 5%:
Sweet pineapple chunk aromas, with a butterscotch note; slightly syrupy, buttery and toffee flavours, balanced by a (very) gentle dry finish. Thin and watery texture, no structure, and, frankly, tastes cheap. *Serve:* fridge cold.

Germany

Others may seek to take the crown for having the most dynamic, progressive approach (the United States) or producing more diverse and unusual beer styles (Belgium), but Germany is still the great brewing nation of the world. Something like 40% of the world's breweries are here, two-thirds of them in Bavaria alone, where small- and medium-sized companies are scattered over the landscape like village churches, creating a density and pattern that would once have been commonplace throughout Britain and mainland Europe. The Germans (and in particular the Bavarians) are dedicated beer drinkers, with an annual capacity of some 140 litres per head, topping the world consumption league with monotonous yearly regularity (until recently toppled by the Czechs).

Many of Germany's breweries are brew pubs, taverns, restaurants, even 'cafes with rooms', where beers are brewed and consumed on site, with little or none being sold outside the premises. This has been the main area for Germany's own beer renaissance in the last 20 years. Over 200 new brew pubs have opened since the mid 1970s. Others maintain the 'brewery tap' approach, attracting visitors to their tavern or café, and selling a limited amount outside. German brewing (and drinking) is still remarkably localized, and people are loyal to their own region's (or own village's) beers, in a way that's almost died out elsewhere. There are very few national brands, of the Boddington's and Carling Black Label sort, and most beer-loving Germans would be horrified at the very idea. Brought up with beer, surrounded by independent little local breweries and brew pubs, they have a natural scepticism about the merits of national brands and the quality of products made by any big national brewery. Having said that, there are beers produced by the bigger regional breweries that appear in bottle over large areas of the country, and there are a handful of truly national brands, including Germany's number-one-selling beer, Warsteiner. Big brewing groups do exist, some owning several names well known in the export trade. There is a mass-market, and there are beers produced for it, but they are kept in their proper place, by and large. And, down at the bottom line, it's also true that Germany's national brands have far more integrity and a lot less hype-based and laddish marketing than Britain's.

This is partly because German drinkers are extremely discerning and can spot quality at 50 paces, but is also down to a historical German insistence on proper brewing with good ingredients. The inheritance of Bavaria's own *Reinheitsgebot* of 1516, which demands that beers be made from malt, hops, yeast and water only, creates a natural standard against which all beers are measured. The 1987 decision of the European Court (boo! hiss!) that Germany must not forbid beer imports on the grounds that they don't meet this simple purity standard was a bit of a blow, but the German Union of 1919 adopted Bavaria's pure beer law and still adheres to it. Germany, despite the EC, is not awash with imports, because there's really no market for them. The position now is that all Bavarian exports are still *Reinheitsgebot*, but north German exports may not be necessarily. Breweries that stick by the pure beer law generally make mention of it on the bottle.

This isn't the only sweeping generalization to be made about the north and south. There are many qualifications to the simple rule that follows, as well as beers that have developed their own regional accent, but in general it's still true that beers from the north have a firmer, harder, drier character: this is the German heartland of the hoppy, clean pilsener style. Southern and Bavarian beers tend to be softer, often with a pale malt creaminess, perhaps fuller bodied and sweeter, with only a gentle hop note.

The German Lager

Germany is often pigeon-holed as a lager-brewing nation. There are two objections to this: one, that Germany does also make fine top-fermenting beers (ales), notably the altbiers associated with Dusseldorf, and the German wheat beer; and two, 'lager' is a primitive and misleading way of describing the wealth of German bottom-fermenting beer styles. British brewers adopted the word 'lager' to flatter their own attempts at a pale, pseudo-Germanic, bottom-fermenting, clean-edged beer style. We also associate imports with 'lager' because the rest of the brewing nations of Europe gave up trying to interest us in anything more interesting – until very recently, that is, when wheat beers, Exports, real pilseners and even bocks began filtering into the British high street. Lager *is* a beer in Germany, but it refers to a very mild mannered, bland, blue-collar quaffing beer of modest alcohol, rather like many of the so-called 'premium' national lagers of Britain, in fact.

Nor are 'pilsener' and 'lager' interchangeable in Germany in the way they have become here. Pilsener has a quite specific meaning, referring to the authentic Czech beer. Officially, German breweries only use the word 'pils', recognizing that it's a Czech trademark; in practice many use pilsener or pilsner despite this sentiment. It was in the Bohemian town of Pilsen (Plzen) that brewers first developed a clear golden version of Bavaria's own invention, the lagered beer. This is where the catch-all term lager comes from: to lager means 'to store'. Bavaria, aside from being the hop garden of Germany, and having over 800 breweries crammed within its borders, also happens to be squeezed in just north of the Alps; its physical isolation, bordered by mountains, hills and forests in all directions, is in large part responsible for its still very traditional culture.

Bavaria happened to invent the Lager Beer by chance, or rather, discovered it by accident. At a time when all yeasts were of the top-fermenting sort, and all the beers of the world were ales, the Bavarians hit upon the idea of overcoming the annual spoilage of their beer during summer by transferring it to the cooler conditions of the Alps, just to the south. And it was in an Alpine cave that a top-fermenting yeast first reacted to the cold by descending to the bottom of the vessel. Bavarians discovered that this procedure meant beers could be kept there for a much longer period than ales would survive outside; that they would mature very slowly in the cool conditions, and would develop different flavours and characteristics.

Lagering had been going on in a fairly make-do, touchy-feely way for a long time, perhaps even 400 years, before one of the great heroes of German brewing, one Gabriel Sedlmayr (of Spaten Brewery), son of the then royal court brewmaster (also Gabriel), developed a scientific approach to lager brewing. Once the nut had been well and truly cracked, the new technique spread from Bavaria to the rest of Europe like wildfire. Anton Dreher in Vienna perfected the amber 'Vienna lager' in 1841. The following year, the Czech town of Pilsen developed its own, clear golden, soft and hoppy style.

Before pilsener took such a hold on European fashion, lager beers were dark lagers. These days, a dark lager is referred to as a 'dunkel' (dark) beer, and perhaps also Munich-style, just as brown malts used in lager brewing are frequently referred to as Munich malts. The colour variation is partly down to the naturally darker colour (at quite low malting temperatures) and maltier character of the 'continental' barley; quite different to the cleaner character of the 'maritime' barley grown and used in Britain and Scandinavia. Pilseners should have lots of hop character, especially in the nose and finish. Northern examples (and this is chiefly a northern style in Germany) tend to be drier, firmer, but are often also restrained, with an elegant dryness all the way through. One of the very driest pilseners in Germany is produced by Jever, who are so far north they are almost in Denmark. Pilseners are also made in Bavaria, but southern lagers have a generally softer, maltier, creamier, subtler character, typified by the Münchener Hell.

Whether of the soft-bodied, mildly malty sort, or the drier, hoppier style, German 'lagers' get their superior character to almost everything appearing under that name in Britain because they (a) use better ingredients, (b) use a proper technique, and (c) lager the beers correctly. It's common in Britain to 'mature' lager for only three days; two weeks if it's lucky. The traditional German period is three *months*, and while not everyone sticks to this period by any means, the better brands have flavours that can only be achieved through slow, cold, steady maturation on residual yeasts, for depth and complexity of flavour. German lagers are often also kräusened, meaning some of the wort (malt sugar suspension) is added to the conditioning tank to enhance secondary fermentation and create spritzy, clean, crisp textures and flavours.

Warsteiner, Germany's number-one-selling beer, comes from a brewery of the same name. It was established in 1753, and 40 years ago was still a small family company. Now they turn out 6 million hectolitres a year of the eponymous lager brand, and export to 40 countries. The brewhouse is a gleaming bank of computer screens, and vast stainless steel vessels, and there are 30 people in Quality Control alone. Both the mass-market lager brand and the Export are made under *Reinheitsgebot*. Bitburger, Germany's number two beer brand, is poised to overtake Warsteiner on the export market, and invested £40 million in the brewery in 1994. The previous year, they also launched Köstritzer Schwarzbier, their newly acquired, formerly East German, classic black lager. Bitburger is light, dry, and highly attenuated, but still retains just enough creamy malt body for good flavours. It's lagered for two months, and filtered but not pasteurized. Northern Brewer, Tettnang, Hallertau and Perle hops are used – a very German assembly of complex aroma and flavour varieties. A third of the brewery's output is now on draught, and there's already a Bitburger Bar at the NEC, Birmingham. Here they come.

But the biggest lager import from Germany to Britain is still Holsten Pils, the brand responsible for creating the 'premium packaged lager market' here. Its full name is Holsten Diat Pils: 'Diat' referring to the very low sugar levels that remain, though this is not (and was not intended to be) a low-calorie beer. 'All the sugar turns to alcohol,' as the famous copyline has it, in what the brewery calls its 'secret double fermentation process'. Holsten Pils first arrived in Britain in 1952. It comes from Hamburg, which along with Bremen, home of rival Beck's, is one of the two most important ports in Germany. Hamburg was historically the great hop market, with great cargoes of blossoms cruising in down the Elbe from the now Czech Republic, and great cargoes of beer cruising out.

The German Export

The biggest volume producer among Germany's many brewing cities is Dortmund, home of both the DAB and DUB breweries, among others. Dortmund is also the world headquarters of the strong lager style known as the Export. 'Dortmunder' is a term restricted to those beers that actually come from the city, so some breweries wishing to claim an authentic Export approach just label their beers as 'Dort'. The original Dortmunder Export (now not much made in its city of origin), suffered a dip in popularity because it had acquired a working-class image, but now seems to be on the rise again, despite the fact that Dortmund's big breweries are presently concentrating on clean, dryish mass-market lagers instead, letting other cities develop the style. The Export gets its name from the fact that, like our English IPAs, this was a beer made to withstand the rigours of overseas travel: the Export's medium to high alcohol levels, yet low level of attenuation, leaving lots of malty body behind, and fairly high hop rates (though it's not a dry style) were all designed for successful export elsewhere. It's typically a fuller golden coloured, higher in alcohol, more robustly flavoursome, strong lager. Rather than hoppy, it tends to have a creamy, malt-accented palate, typically with some alcohol flavour.

Bocks and Double Bocks

Stronger yet, lagers high in alcohol are often labelled as bocks, and have alcohol levels of well over 6% abv. But this doesn't mean that the thin, harsh, turnipy and sweet super-strength lagers stacked up in cans in the local supermarket can grandiosely relabel themselves as bock beers: proper bocks and double bocks are characterized by good ingredients, careful brewing, long lagering times, (generally much longer than the standard three months) to produce medium to high alcohol beers of quite a different order. The style originally comes from Einbeck, where at one time there was a self-contained bock industry. Now only the Einbecker brewery remains. Traditionally, these were dark beers, though golden versions are now also common. There are also some top-fermenting examples left, but not many. Classically, bock beers are richly malty and flavoursome. Traditionally, they were produced on an annual, seasonal basis, and the most important season was (and is) late spring, when Maibocks (May Bocks) are drunk in celebration of summer.

Double bocks (Doppelbocks) seek only to outbock the bockiest single bock, and can indeed be almost overwhelmingly bocky. As bock means 'goat' in German, there's sometimes a goat illustration on the label. More commonly, bocks are identified by a name ending in -ator, following on from the example of Salvator, the original double bock. Like its Munich neighbour Augustiner, the Paulaner brewery, makers of Salvator, were originally a monastic brewery, established in 1634, and Salvator was the strong, rich, nutritious beer they brewed to get themselves through Lent. The new season's Salvator is still launched with civic pomp in Munich every Easter. Hence, the double bock is a beer style intended for drinking in spring, to banish late winter. Double bocks are also highly recommended for banishing late winter *viruses*: half a glass sipped at the first signs of a cold will often nip the lurgy in the bud.

Kulmbach is the home of the very strongest bocks, most famously EKU 28, which is lagered in cold storage for a full nine months, and claims to be the strongest beer in the world, even though it's not as strong as many ales. The strongest *lager* beer, perhaps (although, doesn't the Swiss Samichlaus also claim that honour?). You remember the spectacularly unsuccessful attempt to market an Ice Wine (Eiswein) in Britain, years ago? Well, a similar process has long been used to make the Eisbock (also a Kulmbach style), lowering the temperature sufficiently for the water in it to form ice crystals and be sifted out, so concentrating the texture and alcohol levels. Sound familiar?

The fact that most German brewing (and German village culture) is still run on very traditional lines has left other seasonal beers more or less intact. Probably the best-known across the world is the Märzen, or Märzenbier (March beer), a reference to the pre-refrigeration days when March was the last safe month for brewing, before the warmth and the wild yeasts of spring interfered. March beers are traditionally drunk in autumn, having been safely lagered all summer, and, if sticking to the classic model, should be medium-strong, amber lagers with a Vienna malt succulence and mild spiciness. But it's becoming depressingly common to use the Märzenbier term however the brewery feels like it. Austrian 'märzens' are infamously crude variants on the style; they are sweetish, often amber-coloured, but there the resemblance ends. Oktoberfestbiers, brewed for the festival originally held to celebrate the engagement of the Crown Prince of Bavaria in 1810, are frequently (but not necessarily) Märzens.

Wheat Beers

Like pilsener lagers, the wheat beers of Germany fall into two general camps: the more parochial survival of the north, Berliner Weisse (rarely seen in Britain), and the now extremely trendy Bavarian wheat beers, which are drunk, imitated and plastered with supermarket own labels all over the world. The Berliner Weisse translates as a White Beer, but white implies the use of wheat, and Weisse is also a term widely used to describe the wheat-rich beers of the south. White, in the case of Berliner Weisse, though, is a near-literal description, thanks to the use of very pale malt, and wheat, and the fermentation method used.

Widely drunk all over the city in distinctive wide bowled glasses, it's a low alcohol (about 3% abv), sharp and fruity, pale and sparkling beer. There may be as little as 30% wheat in the mash, and hops are traditionally added very late, but what makes Berliner Weisse unique is its lactic fermentation. They ferment the beer using a fusion of a top-fermenting (ale) yeast and a lactobacillus, so creating a tart, acidic character, that softens and mellows with cellaring. Nowadays, though, it's more commonly drunk fairly young with a dash of flavouring in the glass, traditionally green woodruff essence, but now more commonly raspberry syrup or another brightly coloured fruit flavour. Fairly young, in this case, means after three to six months of warm-maturation. Some beers are then also blended, young with old, rather like a lambic. Lactic fermentation, incidentally, is by no means unique to Berliner Weisse. Some Belgian beers use it. And some champagnes: the lactic method is famed for its propensity for turning sharp, raw, green flavours into something creamy and moussey. Which is useful, if you live in northern France, and produce acres of otherwise unusably acidic wine (to say the least). But it's also a good incentive to tidy the Berliner Weisse away into a nice dark cellar for a couple of years.

The Bavarian Wheat Beer (it's mostly a southern style, although other areas produce German wheat beers, including Britain and the USA) is an entirely kinder, softer, more populist creature. Wheat beers in general have been made for thousands of years, and probably originate (in this form) from the days when fields were sown with a mixture of grains, barley and wheat among them. Barley is the most versatile and sweetest of brewing cereals, but of the remaining cereals, wheat, though notoriously difficult to work with, has the most versatility of flavour and texture. Wheat brings all sorts of subtle variants of character to the wheat beer style, but classically a typical creaminess, thanks to the tiny bits of wheat protein in suspension, as well as apple and orange fruit flavours, and citric, zingy freshness. Fruit is given added complexity by the action of the top-fermenting yeast. Clove spice notes are also yeast-created. Yeasts vary with every brewery, but it's always a top-fermenter that's used for the first ('primary') fermentation. Usually wheat beers are only lagered for a fortnight at most, but then go on to a further fermentation in the bottle, in the case of the Hefe (sedimented) style; the Kristall versions are filtered. It's now commonplace to use a bottom-fermenting yeast for the bottle, for a tidier result.

There may be as much as 60% wheat in the wheat beer mash, though some breweries use a lot less. In the north–south divide, it's the south that tends to use the high wheat percentages; the north, true to its taste in lagers, prefers something crisper in texture. And, of course, the main difference between German and Belgian wheat beers is that the *Reinheitsgebot* insists all cereals used be malted. Malted wheat is used in German wheat beers; unmalted wheat in the Belgians, as well as a great variety of spices: added spice or, indeed, added *anything*, is forbidden in the German variety, which must make its fruit, sweet and spice flavours out of yeast action and other perfected bits of methodology.

But the great race to make increasingly delicious and complex examples is a relatively new phenomenon. Twenty-five years ago, wheat beer seemed to be almost on its last legs as a style, looked upon by the fashionable rather as a British foodie looks upon a bottle of British cream sherry. Almost miraculously, it has since become extremely popular, in a way that seems set to endure beyond mere fashion. Partly this is down to its rediscovered deliciousness, lightness and versatility (nothing like a British cream sherry). Depending on the maker, wheat beers can be warming and spicy in winter, quenching and zingy in summer. The latter sort is now more or less the (unofficial) official beer of the German beer garden season. If Bavarians had Wimbledon, they would drink gallons of cool, fruity wheat beer at it. Meanwhile, it has now become the done thing to drink it at breakfast in summer, a tradition that makes all us Brits, conscientiously waiting for the sun to go over the yard-arm before we head for the bottle opener, look a bit feeble.

A whopping 30% of all the beer drunk in Bavaria is now wheat beer, and there are several Bavarian breweries that make nothing else. The classic wheat beer brewery, Schneider, is one of these companies, and they were instrumental in the popularizing of both the light (hell) and dark (dunkel) wheat beer styles, with their Schneider Weisse and Aventinus brands. Schneider Weisse gets its distinctive tan colouring from the use of a little Vienna and dark malt. It's made from 50/50 wheat and barley malt, Hallertau and Hersbrucker hops, and a little hop extract. Aventinus uses caramalt, a kind of crystal malt made in Bamberg, which accounts for the slight smokiness of its chocolatey, fruity, clovey flavours. Aventinus is also, at 8% abv, strictly speaking a Weizenbock. Interestingly, Schneider are now expecting sales growth in Britain on the basis that the reassertion of the cask ale market here has provided fertile ground for wheat beer to really take off. They're already the market leader, despite arriving in Britain only in spring 1994.

In Germany, the best-selling wheat beers are those made by Erdinger, the largest wheat beer brewery in the world. They too only make wheat beers, of a fairly populist, clean-edged sort: a letter from the brewery while researching this guide innocently points out that it's the fact that their beers have fewer hops and more carbon dioxide in them that make them more palatable. (Can't imagine any British brewery being so disarmingly honest.) Erdinger were the first to launch a national German advertising campaign for wheat beer, back in 1970. They use a particularly low-protein wheat variety (less bits, less cloudy) and Hallertau aroma hops in their Erdinger Weissbier, which, like all good wheat beers, is unpasteurized, though it is lightly filtered; *mit feiner hefe*, in other words. They also make a dunkel, and a weizenbock.

Most standard strength wheat beers are in the 5–5.5% abv category. Often there are two wheat beer brands of the same alcoholic strength, very similar but perhaps with different coloured labels, like Löwenbräu's orange and white-badged twins. One will be yeast-sedimented to some degree: the Hefe Weissbier/Weizen. The other will be a thoroughly filtered, Klares/Kristallklar (crystal clear) version. These tend to be a bright, full gold in colour, and have more of a hybrid, wheat beer-lager flavour and texture. They're a good introduction to nervous wheat beer novices, and make excellent summer quenchers in their own right. Some people have been known to drink either sort of wheat beer very cold with a slice of lemon. But not very many Germans.

Altbiers

German wheat beers are strictly speaking ales, though there is little about their flavours that suggests an ale in the British sense. But Germany also has a unique ale style that does have a touch of the British style, and is made all over the world (but particularly in America), the Düsseldorf Altbier. The style isn't restricted to Düsseldorf any longer. These ales are called altbiers (old beers) because they hark back to the 'old' ale brewing style, before bottom-fermentation took the reins of the German beer wagon. Altbiers have been widely enjoyed and copied around the world because they combine classic top-fermentation with cold-conditioning, which is to say, they are made like an ale, but then matured like a lager, although not usually at quite such low temperatures. It's this cold-maturation period that's responsible for the silky, smooth, mellow, rather reined-in and elegant character of the style: there's ale complexity and recognisable ale flavours there, but the fruitier, wilder excesses of the British ale style are prevented. Traditionally altbiers are a rich, dark copper in colour, and have a fairly hoppy character, but not the fruit depth and roundedness of the British ale. Modern American and Japanese altbiers can just as easily be coffeeish with chocolate malts, succulent with amber malts, and only very subtly hopped. Wherever they come from, altbiers are the cleanest and smoothest of the world's ales. If the label promises an altbier, the beer within should have these specific characteristics. Some of those beers simply labelled 'alt' refer only generally to the old style of brewing, the ale style. Others are altbiers proper, but which have politely refrained from using Düsseldorf's own label.

There are at least five other regional specialities Germany can confidently call her own: the smoked beer, the stone beer, the rye beer, the black beer, and the Kölsch. The smoked beer (rauchbier) is a speciality of the area of northern Bavaria called Franconia, and most particularly, the town of Bamberg. A percentage of the malt used in smoked beers is made by kilning it over a real fire; just how much varies from beer to beer. This is an area rich in peat, and in beechwood, which is used in the malting: the smoke passes through the barley grains, more or less kippering them. The best-known brand is Schlenkerla Rauchbier, which is bottom-fermented, and has been made this way since 1678.

A variant on the rauchbier theme is the stone beer (steinbier), which has been made in its modern incarnation only since 1982, when an enterprising brewery saw that a drinking public enjoying the smoked beer style might also appreciate the smoky flavours of this ancient rustic brewing method. The approach dates from the days before metal brewing kettles, when wooden vessels were used. Not being able to put a fire underneath the pot, the beer was brought to the boil by plunging red hot stones into it and heating from the inside. The hot rock makes the malt in the mixture singe and caramelize, and the malty rocks are then added to the conditioning vessel later on, which helps spark off a further fermentation. The Steinweizen applies this process to a wheat beer, as you might expect (though in fact even the Rauchenfels Steinbier is 50% wheat).

Another Bavarian speciality is the rye beer. Rye beers have been made for hundreds (perhaps thousands) of years, and still feature strongly in the Finnish drinking scene, but this example, Schierlinger Roggen (roggen meaning rye) has only been made since 1988. Usefully, the Schierlinger brewery is part of the Thurn und Taxis empire, so the wheat beer yeast used to ferment the roggen bier (which makes it an ale) and the wheat beer wort used to kräusen it are readily available. Schierlinger Roggen is made from 60% rye malt, but is surprisingly (for anyone who's eaten rye bread, at least) light of touch and delicate of flavour.

The fourth regional speciality is the famous black beer (schwarzbier) of the Köstritzer Brewery of Bad Köstritz, in the former East Germany, now owned by Bitburger. This is a bottom-fermenting lager made with dark malts, and has delicious creamy, chocolatey body, thanks to quite modest attenuation. Black beers, like altbiers, are big in Japan.

The final regional speciality, very rarely seen in Britain, is the kölschbier. Kölschbier means Cologne-beer, and this is a trademarked, protected title for the pale, top-fermenting, elegantly fruity, dry-finished ales of Cologne, a city with more breweries than any other in Germany.

Alt Bamberg Dunkel***

50cl Bottled 5.2%:

Ruby-black, dryish, smooth altbier, with tea-style savoury sweetness, and a fat, rich yeasty tang, all subsumed within an elegant malty mellowness. Rather delicious, with a subtle hop finish that develops within minutes into something still soft, but moreish and lingering. *Serve:* room temp/larder cool. *Avail:* specialists.

ARCOBRÄU CORONATOR DOPPELBOCK***
Arcobräu, Bavaria. 33cl Bottled 7.5%:
Rich auburn brown, with a slightly sour-sweet, leathery, yeasty nose, and a you-either-love-it-or-you-don't flavour which has been variously described as strongly tasting of dates and figs, and of Fishermans Friend lozenges; certainly there's something ever so slightly cold-cure-like there. There's also dry malt character, a clean, spritzy texture, but something slightly off-puttingly cheesey in the treacle toffeeish in the finish. *Serve:* larder cool. *Avail:* BeerC.

ARCOBRÄU DUNKLE WEISSE***
50cl Bottled 5.2%:
Hefe (sedimented) wheat beer of cloudy deep amber-brown colour, and Chinese Five Spice and Arbroath Smokey aromas. Wonderfully spritzy and soft, thanks to well-judged bottle-conditioning, with a pure, clear kipper flavour, framed in summery citrus and cooking apple notes in typical wheat beer style. Kipper flavours fade after a little while, allowing cinnamon and nutmeg spice to flower, along with a little soft clove. *Serve:* larder cool. *Avail:* BeerC.

ARCOBRÄU MOOSER DUNKEL**
50cl Bottled 5.1%:
Pungently sweet and sour Coca Cola cube and pear drop sweetie aromas on the nose, along with some chocolate and red wine, raising expectations tremendously. Curiously, the middle is almost absent from this dark lager, though the texture is smooth and firm. Wait half a moment, and just before the finish there comes a great wave of cocoa, plummy fruit and a softly drying hop character. Almost a three-star beer. *Serve:* larder cool. *Avail:* BeerC.

ARCOBRÄU MOOSER HELL**
50cl Bottled 4.8%:
It may sound like a Canadian curse, but actually this is a *Reinheitsgebot*-brewed, bright metallic-gold beer with citric, fresh grapefruity aromas, than grainy and creamy on the palate with sharp but soft fruit, and a little sweet pineapple. Just a tad unclean and sticky at the finish, though? *Serve:* light fridge chill. *Avail:* BeerC.

ARCOBRÄU PILSENER**
33cl Bottled 4.7%:
Simple, tasty pilsener with good barley sweetness in the mouth, and a gently dry, slightly floral finish. Good, sound stuff, if on the under-exciting side. *Serve:* light fridge chill. *Avail:* BeerC.

ARCOBRÄU URFASS***
Premium Hell 33cl Bottled 4.9%:
Orange and lime aromas lead into a deliciously soft, pale and biscuity, creamy malt and butter-toffee flavour, shot through with a little enlivening melon and grapefruit, and a gentle, bittersweet hoppy finish, with an astringent, grapefruit-pithy aftertaste. Rich and satisfying, quenching lager with good structure. *Serve:* fridge cold. *Avail:* BeerC.

ARCOBRÄU URWEISSE***
50cl Bottled 4.8%:
Unfiltered Bavarian wheat beer, cloudy gold in colour, with freshly-squeezed apple juice aromas and a big crusty head, which slowly peters away. A fresh, quenching beer with good understated fizz, and (apple charlotte!) autumnal cooked and spiced apple flavours, a little bready wheat, a little lemon, just a touch of something pleasantly sulphurous, and lots of nutmeg spice at the finish. *Serve:* larder cool. *Avail:* BeerC.

ASDA PILSENER GERMAN LAGER***
Dortmund. 33cl Bottled 5%:
It's DUB! Or is it DAB? Recognizably the Dortmund Flavour, at any rate: a pale, shiny gold lager with pronounced grain store aromas and flavours, fresh and appetizing. Creamy, grainy malt, barley sweetness and firm, but kind hop dryness in the finish. A class act. *Serve:* light fridge chill.

ASDA PILSENER GERMAN LAGER**
50cl Canned 5%:

Reinheitsgebot German canned lager of quality, soft but dry, clean but tasty, with a good fresh hop nose, a spritzy liveliness, and a nice dry hop and husky barley character in the finish, as well as a touch of nectarine-style fruit juice. Not as fresh and immediate as the bottled version, but still an excellent own brand supermarket choice. *Serve:* light fridge chill.

ASTRA

Bavaria St Pauli, Hamburg. 25cl Bottled 4.9%:
Not a car, not a satellite dish, but a seriously disappointing lager, probably having a very bad day. Bakewell tart and golden syrup aromas, with just a hint of something industrial; pronouncedly mineral in flavour, with more than a touch of aspirin. Just a teensy hint of buttery grain before all senses are overwhelmed in a massive hop dryness attack. And more aspirin. Painfully long and lingering. *Serve:* light fridge chill. *Avail:* Asda.

AVENTINUS****

Weizenstarkbier Schneider, Munich. 50cl Bottled 8%:
Strong malt wheat beer, bottle-conditioned. Opaque reddish-brown, with malt loaf and pastille aromas, and lively, prickly sparkle. To taste, slightly sour and smokey (actually it has a decidedly kippered quality), with bags of baked banana, cherry and dark bruised malt fruit, and a little chocolate and warm, musky clove at the finish. A world classic. *Serve:* larder cool. *Avail:* Odd.

BECKER'S EXPORT***

Becker, St Ingbert. 33cl Bottled 5.2%:
Refreshing, malty dryness, a creamy biscuity finish, and ripe buttery barley, all elegantly restrained. *Serve:* light fridge chill. *Avail:* specialists.

BECK'S**

Bier Bremen. 27.5cl Bottled 5%:
Typically mild-mannered, mass-market German export. Soft, pale malty body, lightly spritzy (the beer is kräusened), elusively nutty, with an emphatically dry hop finish. *Reinheitsgebot* – malt, hops, yeast and water only – and wholesome, if lacking in excitement. *Serve:* light fridge chill/fridge cold. *Avail:* widely.

BERLINER KINDL*

Pilsener Berliner Kindl, Berlin. 50cl Canned 5.1%:
Curiously pungent, sweaty, fishy, almost doggy-smelling *Reinheitsgebot*-brewed beer from a major producer. To taste, dry and subtle with a gentle, light texture, a peachy middle which tends to the sweaty again, and a gently floral finish. Very pale. Very dull. *Serve:* fridge cold. *Avail:* Sains.

BINDING EXPORT PRIVAT***

Binding, Frankfurt. 33cl Bottled 5.3%:
Deep golden, classic Export-style lager with toasted grain, honey and over-ripe pineapple alcohol on the nose. Flavours combine sweet, ripe barley with more spiritous alcohol and tropical, guava fruit notes, but also lots of creamy, pale, textured malt body on the tongue. The finish is mildly whiskyish, soft and perfumey like a mellow lowland malt. A refined and subtle Export. *Serve:* light fridge chill. *Avail:* specialists, Selfridges.

BITBURGER***

Premium Pils Bitburg, Eifel. 33cl Bottled 4.6%:
'Klassisch herb', in the classic extra dry style, and an extremely elegant pilsener of great character. Aromatically floral on the nose, pale malt dry-textured softness initially in the mouth, swiftly followed by a compellingly herbal, lingering and deepening finish, with perfumey rosemary and parsley, and fresh green hay notes. Moreish and delicious. Almost a four-star beer. *Serve:* light fridge chill. *Avail:* Asda, Tesco.

DAB**

Original Dortmunder Actien Brauerei. 50cl Canned 5%:
Fresh, wholesome aromas, a soft-bodied malt dryness – terrific texture for a canned beer – and a little herbal flavour in the finish, but too gassy for quaffing. Good with fish pie, though.

Serve: fridge cold. *Avail:* Asda, Co-op, Odd, Tesco.

DORTMUNDER UNION ORIGINAL***
Original DUB (Dortmunder Union Brauerei). 33cl Bottled 5%:
Pale gold pilsener, with a good lively texture thanks to kräusening, and a fresh barley malt nose, vividly grain store-like. On the palate, it starts out with rich buttery grain, developing a husky (slightly mineral) accent, and a hop resiny, slightly austere, perfumey finish. An excellent aperitif pilsener. *Serve:* light fridge chill. *Avail:* Maj.

EDER'S ALT***
Eder's, Grossostheim. 50cl Bottled 5%:
Tastes more like an English bitter than any other German beer in this guide. A top-fermenting altbier, warm-fermented and cool-conditioned, bright golden-amber in colour with a slender head. Aromas are slightly sour and fruity, with chestnut wood and faintly hoppy smells; flavours, smooth and velvety, drily nutty, and very gently spicy. Delicious. *Serve:* larder cool. *Avail:* Beer Paradise, specialists.

EICHBAUM PILS*
Eichbaum. 44cl Canned 4.8%:
Canned version of the beer below, also quite severe, but a bit thinner with an apple fruit note in the finish. Light and tinny drinking. *Serve:* light fridge chill. *Avail:* specialists.

EICHBAUM UREICH PILS**
33cl Bottled 4.8%:
Austere, puritanically dry lager, with a fresh nose and a firm hoppy astringency all the way through, finishing in glowing Extra Strong Mint style. So blinkered in its dryness, it's actually a bit monotonous. *Serve:* light fridge chill. *Avail:* specialists.

EINBECKER MAIBOCK***
Einbeck. 33cl Bottled 6.5%:
Or Mai-Ur-Bock, as it says on the label. Brassy gold-coloured, strong springtime lager with dry, faintly fruity flavours, clingy, creamy pale malt, and a hard, high spirit note in the finish, when more tropical fruit notes also chime in, along with just a moment of that familiar whiskyish flavour that so often accompanies well-made strong lagers. *Serve:* room temp. *Avail:* specialists.

EINBECKER URBOCK***
33cl Bottled 6.5%:
Pale lemony gold beer with a sweet, pale malty, biscuity nose, and delicious, full-bodied flavours, creamy and Madeira cakey, with refined alcohol notes and just a little lemon. There's fruit in the finish, a little apple and melon, leading into a soft dryness that builds into a firm, florally hoppy aftertaste. Decidedly moreish, delicate drinking. *Serve:* larder cool. *Avail:* specialists.

EKU EXPORT**
Erste Kulmbacher Actienbrauerei, Kulmbach. 33cl Bottled 5.6%:
A rather dull and slightly sweaty Export which really only improves in the finish, when flavours develop buttery, grain and vanilla notes, with a touch of potent Export alcohol, leaving apple and nectarine fruit notes in its wake. Otherwise, on the sweet side, a little thin and lacking in complexity. *Serve:* larder cool. *Avail:* Maj.

EKU PILS**
33cl Bottled 5%:
A light but tasty soft German lager, more Bavarian than pilsener in flavours and textures, with creamy pale malt in the mouth, and a sharper, toasted grapefruit citrus edge, with a very gentle hop dryness in the finish. Likeable but modest drinking. *Serve:* light fridge chill. *Avail:* specialists.

EKU (HEFE) WEISSBIER HELL**
50cl Bottled 5%:
Cloudy greenish gold bottle-conditioned wheat beer with a crusty white head and hardly any nose. Clean-edged (rather than creamy) and refreshing, lagerish wheat beer flavours, with bready, grain husky, very mildly orange-squash-like notes. Probably good cold with a slice of lemon. Or orange. *Serve:* light fridge chill. *Avail:* specialists, Selfridges.

Eku 28*

33cl Bottled 11%:
Still labelled as the strongest beer in the world, and it does have the highest original gravity of any regularly brewed bottom-fermented (lager) beer in the world. Rather off-putting aromas of overripe blue cheese (that's esters for you) preface a remarkably sweet, dense, alcohol-rich, caramelized and, yes, estery flavour. Actually we're well beyond mere flavour and into the realms of phenomenon here: that it's almost undrinkable is hardly the point of the exercise. *Serve:* room temp. *Avail:* Somer.

Erdinger Pikantus***

Erdinger, Erding. 50cl Bottled 7.3%:
Bakers yeast aromas rise from this dark russet-amber coloured weizenbock. Flavours offer succulent amber buttered malt, a little spice and oak, something brown-bready, and, after a few moments, alcohol flavours, which are present but not intrusive. Smooth, lively, tasty, strong, dark wheat beer. *Serve:* larder cool. *Avail:* specialists, Selfridges.

Erdinger Weissbier***

50cl Bottled 5.3%:
Bavarian wheat beer, the best-selling brand in Germany, and approachably populist in style. Only very slightly translucently gold, with a delicious sherbety and orange zest nose and flavour, seasoned with a little sweet pineapple. Smooth and creamy, with some sweet malty Ovaltine-like notes; altogether a smooth operator. *Serve:* light fridge chill. *Avail:* Wait.

Erdinge Weissebier Dunkel**

50cl Bottled 5.6%:
Dark sibling to the beer above, darkest ruby in colour with spiky sparkle, blunted malt-cocoa flavours, and a touch obvious with the cough linctus notes, but the sort of cough linctus (Hactos!) that's full of spices and molasses and popular with ruddy-cheeked farmers (or possibly just their cows?). *Serve:* larder cool. *Avail:* Wait.

Frankisches Kristallweizen**

50cl Bottled 4.9%:
Brewed and bottled on behalf of the Scherdel Brewery. Tangerine and Cox apple, with a little sour note in the finish, along with a little oak, wheat cereal notes and touches of warm spice. Extremely gassy thanks to a rather enthusiastic addition of carbon dioxide. *Serve:* light fridge chill. *Avail:* specialists.

Franziskaner Hefe Weissbier***

Spaten, Munich. 50cl Bottled 5%:
Bottle-conditioned Bavarian wheat beer from a historic brewery, one of the great innovators. Amber-coloured, cloudy beer with spritzy, gently sherbety, mild and sweet flavours, offset by clove, orange and vanilla. A dry, clean and refreshing texture means it makes an ideal aperitif. *Serve:* larder cool. *Avail:* Coop, Sains, Somer.

Gilde Deluxe**

Gilde, Hanover. 27.5cl Bottled 5.1%:
Perfectly acceptable, but rather boring table lager, fine for food but too dull for rumination. Deluxe is certainly a misnomer here. *Serve:* light fridge chill. *Avail:* Tesco.

Gilde Pils**

50cl Canned 5.5%:
High marks for a canned lager. Pale gold, soft-bodied, with pale dry-textured malt, balanced by fresh, slightly sour apple notes, and just a touch of piney greenwood. Tongue-tickling tiny bubbles, and a dry hop finish help create a refresher of some character. Surprisingly strong stuff, in all-the-sugar-turns-to-alcohol mode. *Serve:* fridge cold. *Avail:* Asda, Co-op, Safe, Somer, VicW.

Harry D's Cloudy White Pils***

Hofbrauhaus, Friesing. 50cl Bottled 5.3%:
This is presumably a (made for America?) fresh marketing angle on the wheat beer style: there's plenty of talk on the label about the merits of bottle-conditioned, unpasteurized 'white pils' (whatever that is) but this is unmistakably a wheat beer once the top's off the bottle. Milky pale apricot in colour, with appetizingly fresh

aromas, it has a straightforwardly wholesome and uncomplicated orangey character, wrapped in a pleasantly grainy, bread doughy but refreshing flavour. Light, satisfying summer drinking. *Serve:* light fridge chill. *Avail:* specialists.

HB HOFBRAUHAUS MÜNCHEN**

Premium Lager Hofbrau, Munich. 50cl Bottled 4.9%:
Brewed in Munich at the famous beerhall of the Bavarian Royal Court brewery, but bottled in the UK, which is probably responsible for taking the edge off the flavour. *Reinheitsgebot* (malted barley, hops, water and yeast only), and appetizingly golden with a nice German rocky head (which disperses pretty quickly). Yeasty, citrussy aromas; clean tasting with a little hop and barley balance, and a bitter finish refreshed by a tart note. *Serve:* light fridge chill. *Avail:* Odd, VicW, Wait.

HOLSTEN BIER*

Hamburg. 33cl Bottled 5%:
Glamorously plain packaging, in a skinny brown bottle with just a Holsten brewery seal over the cap, raises the hopes overmuch in this case. The single-star rating is a bit wobbly: two samples tested provided (a) a no-star rating and (b) a two-star, so we have settled at a single in compromise. The better bottle was lively, but not overfizzed, with a lemon barley water, fruity, barley ripe flavour and an underlying, gentle dryness, ending with a tart, sweet note. The other tasting was over-sweet, almost cloying, slightly sprouty and vegetal, with a wet cardboard, mineral finish. *Serve:* light fridge chill. *Avail:* Tesco, Thres.

HOLSTEN EXPORT

44cl Canned 4.9%:
Brewed in Britain (actually) under licence, and under *Reinheitsgebot* pure beer rules. Despite this, and the interesting fruity, malty aromas that emanate from this golden beer when it's provoked, there's something sickly in the flavour, and a very dry, wet cardboardy, beechwoody finish which lingers far too long. *Serve:* light fridge chill. *Avail:* Thres, VicW.

HOLSTEN PILS**

33cl Bottled 5.8%:
Far and away the biggest German exporter to our shores. Orange fruit on the nose, with a little barley sugar (you can smell the famously transmogrified sugar-into-alcohol), and a gentle, soft malt and fragrant hop character. Very simple and clean, but the finish is perhaps a little sweet and disappointing. *Serve:* light fridge chill. *Avail:* widely.

HOLSTEN PILS**

44cl Canned 5.5%:
Imported canned Holsten is greatly superior to the made-here 'Export' sort, clean and with no nasty off-flavours, fairly rounded in smooth international style, but with a reassuringly German floral hop finish, and a moreish dryness that chimes in well before the end. *Reinheitsgebot. Serve:* light fridge chill. *Avail:* specialists.

HOPF WEISSE EXPORT***

Hopf, Miesbach. 50cl Bottled 5.3%:
Translucent gold bottle-conditioned wheat beer, with a bubblegummy nose, and just a touch of bubblegum sweetness among its subtle, savoury, apple and pear flan flavours. Plus a little nutmeg, coriander, warm spice, and a sprinkling of dusty white pepper. One of the least sweet, and most elegant of wheat beers. Subtle, light, wheaten doughy flavours grow nutty and brown bready in the last (yeasty) glass. *Serve:* larder cool. *Avail:* BeerC.

KAISERDOM EXTRA DRY**

Kaiserdom, Bamberg. 33cl Bottled 4.9%:
Dry, yes, but not hoppy exactly; more of a persistent, firm bitterness, all the way through, with a warm, Polo-minty finish, growing warmer and mintier with drinking. There's an intriguing apple-like fruit note just before the mint sets in, but otherwise this is so simple and blinkered a beer as to represent a really upmarket mouthwash. *Serve:* fridge cold. *Avail:* specialists.

KAISERDOM PILSENER***

50cl Bottled 4.8%:
A delicately pale gold pilsener of real quality. Flavours combine a delicious creamy, biscuity malt body with a spritzy, prickly texture that carries through into the firm, dry, herbal hoppy finish. There's also a fresh coconut note in the aftertaste. *Serve:* light fridge chill. *Avail:* specialists.

KAISERDOM (HEFE) WEISSBIER ***

50cl Bottled 5.3%:
This wheat beer produced the most fizz, and, the most enormous great duvet of a head. Pour very gently. It's worth the wait. From this richly cloudy, apricot-coloured beer comes an appetizing tangerine and red apple skins nose, and wheaten, brown bready, mildly orangey flavours with plenty of spice and bite, and a grain husky, oaky edge, finishing with honey-baked apple notes. *Serve:* larder cool. *Avail:* specialists.

KAISERDOM WEIZEN KRISTALLKLAR**

50cl Bottled 5.3%:
An undemanding, but ideal introductory wheat beer, golden bright and fizzy, and tasting rather as if Cox apples and oranges have been infused in a tasty, full-bodied lager. Very softly fruity, only mildly wheaten, rich, sweet and clean drinking, with little in the way of grain and hop flavours to complicate matters. *Serve:* larder cool. *Avail:* specialists.

KÖNIG PILSENER**

König, Duisburg. 33cl Bottled 4.9%:
There's not much information on the label, but it does say 'Best Before' in eleven languages. Faintly appley and melony lager with a mildly drying finish, soft and short with a little dusty white pepper. It acquires a drier, even mouth-coating pilsener finish by the end of the glass. Pleasant, quaffable, but forgettable. *Serve:* light fridge chill. *Avail:* specialists, Selfridges.

KÖNIGSBACHER PILS*

33cl Bottled 4.8%:
Surprisingly fruity, sweet lager, with apple and pear juice flavours, slightly overripe, and not reined in sufficiently by the very gently drying finish. Rather fat and flabby where it should be sleek, and not remotely pilsener-like. *Serve:* light fridge chill. *Avail:* specialists.

KÖSTRITZER SCHWARZBIER***

Köstritzer, Bad Köstritz. 33cl Bottled 4.8%:
The 'black beer with the blonde soul', from the former East Germany. Now owned by Bitburger, it has acquired a touch of house style, with wholesome, creamy malt and a firm hop finish at the heart of both, though the black twin is less attenuated and has more body. In fact it's really only brownish black, mildly spritzy, with a scrumptious, satisfying chocolate and cocoa character, offset by faintly porterish coffee and black malt notes, lots of ripe sweet barley, and gentle, floral dryness. It manages to be rich but light, tasty but also eminently quaffable. But still difficult to find in Britain. Come on Oddbins! *Serve:* larder cool. *Avail:* specialists.

KUTSCHER ALT***

Binding, Frankfurt. 33cl Bottled 5%:
Top-fermented but then cold-conditioned, in the classic altbier style. A dark russet ale with lots of dark malt, and coffee aromas and flavours, with dark biscuity character and restrained fruity yeast, and gently drying malt and soft hop flavours in the finish. Smooth, mellow and light, but also rich, with a hint of spice and liquorice as it warms. For goodness sake don't chill it. *Serve:* room temp. *Avail:* BeerC.

LÄMMSBRÄU ORGANIC PILSNER***

Lämmsbräu Neumarkt. 50cl Bottled 5%:
Ostensibly the same beer as appears under the Sainsbury's Bavarian Organic label (though retailers generally get their own brands reformulated to personal tastes), this version presents lovely yeasty citric smells balanced with fresh hop aromas. It is a translucent pale amber in colour (thanks to only light filtration) and offers mouth-filling dry bubbles, swiftly pursued by orange water, floral and herbal flavours, with a little buttery barley, a touch of clove and aniseed.

Delicious and delicate drinking, with a lingering dry finish. But not quite as wonderful as Sainsbury's version. *Serve:* light fridge chill. *Avail:* Odd, Wait.

LÖWENBRÄU HEFE WEIZENBIER**

50cl Bottled 5.3%:

Only very slightly cloudy, populist unfiltered/unpasteurized wheat beer from the best known of the Munich breweries, made with Löwenbräu ale yeast, malted wheat, two-row spring barley and Hallertau hops. It has a clean and spritzy texture, and a fairly sweet, certainly easy flavour, with more zing and fruit (a little lemon, orange, honey) on the nose and palate than its Klares sibling, reviewed below. *Serve:* light fridge chill. *Avail:* Maj.

LÖWENBRÄU KLARES WEIZENBIER**

50cl Bottled 5.3%:

Filtered ('clear') version of the sedimented weizenbier listed above, and a wheat beer style becoming increasingly popular in mainland Europe. First impressions are of a bright sparkling gold beer with hardly any nose. The flavour is only just discernably wheaten; the experience is more like drinking a wheaty lager in general effect. A decent, tasty, smooth and notably clean-edged one, though. *Serve:* light fridge chill. *Avail:* Maj.

LÖWENBRÄU OKTOBERFESTBIER**

Festive Beer 50cl Bottled 5.8%:

Bottom-fermented *Reinheitsgebot* beer, originally brewed for the Münich Oktoberfest in 1994. The nose is slightly boiled sweetish, with a pear drops note and amber malt aromas; the flavour buttery, caramelly, sweet and clean, with a little sultana and orange. There's little in the way of finish, but for a seasoning of hop floweriness. Subtle, light, and dangerously quaffable for a 5.8% beer. *Serve:* larder cool/light fridge chill. *Avail:* Maj.

LÖWENBRÄU PILS**

27.5cl Bottled 6%:

Brewed in Britain (actually), an 'original strength' pils style lager, highly attenuated in the diat style. Most of the sugar has been converted to alcohol, leaving a dry, subtle, very clean beer with little indication of its potency in the flavours. Very gently creamy, with a mild fruit note, and a lasting dry finish, more straightforwardly bitter than hoppy as such. Rather over-subtle. *Serve:* fridge cold. *Avail:* Davies, Maj, VicW.

LÖWENBRÄU PREMIUM BIER**

27.5cl Bottled 5.2%:

Reinheitsgebot-brewed lager beer made from spring barley, Hallertau hops, yeast and water. This Löwenbräu is surprisingly High Brow actually, made in Munich under the Bavarian pure beer law, even though it may sound like something brewed in England under licence. The gentle, soft palate is its main feature, with dry-textured (almost tongue-coating) pale malt, a clean, refreshing quality, and a gentle hop note on the finish. *Serve:* light fridge chill. *Avail:* Maj, Wait.

LÖWENBRÄU PREMIUM BIER*

44cl Canned 5.2%:

Disappointingly tinny and thin canned version of the previous beer. Very mildly malty, with an oddly flavoured, drying finish: this certainly doesn't taste up to its 5.2% strength. Doesn't taste up to much at all, actually. *Serve:* fridge cold. *Avail:* Asda, Tesco, VicW.

MARKS & SPENCER ORIGINAL**

Premium Pils Bavaria St Pauli, Hamburg. 50cl Canned 4.9%:

Made for M&S by a brewery from an area with a tradition of very dry beers (Hamburg is the great local hop market), and this is a typically workmanlike if uninspiring example of St Pauli's canned output. It's *Reinheitsgebot*, at least, containing summer barley and Hersbrucker hops, yeast and water only; the nose is clean and fresh, the flavour soft (if a little thin), with barley and hop notes, the finish good and dry. *Serve:* fridge cold.

Marks & Spencer Premium German Pilsener Lager **

Bavaria St Pauli, Hamburg. 25cl Bottled 4.9%: Brewed in Hamburg but bottled in the UK. Phenolic aromas of an industrial sort disperse after a few minutes, leaving a decent, robust quaffing lager with a good bitter finish, complete with Hallertauer hop 'bite' and a long dry aftertaste. *Serve:* fridge cold.

Neu Brandenburger Pilsner**

Neubrandenburg. 50cl Bottled 4.2%: Pleasant but not inspiring soft German lager, which tastes as if made for the local mass-market rather than serious attention (a sort of German equivalent to the Czech Staropramen). Golden and sparkling, mildly malty, with a gentle hop character all the way through, although not particularly at the end, where there's instead a little red apple flavour. A little thin-bodied, perhaps, but a good value lager to accompany a light supper, certainly. *Serve:* light fridge chill. *Avail:* Tesco.

Paulaner Hefe Weissbier***

Paulaner, Munich. Bottled 50cl 5.5%: Bottle-conditioned wheat beer of a satisfyingly rounded, tasty sort; Paulaner's populist approach has been instrumental in making wheat beers fashionable in America. Translucently pinkish gold in colour, it has sweet apple and spice aromas and a soft creamy head, leading into apple, honey, and warm fresh bread flavours, just a pinch of clove, and a tart sherbet lemon note at the finish. Delicious, easy drinking for a warm summer evening. *Serve:* light fridge chill. *Avail:* BeerC.

Paulaner Original Münchener***

Premium Lager 33cl Bottled 4.9%: Faintly malty and appley on the nose and with initially rather modest, if wholesome flavours, but growing more sumptuously creamy with even a short acquaintance, introducing lemon and hop notes that increase and form a delicious, moreish dryness. A beer with an afterglow of good flavours. *Serve:* light fridge chill. *Avail:* BeerC.

Pschorr-Bräu Weisse***

50cl Bottled 5.5%: Classic Bavarian bottle-conditioned wheat beer, dense amber in colour with a good wheaten haze, and an inviting rocky white head. Swirl the yeast sediment in the bottle and add it to the glass and delightful clove and sweet mandarin aromas rise. Clean and refreshing, but with very little fizz; red apple, pomegranate and dry orange flavours add weight to the farm cider comparison. Wheaten delicacy and notes of clove spice declare it unmistakably not. A perfect partner to fresh apple pie. *Serve:* light fridge chill. *Avail:* Odd.

Radeberger Pils**

Radeberger. 33cl Bottled 4.8%: A sweet, faintly malty nose leads into a spritzy, lively, mildly malty palate, with a mildly hoppy finish. Very mild-mannered altogether, and a bit thin and watery. *Serve:* light fridge chill. *Avail:* specialists, Selfridges.

Rauchenfels Steinbier***

F. J. Sailer, Marktoberdorf. 50cl Bottled 5%: Hot stones plunged into the mash caramelize the malt of this minor classic, creating smokey flavours that have a dedicated following. The nose is only slightly smokey, with buttery malt and fruit, and spice, but the flavours are imbued with an Austrian smoked-cheese-style flavour, though lighter and drier with a darker, tannic, oaky edge, and dried banana chip and vanilla extract sweetness. *Serve:* larder cool. *Avail:* BeerC.

Rauchenfels Steinweizen**

50cl Bottled 4.9%: Stone-brewed wheat beer with a flip-top, like its sibling above, and a similar deep, luscious copper colour. The smoked palate is kinder and softer, with its bready, wheaten flavours, and slightly appley, clovey, warming finish, and it is lighter all round. Consequently, the stone-brewing is more directly evident, and the beer thinner and less interesting. *Serve:* larder cool. *Avail:* BeerC.

RITTER FIRST**
Pils Dortmund. 33cl Bottled 4.8%:
Palest gold, sparkly pilsener with fresh barley grain aromas and clean flavours, with more barley grain notes. It has the most unusual finish, bitter rather than hoppy, with pronounced mint flavours and an afterglow of the Trebor Extra Strong mint sort. *Reinheitsgebot*-brewed, and an intriguing aperitif, though on the dull side until the finish. *Serve:* light fridge chill. *Avail:* specialist.

RÖMER PILS***
Binding, Frankfurt. 27.5cl Bottled 5%:
A popular brand in central Germany, now imported and bottled in Britain. A quality pilsener, with a pale malty, tasty delicacy, good aromas (calvados and hop resins), and a delicious and very dry hop finish with a little mango and pear. Really good drinking. *Serve:* light fridge chill. *Avail:* specialists, Selfridges.

SAFEWAY GERMAN PILSENER***
Dortmund. 33cl Bottled 4.9%:
Reinheitsgebot-brewed, delicious pilsener with a florally herby hop nose, developing fresh green hay over a few minutes. To taste, this well-structured beer starts out with vivid grain store freshness, develops buttery vanilla, and finishes with a drily hoppy, rose-floral, butter toffee, honeyed complexity, which leaves a long drying-hay and herbal aftertaste. Dortmunder Union, no doubt. *Serve:* light fridge chill.

SAFEWAY LOW ALCOHOL GERMAN LAGER
See Sainsbury's German Low Alcohol Lager.

SAINSBURY'S BAVARIAN ORGANIC PILSENER****
Neumarkter Lammsbräu. 50cl Bottled 5%:
Wowee! Wondrous from start to finish, it has delicious (new-mown hay) aromas as it's poured, and a genuinely fresh, buttery barley flavour at the front, but it's the finish that really excels, exploding like a firework to produce complex flavours, at once buttery, creamy, floral, fruity, with spice and vanilla to season. Clean, but not conventionally dry, it's more properly composed of strands of flavour that together create a dryness, with just the right degree of sparkle and vitality. Organically produced barley and hops; unpasteurized and with only a light filtration. *Serve:* light fridge chill.

SAINSBURY'S DIAT PILS**
Hanover. 44cl Canned 6.2%:
Strong, bocky lager from the great Bock region itself. Bright yellow-gold, with a fresh apple and pineapple smell, it's clean and refreshing at the first gulp, drying on the palate as it goes down, in a soft, pale-malty way, but with a distinctive strong alcohol barley-sugary fruit sweetness, perhaps over-emphasized in the canning procedure. Low in sugar, in the true 'diat' style. *Reinheitsgebot*-brewed. *Serve:* light fridge chill.

SAINSBURY'S GERMAN LOW ALCOHOL LAGER**
Binding, Frankfurt. 33cl Bottled 0.5%:
Clausthaler, the best low/no alcohol lager in the world. Fresh grain aromas and flavours, mild-mannered but clean in the mouth, it's fully brewed, and *Reinheitsgebot* (water, barley malt, hops and yeast only). Surprisingly beer-like considering it has almost no alcohol, and it's low in calories too (85 a bottle), so excellent for fat drivers. *Serve:* fridge cold.

SAINSBURY'S GERMAN PILSENER***
Hofbrauhaus, Brunswick. 33cl Bottled 4.9%:
Bright, yellowy-gold pilsener from the Royal Court Brewery of Brunswick, in northern Germany. Grainy, lemony aromas, and just the right kind of fizz and sparkle. Delicious and delicate flavours, florally dry and citric on the finish. Emphatic perfumey hop character lingers on the palate, stopping just this side of austere. Moreish. *Serve:* light fridge chill.

SAINSBURY'S HEFE WEISSBIER**
Hof, Bavaria. 50cl Bottled 4.9%:
Brewed for Sainsbury's by the Scherdel brewery. Translucent gold, with a dense foamy white head at the start, and barley

grain character offsetting the delicately bready, wheaten quality. Just a little too grain husky. But it does have an appetizing slight sourness, and warm clove notes at the finish. *Serve:* light fridge chill.

St Magnus Heller Bock***
Allgauer Bräuhaus. 33cl Bottled 7%:
Reinheitsgebot-brewed bock beer with strong, alcoholic, mildly lowland whiskyish flavours (and colours), but also very elegant and restrained. Flavours are delicate, with faint coconut notes and an almost mead-like honey liqueur character, sharpened by a touch of soft lemon, before drying impressively in the finish. A delicious sipping beer, rich but refreshing, thanks to its very gently spritzy texture. *Serve:* larder cool. *Avail:* specialists and Selfridges.

St Pauli Girl**
St Pauli Girl, Bremen. 33cl Bottled 5%:
Reinheitsgebot-brewed lager with perryish, pear fruit aromas, and a palate that suggests cracker-dry and creamy pale malt, and a firm but gentle hop finish. But doesn't get much beyond suggesting them. A bit thin and ordinary. *Serve:* light fridge chill. *Avail:* specialists, Selfridges.

Salvator****
Paulaner, Munich. 33cl Bottled 7.5%:
A tasty, drinkable double bock, the original and best. It's a clear, dark amber, with appetizing roasted malt and fruit aromas. Flavours are similarly delicate, with soft malt and fruit richness, a natural dark sugar note, plum and orange, and just the faintest hop finish, with subtle, sweet alcohol. *Serve:* room temp. *Avail:* BeerC.

Scherdel Doppelbock**
Hell Scherdel, Hof. 50cl Bottled 7.5%:
Fearsomely strong, dark-golden lager beer, with a blackcurranty nose that grows appley as it warms in the glass, and fruity, alcoholic flavours, with a little roast swede sweetness, but also vanilla, butter-toffee, tropical fruit notes and a good whack of tannins. Concentrated in flavours, but unfortunately it also grows flabby and cloying, and lacks structure for a beer of this strength and scope. *Serve:* larder cool. *Avail:* BeerC.

Scherdel Premium***
Pilsener 50cl Bottled 4.7%:
Pleasingly puritanical pilsener refresher with a fresh, appetizing nose and a hoppy, dry, slightly savoury grain flavour well balanced with a pale, creamy malt body; the finish lingering and with a pink grapefruit twist. Moreishly dry; very good at six o'clock with crudités and nibbles. Won the Gold Medal at the IFE London Beer and Cider International summer 1995, in the pilsener lager class. *Serve:* light fridge chill. *Avail:* BeerC

Scherdel (Hofer) Weissbier ***
Hell 50cl Bottled 4.9%:
Full peachy gold in colour with a big fluffy head, and appetizing sherbety, fresh orange aromas. In the mouth, an uncomplicated summer quaffer, with freshly-squeezed tangerine flavours, juice, pith and all; a more sophisticated winey note, and then growing wheat-grainy with faint hop notes in the finish. The last glass is the best: when the yeast is swirled and added, and more pithy, savoury, grainy notes and a leathery background flavour are introduced. *Serve:* light fridge chill. *Avail:* BeerC.

Scherdel Weizen**
Kristallklar 50cl Bottled 4.9%:
Yellow-labelled, filtered wheat beer, amber gold and overly fizzed, but otherwise similar to the Scherdel Hofer Weissbier reviewed above. Except there's more pear fruit, with subtle clove and mild, smoky spice, drying at the finish. *Serve:* light fridge chill. *Avail:* BeerC.

Schierlinger Roggen***
Bavarian Rye Beer Thurn und Taxis. 50cl Bottled 4.7%:
Bottle-conditioned rye beer, of cloudy reddish-amber hue, and a sticky rye-bread nose and a spritzy bottle-conditioned texture. Apply rye

bread flavours to the general German wheat beer style and you have it: grainy, yeasty, mild and milky-sweet savoury flavours, but also a discernible smoked ham flavour, though of a subtle, light sort. Thin-textured, possibly, and elusive (even, dare we say, dilute), with no real finish to speak of perhaps, but a classic none the less. An acquired taste, certainly. And excellent with smoked ham sandwiches. *Serve:* larder cool. *Avail:* Tesco.

SCHLENKERLA RAUCHBIER***
Bamberg. 50cl Bottled 4.8%:
Bottom-fermented 'smoke beer', brewed this way since 1678, in the baroque town of Bamberg, Franconia. Smells like the warm remains of a chestnut log fire, and tastes strongly of those aromas, smokey with fatty smoked Austrian cheese-style flavours, robust and mouth-filling, with a strong, dry, woodsmokey, gently kipperish aftertaste. *Serve:* larder cool. *Avail:* Odd, Sains, Wait.

SCHNEIDERWEISSBIER****
Hefe Weizenbier Schneider, Munich. 50cl Bottled 5.4%:
Bottle-conditioned Bavarian wheat beer, translucent mid-tan in colour. Initially a great duvet of a head, which fizzles away, leaving classic wheat beer aromas and flavours: wheaten and bready, sweet pear, tart fruit, soft orange, a little spice and a lovely honeyed finish. Quite gassy, not for gulping. May cause uncontrollable cravings for spicy German sausage. *Serve:* light fridge chill. *Avail:* BeerC, Odd.

SCHOFFERHOFFER HEFEWEIZEN***
Schwangen, Schwetzingen. 50cl Bottled 5%:
Unfiltered, translucent gold wheat beer with only a very light yeast sediment. A spritzy, lively texture '*das nach Sommer schmeckt*', as the label says, and delicious flavours of tangerine, lemon, delicate bready wheat, a little clove and coriander. Clean but creamy, wholesome tasting. *Serve:* light fridge chill. *Avail:* BeerC, Odd, Safe.

SCHOFFERHOFFER WEIZEN***
50cl Bottled 5.1%:
The filtered version (white label) does a good impression of a sparkly gold pilsener in the glass, and has a pils-ish ripe barley aspect, though the nose is yeasty and fresh with a little spice, and there's plenty of delicate clove and nutmeg in evidence, before the clean hoppy finish. Excellent aperitif material, perhaps with a slice of lemon. *Serve:* light fridge chill. *Avail:* BeerC, Thres.

SCHONBRAU*
see Marks & Spencer, BRITAIN

SOMERFIELD BAVARIAN WHEAT BEER**
44cl Canned 5.3%:
That's not a typing error, no, and this is a CANNED wheat beer, yes. Expectations were not great. But – surprisingly – this is a decent, if slightly neutered, wheat beer, authentically hazy and apricot gold, with a sweet tangerine, bready, spicy nose and palate. Refreshing, clean, an ideal summer beer, though not exactly quaffing material at 5.3%. Perhaps very cold, on a shady verandah, with a slice of lime, a cane chair, and the latest Joanna Trollope? *Serve:* fridge cold.

SOMERFIELD GERMAN PILSENER***
Jever. 33cl Bottled 5%:
An own-brand supermarket pilsener of class from one of the finest German pilsener brewers. Clean, but full-bodied and tasty (tasty but not too sweet), properly lagered, mature, smooth and mellow beer with an arrestingly hoppy, dry finish, and a hard grain edge that really works. Wholesome, *Reinheitsgebot*-brewed, moreish. *Serve:* light fridge chill.

STAUDER***
Spitzen Pilsener Beer Jacob Stauder, Essen. 33cl Bottled 4.6%:
Reinheitsgebot-brewed pilsener with a barley-sweet nose, and barley grain-soaked, sunshine flavours. It's a subtle beer, softly malty with an apple note, just a touch of floral hop resin, but then the dry finish comes in like

a low flying aircraft in the hills, seemingly from nowhere, and leaves a positive glow of soft astringency, which builds and moves into the middle before the glass is empty. Firm, likeable, wholesome drinking. *Serve:* light fridge chill. *Avail:* Tesco.

T.A.G.**
Jacob Stauder, Essen. 33cl Bottled 5.3%: A curious raw-potato-juice-like quality hangs around the nose and flavour of this palest gold Rhineland pilsener. That aside, there's also dry malt and a little floral hop to the aroma, and a soft-bodied, textured pale malt flavour, at once dry and gently fruity, that's pleasing and moreish. The finish is oddly unclean, but fairly pleasantly so. *Serve:* fridge cold. *Avail:* Safe, Sains, Tesco, VicW, Wait.

TESCO GERMAN PILSENER***
Dortmund. 33cl Bottled 4.9%:
Good northern pilsener with clean, barley malt, freshly hoppy flavours and a decently dry finish. In the familiar tall green bottle of the Dortmunder Union. *Serve:* light fridge chill.

TESCO WHEAT BEER**
Hefeweiss 50cl Bottled 4.9%:
North Bavarian wheat beer, brewed by Scherdel, *Reinheitsgebot*, and ostensibly bottle-conditioned, though it seemed curiously flaccid and limp in tasting. Still, on the bright side, there are appetizingly yeasty, orange marmaladey aromas, and a mild-mannered, sweet-dough wheaten, slightly orangey flavour. 'Sallright. *Serve:* larder cool/ light fridge chill.

THURN UND TAXIS (HEFE) WEIZEN**
Thurn und Taxis, Regensburg. 50cl Bottled 5.3%:
Bottle-conditioned wheat beer with Cox apple, tangerine and clove on the nose, a spritzy, refreshing texture, and flavours more savoury than sweet, but fruity: reminiscent of pomegranate. The finish has lots of wheaten grain-husky flavour, clove warmth and masses of coriander and pepper: too much, actually. One of the least sweet mass-market wheat beers. *Serve:* larder cool. *Avail:* Tesco.

THURN UND TAXIS (KRISTALL) WEIZEN ***
50cl Bottled 5.3%: A really tasty example of the filtered 'crystal clear' wheat beer at its best. Rich, clear gold in colour, with a huge foamy head that takes a minute or two to disperse, and tantalizing aromas of summer fruit, honey and a very faint tarry smokeyness are a good start. Flavours are sherbety, sharp and sweet, with both tart and ripe orange, honey, that slight tarriness again, and soft, gentle hop finish. Rather yummy. *Serve:* light fridge chill. *Avail:* Tesco.

WAITROSE BAVARIAN PILSNER LAGER***
33cl Bottled 5.1%:
Phenolic aromas thankfully settle and give way to a clean, bitter, slightly prickly and dry mouthful with a more interesting finish in which buttery barley, hop resins and floral notes grow expansive and lead into a lingering astringency. *Serve:* light fridge chill.

WAITROSE GERMAN LAGER*
Hessen. 33cl Bottled 4.8%:
Reinheitsgebot-brewed, with an appealing floral and citrus nose, and old gold colour, but a less impressive flavour. Grainy, clean and refreshing, rather than interesting, with a short finish. *Serve:* fridge cold.

WAITROSE WESTPHALIAN LAGER***
33cl Bottled 5%:
From a province in the north-west of the country, bordering the Netherlands, and with Dortmund, a great brewing city, at its heart. Pale in colour, with an aromatic yeasty nose, and extraordinarily floral, hop resin and husky barley flavours (almost too savoury in effect), with a pot pourri, superdry and lingering finish. Spritzy, but also very soft-textured, with drying pale malts and huge handfuls of fresh hops, it's almost briney and a little austere for lazy palates. *Serve:* light fridge chill.

WALKABOUT BAVARIAN HELLES BEER**

44cl Canned 5%:
The German can in the Walkabout variety pack of four beers, the others being British (not at all bad), Belgian (pretty dire) and Italian (a bland strong dark lager). But the Bavarian is a decent canned lager, with barley, honey and lemon on the nose, grainy barley flavours, a creamy, almost coconut softness and mild hop dryness, with good floral character peeping through. *Serve:* light fridge chill. *Avail:* Wait.

WARSTEINER**

Warsteiner. 33cl Bottled 4.8%:
Germany's best-selling brand. A little disappointing: Bitburger class it's not. Not a pilsener-style lager at all, in fact, but a softly fruity, faintly apple-juicey, mildly-malty beer with a husky hop finish. Perfectly acceptable, but terribly dull. *Serve:* light fridge chill. *Avail:* specialists.

WELTENBURGER KLOSTER**

Berock Dunkel 50cl Bottled 4.5%:
Smokey-brown, softly malty, light and spritzy, almost like a good British Mild in flavours, with a definite malt accent, a fruity note, and a very gentle finish, full of soft water character but with a faint hop dryness. Subtle, kind and comforting. *Serve:* room temp. *Avail:* specialists.

Greece

Greece's historic links with Germany were in large part responsible for the Greeks, like the Norwegians, having a beer purity law which forbade the use of unwanted ingredients. This strictness has now been relaxed. At the same time, demand for beer in Greece is at an all-time high: 23% of all purchased drinks are now beer, far outpacing all other alcoholic drinks available. Breweries are responding by producing more and more lowish-alcohol, refreshing lagers of little character, intended to be thoroughly fridge-chilled and drunk very cold. Being low in alcohol, these products are also fairly cheap, though the breweries make their expected, standard 5% abv bland international bottled beers too. There are only three brewing companies: Athens Breweries (three breweries, 3 million hectolitres a year), Henninger Hellas (also three breweries, but only half the output), plus Löwenbräu Hellas, with just one plant and an output of around 1 million hectolitres.

Aegean

Lager Beer Northern Greece Breweries (Henninger Hellas), Thessaloniki. 33cl Bottled 5%:

The ingredients list is promising: water, malt, hops and yeast only. It looks nice: golden and fizzy. But this beer tastes oddly cereally for a 'pure beer', grain semi-sweet, thin, with a hard, husky, almost savoury edge, and a dryish, lemonadey finish that's also decidedly mineral in character. Tastes like it's been in the bottle too long (and perhaps it has). *Serve:* fridge cold. *Avail:* BeerC.

India

Partly because of its colonial past, India has a surprisingly well-developed brewing industry. Its beers tend to be lagers of a sweetish sort (ideal for partnering spicy foods) and of the thin and clean textured type, for refreshment in high temperatures. There are no beers worthy of serious attention, but one or two drinkable ones. Cobra is brewed entirely for export. Kingfisher, which has been marketed heavily at the Indian restaurant trade in Britain, is also made here under licence; it's a classic two-star, clean and fairly tasty, drinking-with-curries beer, but difficult to find in bottle. Lal Toofan, the other brand available in Britain, was until recently also sold in Indian restaurants, but has the benefit of being a genuine import, in bottle at least (the draught version is made by Ushers in Wiltshire). Its distributors are just beginning to look to British retail outlets, a move prompted by the astonishing statistic that in the first ten months of its availability, Lal Toofan sold 1 million pints. It's brewed by four subsidiaries of Shaw Wallace & Co. Ltd, Calcutta, now India's second-largest brewery group. They also make lager brands called Haywards, Royal Challenge, Taurus, Typhoon and Black Prince. Lal Toofan, which has only been exported to Britain since late 1993, is typical of the Indian approach to lager brewing, using a high percentage of rice, as well as Indian maize, plus at least a proportion of barley and hops. High rice and corn levels are competently managed, producing a refreshing, spritzy, crisp lager, good for washing down a poppadom but not designed for much closer scrutiny.

COBRA*

Indian Lager Mysore Breweries, Bangalore. 33cl Bottled 5%:

Brewed for export to Britain. Perhaps stock is lying about too long: both samples tasted had a slight, but harsh, phenolic note and a hard mineral finish, though orange water struggled through on the nose, and the middle seemed decently sharp and clean, if a little thin, bland and fizzy. Perhaps, though, it's a bottling/ export-handling problem. You might be luckier. Then again, you might not. *Serve:* fridge cold. *Avail:* Wait.

LAL TOOFAN**

Indian Pilsener Beer Skol Breweries, Uran, Maharashtra. 33cl Bottled 4.8%:

'Red Storm' is effectively packaged and designed for export, with its striking frosted glass bottle and ethnic typeface and graphics. It's pale and fizzy, with a distinctive rice-brewed palate, though this thin, savoury grain flavour is flattered by lots of melon fruit, and a pinch of ginger, leading into a peppery hop finish. Refreshing and clean. *Serve:* fridge cold. *Avail:* specialists.

Indonesia

Bintang**

Bintang. 32cl Bottled 5%:
Indonesia's export brand is a golden lager with an appropriately pineapple and coconut nose, and lots of appetizing tangerine aromas. Flavours are creamy with good malt presence, biscuity on the tongue, but otherwise light and refreshing, soft-bodied and slightly sweet, drying with a tart note in the finish. *Serve:* light fridge chill. *Avail:* BeerC.

Ireland

There's probably been brewing and the production of other alcoholic drinks in Ireland since the Bronze Age. Beer was always made, but distilling was the most persistent of the old vernacular Irish traditions. By the early 17th century, so great was the proliferation of stills that King James I decided something had to be done. The introduction of licensing came in 1608, and the first licence was issued by the King's Lord Deputy in Ulster, Sir Thomas Philips, to himself, for Old Bushmills, which is consequently the oldest licensed whiskey distillery in the world.

The oldest surviving brewery in Ireland is Smithwicks of Kilkenny, established in 1710, and now part of the Guinness empire. Guinness was founded in 1759. By the 1770s, such was the scale of the success of the 'new' beer style, porter, which had been imported from London, that there was more than a mild panic among Irish breweries. It seemed for a time that the English porter style was the only beer the Irish would ever want to drink. But Guinness started its porter brewing in 1799, and the rest is history. By 1820 they had launched a second, 'Extra Stout Porter', the grandfather of the modern stout style, and didn't stop making porters altogether until 1974. They were not alone in the Irish stout and porter market. Beamish & Crawford, of Cork, had been founded in 1792, and Murphy's followed in 1856, by which time the original English rival was well and truly vanquished. This pre-eminence was enhanced by the international (but particularly Australia-, Canada- and America-bound) migration of the Irish people, and at home by the fact that the Irish brewing industry escaped the near-shutdown of the mainland brewing industry during the First World War. The popular conviction that Guinness is Good For You, and the historical accident that partnered the poverty oyster diet with cheap, nutritious stout – and found them ideal partners – have also helped boost the Guinness phenomenon. Even today, half the beer consumed in Ireland is stout, and beer is still a crucial part of the Irish economy. Over 80% of the malting barley crop grown goes straight into whiskey and beer production. Only one pint in nine is imported. And over a million visitors a year list a trip to the famous 'singing pubs' of Ireland as one of their top tourist priorities.

Guinness today is very much in charge of Irish brewing. Bass may have an Ulster brewery outpost (churning out millions of gallons of Caffrey's Irish Ale), Heineken may own Murphy's, and Courage may own Beamish, but

Guinness is master of just about all else it surveys. Hilden Brewery, in Northern Ireland, is not simply the only microbrewery on the whole island, it's also the only independent brewery of any size, anywhere in Ireland, north or south.

When Arthur Guinness came to Dublin from County Kildare in 1759 he had only £100 to his name, a legacy recently awarded from his godfather's will. He used the money to buy a defunct and badly-equipped brewery at St James's Gate on a 9000-year lease, with an annual rent of £45. (Guinness are at pains to point out that the rent has since risen. But a 9000-year lease! What a committment for a small business.) In the 1770s, porter (so called because it was the favoured drink of the market porters of Covent Garden) arrived in Ireland and effectively displaced the Dublin Ale Arthur had been brewing. The new beer was initially called Entire, because it came from one barrel, specially brewed to have dark, roasted flavours; until then the dark style had to be blended from three different ales, and was often called Three Threads. By 1920, production in Dublin had reached a dizzy 3 million barrels, and it was decided that a London brewery would have to be built. The then green field site of Park Royal in north-west London was chosen, 100 acres in 'almost pastoral surroundings', previously used as an agricultural showground which had been visited by King Edward VII in 1903. The design of the new brewery was finally awarded to Sir Giles Gilbert Scott, better known for his Battersea Power Station. The brewery took three years to build, before opening for business in 1936.

Almost all the Guinness brands we buy in Britain are brewed here, at the Park Royal brewery. This includes the successful canned Draught Guinness, launched in 1989 after five years, 100 discarded prototypes and £5 million had been lavished on developing the widget, a Guinness invention. Shortly after it was launched into the marketplace, all the other big breweries were maniacally cutting open the tins to find out how they did it (idle speculation, but probably not far off the mark). In 1991 Guinness earned a Queen's Award for Technological Achievement for their widget . The mass-market widget beer – bane of the beer taster's life when it's used to 'recreate the taste of draught beer in the pub' – is, in short, all their fault, but 'Draught Guinness' has the advantage over many massacred English ales in being fairly at home in a sea of micro nitrogen bubbles. The Guinness widget (or 'in-can system') works by placing a plastic chamber with a minute hole at the bottom of the beer can. The can is then pressure-filled with beer containing dissolved gas. Once the can is sealed, pressure pushes some of the beer into the plastic chamber. When the can is opened, the pressure drop in the can forces beer and gas out of the chamber through the tiny hole (hence tiny bubbles), causing the characteristic surge (have that glass ready).

Guinness are by no means confined to brewing in Britain and Ireland. Their list of countries under the heading Guinness Brewing Worldwide Presence Around The World starts with Australia and end 46 lines later with Zaire. Many of these associations are straightforward licensing agreements, though there are Guinness-owned breweries in Africa and Malaysia. Of those 46 countries, there's a particular Guinness presence in obscure corners of Africa and the Tropics and, to a lesser extent, the West Indies. In a similar vein, the list of Principal Brands at the back of the annual report includes the 29 Scotch whiskies as well as other spirits (like Gordon's gin) which come under the United Distillers banner, various foreign beers – some owned abroad (like Cruzcampo, Spain, and Red Stripe, Jamaica), others brewed under licence, like Carlsberg and Budweiser – and a 34% stake in Moët Hennessy, the champagne and cognac company. Worldwide sales continue to surge forward, particularly in continental Europe, and most particularly in Italy. Group profit before tax for the six months to June 1994 was £320 million.

The foundation of this fortune is the Irish Dry Stout style, a stouter, bigger-bodied, drier variant of the original porter beers of the 18th century. Guinness Stout, easily the best of the surviving Irish stouts, is brewed with all natural ingredients – no corn, no sugar. It's made by first milling the malt and roasted barley and mixing it with flaked barley before mashing. Each mash is left to infuse for about 70 minutes, and takes 19 hours to drain off. The resultant wort is then boiled with the hops for 90 minutes, before filtering and chilling to 17°C, after which it goes into the fermentation vessels where the yeast is added. The unique Guinness yeast strain is officially top-fermenting, but seems to like a half-and-half position best; in suspension, it gobbles up sugars in a very even-handed way, and has underneath-fermenting mellowness to add to above-fermenting fruit complexity. A little of the wort is taken aside and kept at a low temperature, ready to be used later for blending. The remaining wort ferments for 40 to 60 hours, and the carbon dioxide made by the fermentation is collected, purified and liquefied, before being used again in the dispensing system for draught Guinness. The young beer is then cooled and centrifuged to remove the yeast, before being transferred to storage vats in the Vat House, where it's left to mature for just a few days. It's here, in the Vat House, that the blending takes place (using the wort reserved from earlier on) to ensure consistency of product. Foreign Extra Stout gets a good deal of its complexity from being blended – old ('stock') ale and young green beer together. After blending, the Guinness is packaged up ready to go.

Guinness make their stout for export, as well as in overseas breweries. The Guinness made for America is stronger than the British version. The Guinness made for Belgium ditto. The Guinness made for Germany is pretty terrible, as roast unmalted and flaked barleys are not permitted to be used under the malted-cereals-only rules of the *Reinheitsgebot* (even pure beer laws have a downside). Tropical stout, of a dizzying strength and a fruity, alcoholic intensity of flavour, has been specially made for the Caribbean since 1800. All good stouts have a malt body (from the high level of unfermentable, highly roasted malt and barley) and a generous level of hopping in common, and Guinness has these, albeit adapted to the demands of the mass-market. Heavy hopping was also, of course, a procedure designed to preserve the beer during long journeys to export markets or in a long maturation in wood anywhere. Prolonged wood maturation is also responsible for that elusive but distinctively stouty 'horse blanket' aroma and flavour which results from a positive, welcome sort of microbiological infection with the famous Brettanomyces. Something muskily, woodily, warmly horsey (get your snout under that warm saddlecloth!), in collaboration with a yeasty acidity, are the flavour factors that, together with rich (but also burnt toasty) malty body and hop dryness, make up the quartet of the classic stout characteristics.

But Irish Ale generally doesn't mean dry stout when referred to across the world. Export markets understand an Irish Ale to be smooth, amber malt-sweet variant on the English bitter, and of characteristically 'red' hue, though often this means more of an auburn tint. The malt accent, like that of Scotland's beers, is down to the agriculture of a barley-growing, whiskey-making climate too hostile for hop gardens. 'Irish Ales' of this specific sort appear in Belgium, France, Australia and Canada, but proliferate particularly in the United States, where the microbreweries are developing more characterful Irish Ales than have probably ever been seen in the home country, effectively culturing up a world beer style from very little substance. Kilkenny Irish Beer (Smithwick's is based in Kilkenny) is widely exported by Guinness, as is the Smithwick's brand itself. Better examples have a buttery succulence. The French Irish Ale, George Killian's, is top-fermenting and 6.5% abv; it's made by Heineken at their Pelforth brewery. Another version, using lager yeast, is made by Coors in the States. The rights to use the name were cannily granted by a member of a defunct family brewery, Lett's (the licensing body is George Killian Lett), in County Wexford.

The Irish Ale we see in Britain is generally a smooth, blandly-sweet product of one of the old family breweries that now form the subsidiaries of Guinness, most likely Cherry's or Smithwick's; the other is Macardle. Since absorption into the Guinness empire, they have begun to use roast barley in their beers. They also use varying degrees of corn syrup, an adjunct ideal for creating smooth, blandly-sweet, light-bodied canned products.

BEAMISH DRAUGHT**

Beamish & Crawford, Cork. 44cl Canned 4.2%:

As the advertising is at pains to emphasize, this is the only Irish stout that is made only in Ireland, although the brewery is owned by Courage, and thus, ultimately by Foster's of Australia. It is 'caskpour' widget beer which makes a pretty black and beige picture in the glass. Beamish is a chocolate malt (rather than roast malt) led beer, so I was expecting something bland and sweet, and was surprised to find vaguely sweet, but also treacle-toffeeish and hop aromas, and vaguely sweet, but also figgy, tarry flavours, with a decided cough mixtureish note. Some malted wheat is used for creamy lightness, and some German (Hersbruck) hops are used among the Goldings and Challengers. But the chill required of the widget is death to these warm, dark, generous flavours. And the widget cream is so dense it makes you thirsty. *Serve:* fridge cold. *Avail:* widely.

CAFFREY'S IRISH ALE

Caffrey's, Co. Antrim. 44cl Canned 4.8%:

A new canned contender in the arena of Irish fashion beers (or as the major players would see it, the Irish traditionals) from Bass's Irish brewery. Supposedly made to a traditional recipe, and 'matured longer than other premium ales', but also 'specially brewed to be enjoyed cold'. In other words, another horrendous hybrid between a shaving foamy widget lager and a light ale. Caffrey's makes a pretty picture in the glass, but tastes of almost nothing, other than very faintly malty, very faintly dry. With Caffrey's, Bass have jumped on the Guinness bandwagon: this beer is all about dreamy Celtic marketing, and not about flavour and character. Which is just as well. *Serve:* fridge cold. *Avail:* widely.

CHERRY'S DRAUGHT BITTER

Guinness. 44cl Canned 3.7%:
Brewed by Macardle Moor, a 200-year-old brewery now part of the Guinness group. And it's a typical Guinness product, insofar as there's more texture than flavour, thanks partly to the 'Guinness-in-can-system'. Madeira cake and sweet buttercream on the nose, and a flavour that's similar, with pronounced vanilla extract, nutty, sweet flavours, creamy and supersmooth. There's no contrast in the finish, which is consequently on the cloying side. We're instructed to chill it for two hours, which only adds to its problems. *Serve:* fridge cold. *Avail:* Wait.

ENIGMA

Draught Lager Guinness. 44cl Canned 5%:
The name (sorry, the *concept*) is a clear candidate for another brilliant advertising campaign, but unfortunately there's little Pure Genius at work in this product. It's awfully pretty, though, photogenically golden, with a crisp half-inch of white head. There's lots of texture, but little flavour, and it comes across more like a widgetized, creamy whipped-up draught 'lite' ale than anything else. Vaguely hoppy, grain husky, a tad sweet, but all experienced through a now familiar veil of nitrogen fog. *Serve:* fridge cold. *Avail:* widely.

FOREIGN EXTRA STOUT****

Imported Guinness. 33cl Bottled 7.5%:
The complex and strong Guinness stout the world has enjoyed, now imported in response to great demand. Pretty strong by stout standards, it's also more complex than almost anything else you're likely to taste under the stout and porter banner. The difference is apparent from the very start, in its much sweeter, fruitier nose, with orange notes and heaps of vanilla. Burnt blackcurrants, black coffee, fresh pod vanilla, liquorice, citrus, mocha chocolate and treacle toffee congregate on the palate, but there's also a ravishing astringency, which creates a beer both rich and quenching. A classic. *Serve:* larder cool. *Avail:* Asda, Sains, Tesco.

DRAUGHT GUINNESS**

44cl Canned 4.1%:
The famous flavour is stunted by canning and over-chilling (they recommend at least three hours in the fridge), but draught canned Guinness still falls naturally into the ranks of two-star beers, and can't help edging towards the three-star rankings, despite itself. The sheer weight of good ingredients propels it forward: no other stout brewery uses so much roast barley, for a start. The widget gizmo produces a million teeny micro-bubbles, so very numerous and insubstantial that the stout doesn't actually feel fizzy in the mouth. Once settled out, this dramatic black beer, with its small creamy head, has the texture of cold Gaelic coffee and, despite the widgetized creaminess, distinct dark coffee beany, burnt toast, espresso, bitter chocolate and (finally) arrestingly dry hop flavours signalling through the fog. *Serve:* fridge cold. *Avail:* widely.

GUINNESS DRAUGHT BITTER

44cl Canned 4.4%:
They really should stick to their traditional product. This whipped-up widget bitter, burnt orange in colour with a pretty creamy head, starts unpromisingly in giving off dream topping aromas. It's sweetish, malty, slightly caramelly, with a little woodiness, and barely any hop flavour until the finish. Monotonous, cloying and oddly synthetic-tasting. *Serve:* fridge cold. *Avail:* widely.

GUINNESS EXTRA STOUT**

44cl Canned 4.2%:
The Northern Irish version, made in Dublin but canned in Belfast, is familiar stuff, coffeeish, with dark malts, and drying roast grain and hop flavours in the finish. No widget, so

refreshing rather than creamy. Drinkable, but just a bit dull. *Serve:* light fridge chill. *Avail:* Northern Ireland.

GUINNESS FOREIGN EXTRA STOUT**

Guinness Nigeria. 55cl Bottled 8%:
Not to be confused with the plain Foreign Extra Stout that's not brewed in Nigeria to tropical strength, or with the Guinness of the same strength, but completely different character, that's brewed in Dublin for Belgium (Guinness Special Export). This Guinness has rich, concentrated flavours, pungent, musky alcohol, root vegetable and something cough linctus-like among its fig and prune, liquorice and black coffee. Almost overwhelming. *Serve:* room temp. *Avail:* BeerC.

GUINNESS ORIGINAL***

33cl Bottled 4.3%:
Everyone complains that Guinness Original isn't what it used to be now that it's no longer bottle-conditioned, which is true, but this is still a delicious beer. Its texture is prickly dry and refreshing, nicely offsetting the dense, deep coffee and liquorice flavours, and the finish is full of vanilla succulence. An excellent choice to accompany a cold chicken or sandwich lunch. *Serve:* larder cool (not fridge chilled, as they suggest on the label). *Avail:* Asda, Sains, Tesco.

GUINNESS SPECIAL EXPORT****

33cl Bottled 8%:
Absolutely glorious, rich and delicious Guinness stout made in Dublin for Belgium, as commissioned by the famous John Martin of Antwerp. Fresh chocolate truffle, sweet vanilla, coffee and strawberry on the nose prepare the palate for the silkiest, mellowest, most quaffable of 8% abv beers, with rich but refined coffee, chocolate (masses of chocolate), cream and vanilla, a sweet, fat yeasty tang, and, as it warms, a seductive strawberry-fool flavour. All reined in and restrained by a firm but kind hop floral bitterness in the finish. So why must we reimport this classic beer from Belgium? *Serve:* room temp. *Avail:* specialists.

HARP

Guinness. 50cl Canned 3.6%:
According to the can, 'brewed and matured by traditional methods, from the original recipe perfected by German brewmaster Dr Muender'. According to the *Guide*, a bland, gassy mass-market beer with husky grain, a little barley sugar sweetness, and no finish to speak of, other than the faintly mineral, grain husky echo of a cheaply-made lager. *Serve:* fridge cold. *Avail:* widely.

HARP*

44cl Canned 4%:
The Harp lager that Guinness brew in and for Ireland is not only slightly stronger, but a far superior product, verging on two-star status. This isn't saying much, certainly, but at least this version has a little flavour, and a mildly barley-butter note in the finish. They use Irish barley and Hallertau hops. *Serve:* fridge cold. *Avail:* Ireland.

KALIBER*

Guinness. 44cl Canned 0.05%:
As alcohol-free as drinks get: apparently apples have more alcohol in them than this. Made of water, malted barley, sucrose, hops, yeast, carbon dioxide and E405 (stablilizer). Nothing unusual there. Fully brewed, rather than constructed from the bottom up, as it were, which may explain why it's the UK number one in this category. Flavours are similar to a standard weak lager, faintly appley, with a gentle hop note in the finish, but also an aftertaste that grows decidedly sticky with knowing: caused by the sucrose, no doubt. *Serve:* fridge cold. *Avail:* widely.

MURPHY'S IRISH STOUT*

Whitbread. 44cl Canned 4%:
Whitbread's entrant in the Irish Ale stakes, brewed in England and Wales under licence from Heineken, who own Murphy's of Cork. The Draughtflow System widget gives this dense black beer its pretty beige head, which has the intended staying power. Unfortunately the flavours don't. It's very mildly stouty, beyond the nitrogen micro-fizz, and is

required to be served far too cold, only improving as it warms a little, when bitter notes along with the expected bitter chocolate and black coffee flavours chime in half-heartedly (perhaps to be expected of an ale that prides itself on not being bitter). In short, Murphy's tastes like a sort of neutered Guinness. *Serve:* fridge cold. *Avail:* widely.

MURPHY'S*

Whitbread. 50cl Bottled 4%:
Brand new as I write, this bottled version of Murphy's Stout contains one of the new generation bottle widgets, but unfortunately the sample bottle was a dud (the perils of making beer technological), and what fell into the glass (with a thud) was consequently a bit of a blackish-brown pond. Flavours and textures reflected this, though probably when on form this is a classic two-star beer. Flavours show more promise than the rather dire canned version, with rich black coffee, lots of bitter dark chocolate, a yeasty note, and a short, bitter (as opposed to hoppy) finish. But it's a pity it still needs to be chilled. *Serve:* light fridge chill. *Avail:* Asda.

SAINSBURYS STOUT**

Cork. 44cl Canned 4%:
Widget-free supermarket own-label stout, brewed in Cork for Sainsbury, presumably by Beamish, though it doesn't taste much like either Beamish or Murphy's. There's no head to speak of, and it falls into the glass rather limply, like something on its way to being flat. The flavour's sweetish – black coffee with three sugars – with chocolate and vanilla, and a squeeze of citrus, before drying gently at the finish. All very kind and moderate, but the texture lets it down. *Serve:* larder cool.

SATZENBRAU PREMIUM PILS*

Guinness, Belfast. 44cl Canned 5.5%:
Rather self-regarding, smartly-packaged canned lager, marketing itself to Northern Irish fans of the 'all the sugar turns to alcohol' style. Amber gold in colour, it has a mildly sweet and beery nose, but tastes of . . . virtually nothing. A bit fizzy, fairly smooth, with the faintest echoes of strong lager character, but echoes only. And the finish is a bit tinny. A strangely absent lager (not even the answering machine is on) as quaffable as pop. And just as complex. *Serve:* fridge cold. *Avail:* Northern Ireland.

SMITHWICKS**

Guinness. 44cl Canned 4%:
Auburn canned ale made in Ireland. No head, hardly any nose, and very modestly flavoured, but this is a very likeable beer, subtle rather than bland, with a refreshing, quiet dryness that builds in the finish into an almost austere, quininey astringency. There's lots of tonic water-like flavour on the aftertaste, too: a sharp, dry, mineral twist that's moreish. *Serve:* larder cool. *Avail:* Ireland.

SOMERFIELD GENUINE IRISH STOUT**

44cl Canned 4.1%:
Brewed in Cork for Somerfield, presumably also by Beamish. Widget bearing, so it needs to be chilled: the reward is a decorative creamy head. Flavours are biscuity, faintly coffeeish, with sweet tarry notes, cold tea and pastille flavours, all whipped up into a creamy froth. Mild and inoffensive, but oversweet. Chilling doesn't help. *Serve:* fridge cold.

STEIGER LAGER *

44cl Canned 3.3%:
Very cheaply packaged, in a luridly coloured tin, but the flavours, though undeniably modest, are at least more detectable (and more honest) than the pretentious Satzenbrau stablemate's. Clean, quaffable table lager with just enough buttery cereal in the finish to stop it being completely featureless. *Serve:* fridge cold. *Avail:* Ireland.

Israel

The Israeli brewing industry is easy to describe. Currently it consists of just one product: Maccabee, a kosher beer made in the factory-friendly conditions of the new Netanya industrial zone. The brewery, Tempo Beer Industries (established 1954, also make soft drinks and plastics) act as sole agents for Heineken in Israel, but Maccabee has a comfortable grip on 90% of its home beer market. It's one of the very few alcoholic drinks made in Israel.

MACCABEE**

Tempo Beer Industries, Netanya. 33cl Bottled 4.9%:
Kosher lager made from malt, cereal, hops and water, with fresh aromas and more than a hint of green bean on the nose. Slightly apple juicey, thin and clean, suggesting a high corn and/or rice content. Refreshing rather than interesting, it's notably fresh and clean-edged, inoffensive stuff. But increasingly difficult to find in Britain: nothing political, surely? *Serve:* fridge cold. *Avail:* specialists.

Italy

As far as much of Italy's youth is concerned, wine is hopelessly old-fashioned, unhip, uncool, and strictly for their parents generation. Perhaps, when they too are too decrepit to ride a scooter, at say 35, and have to give in to the conformist pressures of old age, they will also give in to their native wine culture. But until then, they are beer drinkers.

Beer has become extraordinarily fashionable in this wine-drinking, wine-making country, which only started brewing 120 years ago, when Anton Dreher kick-started the industry here. Italian beer is fine, but those seeking extra style points at the street café should equip themselves with a beautifully-packaged import. German, Czech and English beers are all popular here, and all things Scottish are deeply trendy, but Northern French styles are particularly 'of the moment': not for nothing is the 75cl bottle of Lutèce bière de Paris smothered in Italian language information. In the wake of all this, Italian breweries are beginning to produce their own versions of European beer styles, almost all of them lagers of various sorts and colours: malty lagers, brownish Munich lagers, reddish Vienna lagers, and in one case even a red Irish ale. Many are doppio malto – strong beers – intended for posing with in public places, and savouring rather than quaffing. Italy's native beer style is very much for quaffing, though.

Italian lagers found in Britain are almost certainly going to have come from either Moretti or Peroni. Peroni is the biggest company, and responsible for the very widely exported Nastro Azzuro. Moretti was an old family company, but is now owned by Labatt of Canada. Both companies make the classic Italian bottled (always bottled) lager, which is gossamer light, with a distinctive mineral water texture and flavour and a characteristic lively spritzy fizz. Malt and hop flavours are rarely much in evidence, and yeast never is. The emphasis is on the clean and refreshing, and these are certainly ideal beers for washing down a pizza or pasta dish; beers that make little comment of their own when faced with strong flavours. The newest Italian lager to reach our shores, Menabrea, has been available in Britain only since spring 1995; previously only a local beer, the product was launched nationally in Italy and in the United States in the same month. It's made by the brewery of the same name, which was established in 1860, and is now Italy's only wholly Italian brewing company. The importers are directing its marketing at the 'premium' end of the bottled lager market, where so far, they say, 'Italian beers are only notable by their absence.'

MENABREA**
Menabrea, Biella. 33cl Bottled 4.8%:
Palest gold beer with an initially Persil-white fluffy head, and lots of Italian lager character: very mildly malty, with a notably robust, mineral water finish. It has the driest aftertaste of all the Italians available in Britain, almost pilsenerish, hay-like, dry and lingering. But otherwise a classically Italian spritzy refresher. *Serve:* fridge cold. *Avail:* specialists.

MORETTI**
Birra Friulana Moretti, Udine. 33cl Bottled 4.5%:
Light, fresh and spritzy in the classic Italian style, slightly appley and crisp, but also just a little watery and thin, with a lingering white peppery, hop finish. Altogether a perfectly decent summer barbecue quaffer: surprisingly full-bodied (even though it isn't) for an Italian 'pilsener' (which it isn't either). Brilliant label, though, complete with Moretti's trademark moustachioed drinker. *Serve:* fridge cold. *Avail:* BeerC, Wait.

NASTRO AZZURO*
Peroni. 33cl Bottled 5.2%:
Cereal sweet aromas emerge from this delicately pale gold beer, but flavours are less easy to detect and name – surprisingly, since it's of slightly above-average strength. This is a beer so serious about not offending anyone that it barely tastes of anything beyond a spritzily clean and refreshing, ever so slightly hop-tinged mineral water. Which is probably exactly what was intended. *Serve:* fridge cold. *Avail:* Asda, Maj, Sains, Tesco, Thres, Wait.

WALKABOUT: ITALIAN DARK LAGER BEER*
Walkabout Pack 44cl Canned 7%:
This strong dark Italian lager should have been the highlight of the Walkabout Pack of canned beers from around the world (others are Belgian, British and Bavarian), but has the twin problems of (a) not tasting anything like a 7% abv beer, and (b) tasting like a beer too strong and potentially complex to contemplate canning and chilling. Dark, malty, with plenty of Vienna lager spice, but also a bit tinny, it improves as it warms, but not enough to save the day. *Serve:* larder cool/light fridge chill. *Avail:* Wait.

Japan

They've had Western-style beers in Japan since the late 19th century, but it's only recently that, as in other disciplines, the Japanese are seeking to perfect and rationalize the science of brewing in their own image, and take it back to the world marketplace. Now that 75% of all alcohol sold in Japan is beer, and Belgian Trappist imports have a cult following, who knows what could happen next?

Japan has four huge breweries, and one smaller one. The big three – Kirin, Asahi and Sapporo – control 90% of the home market. Then there's Suntory at number four, with Orion trailing behind in a very late fifth place. It's probably Sapporo we know best in Britain, but at home Kirin is the undisputed giant of Japanese brewing, besides being one of the world's biggest brewing companies. Japanese interest in making beer dates from the arrival of Americans bearing bottles in the 1850s. Kirin, originally an American venture, was the first to be founded, and is now in Japanese hands. Sapporo was the first all-Japanese company, established in the 1870s when the government was determined to create business on the northern island of Hokkaido. Sapporo town was designed by an American.

Just a few years ago, Japanese brewing could be described in a few words. It was a simple affair, producing one or two rather quaint hangovers from the 19th century, perhaps, but otherwise taking its cue from American mass-market products, brewing to impeccably hi-tech specifications, lagering for 4 to 8 weeks, and coming up with a stable of only very slightly different, but all characteristically super-clean lagers. However, things are now becoming intriguingly complicated by recent cultural developments in Japan. Firstly, to distinguish all these canned and bottled lagers from each other, and in response to the young Japanese beer-drinker's craving for novelty and chic, the megabreweries started to launch seasonal beers, new ones every year: a spring collection, say, mirroring the structure of the fashion business. This was (and is) a huge success. But because Japanese breweries effectively operate as an oligopoly, there was actually a disheartening uniformity of approach, packaging and price. Only the most afflicted fashion victims were truly happy.

In fact, the change goes beyond simple fashion. Japanese youth seems at present to be, rather belatedly, going through a period of questioning the old order, and are making declarations about their own individuality. Individualism is a rather novel (and to many, extremely subversive) concept in Japanese society, but in this case it's not so much a 1960s influenced movement, as a 1960s–1980s hybrid, expressed as much in terms of consumer choice as ideology: not so much flower power as label-power.

So what happened next? The young Japanese, having been primed to expect change and value something new for its own sake, stampeded off in search of beers so different and so new that they weren't even Japanese, and the breweries were given a rather hard lesson in the dangers of creating a fashion-led beer market. They still hold sway in their own country, certainly, but they are aware that this hold might not be permanent. Their assumptions have been questioned. They're nervous. So Japanese breweries are now looking to the export market in an urgent and wholehearted way.

Meanwhile, imports are flooding into Japan. The 'reassuringly expensive' sort are very popular as a statement of one's affluence. The cheaper ones are also very popular, for more obvious reasons. Simple fashion created a craze for Corona, a cheap yellow Mexican beer that barely tastes of anything, and the demand for something wacky has proved to be enormous: Crazy Ed's Cave Creek Chili Beer, from the USA, complete with a whole chilli in the neck of the bottle, has been an unprecedented hit. In response, a whole new network of discount *sakaya* (wine and spirit stores) has sprung up to service the insatiable craving for better and more unusual world beers at reasonable prices. Sensing a major craze at work, the big breweries have started importing masses of beer as well, so now there's even more flooding into the country. Belgian ales are apparently very hot this year.

The advent of the Japanese microbrewery is also making a huge impact. It was actually illegal to set up a small brewery in Japan until 1994. For reasons that aren't even clear to the Japanese themselves, a law of 1940 permitted brewing only on a huge industrial scale, producing a minimum of 2 million litres a year. At the time there were only two breweries in the country, Kirin and Dai Nihon Biiru, which later split into Asahi and Sapporo. There are now 37 breweries, averaging 200 million litres a year each. But in 1994 the law was amended, lowering the limit to 60,000 litres, in line with *sake* production rules. Now, Japan is enjoying its first flowering of independent, local micros making what translates as 'local beer' (*ji-biiru*). Actually, it's been a painfully slow start: it will take some little while for Japanese bureaucracy to catch up with demand. Meanwhile, enterprising American microbreweries – or rather their agents and wholesalers – are moving in to fill the gap between fashion and availability. One or two are even making beers specifically tailored to the Japanese market. Contract brewing is also burgeoning, with Japanese non-brewing beer companies springing up like daisies, and commissioning beers of their own from the American microbreweries. A famous speciality beer bar on the island of Hokkaido (where Sapporo are based, and for which they are also making 'local beers') has recently commissioned a small US brewery, Rogue Ales in Oregon to produce 'English-style' beers: White Crane Bitter Beer, North Fox Red Beer, Brown Bear Black Beer, all in prettily painted bottles, have been the result. Like Sapporo, the other big breweries have responded to the success of *ji-biiru* by re-packaging their usual beer range in a variety of 'local' liveries for local markets, changing the labels to reflect regional customs, names and wildlife. They also continue to experiment with various world beer classics, in the search for something with mass-market potential. German altbiers are being worked on at the moment: the combination of an old European style, a top-fermenting ale, with cold maturation, creates beers of rich flavour, but also a mellow smoothness that particularly appeals to the Japanese palate.

Kirin's flagship brand is its Kirin Lager Beer, now being made under licence abroad (including here) and embarking on a major marketing push. Made with Hallertau and Saaz hops, it has the fullest flavour of the Japanese 'pilsener style' lagers, and is apparently lagered for a full 8 weeks. It's Japan's number one brand, though now closely followed by Asahi Super Dry. Like the other big breweries, Kirin also makes a Black Beer, a bottom-fermented very dark lager style that appears to have been imported by German brewers about a century ago. Dark (but clean) malty lagers and liquoricey stouts might also be in the range, as well as perhaps a nutty (but clean) Vienna amber lager, and a whole selection of pale beers, from the delicately hoppy to the delicately malty (or, from the Czech Republic to Bavaria, but only in the most mass market way). Kirin's products tend to make prominent use of (very fashionable) English on its labels: its new canned Ice Beer is a case in point. It happens to be contract brewed in America, by Anheuser Busch. Another of their new canned products is Kirin Shout (also in English with Japanese subtitles), a tremendously spritzy summer thirst quencher packaged like lemonade.

Asahi, which used to be number the three brewery, has now nudged Sapporo out of runner-up position, and reduced Kirin's share from its decades-old 60% to just under 50%, a fact that's caused upheaval and soul-searching in the industry, because it's pretty much done it with just one product. Asahi Super Dry helped create the huge beer boom of the late 1980s (people still talk about the Dry Wars of 1987 in hushed tones) and its phenomenal success has now given the company the confidence to export to Australia, where a deal with Foster's has provided a ready-made distribution network. The Dry style – a creature bred for texture as much as flavour, super-clean, drying in the mouth, and almost bypassing questions of flavour and finish – is one that Japan can proudly claim to have given the world. Whether or not we are grateful is another matter. Asahi Super Dry has now officially disappeared from all national British retailer listings, owing to lack of interest, and is thus not listed in the tastings below. (Yesterday's fashion – we're into ice beers now.) But I can tell you it tastes of virtually nothing, instead concentrating on a mouth-drying, tongue-coating texture that scores one star for novelty and none for pleasure.

Asahi's more recent launches include a Germanesque (in marketing at least) 'beer-hall style' canned beer called Nama Itcho. Nama Itcho is the idiomatic name for a glass of fresh, unpasteurized draught lager as sold in the beer bars. Unpasteurized, micro-filtered keg lagers are the norm in Japan. But

Asahi also makes a rich and sweet black beer, and a top-fermenting stout. Sapporo is best known overseas for its spritzy but rather hit and miss quality lager, Original, and even better known for the post-modernist tin it comes in. They make more characterful lagers for the home market, and also a famously good, coffeeish and malty black beer. There's also Baisen, meaning 'deep roasted' (it's made with coloured barley), and Kuradashi (meaning matured) canned beers, among other brands. New developments include a winter beer, The Winter's Tale (not actually much different from their other products), Calorie Half, a malty low-alcohol lager, and Ginjikomi. Ginjikomi is the first example of a new style that treats the barley grain in the same way a grain of rice is prepared for *sake*-making, removing its outer husk entirely before brewing, and just using the soft, mild, inner heart of the grain, for a naturally smoother, cleaner, subtler flavour and texture. Perhaps we'll get this next, once both Ice and Dry are finally declared obsolete.

Suntory are better known internationally for having the world's biggest whisky distillery, and they only started brewing 30 years ago. Their products have had a rather uneven quality, but the company are also great innovators, and the world may yet come to know and appreciate at least one Suntory invention, perhaps their very creditable Japanese Wheat Beer. Suntory's Malt's brand name beer has been a great success (soft and malt-accented as the name suggests), and their canned ice beer, Hyoten Chozo, was actually launched in Japan before the American ones arrived *en masse*, and perhaps because of this is richer and more bitter than the now-accepted US model of super-mellowed out innocuousness.

KIRIN**

Kirin, Tokyo. 33cl Bottled 4.8%:
Made by Charles Wells of Bedford (actually) under licence. Pale amber, with a sweet, roasted-parsnip nose, and sweet on the palate too, in a rich buttery style which couldn't be more contrasting with the Japanese Dry Beer model. It's also a little barley sugary, and has no finish to speak of. Made by 'the traditional Japanese recipe of blending rice with the finest malted barley and hops'. *Serve:* light fridge chill. *Avail:* Asda, Safe, Sains, Tesco.

SAPPORO*

Imported Draft Beer Tokyo. 50cl Canned 4.7%:
The Alessi kettle of the canned beer world, in its distinctively-shaped silver tin. The aroma is fruity, with subdued, warm undercurrents. The sample tasted had a flavour that started out just like the bottled version, if a little creamier and with a coffee bean note, but was then quite suddenly invaded by a spiky off-flavour, with wet cardboard and damp dog combined. *Serve:* fridge cold. *Avail:* widely.

SAPPORO**

Original Draft Beer Tokyo 33cl Bottled 4.7%:
Clean, sweet and (cornflakes) cereally at the front, with a honeyed, golden syrup note, swiftly followed by a mouthdrying textured finish which makes craquelure of the tongue, like a super-ice beer. Texture eventually overwhelms the flavour altogether. *Serve:* light fridge chill. *Avail:* BeerC, Thres, Wait.

Korea

Crown Super Dry*

Chosun Brewery, Seoul. 33cl Bottled 5.1%: 'Dry' is the word that dominates the label here, in recognition of the Japanese love affair with the dry beer style. It's made of corn and rice, as well as barley and hops; nothing unusual there, but in truth a cup of lapsang has more structure than this. Not remotely dry, other than in having no finish at all, it has sweet and husky grain, a little savoury rice water, and a slightly resiny character, initially light and fizzy, but losing its vitality too quickly and turning limp in the glass. *Serve:* light fridge chill. *Avail:* BeerC.

Luxembourg

Luxembourg, not to be confused with the bordering Belgian province of the same name, is a tiny country and has just five breweries. Historically its lagers are German in influence. There's a pure beer law of sorts, although it also admits adjuncts – more of a natural beer law in effect. Adjuncts feature strongly, especially in the lighter, cheaper lagers, which get their thin body from a corn content that might be as high as 25%. Present-day commercial trends are keenly observed in Luxembourg, as in just about everywhere else, and their exported lagers tend to be of a bland, international sort, typified by Mousel, the second-largest brewery's 25cl bottled beer. These are beers that have much more in common with the light, refreshing character of a bière d'Alsace than with Germany. The classic Luxembourg brewery range includes a so-called pilsener, or light lager, plus a stronger lager approximating the Export style, and a bottom-fermented product of the Bock sort. The better beers show strong German influence, at least. The biggest brewery is called Diekirch; their biggest brand, a bottled lager called Diekirch Pils.

Henri Funck**

Lager Beer Brasserie Nationale. 25cl Bottled 4.8%:
Strongish alcohol, sweet aromas with grain and citrus, and the flavour is also dominated by potency, despite its 4.8% abv. Alcoholic sweetness, with just a hint of roast turnip, leads into sweet and savoury, honey and butter grain huskiness, followed by a gently dry-malt finish. The aftertaste is a little pungent and tannic. In effect, a conventional strength lager displaying Export characteristics. *Serve:* light fridge chill. *Avail:* Asda.

Mousel

Premium Pils 25cl Bottled 4.8%:
Two samples from different sources were both afflicted with the same problems: wet dog, slightly chloriney aromas, a touch of TCP on the palate, a little bitter grapefruit pith in the finish. Either there's a bottling/keeping problem here, or this is just a terrible beer. *Serve:* light fridge chill. *Avail:* Safe.

Mexico

South America is not particularly renowned for its beers in Europe, but this is a region of the world with a major brewing heritage and an active brewing culture. Brazil, for example, has over 100 breweries, or did at the last count, but that's not allowing for inflation. Despite this, we see little Brazilian beer in Britain, although for a time there was a brownish black, tasty lager called Xingu, brought over by Victoria Wine. Possibly England wasn't ready for a stout-dark lager supposedly brewed by Amazonian Indians. In general, Latin America is awash with what we might sociologically label Blue Collar Beer – cheap and cheerful stuff for mass consumption rather than gastronomic attention. Ancient German influences have their own echoes, but only in the most dilute way. Most of the beer is a light, quaffable working-class drink, typically corn- and adjunct-rich, with the great majority of brands distinguishable only by their label.

Mexico, however, was not only the first South American country to get its own brewery (back in the 16th century), but it is now confidently staking out its own territory. Ever since the first mediocre bottled beer became an overnight sensation in the southern states of the USA, Mexican breweries have been aware of two things. One: their extremely cheaply made, working man's beers have an inverted snobbery chic among rich kids everywhere. Two: as this seems to be what sells abroad, there's a strong case for making lots more beer like this, and giving up trying to make beer that Germans would like. The German and Austrian brewing culture is a particular focus of standards here, a legacy of empire and the work of its colonial brewers during the last century.

Not every brewery in Mexico is churning out dreadful rubbish in tall glass bottles, but enough *are* to have created a bit of a syndrome in Mexico's brewing culture. The first brand to cross the border into the perverse territory of western fashion was Sol, which comes from Moctezuma, Mexico's main export brewery. A lot of rice (and also corn) is used to create the light, thin thirst-quenching quality America appreciates so much. Sol is a seriously mediocre beer, but is nothing like so unbelievably dreadful as the current (or possibly passé, by now) bottled export, Corona, a thin yellow corn-based lager that tastes only of all the money and effort saved, and which has taken the north by storm.

Moctezuma, apart from making Sol for export, brews better beers for the home and speciality overseas market, notably Dos Equis. Cuauhtemoc, Mexico's second-largest brewing company and sibling to Moctezuma, makes a range of lagers of varying quality, like Tecate, but including the drinkable

Bohemia (named, like other Bohemia and Bavaria companies and brands around the world, to lay claim to authenticity of style). Modelo, the largest of Mexican breweries, turns out a fairly predictable range of beers, the standard of which is raised several notches by flagship brand Negra Modelo, a rich, creamy, chocolatey dark lager with a much more deserved international following than most other well-known Mexicans. Mexico likes dark lagers, of the (brown) Munich and (amber) Vienna type, a passion partly originating from Germanic and Austrian influences, but continuing to thrive because the soft, clean, chocolatey character of the Munich style, and, most particularly, the buttery, gently spicy flavours of the classic Vienna lager go so well with robust, spicy food. Most of the rest of the Mexican brewery range is typically made up of bland international lagers of the quaffing sort, reflecting the priorites of a hot and dusty country.

CORONA

Extra Modelo. 33cl Bottled 4.6%:

If there were also minus star ratings, Corona would have plenty of medals to wear. Palest yellow gold, with a curiously resiny smell and slightly pine resin flavour, it's otherwise emphatically bland and watery, flat and lifeless, with a starchy, cereal and raw potato peelings finish. Extraordinarily, this cheaply made, blue-collar Mexican beer has become a laddish cult in the USA, and is terribly popular with beer fashion victims here. Or was. The wind has changed. *Serve:* fridge cold. *Avail:* Odd, Thres.

DOS EQUIS XX**

Moctezuma. 33cl Bottled 4.8%:

Copper-red Vienna-style lager with faint hints of banana on the nose, and a bland, cereally, semi-sweet flavour, offering a little dark and chocolate malt, but with a hard, mineral-water edge, and a drying, slightly tannic (corn-influenced) finish. Drunk too cold, it approximates the English fizzy keg beer style quite well. *Serve:* larder cool/light fridge chill. *Avail:* BeerC, Tesco.

NEGRA MODELO***

Modelo. 33cl Bottled 5.3%:

'Special black beer' in an exciting plump cone of a bottle. In fact it's more very dark amber than black, with shades of both the Munich and Vienna lager styles – the first soft and chocolatey, the second nutty and spicy. There's banana, pear and dark malt on the nose, and flavours combine the soft, cocoa notes of Munich with buttery, amber malt succulence, complete with sultana, a touch of fruit and Vienna spice. All this expressed in the most subtle, spritzy and refreshing way. *Serve:* larder cool/light fridge chill. *Avail:* specialists.

SOL

Moctezuma. 33cl Bottled 4.1%:

Another Mexican fashion brand. Sunshine yellow, high-rice and corn beer, with lots of bubbles, an encouragingly tropical fruity nose, but a discouragingly watery, bland, slightly flowery (stale pot-pourri) flavour, redolent of fizzy water with a slice of lemon, gone warm in the glass. A bit dish-watery, even, as if it were made from the fourth or fifth mash (you really can't get away with using a teabag this often). Truly has nothing going for it except fashion. Dos Equis is a three-star beer compared to this. *Serve:* very cold. *Avail:* Asda, Sains, Wait.

TECATE

Cuahtemoc. 35.5cl Bottled 4.5%:

Either something has gone wrong somewhere along the line, or this is a seriously bad beer. Phenolic and industrial aromas and flavours, TCP and nail varnish, with just a hint of old vegetables, and very little lager flavour underneath. *Serve:* light fridge chill. *Avail:* specialists.

Netherlands

The Netherlands has as long a beer tradition as anyone else in this corner of northern Europe, but has also suffered more than most from the dreaded rationalization of the post-war years. By 1975 (also a turn-around period in many other brewing nations) there was pretty much only Heineken left, plus a clutch of survivors turning out mostly rather dull beers in the Dutch regions. But things have improved since, in leaps if not bounds. Historically, artisanal brewing in the Netherlands has been a southern tradition, a feature of the traditionalist, rural, Catholic provinces bordering Germany and Belgium, but a small number of the 20 new breweries that have sprung up in the last ten years are scattered across the sober, Protestant north. Even so, there are still only 32 breweries in the entire country, some of them extremely tiny.

Heineken remains the undisputed giant of Dutch brewing, closely followed by our own Allied Breweries' Oranjeboom. The remaining 30 names comprise a mix of old medium-sized companies and a pleasing crop of more adventurous, newer, smaller ones: the microbrewery has arrived, albeit discreetly. It's Heineken, though, which holds the real power in Dutch brewing. Famous for their merciless takeover and closure programme, they have also ensured their ultimate control of the distribution network in the Netherlands. Allied/Oranjeboom has carved its own comfortable niche, but is none the less dwarfed by Heineken, which happens to be the world's number two brewery, after the USA's Anheuser Busch. The American is comfortably ahead on volume, but Heineken is the world's biggest exporter (Busch having so vast a home market to contend with). Heineken was founded in 1864, and is still partly family-owned. It took over its neighbours and rivals Amstel in 1968, and still uses a different yeast (in fact, a different brewery altogether) to make the Amstel lager brands. Heineken lager, now called Heineken Export to distinguish it from the weak and bland Heineken 'ordinary' made in Britain under licence by Whitbread, has been a huge success around the world and is now made by many other breweries at various global staging posts.

The other major player in the Netherlands is Allied (or Allied-Domecq, or whatever they are calling themselves this month), known in their local materialization as VBBR, or Verenigde Bierbrouwerijen Breda-Rotterdam. Originally the company put all its backing behind a dreadful lager called

Skol, and bought up masses of production facilities in the hope that the stuff would become a ubiquitous worldwide brand, a lager equivalent to Watney's Red Barrel. Now they are pinning their hopes on Oranjeboom. Originally Allied bought up both this and another brewery, called Breda. Oranjeboom was promptly closed down. Breda facilities are still used, but under the Oranjeboom ('orange tree') name.

Along with Heineken, Amstel and Oranjeboom, the final lager brand in the Dutch mass-market quartet is Grolsch, made by the Grolsche Brewery, who are the second-largest Dutch independent, and now also own our very own Ruddles Brewery. Famous for its glass bottles with the rubber flip-top openers, which make a satisfying pop when first released, Grolsch is the nearest thing the Netherlands has to a mass-market pilsener, and is a subtle, but fresh and wholesome beer, partly thanks to its remaining unpasteurized. There is an apocryphal story that some years ago the brewery tried to get rid of these expensive and fiddly bottle tops (before they became the lager's trademark) and it was drinkers from the northern provinces (famously thrifty, like all northerners) who were ready to demonstrate in the streets – because they used the rubber stop to reseal the beer and keep it for another time. Presumably not even noticing that all the zizz and condition had gone out of the product when it was opened again.

Grolsche, like the other large companies, also produce a short series of beers targeted at the tastes of their home audience. Whilst something like 90% of the beer sold in the Netherlands is pale, mass-market lagers – many claiming to be 'pilseners' – and whilst most Dutch lagers have up to 25% adjuncts in their ingredients, all-malt brewing is acquiring a high status, and speciality and traditional beers are acquiring a strong (if minority) following. Heineken took the world somewhat aback a few years ago by switching from high-adjunct brewing to an all-malt policy, and this is the reason Heineken Export is so much nicer to drink now than it used to be. An all-malt policy, undertaking to use no rice, corn, torrefied wheat or any of the much less appealing adjuncts that are commonplace elsewhere, is considered rather extraordinary (not to say, eccentric) by the other big breweries of the world.

An even greater impact has been made by the mini micro revolution in the Netherlands. The new wave of companies are primarily ale breweries, perhaps also making one or two bottom-fermented 'lager' products, but with their real interests very evidently riding on top of the fermenting vessel. Not so long ago, the proto-typical Dutch brewery beer range would have rested on three or four products: perhaps a traditional sweet, weak, brown table lager called an Oud Bruin, a lager self-described as pilsener (but probably just a lager), a strong lager which may or may not have deserved its 'Dortmunder' label, and a traditional Dutch brown bokbier. These days, the micros are setting an altogether more sprightly pace, possibly including the Oud Bruin, but also a more authentic pilsener, a more authentic Dortmunder Export-style lager, a pale ale or an amber ale, and at least two bock beers, a pale and a brown. There might also be a wheat beer, a winter ale, a Düsseldorf style altbier, a Cologne-style Kölsch, an English bitter, and other daring experiments. Dutch microbrewing is learning to be cautiously dynamic.

Germany is certainly a major influence on the new generation, but the pull of the Belgian tradition often appears greater. This is natural enough, when you consider that the two were once one country; it's the ancient Dutch merchant tradition that's responsible for the Belgian love of spices and exotic ingredients like curaçao orange peel in their beers. The Dutch merchant tradition has also led to an export-based brewing culture, and thus the development of a series of bland, mild-mannered, weak lagers made to broadcast to the world.

Lagers

Despite the all-malt policy of Heineken, most Dutch mass-market beers come from the very heart of Adjunct City. At their worst, Dutch lagers are the most painfully undrinkable in Europe, with a dinstinctively unclean, flabby, sticky-finished palate and a characteristic 'Dutch' flavour that's pungently saddle-soapy. In general the 'Dutch Lager' soubriquet is to be regarded as a warning when buying cheap beer and supermarket own brands. But the Netherlands also boasts a wider range of lager styles than its Belgian mentors, some of them very decent, but very few of them available here. The outstanding pilsener brand, Christoffel, is also better than anything Belgium has so far come up with. It's called Christoffel Blond in bottle, for which it's unpasteurized and only lightly filtered; Christoffel Bier (filtered) on draught. This microbrewery, based in Roermond, was set up about ten years ago by former family members of the Brand brewery (now part of Heineken). There's a sibling, amber brew called Robertus, which is also all-malt, unfiltered and unpasteurized. Another fine all-malt Dutch pilsener goes by the name of Gulpener X-Pert, from the Gulpen Brewery, which was founded in 1825 and is one of the most innovative of established companies.

Brand Brewery, the oldest of Dutch survivors with late medieval origins, was gobbled up by Heineken in 1990. The Brand brand (so to speak) pilsener lagers are still made there; the best of them a beer called Brand UP (Urtyp Pilsener). We get a beer in Britain called Royal Brand, a reference to Queen Beatrix's praise of the company back in 1971 (in its independent guise, in other words). Heineken itself make a Special Dark Lager for export, and under its other brand name, a superior, all-malt lager called Amstel 1870 that we have yet to see in Britain.

A lager brewery that is still family owned, Alfa, in Schinnen, dates from 1870, when there were still over 1000 working breweries. They still make their Alfa Holland Bier with 100% malt, plus Hallertau and Czech whole hops, and claim to lager for a full 3 months. Another Limburg name is Lindeboom ('lime tree'), also established in 1870, originally to make ales; pilsener-style lagers took over in 1926. Lindeboom brand lager is made with Dutch and Flemish barleys, Hallertau, Tettnang and Saaz, and is lagered for 8 weeks. It is then filtered (but not pasteurized) before bottling. But perhaps the best-known independent brewery in Britain – you've probably drunk their lagers without knowing it – is Bavaria, from Lieshout, who happen to be not only the largest independent brewery in the Netherlands, but also one of the largest privately-owned breweries in the world. They are responsible for a lot of the own-brand, own-label Dutch lager that sloshes onto our shores, from their huge modern factory, which turns out over 3.5 million hectolitres (purely of lager) a year. They can fill 300,000 cans and 225,000 bottles an *hour*. Bavaria, established in 1719, and named in honour of South German brewing traditions, say in their brochure that they'll make all-malt, adjunct-free beers to special request. But it's more expensive, naturally. Not that many people ask.

On the speciality lager front: Vienna lagers, with their full amber colouring and mildly spicy-sweet palate, are very popular in the Netherlands. Dutch interpretations of the strong 'Export' lagers of Dortmund are usually more potent than the originals. Alfa Brewery make the strongest, Alfa Super Dortmunder, at 7% abv. Gulpen has been brewing its fine Gulpener Dort (6.5% abv) since 1953. Some breweries also make soft brown lagers, approximating to the Munich style. Sweet, weak Oud Bruin table lagers are still widely available.

Bocks and Boks

It was a bokbier that 15 years ago really ignited the microbrewery movement in the Netherlands. The traditional Dutch brown bok had virtually disappeared, but was brought back from the brink of extinction, gained a following in the cafés, and became the focus of the independent breweries' struggle for market share. Then, looking about for novelty, brewers hit upon a Dutch version of Germany's here-comes-spring beer, the Maibock, which they rechristened the Meibok (or even Meibock). Often these pale-ish, perhaps amber-coloured beers have a sweetish accent, and are sometimes labelled as Lentebok. Both Alfa and Oranjeboom make Lenteboks. Kroon, one of the old school of independents, makes a fine Meibock, at 6.5% abv, the average Meibock strength. So does Grolsche.

But the original, brown Dark Bok (often just called a bokbier, as opposed to a Meibok) is a Dutch style in its own right. Typically, it's dark brown and characteristically fairly straightforward in its flavours. Mass-market examples are often very soft and elusively malty, with a smooth drinkability, and only very lightly hopped. Traditionally boks were made in spring, matured all summer and launched in the autumn, but they're now made and drunk all year round. Just about every independent and microbrewery produce at least one beer in the bock/bok style, and just about every brewery's bok is 6.5% abv. Grolsche and Amstel produce popular dark bokbiers. So do Bavaria and Alfa. Kuipertje, a micro established in 1988, which specializes in bottle-conditioned ales, makes a rich and succulent one. A few others make more identifiably Germanic bocks, even double bocks in one or two cases.

Alts and Others

The great love affair of Dutch microbrewing is with the ale. The Netherlands makes a few top-fermented, cold-conditioned altbier-style beers, some of these in open homage to Düsseldorf, others in the more international, more widely defined 'Alt' ('old') style. Others make Kölsch-style or Kölsch-inspired ales, the pale, delicate beers unique to Cologne. A fine exponent of both these Dutch interpretations of German classics is Budelse Brewery, at Budel, near the Belgian border, a smallish independent founded in 1870. Their mellow, tasty, brown Budels Alt, and pale, creamy, fruity Budels Parel should be more widely available in Britain. They also make an excellent Dubbel called Capucijn (not a reference to coffee flavours, but a monk's cowl), which is also top-fermented, and then cold-conditioned, altbier style, as well as a dark Dutch bok and a decent, hoppy pilsener. Budelse offer easily the most interesting imported Dutch beers currently available in Britain.

Pale Ales are also becoming increasingly ubiquitous among the independents. Typically these are a pale or full amber, smooth and rounded, perhaps with toffee or fruit sweetness, and either a soft or strong dry hop finish. Grolsch Amber (5% abv) is a decent mass-market example, of altbier mellowness. Probably the best pale ale is made by Us Heit Brewery, established in 1985 and right up in the north of the country. Their Frysk Bier (6% abv and wonderfully named for English drinkers, or would be if we could get it) is generously rounded and nuttily dry. Us Heit make rather dull but competent lagers and delicious ales: the New Dutch Brewery typified. There's a sense of pressure being applied to the mass-market, too. Even the rather workaday Leeuw (lion) Brewery, historically a rather stolid lager producer, is now turning out a wheat beer and an alt, as well as a dark bok.

The other kind of ale that's really taking off in the Netherlands is the strong, complex, mature old ale that straddles the traditional English and Belgian styles. Most producers have gained much of their inspiration over the border in Belgium, however. Spiced ales are the particular speciality of the Maasland Brewery, established 1989. Their flagship spiced ale is called D'N Schele Os Tripel (7.5% abv), and their delicious Easter Beer (Paasbier) is currently available at Oddbins. The micro now known as Drie Ringen (three rings), established 1989, makes an 8% abv Winterbier with more of an English, or rather American micro accent. But probably the connoisseur's choice of ale brewery in the Netherlands would be the disconcertingly abbreviated 'T Ij Brewery, established in 1984 in Amsterdam docks, who make a full and inspiring range of ten beers, all in small (and unexported) quantities. Incidentally, Amsterdam only got its first brew pub, the Amsterdam Brouwhuis, in 1992.

Wheat Beers

Wheat beer, commonly called Wit Bier (white beer, equivalent to Germany's Weissbier), or else Bière Blanche, but occasionally given its literal translation of Tarwebier, is made in both the Belgian and German manner, that is to say with either unmalted or malted wheat. Or both together at the same time. Many are quite low in wheat, at around 30%. Ever with a watchful eye on the export markets of their neighbours, Dutch brewers have been inspired by the runaway success of Hoegaarden White. Ridder's Wieckse Witte, widely felt to be the quintessential Dutch wheat beer, has been part of the Heineken portfolio since they took over the brewery in 1982.

Heineken are also responsible for a daring innovation on the bok front: the Tarwebok, the first bottom-fermented wheat bok, which they launched in 1992. Thirty per cent wheat is used in the mash. Dutch wheat beers are probably available somewhere in the British Isles; exclusively in a small off-licence in Elgin, perhaps – who knows?. But they are certainly hiding well. Which is a pity, because the Dutch approach produces likeable, toffee-sweet, slightly honeyed, pudding-friendly wheat beers that would probably find an audience here. The small band of Dutch microbreweries, meanwhile (around 20 at the last count) are coming up with wheat beers of a more challenging and complex sort.

Abbey Beers

There are Abbey Beers aplenty produced by secular breweries in the Netherlands, either under licence from surviving abbeys or under their own steam, referring with varying degrees of authenticity to the brewing traditions of extinct monasteries. And there is also Schaapskooi, the sixth Trappist Monastery (the other five being in Belgium). At Schaapskooi they produce Trappist ales under the Koningshoeven (King's Gardens) and La Trappe brand names; indeed, they were the only ale producing brewery in the Netherlands for a very long time, until Arcen, the pioneer micro, was established in 1981. They are also easily the most commercially minded of all the Trappist breweries. The five Belgian operations are rumoured to be up in arms at the decision of Schaapskooi to allow La Trappe ales to appear under the labels of others, something they themselves would never allow. Sainsbury's Trappist Ale is largely responsible for this hoo-hah. Schaapskooi (which means sheep's pen) produce an accessible, drinkable series of beers, which appear under the Koningshoeven brand name at home, under the La Trappe brand name when imported by Allied into Britain, and under the La Trappe Koningshoeven joint brand name when sent here by hte famous beer broker, John Martin's of Antwerp. There appear to be further versions and labels about.

There are four products, all top-fermented and bottle-conditioned, in the Trappist way. The core two are the La Trappe/Koningshoeven Dubbel and Tripel, of 6.5% (Dutch Dubbels are always 6.5%) and 8%abv respectively, the first a brune, the second a blonde. A Quadrupel (10% abv) was introduced in 1992, in response to the Dutch (and export markets') love affair with seriously strong ales. There's also a newish 'single', called La Trappe Koningshoeven Ambrée, at a modest 5.5% abv, coming in through John Martin's. Trappist monasteries give an initial impression of great age, but Schaapskooi brewery is currently celebrating its centenary year. It was set up to raise money to build the monastery, which is consequently even younger.

The fact that there are still only 32 breweries in the whole of the Netherlands is rather sobering: compare and contrast this with Germany's 1200! But the fact that two-thirds of these have emerged in the last ten years is very encouraging. The hope is that more, making more and more interesting beers, are now waiting in the wings. However, the fate of two of the original microbreweries gives a measure of what they're up against. De Raaf, established in 1983, makers of a good wheat beer among other products, are now owned by Allied/Oranjeboom. But this is as nothing to the fate of Arcen. The pioneers of the whole Dutch micro revival, the founders of Arcen Brewery set up their company when Allied closed Arcen's village brewery and made them redundant in 1981. The new Arcen brewery became a great success. Such a success that in 1991 Allied took it over.

ALFA PREMIUM HOLLAND BEER**

Alfa Brewery, Schinnen. 50cl Bottled 5%:
Golden lager with an initially impressive rocky white head. Made from malt, hops, yeast and water only, with bubble-gum aromas and the illusion of just a little corn on the palate, which is fairly sweet and barley grainy. There's bubble-gum here too, with Juicy Fruit-like notes in the finish, and Cox apple and orange fruit flavours. But otherwise a bit thin and lacking in structure. *Serve:* light fridge chill. *Avail:* specialists.

AMSTEL**

Bier Heineken. 33cl Bottled 5%:
Bright golden lager with surprisingly appetizing aromas and perfectly acceptable, if unexciting, flavours. A decent lunchtime sandwich lager. Medium-bodied with a rounded sweet grain palate, and a fairly clean, slightly honeyed finish, but with just the faintest touch of something Dutch, in the saddle-soapy, slightly resiny sense. *Serve:* fridge cold *Avail*: Asda, Odd.

BAVARIA*

Dutch Lager Bavaria, Lieshout. 25cl Bottled 3%:
Low in alcohol, thinnish in body, mildly sweetly malty, with a floral note at the finish, which is otherwise a bit sticky and sugary. Initially seeming clean and simple, it becomes oddly sappy and develops raw-dough flavours about halfway through. *Serve:* fridge cold. *Avail*: Safe, Spar.

BAVARIA*

Strong Pils Lager 25cl Bottled 5%:
Similar to the canned version, below, but not so sweet. Hugely frothy, with a white foamy head, it has a little citrus on the nose, and is a little drier at the finish, but still very bland stuff. *Serve:* fridge cold *Avail*: Safe.

BAVARIA*

Strong Pils Lager 44cl Canned 5%:
Not particularly strong, and not a pilsener. Aromas are sweet and vaguely malty, with barley sugar and a little golden syrup; flavours ditto. No real finish, just comes to a dead stop. Oversweet and lacking in body, but without the classic Dutch cheap lager 'taint', at least. *Serve:* light fridge chill. *Avail:* Co-op.

BUDELS ALT***

Budelse Brewery. 30cl Bottled 6%:
Deep amber in colour, with a fruity malty nose, plus a little pineapple, and sweet and sour notes. In the mouth, there's pale, creamy malt; drier, nutty, 'cured' malt flavours, woody with notes of orange, but also smooth and silky alt character, with a drying malt and hop finish. Perilously drinkable for a 6% beer: tasty, medium-bodied and spritzy. *Serve:* larder cool. *Avail*: BeerC.

BUDELS PAREL***

30cl Bottled 6%:
Unusual and moreish pale gold 'blonde' made with more than a nod to the German Kölsch style. Aromas are creamy sweet, vanilla yoghurt, lemon custard-like with a delicate fruitiness. Flavours are similar, creamy and biscuity with good pale malt body initially, but

growing sharper and drier at the back, when a lemony sour note precedes a notably floral hop finish. Nice texture, too, both coconut creamy and refreshingly semi-spritzy. A delicious and intriguing beer that might also appeal to Malibu drinkers. *Serve:* larder cool/ light fridge chill. *Avail:* BeerC.

CAPUCIJN***

Budelse Brewery. 30cl Bottled 6.5%:
Opaque amber, bottle-conditioned ale with a smug-looking monk on the label (as well he might be). Roasting chestnuts, banana and citrus on the nose, and extraordinarily delicious to taste, sweet and puddingy but also sophisticated: sticky-toffee pudding cravings can be satisfied here. Good texture, with a prickly hop backdrop, and a light fruitiness, followed by buttery, honey-drenched sultana and orange cake, leading into a full vanilla toffee flavour, before returning to fruit, and a very gently drying hop finish. Could easily be a four-star beer, were it not for the fear that a sweet tooth was in charge of that decision. *Serve:* larder cool. *Avail*: BeerC.

CLASSE ROYAL

De Vriedenkring, Breda (Allied/Oranjeboom). 25cl Bottled 3%:
Camembert, Cheddar and Brie skin all gather in the cheesy nose of the 'naturally brewed' bright-gold, gassy lager. Flabby and bland. *Serve:* fridge cold. *Avail*: VicW.

GROLSCH***

Grolsche Brewery. 45cl Bottled 5%:
In the famous flip-top bottle. Dry with grain flavour and texture, clean and quaffable, but quite astringent at the finish, when it dries up suddenly and dramatically – but which also introduces a tropical note quite evident on the nose. Pure beer: just malt, hops, water and yeast. Good aperitif material, will have you reaching for the peanuts. *Serve:* fridge cold. *Avail*: widely.

GROLSCH***

Premium Lager 50cl Canned 5%:
Made in England (actually), from water, malted barley, hops and yeast only. These ingredients lift expectations, rightly as it happens, for this is a surprisingly decent canned lager, with barley sweet, hop dry balance, and no metallic taint at all. Sweeter than the bottled import, it's none the less clean and refreshing, good with a lunchtime sandwich or with garlicky delicatessen treats. *Serve:* fridge cold. *Avail*: widely.

HEINEKEN

44cl Canned 3.4%:
The green tin is possibly the most distinctive feature of this lager, made in England (actually) by Whitbread, like the canned 'Export'. Sweet-nosed, thin and sugary, grainy, and over gassy. *Serve:* fridge cold. *Avail*: widely.

HEINEKEN EXPORT***

33cl Bottled 5%:
Not having opened a can of Heineken for a few years, I was sincerely astonished to like this so much more than the high-profile rival, Oranjeboom. It's the 'original continental recipe', as this is the standard Heineken; the weaker, ordinary canned lager (above) was devised for feeble English palates. Pale gold in colour, with a delicate pale malt and hop, and (hey!) a tasty well-balanced flavour. It's not a pilsener, but drily, fragrantly malty, a little nut-woody, clean and rounded with a drying malt and hop finish. Nothing fancy, but honest and wholesome. Now also available (Asda) in a useful 65cl size. *Serve:* light fridge chill. *Avail*: Asda, Safe, Somer, Tesco.

HEINEKEN EXPORT*

44cl Canned 5%:
Like Heineken 'ordinary', this is made by Whitbread (actually) under licence in Britain. Has some flavours in common with the bottled version, sweetish and reasonably rounded with a medium dry finish. Not turnipy or tinny at keast. *Serve:* fridge cold. *Avail*: widely.

LANDENBROUW**

Bavaria, Lieshout. 44cl Canned 2.4%:

A bit of a find, this, a low-alcohol Bavaria-brewed supermarket lager which is good to drink and makes a very decently workaday table beer. Packaged for Spar/Landmark, it has a sweet, fresh nose and malty, refreshing, faintly honeyish flavours with an admittedly subtle, but pleasing, biscuity creaminess in the texture that's unusual for a beer of this low strength and low price. Plain, but useful lager, worth stocking up in the lager. *Serve:* light fridge chill. *Avail*: Spar.

LINDEBOOM**

Lindeboom, Limburg. 50cl Bottled 5%:
Commendably all-natural ingredients, but just a little dull. Fresh, wholesome, quaffable, but tentative beer with a mildly malty, mildly hoppy, clean palate. Another good sandwich lager. *Serve:* light fridge chill. *Avail*: specialists.

ORANJEBOOM*

Premium Lager Breda (Allied). 33cl Bottled 5%:
Diappointing so-called 'premium' lager with a soft, almost soapy texture, bland and watery in the middle, slightly dry but also slightly cloying at the finish. Tastes like canned beer. Doesn't really deserve a star. *Serve:* fridge cold. *Avail*: widely.

PAASBIER***

Maasland Brewery. 33cl Bottled 6.5%:
A traditional Dutch Easter beer, made from barley and wheat malts, Styrian Golding and Challenger hops, plus ginger and orange. Bottle-conditioned, a translucent reddish-brown, with an appealing spicy nose, and a dry, succulent but spritzy texture, with a creamy, wheaty, woody, vanilla-sweet, egg-noggy, mellow orange flavour that's absolutely irresistible. *Serve:* room temp. *Avail*: Odd.

ROYAL DUTCH

De Posthhorn, Breda (Allied/Oranjeboom). 25cl Bottled 3%:
Big brewery lager in a little bottle, with, as they claim, 'distinctive Dutch quality'. The quality of being one of the least drinkable cheap lagers in Eurôpe, that is. Icky, sticky, caramelly, adjunct-laden stuff with nothing to recommend it. *Serve:* fridge cold. *Avail*: Somer.

SAFEWAY DUTCH LAGER

50cl Canned 3%:
Big bubbles settle on the top of this brassy gold lager (o-oh . . .) and it tastes, well, cheap, frankly. Slightly sweet, a bit sugary (not hoppy, not malty, not yeasty), wet, cold and fizzy. Having tasted this and the Sainsbury's version, below, the only question that springs to mind is why do we import this rubbish, and who buys it, for heaven's sake? *Serve:* fridge cold.

SAFEWAY EXPORT STRENGTH LAGER

50cl Canned 5%:
The nose of this Dutch-brewed own-label beer is corn cereally, and a little peppery; its flavour is initially pineapple fruity – rather sickly – before dissipating into corn cereal flavours, and dying away completely before the finish, which is simply tinny and slightly tannic. *Serve:* fridge cold.

SAINSBURY'S DUTCH LAGER

50cl Canned 3%:
Modestly low-alcohol lager in the bright green and yellow tin. Bubbly, cereal husky stuff, with savoury and woody grain notes and not enough malt sweetness (and no discernible hop, for all that matter). Actually very little flavour at all. Truly dismal. *Serve:* fridge cold.

SAINSBURY'S TRAPPIST ALE***

50cl Bottled 8%:
Stone-flagonned Konigshoeven (La Trappe) Trappist ale, a cloudy full apricot in colour, with a spirity, fruity, peachy nose. Flavours are sweet and bittersweet, rich but light, with a citric, peachy accent, wheat-beer yeastiness, and a fino sherryish note further sharpened by just a touch of Seville orange. The most refreshing and summery of Trappist ales, spritzy and clean-edged, very softly dry and very drinkable. But for goodness' sake

don't chill it for two hours, as Sainsbury's recommend. *Serve:* larder cool.

SPAR BRAU

Bière de Luxe Bavaria, Lieshout. 25cl Bottled 5%:

Luxe can be deceptive. This is very Dutch, lightly malty, bland lager with acidic grapefruit notes in the finish and on the nose, and a flabby, unclean edge to it. Grainy, mediocre stuff at best. *Serve:* fridge cold.

SPAR IMPORTED DUTCH PILSNER LAGER

Bavaria, 44cl Canned 3%:

Quite why this should be so bland and ordinary, and the Landenbrouw so nice is a mystery, but here's a not too afflicted cheap Dutch lager with a bit of a sticky end, and saddle soapy/resiny notes in the finish, of the classic Dutch cheap lager sort. *Serve:* fridge cold.

SPAR DUTCH SUPER STRENGTH*

44cl Canned 8.6%:

Bavaria's famous 8.6 Lager could have been dreadfully alcohol-sweaty, turnip-haunted stuff, but instead turns out to taste and smell remarkably like tinned peaches, or rather the syrup they come in, complete with evaporated milk stirred in. The expected alcoholic, whiskyish kick arrives after a minute or two, though. Weird, but better than homegrown Supers. *Serve:* fridge cold.

TESCO DUTCH EXPORT LAGER*

Bavaria. 44cl Canned 3.2%:

Better than the usual Dutch tinned beer, even though a cheap adjunct, maize grits, is listed as one of the ingredients. (Don't be put off; to use just one adjunct shows positive restraint in value-lager-making.) It has a sweet malt, slightly pineapple-juicey nose, dry textured malt and a little apple sweetness on the tongue (along with the corn), and a gently drying, slightly malt-accented finish. In supermarket own-brand Dutch canned lager terms, one star is an accolade. *Serve:* fridge cold.

LA TRAPPE***

Schaapskooi, Koningshoeven. 33cl Bottled 6.5%:

Bottle-conditioned Dubbel from Holland's only Trappist monastery. Allied have import rights over this bottling, which appears to be not only different in flavour, but different in colour to the second version, reviewed below. It's deep ruby in colour with a creamy pillow of a head, crackling as it disperses in the glass. Appetizing yeasty, fruity aromas, cherry and banana rich. To drink, soft, soft water and tiny prickly bubbles deliver dark, slightly smokey and sour fruit flavours, with muscovado and prune, and floral hop dryness in the otherwise rich and satisfying finish. *Serve:* larder/room temp. *Avail:* VicW, Wait.

LA TRAPPE KONINGSHOEVEN***

John Martin's, Antwerp. 33cl Bottled 6.5%:

The La Trappe Koningshoeven Dubbel, imported via famed beer-broker John Martin's of Antwerp. Bottle-conditioned, top-fermented ale, burnt orange in colour, and with fresh tangerine cheesecake aromas. This fruity, yeasty curdiness gives way to orange and sultana cake flavours, growing a little figgy, with vanilla sweetness and a sherryish note in the finish. Light, dry, semi-spritzy, summery and refreshing. *Serve:* larder cool. *Avail:* specialists.

LA TRAPPE KONINGSHOEVEN AMBRÉE**

John Martin's, Antwerp. 33cl Bottled 5.5%:

Serve chilled, it says on the bottle: please don't. The beer itself is also something new, and in experimental mood. Clear amber in colour, it's a rather disappointing, slightly flaccid beer, with orange marmalade and whiskyish notes, vanilla sweetness and a faintly smokey edge. *Serve:* larder cool. *Avail:* specialists.

LA TRAPPE KONINGSHOEVEN TRIPLE***

Blonde John Martin's, Antwerp. 33cl Bottled 8%:

The beer that also appears as Sainsbury's

Trappist Ale, although tasting rather different, and not in its public relations stone-bottle uniform in this case either. Barley-sugar-coloured, creamy, with sweet and bittersweet, orange fruit notes and a Calvados alcohol kick in the finish, all expressed in a light and drinkable fashion. Quite unusually quaffable, for an 8% ale. *Serve:* larder cool. *Avail:* Asda.

WAITROSE DUTCH LAGER

50cl Canned 3%:
Back to the usual Dutch canned lager style. Aroma: slightly leathery, even sweaty. Flavour: sugar-sweet, and of the sugar itself (demerara style), barley sugar and corn. The finish, a particular problem with cheap Dutch beers, is sticky and adjuncty. Icky is the technical term. But it is under 45p a tin. *Serve:* fridge cold.

New Zealand

As the Australian introduction explains, New Zealand is far from content to make beer for home consumption. Instead, like its lamb and apples and excellent wine, New Zealand beer is exported to the world. It's just that most of it is actually brewed over in Australia, by companies owned by the enormous Lion Nathan Brewing Group.

But there is also, naturally, a native New Zealand brewing industry, more or less divided up between Lion Nathan's imaginatively-titled New Zealand Breweries and the deadly rival, Dominion, whose Kiwi lager is occasionally to be found here. Steinlager is NZ Breweries' flagship brand, a best-seller at home and exported to 40 countries, including Britain. It's been brewed since 1958, and was the first export-class lager to be made in New Zealand. Only one in ten beer bottles leaving the country contain something else.

Steinlager is brewed with the intention of making a lager in the traditional European style. The barley for malting is grown on the Canterbury and Manawatu plains. The hops are also New Zealand grown; Green Bullet, a New Zealand-developed super-alpha variety, is the main aroma/bittering hop. Though they did once use a continuous fermentation technique to make the beer, it's now once again made by a traditional batch brewing process, using traditional German Steineker equipment. Bottled (rather than canned) New Zealand beers can be rather vulnerable to travel and storage damage, but if the bottle has been well protected from light, and is drunk at 5–7°C, it should then, according to the brewery, display a good malt/hop balance, zesty carbonation, a grassy undertone (rather like a New Zealand Sauvignon?) and a hint of dimethyl sulphide (yum).

The same company's Lion Ice Beer, launched at home in October 1983, is their newest export, arriving on our shores in autumn 1995. Lion Nathan are convinced that theirs is the smoothest ice beer in the world. To these ends, they use 'super refined hop extract' with the malt in the kettle. The beer is transferred to vast, purpose-built stainless steel tanks, which are blanketed in thick, impenetrable ice. Inside these ice chambers, huge clusters of ice crystals form on a maze of refrigeration coils. In the classic ice beer style, water is drawn from the beer, plus what they call 'natural impurities' (and what others call flavour). Super-chilled filtering then removes the ice, and any 'impurities' that previously escaped.

New Zealand also has a thriving microbrewery culture, which began in

1982, two years before the Australian movement got going. The first New Zealand micro was set up by a former All Black, who had been inspired by world tour experiences, especially in England. Brew pubs are a particular hit in New Zealand and are popping up like daisies. They often produce variants on the brown lager theme – slightly brownish-amber, slightly malty lagers being an unofficial New Zealand trademark – as well as pale quenchers, and perhaps a pale ale or bitter, plus darker beers generally in the mild, Scotch or porter style, and maybe also a wheat beer.

DB NATURAL**

Dominion, Auckland. 33cl Bottled 4%:
Unpasteurized, micro-filtered beer that only mentions it's an ale in passing on the rear label. Perhaps the word would scare off half of their target market? Certainly it seems that real ale character would. Amber brown in colour, it has faint roast and amber malt flavours, with a mildly buttery, yeasty tang, sweetish but with a coffee bean, roasty note, and a sour, grainy and delicate hop finish. The whole beer has a lightness of touch – too light (in fact verging on watery), but still a likeable, if nervous, beer of a sort we've not seen from New Zealand before. *Serve:* larder cool. *Avail:* specialists.

STEINLAGER**

New Zealand Breweries, Auckland. 33cl Bottled 5%:
Imported bottled lager, apparently 'renowned around the world for its clean, fresh taste'. But our tasting found it in a sweet-nosed, caramelized vegetal mood, with pumpkin sugar flavours and a finish at once drying and cloying. Remarkably unclean in fact, and not remotely fresh either. *Serve:* fridge cold. *Avail:* Safe, Sains, Thres.

Norway

Ancient Scandinavian literature, but particularly the sagas, reveal that the Vikings made fermented barley drinks. Indeed, it's their word for beer, *aul* (or in Sweden *öl*, in Danish *øl*, that gave us our word 'ale' for beer. These are countries far too chilly for the vine, so brewing of one sort or another has always been of central importance. We think of Scandinavia as a rather severe, Lutheran Protestant world, serious about its work and about family and community, and rather sober in its pleasures. This is a view enforced by the region's restrictive, conservative alcohol legislation. But in concentrating on this aspect of Scandinavian (and especially northern Scandinavian) life, we might easily forget to mention the other strongly traditional aspect of beer drinking here. Home brewing.

Norway is traditionally the headquarters of Scandinavian home-brewing. This phenomenon has been given fresh impetus by the very real difficulty entailed in going out and buying beer. In the rural areas of the west and north especially, home brewing is still a living, thriving tradition. We're not talking kits from Boots here, either, but real beer-making on a small (or perhaps not so small) scale, in the home or farm brewhouse. The open fire used for cooking and for smoking meat and fish might also be the site where the direct-fired copper (actually more of a cauldron) is placed for boiling up the mash. Herb beers are still very widely made, and in particular juniper beer. Juniper has its own distinctive flavour, and a preservative value not unlike the hop that long ago superseded it in most of the rest of western Europe. Even if Norwegians don't make their own beer, home drinking is the norm everywhere: there's high taxation on beers, and not much of a pub culture to speak of.

Norway is one of the very few countries in the world to still enforce its very own Pure Beer Law. All commercial brewing is of the 100% malt sort, and as you might expect of such a cold country, bottom-fermenting (lager) brewing is very much the norm. Generally Norwegian lagers are given a good long lagering, but local taste clearly runs to the light, crisp and clean. The average brewery's range is deeply conventional. If world beer styles are represented, they tend to be a softened, mild-mannered, smooth and mellow sort. Dark rich bock beers – here called Bokkøl, and often long-matured – and a jewel-red Christmas beer (Jule Øl), are perhaps the most interesting aspects of the traditional Norwegian beer range, which might also include a soft, malty

Bavarian style lager, an amber/Vienna lager or a strong, sweet Export, as well as the ubiquitous clean pilsener-style lager. There are only nine breweries in the whole country. Aass is the oldest survivor, Ringnes the biggest brewing group (it also owns Arendals, Dahl, Nordlands and Tou) and the keenest on export. Breweries are mostly clustered around Oslo, but in Bergen, on the west coast, there's the Hansa brewery, which produces Ludwig Pils. There are one or two new microbreweries trying daring beer styles in the German or even British manner. And Norway boasts the world's most northerly brewery, Mack, in Tromso, well within the boundary of the Arctic Circle. Its most famous beer, Mack Øl, is traditionally accompanied by seagulls eggs in spring.

RINGNES***

35.5cl Bottled 4.5%:

Probably the freshest, cleanest-tasting lager in the world. Lots can claim to be clean, and often this is a euphemism for a lack of flavour and body, but in this case freshness and cleanness and refreshment are positive virtues. This invigorating lager tastes like it's been made with clear, zingy mountain water (which it probably has), as well as offering mildly sweet malt, mildly hoppy dryness, and moreish mineral water character. Bet they love this beer in Italy. *Serve:* fridge cold. *Avail:* specialists.

Peru

Peru Gold**

Campania, Arequipa. 35cl Bottled 5%:
Let the label tell the story: 'beer has been brewed in Peru for centuries. The Incas produced a potent brew called chicha (known today as corn beer) . . . Arequipa, Peru's second city, is the home of Peru Gold, made only from the purest natural ingredients, and clear spring waters.' Lots of amiable tourist board guff about the Incas follows. Aromas are banana fruity and lemony when swirled. Initial impressions of flavour are of a beer clean as a whistle and made for a hot country, superclean with spritzy bubbles, but there's also a good twist of lime in the middle, and a little soft dryness in the very finish, leaving a clean and gently citric aftertaste. A simple but moreish little beer: two and three-quarter stars awarded. *Serve:* light fridge chill. *Avail:* BeerC.

Poland

Once the dust started to settle from years of political upheaval in Poland, the newly launched Privatization Ministry began to take a long, hard look at the Polish brewing industry. Chief among its concerns was the fact that there are presently only five breweries achieving production levels of 500,000 hectolitres a year; this is unchanged since 1989 (and probably long before). Five years ago, the Ministry were also worried about the structure of Polish brewing. It seemed to take more than twice as many workers to make 100,000 hectolitres of beer than in Germany, for a start. Forty-five breweries were making under 100,000 hectolitres a year; 70% of beer was being made by small breweries. Instead of being delighted by this state of affairs (as we small-brewery-loving countries undoubtedly would) the Polish authorities thought this lamentable and in need of revolutionizing. They still do. The pressure is on for more mega-giant brewing plants, making more mega-giant beer, enough to satisfy Polish needs and create a thriving export trade, particularly to the Russian Federation. And who can blame them?

Polish home consumption of beer was about 35 litres per head per year in 1992, compared with 145 litres by their neighbours, Germany. They drink more beer in the very north and south, but especially the south, which was the area annexed by the Austrian empire and which is still characterized by a Germanic approach to alcohol. In the central region, however, which was once 'absorbed' by the old Russian empire, there is still a strong spirit-drinking culture. Poland in general is number two in the world on the global spirit-drinking league table, just behind the former East Germany, and only 27th on the beer-drinking table. But it's beer that's the big growth area.

There was brewing in Poland as early as the 10th century. A strong monastery-brewery tradition followed, after which the towns obtained royal assent to brew beer and brewing became dominated by the Brewers Guild. This is a pattern repeated all over Europe, of course. Four of the large modern breweries built in the 19th century are still in use. The great decline in the diversity of Polish brewing has come, not surprisingly, since the Second World War. In the early 1930s Poland was also a major exporter of malt and hops to other brewing nations: its hops in particular were renowned for their quality. Poland only began to import its raw materials, mostly from the Czech Republic, in 1992. In the 1930s there were something like 500 breweries in Poland. Now there are 24 companies, who between them have 77 breweries.

Seventy per cent of the beer is produced by ten of them, including the first two breweries to be privatized, Zywiec and Koszalin. Eight have been privatized so far, with another 19 waiting in line. Zywiec, whose beer is now available in Britain, was sold by a public share offer. Most of the breweries are in the south, south-west and Silesia.

Traditionally, beer was drunk at home in Poland, but an increasingly Westernized society is taking to drinking in bars, which is (sadly) putting a lot of the old café-restaurants out of business. In the years between 1984 and 1992 beer consumption rose by 55%. Ten per cent of the beer currently sold is imported. An even greater boom in beer-drinking is expected in the next five years, and the Ministry is determined that most of those profits will come to rest in Polish banks, even though demand for home-grown lagers already exceeds supply, especially in the summer. Only around 20% of the beer is pasteurized, so it has a shortish shelf life. At the moment this isn't a problem: beer doesn't sit on shelves for very long, but when export becomes a major part of the industry, pasteurization will doubtless become the norm. There are already two national brands, Zywiec and Okocim, with others poised to follow. Otherwise, brands are mostly local: 78% of all beer made in Poland goes no further than 30 kilometres from the brewery gate.

Typically, a full Polish beer range includes a brown, weak lager flavoured with dark malts; a roughly 6% abv pale, strong Export-style lager, sweetish rather than dry; a pilsener-style lager of moderate alcohol; an even more moderate (2.5% abv) tart, fizzy lager refresher, and a porter style, dark strong beer of up to 7% abv, with caramel and high hop rates. It might also include a light, weak ale of dry, hoppy character, the only top-fermenting beer made in Poland. The Grodzisk Beer, still made with wood-smoked malt, as it has since the middle ages, contains a high percentage of wheat, is pale and fairly light-bodied, and has a pleasantly sourish, smoky, dry palate.

ZYWIEC***

Zywiec Breweries PLC. 35.5cl Bottled 4.3%: Toffee-nosed with fresh nectarine juice aromas. Was expecting something grainy and blandly international, but this is rather delicious, with toffee at the front of the gulp and mango at the back. Clean-edged, with a prickly, dry hop flavour creeping in after a few mouthfuls, but also with buttery, vanilla richness that returns at the finish, and a tropical fruit accent of succulent mango and guava, that's fruity but dry. Excellent with spicy food; made for partnering mango chutney and poppadoms, and an almondy, creamy chicken curry. The third star is only slightly wobbly because Zywiec has a tendency to turn flat and flaccid before the glass is empty. *Serve:* light fridge chill. *Avail:* BeerC.

Portugal

Brewing in Portugal began in the 17th century, and was greatly affected by the arrival of French, German and Danish influences in the last century. That of the Danes has made most direct impact, and Portuguese lager is generally in the mildly malty style, though they do also produce stronger lagers of the international sort, and one or two soft examples of the darker, malty Munich style. There are two mainland breweries, plus two further companies on the islands.

Seven beers are exported to Britain, all in small bottles: Sagres, Sagres Golden Premium, Coral, Cristal, Cristal Brown, Europa and Super Bock. Sagres is Portugal's number-one beer brand, brewed and bottled just outside Lisbon. Its name comes from the old seaport of the same name from which Christopher Columbus sailed.

CRISTAL*

Pilsener Unicer, Uniao Cervejeira. 33cl Bottled 5.2%:

Sweetish and just very slightly unpleasant bland international lager (but absolutely not a pilsener) with pronounced corn flavours: mild and malty, big fizzy bubbles and no real nose. Mediocre is the best that can be said. Teetering on the brink of star-deprivation. *Serve:* fridge cold. *Avail:* Odd.

EUROPA

Lager Central de Cervejas, Vialonga. 33cl Bottled 5.2%:

The initial aromas coming off this would probably strip paint, but settle down nicely into something closer to wallpaper paste. The flavour starts out with all the right clean and smooth, sweetish-in-the-middle Euro-beer intentions, but swiftly acquire a none-too-flattering industrial edge. The finish is unpleasantly mineral, with aspirin dryness. *Serve:* fridge cold. *Avail:* Thres.

SAGRES**

Central de Cervejas, Vialonga. 33cl Bottled 5.1%:

Undoubtedly the Portuguese lager of choice. A golden, bright beer with fresh, drily malty aromas and tropical fruit notes. In the mouth, it's medium-bodied, tasty, softly but aridly malty again, with sweet notes and a drying finish. Tastes like a good Danish beer: the apotheosis of positive Danish influences in Portuguese brewing? Good with pizza, and with grilled sardines. Almost three stars. *Serve:* fridge cold. *Avail:* Asda, Odd, Somer.

SUPER BOCK**

Unicer. 25cl Bottled 5.8%:

Pale strong lager with a malty, fruity smell, and plenty of nutty malt dryness on the palate, with banana and pineapple notes and robust, slightly vegetal, strong lager sweetness. Let down by a pronounced non-malted cereal character. *Serve:* light fridge chill. *Avail:* Beer C, Odd.

Russia

August*

Russian Premium Lager 33cl Bottled 4.5%: August and Zhiguli are the A–Z of Russian export brewing at present, though much of what was said in the Polish introduction (an industry happy to talk, unlike this one) is equally true of Russia's problems and plans. This is the commemorative beer of the Second Russian Revolution, of 1991, according to the label, but also made using the 'classical brewing techniques as learnt and refined by the Moscow Brewery since 1863'. Yes, it's more than a mite pretentious and gimmicky (though actually I quite like the political art label). The beer itself is clean(ish), a bit grainy, with a melon and apple fruit note, and is fairly creamy in texture. The finish is on the hard, mineral, cereal husky side, though. First and foremost, a fashion brand to be seen with at the café. *Serve:* fridge cold. *Avail:* Beer Paradise.

Zhiguli

Obolon Brewery, Kiev, Ukraine. 50cl Bottled 4.5%:
This seriously weird Eastern European lager is, so the bottle assures us, made by traditional methods, using artesian well water, barley, hops and yeast. But at least two samples have smelled rancid and antiseptic and of old socks, and tasted of overripe banana, pineapple and melon, with a strong apple-juicey flavour. While it's not exactly horrible, it's not exactly pleasant either. More compelling than nice. Probably this is a storage or bottling problem of some kind. Possibly, though, it stems from the brewery itself. *Serve:* fridge cold. *Avail:* specialists.

Singapore

Tiger***
Lager Beer Asia Pacific Brewery. 33cl Bottled 5%:
Bright golden lager with a white head and a slightly citrussy, fresh yeasty nose. The texture's sparkly, the flavours smooth, grain sweet, clean and rounded; it's extremely good with spicy food and in particular chicken, with a sweetness that's almost Kulfi-like. If there's a fault, it's that Tiger is too sweet and lacks balancing dryness, though a soft hop note accompanies the final, lemony wash over the tongue. Heineken own a substantial share in the brewery; hence its international marketing presence. In fact, Tiger has been popular in the West a lot longer, since the colonial days, and in particular since the residency of British soldiers here in the Second World War. The brewery also make a good bottom-fermented stout. *Serve:* fridge cold. *Avail*: Co-op, Tesco, Thres, Wait.

Spain

Spain has been brewing for 400 years (Holy Roman Emperor Charles V was born in Ghent) but it's true to say that, in terms of style and variety at least, it has no more complex a brewing culture than the tiny Duchy of Luxembourg. Certainly Spain produces volume lager for home and international consumption, but its native beer range, such as it exists at all, is confined to about the same pattern as Luxembourg's, with light pilsener-style lagers taking up most of the space, peppered by a few stronger, more flavoursome Export-style lagers, and the odd Bock beer. Naturally, we are in wine country here; even the French beer belt is essentially confined to the north, and so, driving through from the Channel, we have physically left the beer culture of northern Europe far behind. It's therefore not surprising that Spain has not produced a classic beer of its own style, but concentrates on light, quaffable lagers and fashion brands. Although, having charitably let them off the hook, it ought to be added that even Mexico makes a more interesting range than Spain can muster. Rather further south.

The biggest brewery is El Aguila, which is part of Heineken, and based in Madrid. Their Aguila pilsener is now being sold in Britain, and takes its turn in the popular, Spanish lager own-brands that proliferate here. As does Guinness-owned Cruzcampo, which supplies at least one British supermarket (Sainsbury's). Carlsberg and Kronenbourg (BSN) also own big parcels of Spanish brewing, as do several German companies. The one brand that most British drinkers would identify as authentically Spanish, San Miguel, is actually a Phillipine company which also happens to have three vast factory plants in Spain, as well as a brewery back home.

AGUILA**

Pilsener Lager El Aguila, Madrid. 25cl Bottled 5%:
Not a pilsener, but a corn sweet, pleasantly grain savoury, full-bodied and fairly clean Euro-lager, from a brewery established in 1900. *Serve:* fridge cold. *Avail:* Asda, Tesco, Wait.

ASDA SPANISH LAGER**

33cl Bottled 5.4%:
Probably Cruzcampo again (see Sainsbury's Spanish), but supermarkets aren't telling. This is pale gold, reasonably drinkable, very Spanish stuff, straight down the middle of the road, fairly fresh and quaffable, with corn-inspired apple-juice notes in the middle, and a dry finish that grows notably citric-pithy after a little while. *Serve:* fridge cold.

ESTRELLA*

Pilsen Extra Damm, Barcelona. 25cl Bottled 5.4%:
Also made in Valencia, Granada and

elsewhere: a mass-market Spanish brand of the cheap and cheerful sort. Fairly clean and grainy (probably awash with non-malted adjuncts), sweetish and spritzy, with a finish half pleasingly honeyed, half acrid and watery. Certainly not a pilsener, but not entirely to be damm-ed. *Serve:* fridge cold. *Avail:* Odd.

NORLANDER PILS '1920'

25cl Bottled 4.8%:
Cheap cereal nose, big fluffy white head, frankly nasty corn and general adjunct flavours, and a savoury, mineral, almost flinty finish. Could just as easily be manufactured from pencils, shavings and all. *Serve:* fridge cold. *Avail:* Sains.

SAINSBURY'S PREMIUM SPANISH LAGER*

33cl Bottled 5.4%:
A slightly fishy nose gives way to dried orange-peel aromas. Very soft, subtly malty palate, with a tiny hint of buttery vanilla and a drying finish with a fairly tannic whack. There's also something cheap and hard-edged in there; an industrial aspect, you might say, which leaves it with a single star. Also imported as Cruzcampo lager, under its own steam. *Serve:* fridge cold.

SAINSBURY'S PREMIUM SPANISH LAGER II**

33cl Bottled 5.4%:
Yes – the same beer as was awarded one star in the preceding paragraph, but here in a very different mood. This is, of course, pure speculation, but possibly the first sample had been sitting about in Sainsbury's for just a bit too long. This sample: same beer, same label, came direct from the importers and could have been a different beer. Hence its own tasting note. The nose is still a little sweaty, perhaps, but there's much more fruit on the palate, something tropical, with strong lager whisky butter flavours, and a briney almost oyster-like note at the back, finishing with firm hop astringency. Likeable, in short. *Serve:* fridge cold.

SAN MIGUEL**

San Miguel, Madrid. 33cl Bottled 5.4%:
Expectations of this 'premium export lager' are not high, having caught a whiff of a rather industrial, adjunct-laden nose, but things improve. It's not at all bad, with nice light carbonation, strong and clean, with some orange citrus notes, sweet cereal in the middle, quite a lot of body (but then it ought to at 5.4%), and a dry, almost briney finish. Only the adjuncty, rice and corn notes that linger on the finish let it down. *Serve:* fridge cold. *Avail:* widely.

TESCO SPANISH LAGER*

33cl Bottled 5.5%:
Terribly dull cheap Spanish lager with a distinctively sweaty nose, a flabby grain palate with just a touch of golden syrup and honey sweetness, and a vague bitterness in the finish. *Serve:* fridge cold.

Sri Lanka

Sir Samuel Baker, an English big-game hunter, founded a brewery at Nuwara Eliya in 1849, in the course of also establishing an English village there. The village, now grown into a tea-planting town some 6000 feet up in the cool hill country of Sri Lanka, also has a spectacular rock waterfall, and Sir Samuel very sensibly sited his new brewery close to these falls, using the clear mountain water surging past to make English beer. Perhaps tamed by this extraordinary achievement, Sir Samuel gave up big game hunting and instead became one of Sri Lanka's foremost conservationists. As well as its most famous brewer. Recently the Ceylon Brewery has decided to use his name on its established Lion Lager brand, and has also taken this opportunity to increase the strength (and quality) of the beer. There's another lager, which dates from 1983, when it was brewed to celebrate the state visit of the Queen, and is thus labelled Royal Pilsner. Ceylon Brewery's third beer, Lion Stout, is something of a classic. It's top-fermented, and tropical strength, at 7.5% abv, and on its home turf, still cask-conditioned and dispensed by traditional English handpump, as Sir Samuel would have wished. The brewery is still at Nuwara Eliya, despite the fact that the imported ingredients have to trundle along precarious Sri Lankan hill roads to reach the brewery site. An English yeast is still used, as is the mountain water.

There's a second brewery in Sri Lanka, and it also produces a stout; as in Africa and the West Indies, the Sri Lankan stout style owes much to the legacy of colonial rule. The brewery is called McCallum, often known as the Three Coins brewery, and its most interesting beer is called Sando Stout, after Eugene Sandow, a famous Victorian circus strong-man. Sando Stout is bottom-fermented, like many other tropical stouts.

LION LAGER**

Ceylon Brewery. 32.5cl Bottled 4.2%:
The old Lion Lager brand, tasted before it was officially replaced by Sir Samuel Baker. Grain sweet, round and clean, with a little cereal huskiness and a drying finish. Simple, fairly drinkable, of modest strength. *Serve:* fridge cold. *Avail:* BeerC.

LION STOUT***

32.5cl Bottled 7.5%:
Blackish-brown, potent tropical stout with loose-leaf tea and cold stewed-tea aromas, lots of compelling blackcurrant and mint among the usual coffeeish stout flavours, and a little rounding-off tannic oak and dry hoppiness. Good texture, though it could have a little more zizz to balance the richness. *Serve:* room temp/larder cool. *Avail:* BeerC.

ROYAL PILSNER **
32.5cl Bottled 4.5%:
Brewed in honour of the Queen's state visit to Sri Lanka, this is a pale gold lager with promisingly buttery and lemony aromas. Flavours aren't quite as good, though. It's light, mildly spritzy, with a soft hop note, but the (very Asian-style) buttery, fat finish overbalances the flavours a little, leaving the whole effect a bit flabby, though there is also a dry apple fruit note and a touch of lemon. Modest, but pleasant lager, seriously mislabelled as a pilsener. *Serve:* light fridge chill. *Avail:* specialists.

SIR SAMUEL BAKER**
62.5cl Bottled 5%:
The new Ceylon brewery lager has much more pilsener character than the 'Royal' (albeit low-key in style), drier and fresher on the palate with a little hop character. It also comes in a good big bottle. Flavours are subtle (rather than bland), with lots of zingy mountain water and spritzy freshness. No doubt it's terrific in a hot climate, but also tastes quite good on a rainy English day in June. *Serve:* light fridge chill. *Avail:* specialists.

Sweden

Of roughly equal size to California or Spain, Sweden's land area towers above that of Denmark, across the sea to the south, but this is a far less distinguished brewing country. This is partly down to geography: Sweden is a tremendously long country, covering more climatic zones than any other European country except Russia. Half its land surface is covered in forest; the rest is peppered with 100,000 lakes. There are thousands of islands, and 7000-foot-high mountains to the north west; less than 10% of its remaining land area is farmland. There are only 9 million Swedes, and 90% belong to the Lutheran Church. Added together, these are not the most fertile conditions for a great brewing culture.

Publications produced by the Swedish farming and food organizations don't even mention beer, though they do proudly advertise the virtues of sweet arrack punch, a relic of East Indies colonial days, as well as the more famous Schnapps, which arrived here from Russia (who got it from the East).

Unlike Denmark, which happens to be stuck to the north German coast and is the most liberal of Scandinavian countries in its relationship with alcohol, Sweden is very much with the north, and has many of the attitudes that characterize Norway. Like Norway, it's a society that still has living traditions, and has preserved many of its rituals, customs and seasonal festivals. In the more traditional (conservative) Swedish community, the coffee party is still the classic social event; Swedes drink huge amounts of coffee. But things are beginning to change. Immigration into Sweden from the Mediterranean has loosened the formality of Swedish life a little. Drinking in cafés is becoming more widespread, and it's no longer required that hot food be ordered at the same time. Foreign influences (not least from the EU) have also brought foreign beers into the state-controlled off-licences. And two mainstream Swedish lagers are beginning to appear in British retailers.

As in other Scandinavian countries, brewing in Sweden goes back a long way, and Swedish beer has not altogether abandoned the ancient ways of doing things, before the hop plant took hold. You can still find mead-style honey beer here, beers seasoned with bog myrtle and angelica, and juniper beers of various sorts, though these are very much in the minority (and a minority taste). Swedes, like the rest of Scandinavia, prefer light-bodied, crisp lagers, though more interesting beer styles are also produced by the nine brewing companies: three big, three middle-sized, three newish, all pretty conventional in approach.

Pripps is the biggest of the Swedish breweries, and state-owned. Its fine Carnegie Porter, which for a while was available only by prescription, commemorates a Scotsman who founded a brewery in Gothenburg, which later merged with Pripps brewery. It comes in two strengths and is top-fermenting. Pripps also makes other speciality beers, including a Munich-style lager, a malty soft one, and a whole range of pale, inoffensive brands, as well as a flagship pilsener with more character and aroma. There's also a sweet, rich Christmas beer (Jule Øl): Swedes have a collective sweet tooth, presumably because sugar was a rare and expensive commodity for a long time.

The other brand we see in Britain, apart from Pripps, is Spendrup's, which is the brandname of the Grangesbergs brewery. Theirs is an all-malt pilsener: Swedish law demands brewers use a minimum of 70% barley malt, but sugar and corn are widely included to make up the remaining 30% of the mash. There's another state-owned brewery, Falken, which uses the Falcon brand name. Brew pubs are not permitted by law in Sweden.

PRIPPS***

Special Lager Pripps, Gothenburg. 35.5cl Bottled 5.6%:

Smartly-packaged beer that's been brewed for over 160 years, these days from maize and ascorbic acid (E300) as well as water, malt, yeast and hops. Nothing unusual there, except that this is a delicious beer, shiny gold in colour, with appetizing butter and vanilla aromas, and decidedly almond, marzipan notes in its rich, full-bodied flavour, which is also very refreshing and clean, thanks to a tart citric edge. As they say, 'just the right balance of body and bite'. Quite strong, very tasty, should be better known. *Serve:* light fridge chill. *Avail:* BeerC.

SPENDRUP'S OLD GOLD***

Spendrup's. 33cl Bottled 5%:

Two brothers run the show at Spendrup's, and one of them at least is mad for style. This chicly-packaged, ridged bottle has a black label that refuses to mention Sweden, and originally had nothing but the words 'Old Gold' on it, with the contents and strength information hidden away in the gold margins. Certainly one of the handsomest lagers to emerge during these tastings. Aromas are fresh and yeasty with a fruit note, and the flavours fresh and wholesome, sparkling in texture, with a little buttery ripeness, before a clean, lemony dryness takes over. Perhaps just a bit too clean-edged? *Serve:* light fridge chill. *Avail:* BeerC.

Switzerland

Swiss brewing is known to beer producers across the world in the shape of the influential Hurlimann Brewery. To drinkers, however, Swiss beer is like as not notable only for producing the strongest beer in the world, or rather the strongest bottom-fermented, regular-range, standard beer in the world. Or rather, *one* of them. The strongest beer in the world contest is like that. While the other big contender for strongest lager on the planet, EKU 28 from Kulmbach, Germany, has a higher original gravity, Samichlaus, of the Hurlimann Brewery, Zurich, has the highest alcohol by volume. Just.

Hurlimann are yeast culture experts, and well known among brewers for their nice clean (very Swiss) yeast cultures, supplied worldwide. In the course of their work on yeasts that would tolerate high alcohol levels – many won't – Hurlimann produced their own, illustrative example of a successful beer made with just such a yeast strain. They called it Samichlaus because it was made on 6 December, St Nicholas's Day. The beer is still made only on that date, then matured for a year and released for sale the following December. At the other end of the scale, and also as a result of their hi-tech tinkering with yeasts and methodologies, Hurlimann made an alcohol-free beer, and other Swiss breweries have followed suit.

Beyond these specialities, there's a much more conventional face to Swiss brewing, with plenty of light, quaffable, international lagers on offer, and drier, 'premium' beers. There are no 'pilseners' in Swiss brewing, because it's recognized that this is a Czech style, and that the word pilsener ought not to be used elsewhere. Instead, 'Premium' and 'Special' indicate well-made, fuller-bodied, more flavoursome lager beers.

Aside from a short range of light, premium and special lagers, Swiss breweries might produce one or two darker, stronger beers. The altbiers associated with Dortmund (classically top-fermented and cool-conditioned for mellow smoothness) are becoming increasingly popular, and wheat beers are made by four of the 35 or so breweries operating. Some of this number are reasuringly small, though most participate in a trade agreement that is cartel-like in effect. A handful of brew pubs have emerged in the last few years, too.

Perhaps surprisingly, there's no pure beer law in Switzerland, but it wouldn't occur to most of their brewing companies to use anything beyond, perhaps, just a little adjunct support. There's one famous exception in the form of Maisgold, from the Rosengarten (rose garden) brewery, which is proud to be a corn beer. Many beers are all-malt. Lagers are usually lagered for a decent period, and are also often unpasteurized, for the home market at least.

There are four big brewing groups: Hürlimann, Lowenbrau (not related to the German brewery), Cardinal and Feldschlossen. Feldschlossen's beers are (officially) imported into Britain but proved impossible to get hold of for the *Guide*'s tastings. Hürlimann lagers, other than Samichlaus, which is imported, are made in Britain under licence by Shepherd Neame of Kent. Swiss Lowenbrau and Cardinal beers are not presently imported, according to the Embassy.

HÜRLIMANN**

Premium Swiss Lager Hurlimann. 50cl Bottled 5%:

If the broad-shouldered bottle looks more like a Shepherd Neame example, that's not surprising, because the Kent brewers make this lager under licence. It's a light-bodied, pretty tasty, sweet barley grain lager, modest in scope, certainly, and perhaps a little over-sweet and lacking in vigour (and fizz), but fine with food. *Serve:* light fridge chill. *Avail*: Sains, Tesco, VicW.

HÜRLIMANN**

44cl Canned 5%:

Canned version, also made by Shepherd Neame in Kent. Tastes much like the bottled one, sweet and clean, a little bland, with just the faintest alcoholic pungency, creamy in texture and with no adjunct flavours. Reasonable, efficient, and a bit dull (no, I'm not going to say 'much like the Swiss themselves'). *Serve:* light fridge chill. *Avail*: Sains, Tesco. VicW.

SAMICHLAUS**

25cl Bottled 14%:

Accredited in the *Guinness Book of Records* as the strongest beer in the world (within certain qualifying limits), and it's undoubtedly a great achievement, a credit to the Hürlimann yeast scientists, blah blah. But the fact is that Samichlaus (Santa Claus) is pretty difficult to drink, actually. Though having been exposed to it on several occasions and become more acclimatized, I can see how some people get a taste for its particular blend of Bovril and red wine, and the cough mixtureish notes suggest it might also be useful in homeopathy. The finish suggests a particularly good, winey consommé (or is it homemade oxtail soup?). Personally, I can only bear to drink it larder cool. Too warm and too large a glass, and 'hurlimann!' as Billy Connolly might say. *Serve:* room temp/larder cool. *Avail:* BeerC.

Thailand

In Thailand, in the 1920s, beer imports had reached such impressive levels that plans were drawn up for a native Thai brewery, intended to make a proper European lager of sufficient quality to stem the tide of imports. A resident German brewer in Bangkok was used to help set up the Boon Rawd Brewery, makers of Singha lager. Building on Boon Rawd started in 1930. It's a modern brewery, on the banks of the Chao Phya river. Singha, launched in 1934, was the first Thai beer to be brewed, and, despite the local rival, Amarit, it is still Thailand's most popular lager, made in two versions: 6% abv for export (reduced from the previous 6.5%) and 4.7% abv for the home market, which is the strength Thai drinkers prefer. It was named by a public votes process familiar to anyone who has helped name a labrador pup on *Blue Peter*: the world is grateful that Singha, the name of a mythological local lion, was chosen and not the other contender, Rot Fal.

Singha is still made to German specifications – that is from imported (mainly European) hops, malt, yeast and water only. The brewery used to import its malt, too, but after a series of experimental farm projects has now set up its own barley fields in the very north of the country, and malts the grain there to its own specifications. Well water, of an ideal quality for pilsener brewing, is also used (not water from the Chao Phya). Singha is fermented for 10 days, and lagered for a full 8 weeks, before being filtered, pasteurized and bottled. Pasteurization is a fairly recent, rather regrettable innovation, no doubt in the interests of shelf life. The beer seems to have less pilsener hoppiness than it used to, but has retained its succulent and refreshing Eastern character. There is no more ideal an accompaniment to Thai food.

AMARIT**

Amarit Brewery, Bangkok. 33cl Bottled 5.5%: Very pale, rather strong lager with a savoury sweet fruit aroma, suggestive of something tropically exotic, like starfruit. Flavours are light and spritzy, but also smooth, until the finish, which has both an Export lager-like, creamy and spiritous note, and more of that elusive tropical fruitiness. *Serve:* light fridge chill. *Avail:* specialists and Selfridges.

SINGHA***

Boon Rawd Brewery Co. 35.5cl Bottled 6%: Bright, shiny yellow-gold beer made for export. It has appetizingly fruity aromas, and a dry refreshing texture, sparkly lively but not too gassy. Grain sweetness is closely followed by a citric, slightly sour note, which is then chased off by a densely butter-toffee and vanilla finish. A delicious summer beer – but watch out for the strength. *Serve:* light fridge chill. *Avail*: Beer, Thres.

Turkey

Until 1955 a state monopoly controlled brewing, importing and beer sales in Turkey; 1955 brought change, and a new lease of life for private industry. In 1969 there were three breweries operating: two belonging to the Efes Pilsen Group, called Erciyas Biracilik and Ege Biracilik, plus Tuborg, the Danish company now part of Carlsberg. In 1977 a third Efes brewery opened. There's also Tekel Brewery, which is still state-owned, but which only has 3.5% of the market.

There's been a steady rate of increase in beer consumption in Turkey. In 1994, 9.3 litres a head were drunk of which 6.7 litres has been identified as Efes Pilsen beers. The remaining 25% or so of the market is Tuborg's.

Efes is to open a fourth brewery, in Ankara, late in 1995. It also has two maltings, a hop-processing plant and an investment company. By the end of 1995 Efes will boast a 750-million-litre a year capacity. It now exports to 28 countries, including Germany and Russia. Efes get their barley for malting from the plains of Central Anatolia, and process 100,000 tons a year; some of their malt is also exported to breweries in South America and Africa. Their new investment and overseas arm (1993) has among other things set up a new brewery in Romania, and soft drink factories in some of the more obscure and far-flung corners of the Russian Federation. The Efes Group were the very first customers of the new Istanbul Stock Exchange when it opened its doors in 1986. They're also heavily into sponsorship (billiards, tennis) and stage cultural events like the Efes Pilsen Blues Festival, as well as having their very own basketball team.

There are four Efes products: Efes Pilsen, the flagship and export brand; Efes Light; Efes Extra, and Efes Alkolsüz, an alcohol-free beer made mainly for export to Saudi Arabia. Efes also make Löwenbräu under licence.

EFES PILSENER**

Premium Beer Efes Brewery. 33cl Bottled 5%: This brewery, and its flagship brand, take their name from the ancient Ionian city of Ephesus, the Roman capital of Asia. It's a full-bodied, tasty lager in the roughly Budweiser Budvar sweet Czech style, with toffee and honey notes, but lacking the Czech classic's pilsener complexity and dryness. A little samey and lacking in structure, but still a decent little beer, especially good with spicy, herby dishes. A tendency towards wet cardboard notes deep in the finish (staleness, probably) lets the side down a little. *Serve:* light fridge chill. *Avail:* BeerC.

United States of America

Modern American brewing is full of the most intriguing contradictions: this is at once the most conformist and the most progressive of beer cultures, dominated by giant brewery corporations turning out dull mass-market lagers, but at the same time peppered with the seeds of the most varied and vibrant microbrewery culture to be found anywhere.

The United States is easily the biggest brewing nation in the world, if we are simply concerned with volume. The huge beer factories which have developed through repetitive takeover and closure in the last 50 years haven't had to worry about whether their products are popular with the rest of the world, because of the sheer size and sales potential of their own country. The US population has been sufficiently complacent and obliging for a long time, and the wheels of export markets have been oiled by the rest of the globe's continuing love affair with the idea of America. The USA has been very competently turning out cheap quaffing beers aimed at the working man for over 100 years, and in more recent times has succeeded in creating a modern snob appeal out of these humble associations, an achievement epitomized by Budweiser, the best-selling beer in the world.

At the same time, the USA is currently the most dynamic brewing nation in the world: no contest, no argument. This is a recent development: any visitor to the States in the 1970s would have found just 40 breweries carving up the map between them. But there are now 400 breweries – more than 400, and counting – with at least one new microbrewery opening every week, and the pace of this expansion swiftly gathering speed. This is remarkable in itself, but more exciting still is the approach these small breweries are taking. Just as America has become a melting pot of nations, it is now becoming a repository of the world's beer styles. Just about every beer variety ever developed anywhere is now being re-developed here, by hundreds of little breweries spread across the country. Some have set out to produce faithful reproductions, and many have succeeded; others have set out to create new beers, variants on the old traditions that have a distinctive American twist, and are perhaps destined to become new U.S. classics. Perhaps because American brewing and beer-drinking have been so very predictable and lacking in excitement for so many years, the new generation of U.S. breweries has an energy, imagination and spirit of innovation that presently leads the world.

It's also partly down to beer's American image. Because the new beer styles are so very different from the mass-market light-bodied pale lagers America had previously thought interchangeable with the word 'beer' (in fact, they *are* interchangeable with the word 'beer'; America has beers and ales like we have beers and lagers), they have more or less escaped the working-class and macho image many of the canned and bottled national lager brands have cultivated. Instead, American micro beers have managed to slot themselves into a position closer to that of American wine, and have taken their place in American foodie culture much more naturally than anything achieved by British micros. This has been helped very much by the respect some extremely influential restaurants have previously shown to imported beer classics, and are now showing to their own. San Francisco, particularly, is famous for its beer-listing restaurants. California in general is a vitally important arena in the great American beer revival (in fact it has the most breweries of any state), as are the East Coast regions surrounding New York state, but both are slightly overshadowed by the enthusiasm and innovation of the North-West, and in particular the area surrounding the urbane, coffee-house culture of Seattle.

When asked to comment on the nature and pace of change of their native brewing culture, successful small American breweries (often called craft breweries) draw parallels with the way the American wine industry developed 30 years ago, when at first a trickle and then a flood of new names appeared to challenge the previously cosy rule of mass-market wine brands like Gallo and Masson. When it launched, in 1985, the Boston Beer Company – which has risen almost without trace to the status of fourteenth-largest brewery in America in just ten years, and now widely exports its flagship brand, Samuel Adams Boston Lager – joined a beer market that was just about moribund. There were a handful of operating micros, but mostly of cottage industry size: only 103 beers showed at the 1985 Great American Beer Festival. In 1993 there were over 900, and they were the prime products of only 200 breweries. The Boston Beer Company is typical of many of the new generation in discounting altogether the bland mass-market lagers of the national giants as serious competition. They are such entirely different products. Rather, they see their competitors arriving in ships: imports are perceived as the only real rivals for market share.

Samuel Adams

Jim Koch, founder of the Boston Beer Company, comes from an old brewing family, and took the original recipe for Samuel Adams Boston Lager from the papers left by his grandfather, Louis. He was a management consultant at the time, but, like so many other micro-owners, felt the irresistible call of brewing. That's one really noticeable feature of the micro revolution here: the chaps (it's almost always chaps) starting up these little companies rarely seem to be time-served apprentices making a careful transition between their big brewery job and a new little business. Instead, they frequently turn out to be (initially, at least) no better qualified to run a brewery than most other impassioned beer buffs – they have just enjoyed drinking the products, and have caught the micro-brewing bug. Micro founders are often ex-computer boffins, ex-lawyers, ex-Wall Street: they hail from the great drinking professions. Starting up a successful little brewery of your own seems to have become a new American Dream.

But back to Jim Koch. He started by hawking the lager around Boston bars and restaurants in 1985, just a year before Pete Slosberg (same generation, same sort of career-defection) did likewise on the opposite coast with his Pete's Wicked Ale. Like the Pete's brands, the Boston Beer Company's beers are contract brewed at various locations around America, a development that earns them more than a little flak, and puts both companies well outside the perimeter fence of the widest microbrewery definition. Contract brewing for volume and the increasing demands of the export market will probably lead to a contract in Europe before too long.

Currently Boston has a stable of 12 bottled beers, including Boston Stock Ale, Octoberfest, Winter Lager (a weizenbock), Double Bock, both a light and a dark wheat beer, Honey Porter and Cream Stout. The flagship brand remains Samuel Adam's Boston Lager, which is made from pure ingredients, including Bavarian Tettnang and Hallertau hops, and can boast four times the sales of its nearest independent rival (presumably Pete's Wicked). Samuel Adams Boston Ale uses the more English-inspired Fuggles and Goldings, with a dash of Czech Saaz for aroma, and is kräusened. (Incidentally, the original Samuel Adams was the rabble-rouser who kicked off the Boston Tea Party, and also happened to own a brewery in Boston.) Unfortunately, the company has so far resisted their British PR's suggestions that brands besides the Boston Lager would go down well here.

Budweiser

The USA started out, like so many others, as an ale-making country, until 19th-century Czech and German immigrants brought their new traditions. Lager has now been made in America for 150 years. As in most other countries, early American industry particularly favoured the lager-brewing process, as it has in most other countries, simply because lagers are better suited to factory production methods and large-scale retail sale. Anheuser Busch, the world's biggest brewing company, embodies the logical conclusion of that process. Based in Missouri in the Mid-West, but with a dozen brewery plants dotted around the country, Anheuser Busch now produces a staggering 100 million barrels a year. Its Budweiser brand, the world's first mass-market beer and still the world's number-one seller, is typical of American lagers in being high in corn and rice ingredients and low in flavour: much is made of the blend of hop varieties used, but whatever they are, they are certainly used very sparingly. Budweiser is also typical in being lagered only for 21 days, as opposed to the 3 months' maturation awarded to its Czech near-namesake. In fact, 21 days is considered wantonly generous by other mega-breweries.

The brewery has been Anheuser Busch since 1860. Mr Anheuser, a soap baron, had invested in a failing small brewery some years before, only becoming its (extremely unwilling) owner in 1860, when it was otherwise close to complete collapse. His daughter then married Mr Busch (the Busch family are still in control). Mr Busch came up with the idea of modelling their beers on Czech pilseners. Pilsener not being available as a trademark, he chose Budweiser, after the home town of the royal court brewery of Bohemia. The beer was launched in 1876. Busch even invented the refrigerated rail wagon, to transport his beer all over America. Michelob, also named after a Bohemian brewing town, followed in 1896.

Anheuser Busch is still based in St Louis, Missouri, which frequently calls itself the gateway to the Mid-West. This was once the industrial heartland of American brewing, though in recent years its brands have lost more than a little of their original gloss. Big companies like Heileman (now owned by Lion Nathan of New Zealand) and Miller, which is famous for launching the Lite Beer style into the mass-market 20 years ago, and Pabst, once makers of the classic blue-collar cheap quaffer of America (Blue Ribbon), now known for its Ballantine Ale, and Schell, and Strob are all in this region, which, as the names suggest, was a popular destination for German émigré brewers.

The North-West and California

They say that the popularity of ales (as opposed to lagers) in the North-West has something to do with the climate: in Seattle, like Glasgow, it's said to be always raining, or contemplating raining. Certainly the cooler northern regions of the USA are the natural home of the microbrewery, with light and undemanding bottled and canned coolers more unshakeably at home in the hotter southern states. This is also a great barley and hop growing area, and prides itself on its thriving pub culture, in which draught ales of character are particularly prized. Micros and brew pubs abound . . .

Anchor

. . . As they also do further south, in California. The micro revolution really started here, with the pioneer company New Albion, established in 1977 (now defunct), when the only other small independent was Anchor Steam. Anchor brewery is in fact 100 years old, though widely associated with the micro revolution in America. The brewery makes a superb range of beers, including the extraordinarily dry and moreish Liberty Ale. But its flagship product, Anchor Steam Beer, was originally created from a make-do-and-mend solution to the problem of making lager-style beers in a warm climate without refrigeration. The brewery's answer was to use lager yeasts at ale temperatures, in uniquely designed shallow vessels that make for rapid cooling. The 'steam' soubriquet probably comes from the sudden release of gas from this naturally lively beer when the vessels are tapped. The brand has created a unique style, but fiercely protects the 'Steam Beer' name as a personal trademark, effectively preventing a new genre of beer developing. Anchor was in fact saved from the brink of ruin in the 1960s by its now owner, Fritz Maytag, who used his family's washing-machine fortune to rescue an American classic company from dereliction and turned it into an international success. Liberty Ale is a new beer to us in Britain, but was actually launched

20 years ago, to commemorate the bicentennial of Paul Revere's War of Independence-sparking ride from Boston to Lexington. It's been on the permanent range since 1983. Liberty is made from 100% American ale malt, and great handfuls (sackfuls) of rose-floral, fruity, resiny and aromatic Cascade hops. Heavy dry hopping gives it that immense astringency.

Pete's Wicked Beers

Pete's Brewing Company also started out in California. Pete's Wicked Ale, the flagship and first beer made, was developed in 1986 in keen home-brewer Pete Slosberg's kitchen after six years of patient trial runs. He had a real struggle getting his beer into retail outlets at first, but once the Ale had become fashionable in the San Francisco Bay area, demand grew like Topsy. California is also home to Sierra Nevada, a 15-year-old micro that's unquestionably in the inner circle, the élite of American microbrewing, and in the next five years is expected to move into number three position on the micro sales league table (after Boston and Pete's, currently at number five, and ahead of Anchor).

Pete's Wicked Ale is made from pale, crystal and chocolate malts (crystal malt is called caramel malt in the USA), and hopped with Cascade and Brewer's Gold. Pete's Wicked Lager, now reformulated and more characterful, also uses pale and crystal malts, and Saaz, Tettnang and Yakima Cluster hops, before dry hopping with more Saaz. It's the Saaz that's made the difference. It's also krausened for a spritzy, clean texture. Pete's Wicked Red, which only arrived in Britain in summer 1995, is an amber ale made with pale, crystal and Munich malts for a rich red hue, and then hopped with Yakima Cluster and Cascade, before being late-hopped with Tettnang. There are only two other products at present. Pete's Wicked Summer Brew, the newest addition, is a pale ale made with pale and wheat malts and hopped with Tettnang, before being flavoured with lemon. The other, Pete's Wicked Winter Brew, from a recipe devised by a home-brew competition champion, features pronounced raspberry and nutmeg flavours. Perhaps the huge success of authentic-flavoured-iced-tea companies like Snapple will inspire more flavoured American micro beers. Pete's brands meanwhile are currently contract brewed at Minnesota Brewery, St Paul.

Two Californian microbreweries whose bottled products are just beginning to arrive in Britain, via the importer-wholesaler network, are St Stan's and Devil Mountain. The St Stan's range comes from the Stanislaus Brewing Company in Modesto. They specialize in the German altbier style, originally brewing on a hobby basis, then via a brew pub, and now as a fully-fledged independent brewery. The Devil Mountain brewery is situated in the Gold Rush port of Benicia, once famous for its bars and brothels, and is named after the local Mount Diablo. Their unpasteurized beers use hops from the Pacific North-West, Sierra Nevada mountain water, and a very old strain of English yeast. Both companies make a blonde, an amber and a dark.

East and South

Over on the East Coast, meanwhile, a whole network of micros and brew pubs is springing up, in Boston and New England particularly, where British settlers first made ale and where the ale-making tradition is now experiencing a popular revival. As is a taste for real, appetizing, wholesome lagers. In upstate New York, the tremendously influential F. X. Matt, a fourth-generation German family brewer, contract brewer, packager and general fount of wisdom, responsible for getting many small brewery companies on the right road, is currently contract brewing the delicious Brooklyn Lager, among other brands. Down in the south-east, the climate (both literally and politically) favours solid patriotic old-fashioned American brands (thin clean lagers, mostly) designed to appeal to solidly patriotic old-fashioned American men, though there are daring pockets of innovation.

The south-west has a similar brewing environment, though Pierre Celis, of (Belgian) Hoegaarden fame is exerting a positive influence with his Texan brewery, making the rather wonderful American wheat beer, Celis White. Pierre Celis was the man responsible for re-kindling the popularity of Belgian wheat beers, when he opened the De Kluis brewery in East Brabant, a traditional wheat beer area that had lost its last such brewery in the 1950s. Having made Hoegaarden White a huge international hit, Pierre Celis sold out to Stella Artois and moved to Texas, where he has done it all over again with Celis White. To such an extent that not only is his American wheat beer being made under licence in Belgium by Hoogstraten, but (rumour has it as we go to press) Coors have recently purchased at least a large stake in the new Celis operation.

Just occasionally the south comes up with a high fashion statement. Currently it's Crazy Ed's Cave Creek Chili Beer, which is huge in Japan, and features a marinated small green chilli in the neck of the bottle –which, as Crazy Ed says, 'gives the consumer an immediate glow, often to the entertainment of other patrons'. Last but hardly least, there's Coors, down in Colorado, which turns out more volume beer than any other single brewery plant, so making Colorado the highest-volume American brewing state of all. Coors lager has at least the edge over many other mass-market American lagers in using rocky mountain spring water and their own malt and hops, and in filtering rather than pasteurizing the beer. Filtering removes the yeasts without jeopardizing flavour and body in the pasteurization machine, where beers can all too easily be inadvertently cooked.

A World of Beer Styles

The American microbrewery movement, meanwhile, is literally offering a world of beer styles to an eager young (and not so young) audience. Thanks to their efforts, the USA can now be credited with producing some of the most interesting beer in the world: hoppier lagers than are made almost anywhere else, redder and more distinctive 'Irish Red' ales than have probably ever been tasted in Ireland, richer Scotch ales ditto, juicier wheat beers and bockier

Bocks than are produced from many a German brewery, and, perhaps, a carefully researched kölsch (Cologne) or altbier (Düsseldorf); more complex 'British' ales than many of our own breweries offer, as well as superb dark beers, porters and stouts, drily nutty, fruity pale and amber ales, and others besides, in seemingly endless variation.

Probably the most influential British import in the USA micro revolution has been the fine bottled beers of Sam Smith, from Yorkshire. Sam Smith's Nut Brown, together with Scottish & Newcastle's Newcastle Brown, has been instrumental in developing the American brown ale style. Pete's Wicked Ale is classified not as a bitter but as an American Brown Ale, which they define as 'combining caramel richness with hop dryness'. Britain's robustly flavoured, medium-strong bitters are also admired, and Fuller's ESB has been a huge hit. Micro beers have now emerged in this style; Redhook Brewery ESB has developed a good following. The hugely influential Sam Smith's Strong Pale Ale, and Bass Pale Ale are widely cited as classics of the English pale style, and their own, dry and hoppy Ballantine's IPA the classic homegrown India Pale Ale. Exported Scotch Ales are also popular in America: McEwans Export and Belhaven particularly.

Guinness and Murphy's stouts have been a great success in the past, but the creamier, more complex Sam Smith's Oatmeal Stout is the connoisseur's preference. Carlsberg Tetley's made-for-export Watney's Cream Stout is widely available. American-made Porters, in the modern style – with a roasty, fruity aroma and a bittersweet character – are hugely popular, and both Anchor and Sierra Nevada make successful examples. Orval and Chimay are America's favourite Trappist ales at present, and Theakston's Old Peculier has become the mass-market so-called 'English Strong Ale'. Specialist strong imports like Thomas Hardy's Ale are popular; Anchor and Sierra Nevada both make outstanding 'barley-wine-style ales' (as the compromise American idiom has it) of their own. Pilseners and softer lagers from Europe have been a huge hit with the specialist retailers: Pilsner Urquell from the Czech Republic, DAB, and the entire packaged Spaten and Paulaner ranges (lagers, dark lagers and bocks), plus the Mexican amber lager, Dos Equis, from over the border. Sierra Nevada, apart from making the best-known pale ale in America, also brew their own, rather distinguished pale bock. Sierra Nevada are rumoured to be planning a big European push in 1996, so with any luck we'll get to taste it then.

Imported fruit lambics have also been a hit in the States, and American brewers are starting to make their own fruit beers, often using native fruits, like Marin's Blueberry Ale and Samuel Adams Cranberry Lambic (which isn't, of course, a lambic at all). The specialist American market also favours herb and spice beers, both imported and micro-style: Anchor Christmas is the best known of the spicy winter style, while Alaskan Brewery's Smoked Porter is the native answer to the popularity of the imported German rauchbiers. America is also besotted with wheat beers of every sort, and makes its own bottled versions: Samuel Adam's Dunkelweizen is probably the best known. As this New World of world beers grows in scale, takes to the bottle, and begins to look to export markets, traditional producers in Europe might just start to get a bit twitchy.

Certainly the American giants are already keeping a watchful eye on their collective progress, and some have already test marketed more interesting products than they would have previously countenanced. The home beer market is worth some $50 billion, and Anheuser Busch, Miller and Coors still control 77% of that market, so there is no immediate cause for panic. But whereas in the old days (around ten years ago) competition had simply come down to a price and marketing war, the giants have since concentrated on creating new products within the bounds of conventional mass-market styles: ice beers, dry beers, lite beers, genuine draft and the like, to give the impression of choice and novelty within their own beer range. Most of them are even now developing, or considering developing their own versions of some of the ale styles that have taken the micro beer market by storm.

Not that mass-market ales don't exist already in America, although American labelling is complicated considerably by the law that still applies in some states, demanding that beers of over 5% abv be called 'ale', whatever they are, and by the American use of 'beer' to mean lager. Ale in America can also be a bottom-fermented product, though bottom-fermented examples are frequently also warm-fermented (like a traditional ale) to create ale-like fruitiness and complexity. Pete's Wicked Ale is a bottom-fermented beer. Mass-market ales also tend to be lighter and blander than the British model, and Cream Ales even more so – some may even be made by blending a pale, creamy ale with lager for a hybrid effect. Microbreweries are mad for ales and use the word whenever possible (Liberty Ale, Wicked Ale, Boston Ale and so on) to reinforce the message to the home market that this is not a lager, and thus, in American terminology, not a beer either.

ANCHOR CHRISTMAS**

Anchor Steam, San Francisco. 35.5cl Bottled 5.5%:

Makes a good Christmas present, as it has 'Merry Xmas And A Happy New Year' written all over the label. This is very much a spice beer, dark and porterish with apple mint, lemon and nutmeg on the nose, and spicy, savoury flavours, like the equivalent of a cold mulled wine. Spices are joined on the palate by coffeeish and roast malt flavours, with a slight fruit tang, and soft herbal notes in the finish. An objective and a subjective point: objective first – flavours are let down by a flabby, thin texture. And (subjectively) I find the flavours over-spiced and a bit unbalanced. But you could grow accustomed to its face. And it's probably an excellent cold cure. *Serve:* room temp. *Avail:* specialists.

ANCHOR PORTER***

35.5cl Bottled 5.7%:

A in this instance stands for Absolutely Atypical of the general American export to Europe, a welcome despatch from the thriving indie brewing culture of America. There's strawberry jam, chocolate and coffee on the nose, and fizzy, rich and creamy coffee, vanilla and chocolate flavours, before things turn very mildly liquoricey in the soft, persistently but gently drying finish. Rich but refreshing, in the fairly light-bodied, spritzy, classic Anchor style. Virtually handmade from 100% malted barley and whole hops, with an entirely natural carbonation. *Serve:* room temp/larder cool. *Avail:* specialists.

ANCHOR STEAM BEER***

35.5cl Bottled 4.8%:

This shiny amber-russet, all-barley malt beer has now built a reputation almost bigger than it can withstand. It's good drinking, but in a surprisingly modest way, offering arrestingly fresh, prickly bubbles (high carbonation levels are right for the style), ever so slightly sour fruit notes, and more than a hint of Irn Bru, with a dash of tropical juice and a dry malt finish. Good, ingenious and wholesome certainly, but not quite of four-star magnitude. *Serve:* larder cool. *Avail:* BeerC, Sains, Wait.

Asda American Lager**

Evansville, Indiana. 35.5cl Bottled 5%:
From the same brewery as Sainsbury's Indiana Gold, a medium-sweet, clean and quaffable table lager. Aromas are mildly appley and orangey, and there's a hint of fruit on the subdued sweetcorn palate, a faintly resiny note, and just a little pale malt body in the mouth. Not completely thin and 'lite' in style, though it does taste under-strength. *Serve:* fridge cold.

Brooklyn Lager***

35.5cl Bottled 5.5%:
This brand dates only from 1988, but contrives to be brewed with Schaefer yeast, though that brewery, a Brooklyn landmark, closed in 1976. A reddish-orange beer, with pungent, spikily sweet and sour-fruit, Vienna malt aromas. Flavours offer a good firm astringency, soft peachy fruit, malt notes both mildly nutty and buttery, and a floral, dry-hopped finish, which is long and moreish. *Serve:* light fridge chill. *Avail:* BeerC, Beer Paradise.

Budweiser*

Anheuser Busch. 33cl Bottled 5%:
It's hard work to describe much in the way of flavour and character at all in this ghostly pale beer, but straining the senses produces a boiled sweet, slightly sherbety nose, notes of woodsmoke among the thin, sweet cereal and rice flavours, and a deeply mediocre finish, faintly sticky with adjuncts and outstaying its welcome. Frankly astounding that it's 5% alcohol, the same as the Czech beer of similar name. But gosh, they have a good advertising agency. *Serve:* fridge cold. *Avail:* Asda, Maj, Thres.

Budweiser*

33cl Canned 5%:
Quenching, fizzy, clean-edged lager of similar qualities to the bottled version. Crisp, very pale, slightly appley, with beechwood notes on the finish, thanks to the famous Budweiser maturation over beech planks, which help clarify the beer and add a little much needed character. (Charitably interpreted tasting note of otherwise dull, bland beer). *Serve:* fridge cold. *Avail:* widely.

Cave Creek Chili Beer**

Arizona. 35.5cl Bottled 4.7%:
Was expecting to hate this and dismiss it as a gimmick. It is gimmicky, but it works. Originally made to commission for local Mexican restaurants, Crazy Ed's Original Cave Creek Chili Beer has now become an international hit and is currently a cult drink in Japan. The marinaded whole green chilli in every bottle provides a cooked green pepper aroma, and crisp, fresh, raw green pepper flavours, combined with a slow-acting but gentle chilli spice 'glow'. The more you drink the thirstier you get, a cunning selling point. *Serve:* fridge cold. *Avail:* specialists and Beer Paradise.

Celis Pale Bock***

Austin, Texas. 25cl Bottled 5.5%:
Pierre Celis, formerly of Hoegaarden in Belgium, has now made his Austin brewery's Celis White almost a household word in America and, increasingly, abroad. His Texan versions of Belgian beers are now also made under licence in Belgium, by the Hoogstraten brewery. This is one such beer. Made with both wheat and barley, it's smooth and creamy, seductive stuff, with amber malt succulence and spice; is mildly buttery, with a fat, but soft yeasty tang, and a gentle hop finish, with sandalwood notes. A delicious Belgian version of an American micro version of a Germano-Belgian classic. *Serve:* room temp/larder cool. *Avail:* Beer Paradise.

CELIS WHITE***

25cl Bottled 5%:
Made in Belgium (actually) under licence, like the Pale Bock above. Water, malt, hops, wheat, yeast and spices go into this cloudy apricot-gold wheat beer, with its cooked apple nose, faint and fresh. Flavours suggest a baked apple, too, with traces of honey and sultana, and soft wheat beer spice, coriander, nutmeg and pepper, in the finish. A notably smooth example (the way America likes it), easy, mellow and integrated, with no pointy bits whatsoever, but also good and spritzy on the tongue, with a more robust hop tang growing in the finish as it warms. *Serve:* larder cool. *Avail:* Beer Paradise.

COLT 45*

50cl Canned 5%:
Made in England (actually) by Courage. Cheap, cereally, bland, it was initially awarded no star, but on reflection tastes quite convincingly like one of the less palatable American rice-based 'lite' beers, so gets its gong in recognition of this adherence to style. Tastes under-strength, in typical American 'lite beer' fashion, too. *Serve:* fridge cold. *Avail:* Co-op, Tesco, Thres.

COORS EXTRA GOLD**

33cl Bottled 5%:
Made in Britain (actually) under licence. The label's description of a 'full-bodied, robust beer' certainly applies in an American mass-market context. It's tasty and uncomplicated, with fresh, soft pale malt, showing a decent texture in the mouth, medium dry, with a flavoursome hop finish and grainstore barley notes, all under a clean and quaffable fizz wrapper. *Serve:* fridge cold. *Avail:* widely.

COORS EXTRA GOLD**

33cl Canned 5%:
Also brewed in Britain. A surprisingly full-bodied, refreshing, firm little beer, apparently brewed from malted barley, selected cereals and choicest hops. Coors is the most international and modern of the giant US lager brands, clean as a whistle, pleasingly rounded and really quite drinkable. Almost as good as the bottled version. *Serve:* fridge cold. *Avail:* widely.

DEVIL MOUNTAIN DEVIL'S BREW PORTER***

Benicia, California. 35.5cl Bottled 5.4%:
You can't miss the most important word in marketing this range of beers: DEVIL, two inches high on every label. Very, very fizzy, with the biggest, frothiest, wildest head ever, and, as it subsides, subtle alcoholic esters and horse blanket aromas (a good sign for the style). Dense, black stuff with rather good and unusual flavours: markedly bitter edges lead into a soft mocha, coffeeish, slightly tarry porter, with lots of burnt black malt and a hint of strawberry. Rich but (typically, of American micro bottled beers) fairly thin-textured and refreshing at the same time. *Serve:* room temp/larder cool. *Avail:* specialists.

DEVIL MOUNTAIN DIABLO GOLDEN ALE**

Benicia, California. 35.5cl Bottled 4.6%:
Old-gold coloured, with dried banana and coconut aromas, its flavours are disappointingly absent and muffled, though a fresh hop dryness (Mounthood and Hallertau) and sweet orange notes struggle through. Pure beer, made of barley malt, hops, water and yeast only, but a little flat and flabby in the mouth. Don't chill it. *Serve:* room temp. *Avail:* specialists.

DEVIL MOUNTAIN RAILROAD ALE***

35.5cl Bottled 5.9%:
A dark-amber ale supposedly ideally placed to 'locomote you down life's tracks'. It's a darker amber than Stan's Amber, down the road in Modesto, with a peppery, spicy malt nose enlivened by sweet pink grapefruit aromas. Use of the rather rare Galena hop partly accounts for these. Flavours are spicy but sweet (like the ale equivalent of a Gewurtztraminer), oaky but orangey, with lots of cured, nutty malt but also a firm, dry-hop background with nutmeg chipping in at the finish. Aftertastes grow citric, and grapefruit

pithily dry. *Serve:* room temp/larder cool. *Avail:* specialists.

INDIANA GOLD**

35.5cl Bottled 5%:
Bottled 'exclusively' for Sainsbury by Evansville Brewery, Indiana, and the first of their planned new portfolio of 'sub-branded' beers. Made of selected premium grain and hops (not all-malt, in other words), and triple-filtered for clarity, it's a bright-golden lager with corn sweetness on the palate, apple juice notes, and just a touch of honey in the finish. Typical of the better American mass-market lagers in being clean and fairly tasty, without committing itself to actual malt and hop flavours. It also aims to keep its pricing 15% below the competitors. *Serve:* fridge cold.

INDIANA GOLD**

35.5cl Canned 5%:
Canned version of the above, and tastes much like it, only with a very slightly tinny finish. As expected, in other words. *Serve:* fridge cold.

LIBERTY ALE****

Anchor Steam, San Francisco. 35.5cl Bottled 5.6%:
Unlike the sibling beer Anchor Steam Bitter, which uses lager yeast at ale temperatures, Liberty is made with an authentic top-fermenting yeast and then dry-hopped (and how) with Cascade. Its nose is drily woody and herbal, with an alluring hint of orange, and its flavour quite extraordinary in any terms: raspingly dry, with sandalwood and smoke, and a dry, grapefruity citric character, with sour, bitter pith and a briney salt note at the finish. The astringency is of the slow-release sort, still building two minutes after sipping. In balance, there's a rounded, sherryish (oloroso) opulence. Liberty from blandness and dull American mass-market brewing! *Serve:* larder cool. *Avail:* BeerC.

LITTLE KINGS CREAM ALE**

Schoenling, Cincinnati. 35.5cl Bottled 5%:
Pale, rather dense, bottom-fermented beer with strong flavours. Fruity, sweetish, with apricot, banana and pineapple notes, all doused in liqueur, lots of pepper on the finish, and a mildly whiskyish kick. A little sticky, clogged up and flabby. *Serve:* light fridge chill. *Avail:* Beer Paradise.

LONE STAR

33cl Bottled 5%:
The National Beer of Texas, so they say. On this occasion, it had oddly perfumy flavours, like scented lip-gloss on the tongue, growing strongly rose-watery as it warmed. Not altogether what you'd expect of a cowboy beer. *Serve:* fridge cold. *Avail:* specialists.

MICHELOB**

Anheuser Busch. 33cl Bottled 5%:
In the distinctive foil-topped space rocket bottle, meant to be grasped in the hand. A higher ratio of malt to rice gives better, fuller-bodied flavour than sibling brand Budweiser. The sweet candy nose suggests pineapple chunks, leading into more pineapple (carton juice this time) flavours and a toasted walnut finish, thanks to the ancient (and rather rare) Bavarian technique of maturation over beechwood, that Budweiser makes such a fuss about. *Serve:* fridge cold. *Avail:* Co-op, Maj, Sains, Tesco, Thres.

MICHELOB DRY

33cl Bottled 5%:
Supposedly has a 'bold' start and a clean finish, and it's true that there's some flavour at the start and barely any at the end (which is, of course, almost a working definition of the Dry style). Sweet, ripe grain chimes in briefly at the front of the sip, but melts away leaving a remarkably dull and watery finish, with a positively unpleasant, dishwatery aftertaste. Here's the giant brewery looking positively distracted by an empty fashion that's already well past its sell-by date. *Serve:* fridge cold. *Avail:* Tesco, Thres.

MICKEY'S BIG MOUTH*

American Strong Beer Heileman, Wisconsin. 35cl Bottled 5.6%:

Its wide-mouthed, stubby barrel-shaped bottle is the most distinctive thing about this strongish lager, from an American national brewer famed for the undistinctiveness of its products. There's a tropical fruit note amidst the strong, smooth, fairly sweet flavours here, its high-alcohol kick perhaps a little obviously of the turnip sort. *Serve:* light fridge chill. *Avail:* Beer Paradise, Odd.

MILLER GENUINE DRAFT**

Miller, Milwaukee. 33cl Bottled 4.7%:
All natural ingredients comprise malted barley, selected cereal grains and choicest hops. Grain and pleasant: the slightly sugary cereal nose and flavour are at least more robust than other high cereal US imports. There's a little barley flavour stranded in the middle, too, before a rather watery, woody, cereal-husky finish takes hold. But it's lively and fresh. *Serve:* fridge cold. *Avail:* Maj, Tesco.

MILLER PILSNER

44cl Canned 4.2%:
Made in England (actually) by Courage, under licence, supposedly 'by a special process that ferments most of the sugar into alcohol, for a smooth clean taste'. It tastes (if you can get past the rather cat pee nose) sweet and cereally, with a thin sugar syrup aspect, a little malt, but no hops to speak of, and is further let down by a distinctly cardboardy finish. I have to say I found this positively unpleasant. *Serve:* fridge cold. *Avail:* widely.

PETE'S WICKED ALE**

Minnesota Brewing, St Paul. 35.5cl Bottled 5.1%:
Wonderful colour: a delicious dark garnet-jewelled red, with appetizing summer fruit and cocoa powder aromas. Not quite so wonderful flavour: it's lively, smooth, with a dry malt texture, and some fruity, chocolate notes, but is also rather wet and thin, with very little in the middle, where the ingredients ought to to be conferencing. There's a (too subtle, but) soft malty body and drying, chocolate malt finish, though, so almost a three-star beer despite its failings. *Serve:* larder cool. *Avail:* Maj, Odd, Tesco.

PETE'S WICKED LAGER**

35.5cl Bottled 4.9%:
From the self-described premier microbrewery of the States; the label is laden with paragraphs of testament to their technical wizardry (presumably they are really a testament to Minnesota Brewing, who contract brew it?). Two facts emerge from the hype: the beer is Liberty dry-hopped, and kräusened. It's bright amber in colour, tasty and full-bodied, simple and unambitious, but wholesome in flavour, with decent, chewy barley-sweet body and the advertised dry-hop finish. Undeniably straightforward, made for the new micro mass-market. *Serve:* light fridge chill. *Avail:* Maj, Odd.

PETE'S WICKED LAGER II***

35.5cl Bottled 4.9%:
The new formulation puts heavy emphasis on Saaz, and this is a far better beer because of it. Very newly arrived in Britain (look out for Saaz on the neck label), it's crisp, clean, satisfying, tasty stuff, of convincing Czech character, with its butter-sweet, nectarine-edged, rich but florally delicate flavours and hay-like finish. Hop-heads rejoice (dude). *Serve:* light fridge chill. *Avail:* Maj, Odd.

PETE'S WICKED RED**

Amber Ale 35.5cl Bottled 4.9%:
Great label, okay beer. Soft and drinkable micro amber, too subtle and muffled, and too obviously made with the mass-market palate in mind, but with mild amber succulence, a little butter, a momentary note of toffee, and a soft (bland) hop finish. Competent, but dull. *Serve:* larder cool. *Avail:* Odd.

PETE'S WICKED SUMMER BREW**

35.5cl Bottled 4.8%:
Made with pale and wheat malts, Tettnang hops and 'added lemon flavour', this is a dull, rather Snapple-like summer quaffer, mildly beery, with a very subtle lemon note, and finishing with a hint of pepper but not much of

the promised 'crisp hop bite'. It develops a little savoury orange and barley as it warms, though. PS: Although the label states it's a real ale, this isn't to say it's bottle-conditioned. It means 'real' by American mass-market standards. *Serve:* light fridge chill. *Avail:* specialists.

PETE'S WICKED WINTER BREW**

35.5cl Bottled (no abv listed):
The brewery sponsored the 1993 Home-Brewing awards and gave the winner the chance to create a beer for the Pete's range. This is it: a dry amber pale ale with raspberry and nutmeg flavourings. Tasty, but not particularly interesting or complex, with a thinnish texture beneath the surface flavours. *Serve:* larder cool. *Avail:* specialists.

RED EYE*

33cl Bottled 5%:
Packaged up like a beer that expects to be cultish, in a Mexican-style cheap-printed bottle. Like Mexican fashion lagers, it's a yellow beer, high in corn, with fairly clean, sweetcorn beer flavours, but also an atypical bitter, hoppy twist in the tail. *Serve:* fridge cold. *Avail:* specialists.

ROLLING ROCK*

33cl Bottled 4.6%:
An American institution now owned by Canadian giant Labatt, who also brew in England. Water, malt, rice, corn, hops and yeast, a typical US line-up, create a pale yellowy-gold beer with malt and pineapple aromas, and a light, sharp, refreshing texture and flavour, apple-juicey, corny, woodchippy and thin, though with an unattractive cardboardy, watery finish. *Serve:* fridge cold. *Avail:* widely.

ST STANS AMBER***

Modesto, California. 35.5cl Bottled 5.8%:
American micro alt, warm-fermented and cold-conditioned for mellow smoothness. Pure beer, using barley malt, water, hops and yeast only. Aromas are appetizingly oaky and amber sweet, with Seville orange, and whisky marmalade notes. All these are also featured on the palate, which is smooth, succulent but subtle, extremely delicious, finishing with hot prickly pepper and a gentle hop dryness. *Serve:* room temp/larder cool. *Avail:* specialists.

ST STANS DARK**

35.5cl Bottled 6.2%:
There's something unsatisfyingly thin in here, which is all that deprives this translucent, brownish red American alt beer of its third star. There's spice and raisiny malt in the super-mellow, smooth and mature flavours, and warm, spicy, old-fashioned liquorice of the dark, dry sort in the finish, which also has lots of prickly hoppy pepper. *Serve:* room temp/larder cool. *Avail:* specialists.

ST STANS RED SKY ALE**

35.5cl Bottled 5.9%:
There's wheat and barley malts, Cascade, Fuggles and Tettnang hops in this strong, slightly disappointing beer. Things start promisingly, with its pretty reddish-amber colour and banana and peardrop aromas, but flavours are dominated by startlingly unsubtle cherryade and Vimto fruit character. However, there's also spicy malt and sneezy peppery heat in the hoppy dry finish, plus dried banana chips in the aftertaste, and a persistent, pleasing sourness that helps redeem matters a little. *Serve:* room temp/larder cool. *Avail:* specialists.

SAMUEL ADAMS BOSTON LAGER***

Boston Beer Co. 33cl Bottled 4.8%:
Actually brewed in Pittsburgh and Portland on behalf of this large independent (or super-micro). Typical American export hype on the label at least includes ingredients: two-row summer barley, Hallertau and Tettnang hops, lager yeast and water. It's also dry-hopped. The result is a zingily fruity banana and peardrops nose, barley grain and a little sweet fruit (with a touch of honey and raisin) in the middle, and a drying German hop finish. Extremely clean, very refreshing, if not quite 'the best beer in

America'. *Serve:* light fridge chill. *Avail:* Asda, BeerC, Odd.

TESCO BEST AMERICAN LAGER*

35.5cl Canned 4.9%:

Not particularly the 'strong lager' the can promises. Ingredients are listed, and there's (surprisingly) no rice or unmalted cereals, but you can smell the glucose syrup used in brewing on the nose, which is barley sugary with a little fruit. The flavour is affected by glucose, too, fairly sweet, but also appley and crisp, with a little floral hop note at the finish. Gassy, pale and 'lite' in the classic US quaffing style. *Serve:* fridge cold.

British Breweries Directory

This directory lists British breweries in alphabetical order. Each brewery listing features not just the cask ales on offer, but also identifies the keg, bottled and canned ales and lagers made there. Or rather, those the brewery has admitted to. There are plenty of 'commodity' beers listed in the tastings that don't appear here; own brands for supermarkets, that kind of thing.

The convention when listing a brewery's beers is to put them in order of alcoholic strength – weakest first, strongest last. We follow this format, except in the case of the National Brewing Giants, who have so many brands that alphabetical order is better. Ales and lagers are listed separately in the National Breweries listings. Note also that given strengths apply to cask beers; keg versions are often weaker. Many 'cask only' beers listed may also appear in keg format on a small scale, produced to customer request.

Cask-conditioned beers (real ales) are traditionally identifiable in the pub by means of a handpump (unless the barrel's sitting on the counter), keg beers by some form of 'box' with a push button mechanism which electrically pumps the beer (and its added carbon dioxide) into the glass. Things are complicated a bit by (a) the fact that electric pumps are used to dispense real ale in some parts of the country, and (b) the tall fount system in Scotland, an elegant air compressor which has fooled many a southerner into thinking no real ale is available. Generally, though, a handpump on the bar means a real ale in the cellar. If in any doubt, look closely at the pump clip (name label) for clues. Or ask.

Key to terms

Cask Dispensed on draught, cask-conditioned (real ale)
Keg As cask above but brewery-conditioned – not a real ale
Bottled Bottled beers are also keg (filtered/pasteurized) unless . . .
Bottled BC Bottle-conditioned, with residual/added yeast/sugar
Can Canned beer. Canned ales/lagers are always keg beers (despite the possible presence of a 'draught system')
PET Large plastic, screw-top party-size bottle

THE BREWERY LISTINGS

ABC

see Carlsberg-Tetley

ABERDEENSHIRE ALES

Aberdeenshire Ales, Mains of Inverbrie, Ellon, Aberdeenshire AB41 8PX
Tel (01358) 761208

New brewery, established in a converted steading on a farm 18 miles north of Aberdeen. Small-scale traditional brewing includes the use of Yorkshire Square fermenters.

Buchan Gold (4%) cask

ABERYSTWYTH

Aberystwyth Ales, Tregynnan Isaf, Llanrystud, Dyfed SY23 5DW Tel (01974) 202338

Est. 1994. Operates from an ex-cow shed, and has its own well.

Dinas Dark Mild (3.6%) cask
Dinas Draught (3.6%) cask
Premium (4.4%) cask

ADNAMS

Adnams and Co. PLC, Sole Bay Brewery, Southwold, Suffolk IP18 6JW
Tel (01502) 722424

Est. 1872. Victorian seaside brewery, an East Anglian landmark. Their delicious, traditional ales are brewed using East Anglian malted barley, and whole Fuggles and Goldings hops, and routinely dry-hopped. No keg beer, other than that destined for bottling.

Champion Pale Ale (3.1%) bottled
Mild (3.2%) cask
Nut Brown (3.2%) bottled
Best Bitter (3.7%) cask
Old (4.1%) cask
Extra (4.3%) cask
Suffolk Strong Ale (4.5%) can and PET
Broadside (4.7%) cask and bottled (6.3%)
Tally Ho (7%) cask

ALFORD ARMS

Alford Arms Brewhouse, Frithsden, Hemel Hempstead, Herts HP1 3DD
Tel (01442) 864480

Est. 1992 (re-opening), now Whitbread owned, a brew pub with other local outlets. Typical ingredients: malt extracts of five sorts, plus liquorice root and Target hops in the Dark Mild; Target, plus orange and coriander in the wheat beer; and Styrians in the rest, apart from Rub of the Brush, which uses Saaz.

Alford Dark Mild (2.8%) cask
New Cherry Pickers (3.9%) cask
Olde Frithsden (4.2%) cask
Pickled Squirrel (4.5%) cask
Geoff's Wheat Beer (4.7%) cask
Rub of the Brush (5%) cask

ALL NATIONS

All Nations Pub and Brewery (Mrs Lewis's), Coalport Road, Madeley, Telford, Shropshire TF7 5DP
Tel (01952) 585747

Est. over 200 years ago, and in the same family since 1934.

Pale Ale (3%) cask

ANCIENT DRUIDS

Ancient Druids Pub and Brewery, Napier Street, Cambridge, Cambs, CB1 1HR
Tel (01223) 324514

Est. 1984 by Charles Wells of Bedford. Malt extract brewing.

Ellies SB (5–6%, varies from batch to batch) cask

ANN STREET

Ann Street Brewery, Ann Street, St Helier, Jersey JE1 1BZ Tel (01534) 31561

Est. 1992 (re-opening). Owner of Guernsey brewery, and of many island pubs. Nest Egg (5.5%), an island liberation commemorative keg beer, may join the permanent range if popular. They also make Harp Export (5.2%) for Guinness.

Mary Ann Best Bitter (3.5%) keg and can
Mary Ann Brown Ale (3.5%) bottled
Mary Ann Pale Ale (3.5%) bottled

Mary Ann Pilsener Lager (3.6%) keg and can
Old Jersey Ale (3.6%) cask
Mary Ann Special (4.5%) keg, bottled and can
Ann's Treat (5.2%) cask
Winter Ale (7.5%) cask
Mary Ann Jubilee Pils (8%) bottled

ANSELLS

see Carlsberg-Tetley

ARCHERS

Archers Ales Ltd, Station Industrial Estate, London Street, Swindon, Wilts SN1 5DY Tel (01793) 496789

Est. 1979 in the Great Western Railway's former carriage building shops.

Village Bitter (3.6%) cask
Best Bitter (4%) cask
Blackjack Porter (4.6%) cask
Golden Bitter (4.7%) cask
Old Cobleigh's (6.3%) cask

ARKELL'S

Arkell's Brewery Ltd, Kingsdown, Swindon, Wilts SN2 6RU Tel (01793) 823026

Est. 1843. Still a family brewery, run by Arkell descendants.

2Bs (3.2%) cask
Mash Tun Mild (3.5%) cask
3Bs (4%) cask, and can (as Best Bitter)
Kingsdown Ale (5%) cask
Victory Bitter (5%) cask
Noel Ale (6%) cask (Xmas)

ARROL'S

see Carlsberg-Tetley

ARUNDEL

Arundel Brewery, Ford Airfield Estate, Ford, Arundel, West Sussex BN18 0BE Tel (01903) 733111

Est. 1992. Additive- and adjunct-free, traditional Sussex beers. Arundel Gold uses 100% pale malt, but typically it's about 80% pale, 20% crystal, plus whole Fuggles and East Kent Goldings. There's 8% chocolate malt in Old Knucker, which uses only Fuggles and is named after a local dragon. Arundel also makes seasonals and celebratory specials throughout the year.

Best Bitter (4%) cask
Gold (4.2%) cask
Stronghold (5%) cask
Old Knucker (5.5%) cask

ASH VINE

Ash Vine Brewery Ltd, The White Hart, Trudoxhill, Frome, Somerset BA11 5DP Tel (01373) 836344

Est. 1987 in Taunton, relocating in 1989. Recently launched Hop & Glory in bottle-conditioned form, using Maris Otter malt, Goldings and Challenger hops, and their own distinctive strain of yeast, developed here. Looking to export to Sweden, Holland and France, but can presently brew only 20 barrels a week. Also monthly changing specials.

Bitter (3.8%) cask
Challenger (4.1%) cask
Black Bess Porter (4.2%) cask
Hop & Glory (5%) cask and bottled BC

ASTON MANOR

Aston Manor Brewery, 173 Thimblemill Lane, Aston, Birmingham B7 5HS Tel (0121) 328 4336

Est. 1983 by ex-Ansells brewery staff. The three cask ales of 1994 have all been deleted, leaving an operation geared mostly to brewing for plastic bottles, as well as cider and other products.

Bitter (3%) can and PET
Lager (3%) can and PET
Mild (3%) PET
Draught at Home Lager (3.5%) PET
Draught at Home Bitter (4%) PET

B&T

B&T Brewery Ltd, The Brewery, Shefford, Beds SG17 5DZ Tel (01462) 815080

Est. 1981 as Banks & Taylor, went bust in 1994, and rematerialized the same year as B&T Brewery Ltd, with a new owner. Traditional makers of cask ales, using pale and crystal malts, wheat malt in some, roast barley in others, and a mix of whole hops including Hallertau. Like most other medium-

sized breweries, they now also make seasonal specials, including a wheat beer in summer. Bottling is planned for late 1995.
Shefford Bitter (3.8%) cask
Shefford Mild (3.8%) cask
Dragonslayer (4.5%) cask
Edwin Taylor's Extra Stout (4.5%) cask
Shefford Pale Ale (4.5%) cask
Shefford Old Dark (5%) cask
Shefford Old Strong (5%) cask
Black Bat (6%) cask
2XS (6%) cask
Old Bat (7%) cask

BALLARD'S

Ballard's Brewery Ltd, Unit C, The Old Sawmill, Nyewood, Rogate, West Sussex GU31 5HA
Tel (01730) 821301
Est. 1980 in Trotton in a cow byre, moving to Nyewood in 1988. Typical ingredients: Pipkin pale and crystal malts, Fuggles and Goldings hops. Off The Wall, the 1994 Harvest Ale (there'll be a new one in winter 1995), also contains chocolate malt and a sprinkling of torrefied wheat (for the head). All natural brewing. Around 1300 gallons a week.
Midhurst Mild (3.5%) cask
Trotton Bitter (3.6%) cask
Best Bitter (4.2%) cask
Golden Bine (4.2%) cask
Wild (4.7%) cask
Wassail (6%) cask, and bottled BC
Off The Wall (9.6%) bottled BC

BANKS'S

Wolverhampton & Dudley Breweries PLC, Park Brewery, Bath Road, Wolverhampton, W. Midlands WV1 4NY Tel (01902) 29136
Est. 1890 when three local breweries merged. Hanson's of Dudley was bought in 1943, and closed in 1991; Cameron's was purchased the following year. They now own around 1000 pubs. Principally a mild-producing brewery; their cask mild is a classic, though it's now been re-christened Banks's, the term 'mild' being considered too old-fashioned and a hindrance to the progress of the bottled product in particular. The canned Mild (sorry, Banks's) comes in two versions – one Nitrogen Flush, one widget. A 5-litre 'caskie' (complete with its own handpump) of a new unpasteurized party product, Banks's Fine Fettle, is being test-marketed at Oddbins Bristol.
Hanson's Bitter (3.3%) keg
Hanson's Mild (3.3%) cask
Banks's (3.5%) cask/keg, bottled, can and PET
Bitter (3.8%) cask/keg, can and PET
Strong Old Ale (9.1%) bottled

BASS

Bass Brewers Ltd, 137 High Street, Burton-upon-Trent, Staffs DE14 1JZ Tel (01283) 511000
Est. 1777, and now the country's biggest brewer. Eight major brewing plants (in Hampshire, Sheffield, Birmingham, Cardiff, Tadcaster, Belfast and Glasgow, as well as Burton-upon-Trent), plus their only small 'regional', Highgate Brewery, produce over 8.5 million barrels a year, and command almost a quarter of the entire British market. They're also Britain's biggest exporter, and their flagship export brand, Bass Ale, is the best-selling British beer in the USA. In Europe, they own a 34% stake in Prague Breweries, makers of Staropramen lager, and have an agreement with Grolsche's Dutch parent to market and brew Grolsch over here.

Carling Black Label is the biggest selling lager in Britain, with almost 2 million pints sold a day; Tennent's lager is the best-seller in Scotland. Low alcohol products: Tennent's LA (1%) and the alcohol-free Barbican. On the cask ale side of things, Draught Bass is still Britain's most popular premium brand (though Stones easily outsells it), and Worthington Best is apparently the fastest growing mainstream bitter. They also make a limited range of seasonal ales and specials under the 'caskmasters' label. Caffrey's Irish Ale, their Ulster-brewed keg beer, has been one of the company's most successful product launches ever (the canned version is going to be BIG), and £3 million has recently been spent on doubling the capacity of the brewery. In Glasgow, Aitken's 80/- is a new cask ale and the first to be brewed at Wellpark for 25 years.

Contract brewing arrangements: Charrington IPA is brewed by Shepherd Neame, Worthington E by King & Barnes, D.P.A. by Hardy & Hanson, Bass Best Scotch by Thwaites, Tennent's Pale Ale by Maclays.

Aitken's 80/- Cask Ale (Scotland) (4.2%) cask
Aitken's Ale (Scotland) (3.1%) keg
Allbright Bitter (3.2%) keg and can
Draught Bass (4.4%) cask and can
Bass Best Scotch (3.6%) keg
Bass Blue (3.7%) bottled
Bass ('Cask') Light (3.2%) cask/keg
Bass ('Cask') Mild (3.1%) cask/keg
Bass Special (3.4%) keg and can (3.5%)
Bass Special Cask Bitter (3.2%) cask
Brew XI (3.9%) cask/keg
Caffrey's Irish Ale (4.8%) keg and can
Charrington IPA (3.4%) cask
D.P.A. (3.3%) keg
Hancocks HB (3.6%) cask
Highgate Dark (3.2%) cask
Highgate Old (5.1%) cask (winter)
Jubilee Stout (3%) bottled
M&B Mild (3.2%) cask/keg
North Eastern (3.2%) keg
Stones Best Bitter (3.9%) cask/keg and can
Sweetheart Stout (2%) bottled and can
Tennent's 70/- (3.5%) can
Tennent's 70/- Velvet Ale (3.5%) keg and can
Tennent's 80/- (4.2%) keg and can
Tennent's Export (4.2%) keg and can
Tennent's Light (3.1%) keg
Tennent's Pale Ale (3.1%) keg
Tennent's Special 70/- (3.5%) keg and can
Tennent's Superior (4.2%) keg and can
Toby Ale (3.7%) bottled
Toby Bitter (3.2%) keg and can (3%)
Toby Brown Ale (2.8%) bottled
Toby Light (3.1%) bottled
Worthington Ale (4.1%) keg
Worthington Best Bitter (3.6%) cask/keg, and can (3.8%)
Worthington – (3%) cask/keg
Worthington E (4%) keg
Worthington White Shield (5.6%) bottled BC

LAGERS

Breaker Malt Lager (4.8%) can
Carling Black Label (4.1%) keg, bottled and can
Carling Premier (4.7%) keg and can
Carling XD (5.5%) bottled
Charger (3%) can
Grolsch (5%) keg, bottled and can
Hemeling (3.5%) keg and can
Hooper's Ginger Brew (4.7%) bottled
Lamot Lager (3%) can
Lamot Pils (4.8%) bottled and can
Staropramen (5%) keg and bottled
TAG (5.3%) bottled
Tennent's Dry (5.5%) bottled
Tennent's Extra (4.8%) keg and can
Tennent's Gold Bier (5%) bottled
Tennent's Lager (4.1%) keg, bottled and can (4%)
Tennent's Pilsner (3.4%) keg and can
Tennent's Super (9%) bottled and can
Zeiss (8%) bottled

BATEMAN

George Bateman & Son Ltd, Salem Bridge Brewery, Mill Lane, Wainfleet, Skegness, Lincs PE24 4JE Tel (01754) 880317

Est. 1874, and still a family brewery. Their very fine bottled and cask-conditioned beers are made with traditional methods, ingredients and equipment. Fermentation takes place in open squares, using an ancient strain of their own yeast. Typical ingredients: English pale and crystal malts, invert sugar, a little wheat, and Goldings and Challenger whole hops.

Dark Mild (3%) cask
XB (3.8%) cask
Valiant (4.3%) cask and bottled
Salem Porter (4.9%) cask
XXXB (5%) cask and bottled (4.8%)
Victory Ale (6%) cask and bottled

BATHAM

Bathams (Delph) Ltd, Delph Brewery, Delph Road, Brierley Hill, W. Midlands DY5 2TN
Tel (01384) 77229

Est. 1877, and still family owned. Situated to the rear of The Vine public house. Batham's bottled Best Bitter is 'only sold to people we know will appreciate it'!

Mild Ale (3.6%) cask
Best Bitter (4.3%) cask and bottled
XXX (6.3%) cask (winter)

BEAMISH

see Courage

BEER ENGINE

The Beer Engine, Newton St Cyres, Exeter, Devon EX5 5AX Tel (01392) 851282
Brew pub located beside Barnstaple branch railway line. Also owns The Sleeper, in Seaton.
Rail Ale (3.8%) cask
Piston Bitter (4.3%) cask
Sleeper Heavy (5.4%) cask

BELCHER'S

Belcher's Brewery, 100 Goldstone Villas, Hove, East Sussex BN3 6RX
Tel (01273) 324660
Set up in 1990 by David Bruce of Firkin fame, but now owned by Grosvenor Inns. Brew-pub operation behind the Hedgehog & Hogshead public houses; they also brew in the Southampton pub. Ingredients: pale and crystal malts (also coloured and wheat malts in some beers), Styrian Goldings and Challenger hops, plus molasses and cinnamon in New Barbarian.
Brighton Breezy Bitter (4.2%) cask
Bootleg Bitter (5.2%) cask
New Barbarian (5.2%) cask
Hogbolter (6%) cask

BELHAVEN

Belhaven Brewery Co. Ltd, Spott Road, Dunbar, East Lothian EH42 1RS
Tel (01368) 865411
Est. 1719, but actually much older: records exist showing that Franco-Scots troops, garrisoned at Dunbar in the 1550s (and planning to invade England), were supplied with Belhaven Ale. Belhaven has had an up-and-down history, and was languishing in the doldrums before the present management team got hold of it. The spectacularly successful launch of Belhaven Best, a creamy, light 'premium keg ale', helped create the confidence for a successful management buy-out in 1993. The bottled Premium Ale in the Brewer's Heritage pack is St Andrew's Ale.
Light (2.7%) keg
Pale Ale (2.7%) bottled
60/- Ale (2.9%) cask
Belhaven Best (3.2%) keg and can
Belhaven Heavy (3.2%) keg
70/- Ale (3.5%) cask
Sandy Hunter's Traditional Ale (3.6%) cask
Festival Gold (3.8%) cask
Belhaven Export (3.9%) keg and bottled
Belhaven Lager (4.1%) keg and bottled
80/- Ale (4.2%) cask
St Andrew's Ale (4.9%) cask and bottled
90/- Ale (8%) cask

BENSKINS

see Carlsberg-Tetley

BENTLEY'S

see Whitbread

BEOWULF

Beowulf Brewing Co., Waterloo Buildings, 10–14 Waterloo Road, Yardley, Birmingham B25 8JR Tel (0121) 626 2155
New brewery, set up to brew short run bottle-conditioned ales for sale in specialist outlets/delis, as well as cask-conditioned ales for the local free trade. Hero is all-malt, using Maris Otter pale and crystal malts, Fuggles and Goldings whole hops. Wulf also uses malt extract.
Hero (4.75%) cask
Wulf (11.5%) bottled BC

BERROW

Berrow Brewery, Coast Road, Berrow, Burnham-on-Sea, Somerset TA8 2QU
Tel (01278) 751435
Est. 1982, with an expanding local trade. Berrow Porter, the new winter beer, may become known as BP, especially if it's black.
Best Bitter (BBBB) (4%) cask
Berrow Porter (4.4%) cask (winter)
Topsy Turvy (6%) cask

BIG LAMP

Big Lamp Brewers, 1 Summerhill Street, Newcastle upon Tyne NE4 6EJ
Tel (0191) 261 4227

Est. 1982, new ownership in 1990. Blackout (11%) is brewed on an occasional basis.
Bitter (3.9%) cask
Summerhill Stout (4.4%) cask
Prince Bishop Ale (4.8%) cask
Big Lamp Premium (5.2%) cask
Winter Warmer (5.2%) cask
Old Genie (7.4%) cask

BIRD IN HAND

Paradise Brewery, Paradise Park, Hayle, Cornwall TR27 4HY Tel (01736) 753974
Est. 1980, in a Cornish bird park. There are more beers in summer.
Paradise Bitter (3.8%) cask
Miller's Ale (4.2%) cask
Artists Ale (5.2%) cask
Old Speckled Parrot (6.3%) cask

BISHOPS

Bishops Brewery, 2 Park Street, Borough Market, London SE1 2AH
Tel (0171) 357 8343
Est. 1993 by a former Market Porter brew-pub brewer. Malt extract used.
Cathedral Bitter (3.7%) cask

BLACKAWTON

Blackawton Brewery, Washbourne, Totnes, Devon TQ9 7UE Tel (01803) 732339
Est. 1977, and now the oldest surviving brewery in Devon! Very hot on all-natural ingredients and methods, with a policy statement on beer purity. Beers are made using whole grain malted barleys, whole hops, fresh yeast and water only. Devon Gold, the pale refreshing summer brew, is made with pale English malt and European hops. They also brew monthly specials.
Bitter (3.8%) cask
Devon Gold (4.1%) cask
Winter Fuel (4.1%) cask (winter)
44 Special (4.5%) cask
Headstrong (5.2%) cask

BLACKBEARD

A non-brewing wholesaler, its beer brewed by Freeminer and by Hanby.

BLACK BULL

Black Bull Brewery, Ashes Farm, Ashes Lane, Fenny Bentley, Ashbourne, Derbyshire DE6 1LD
Est. 1994 in farm buildings by an enthusiastic home-brewer.
Dovedale Bitter (3.6%) cask
Bitter (4%) cask
Raging Bull (4.9%) cask
Owd Shrovetider (5.9%) cask

BLACK SHEEP

Black Sheep Brewery PLC, Wellgarth, Masham, Ripon, N. Yorks HG4 4EN
Tel (01765) 689227
Est. 1992 by Paul Theakston, after Theakston brewery was swallowed up by Scottish & Newcastle. The brewery was installed in the kiln of the old maltings of the defunct Lightfoot brewery in Masham. It has sprung to prominence in a remarkably short time. Black Sheep Ale, now finding its way into our supermarkets, is typical in being brewed from floor-malted barley, Fuggles, Goldings and Challenger hops, and their own Wensleydale water, and fermented for five days in traditional Yorkshire stone squares. It's a bottled version of Special Strong Bitter.
Best Bitter (3.8%) cask
Black Sheep Ale (4.4%) bottled
Special Strong Bitter (4.4%) cask

BLEWITTS

Blewitts Brewery, Ship & Plough, The Promenade, Kingsbridge, Devon TQ7 1JD
Tel (01548) 852485
Est. 1991. Occasionally brews Blewitts Nose (3.8%), King's Ale (4%), Blewitts Black Balls (4.5%) and Blewitts Brains Out (6%).
Blewitts Best (4%) cask
Blewitts Head Off (5%) cask

BODICOTE

Bodicote Brewery, Plough Inn, Bodicote, Banbury, Oxon OX15 4BZ
Tel (01245) 262327
Est. 1982. Full mash brewing.
Bitter (3.3%) cask
No.9 (4.2%) cask
Old English Porter (4.3%) cask

Triple X (5.1%) cask

BORDER

Border Brewery Co. Ltd, The Old Kiln, Brewery Lane, Tweedmouth, Berwick upon Tweed, Northumberland TD15 2AH Tel (01289) 306115

Est. 1992. All cask-conditioned beers, using only natural ingredients: pale and crystal malt (and chocolate malt in some), Fuggles and Goldings hops, yeast and water.

Old Kiln Bitter (3.8%) cask
Special Bitter (3.8%) cask
Old Kiln Ale (4%) cask
Noggins Nog (4.2%) cask
SOB (5%) cask and bottled

BORVE

Borve Brew House, Ruthven, Huntly, Aberdeenshire AB54 4SR Tel (0146 687) 343

Est. 1988 on the mainland, having moved from Isle of Lewis. The brewery is attached to an old schoolhouse, now a pub. Ingredients: over 90% pale malt, the rest crystal/chocolate; Target and Hersbrucker hops, and Union Street has 4% roasted barley. Borve Extra Strong is matured entirely in American oak bourbon casks.

Borve Ale (4%) cask and bottled BC
Union Street 200 (5%) cask and bottled BC
Tall Ships (5%) cask and bottled BC
Extra Strong (9.5–11%) bottled BC

BRAINS

S. A. Brain & Co. Ltd, The Old Brewery, 49 St Mary Street, Cardiff CF1 1SP Tel (01222) 399022

Est. 1882 as Brains, when Samuel Brain and his uncle Joseph bought the Old Brewery, and has stayed in family hands ever since. Still the largest independent in Wales. Maris Otter and Halcyon malts (and brewing sugar in some beers), and whole hops including Fuggles and Goldings.

Dark (3.5%) cask/keg, can and PET
Bitter (3.7%) cask/keg, can and PET
SA Best Bitter (4.2%) cask, can and PET
IPA (4.5%) bottled

BRAKSPEAR

W. H. Brakspear & Sons PLC, The Brewery, New Street, Henley-on-Thames, Oxon RG9 2BU Tel (01491) 573636

Est. 1799 as Brakspear, and still family owned. An expanded capacity in recent years has now led them to wonder about embarking on some serious bottling. Henley Strong (which is OBJ), the new bottled and canned product, is only available in local supermarkets at present, but there are hopes for a national listing. Typical ingredients: Maris Otter pale, crystal and black malts, plus brown sugar, and Fuggles and Goldings hops.

Dark Mild (3%) cask
Beehive (3.4%) keg
Bitter (3.4%) cask/keg (as Pale Ale), and can
Old Ale (4.3%) cask
Special (4.3%) cask
Henley Strong (5%) bottled and can
OBJ (5%) cask

BRANSCOMBE VALE

Branscombe Vale Brewery, Great Seaside Farm, Branscombe, Seaton, Devon EX12 3DP Tel (01297) 680511

Est. 1992 in a pair of National Trust cow sheds. All beers are cask-conditioned, full mash ales, using village spring water, pale and chocolate (and in one case crystal) malts, micro maize, and Challenger, Goldings and Willamette hops. They also make an own label 'house ale' for local pubs. An Anniversary Ale (4.6%) is produced in December.

Branoc Traditional Ale (3.8%) cask
Own label 'House Ale' (4.6%) cask
Olde Stoker (5.4%) cask

BREWERY ON SEA

The Brewery on Sea Ltd., Unit 24, Winston Business Centre, Chartwell Road, Lancing, West Sussex BN15 8TU Tel (01903) 851482

Est. 1993. Fairly small (2500 barrels a year) but hi-tech in methods and progressive in approach: they have no desire to own any pubs, but work to produce successful wholesale products, and do contract brewing, currently for London Beer Company (for whom they make the old Pitfield brewery

brands), and seasonal specials for East West Ales. There are plans to bottle Spinnaker and Riptide. Occasional beers: Spinnaker Porter (5%) and Tidal Wave (7%), as well as curiosities, including a garlic beer and a tandoori beer. Spinnaker Buzz, which is primed with honey and dry-hopped, has become a best-seller. Spinnaker Ginger is primed with pure ginger.
Spinnaker Bitter (3.5%) cask
Spinnaker Mild/Special Dark (3.5%) cask
Spinnaker Classic (4%) cask
Spinnaker Buzz (4.5%) cask
Special Crew (5.5%) cask
Black Rock (5.5%) cask
Spinnaker Ginger (5.5%) cask
Riptide (6.5%) cask

BRIDGWATER

Bridgwater Brewing Company, Unit 1, Lovedere Farm, Goathurst, Bridgwater, Somerset TA5 2DD Tel (01278) 663996
Est. 1993. Full-mash, all local malt brewing using Challenger and Styrian Goldings hops. Cannonball was commissioned by the Sealed Knot. Occasional beers: Carnival Special (3.5%), Bluto's Revenge (6%).
Blake's Bitter (3.4%) cask
Amber Ale (3.8%) cask
Bosun's Tickle (4.1%) cask
Cannonball (4.2%) cask
Coppernob (4.4%) cask
Sunbeam (5.4%) cask
Krimbel Ale (4.8%) cask (Xmas)

BRITISH OAK

British Oak Brewery, Salop Street, Eve Hill, Dudley, W. Midlands DY1 3AX Tel (01384) 236297
Est. 1988. Originally a brew pub, now owns a second pub and also supplies local free trade. Full-mash, mostly malt (Maris Otter usually) brewing, with Fuggles, Challenger and Goldings pellets and a little wheat. Occasional beer: Castle Ruin (3.8%).
Oak Mild (3.7%) cask
Eve'ill Bitter (4%) cask
Colonel Pickering's Porter (4.6%) cask
Dungeon Draught (4.8%) cask
Old Jones (6%) cask

BROUGHTON

Broughton Brewery Ltd, Broughton, Biggar, Borders ML12 6HQ Tel (018994) 345
Est. 1980 by David Younger, formerly a Scottish & Newcastle man, in this windswept Borders village, where John Buchan spent much of his childhood. All natural brewing, using malted barley, roast barley, flaked maize, pinhead and flaked oatmeal (in the Stout), Goldings, Fuggles and Target hop pellets. They culture their own yeast and use local Tweed valley water. Special Bitter is a dry-hopped version of Greenmantle.
Broughton 60/- Pale Ale (3.1%) keg
Broughton Ale (3.8%) keg
Scottish Oatmeal Stout (3.8%) cask and bottled
Greenmantle Ale (3.9%) cask and bottled
Special Bitter (3.9%) cask
Broughton 80/- Ale (4.2%) cask
Merlin's Ale (4.2%) cask and bottled
Old Jock (6.7%) cask and bottled

MATTHEW BROWN

see Scottish & Newcastle

BRUNSWICK

Brunswick Brewing Co. Ltd, 1 Railway Terrace, Derby, Derbyshire DE1 2RU Tel (01332) 290667
Est. 1991, in the Brunswick Inn. Brewery viewable from pub. Not all of the beers are available at once. Two other occasional beers: Scrooge's Ale (5.4%), and Vicarage Ale (7%), which is also available bottled.
Recession Ale (3.3%) cask
First Brew (3.6%) cask
Pain I' T' Neck (3.9%) cask
150th Brew (4.2%) cask
Second Brew (4.2%) cask
Railway Porter (4.3%) cask
Festival (4.6%) cask
Old Accidental (5%) cask
Owd Abusive (6%) cask

BUCKLEY

see Crown Buckley

BUFFY'S

Buffy's Brewery, Mardle Hall, Rectory Road, Tivetshall St Mary, Norwich, Norfolk NR15 2DD Tel (01379) 676523

Est. 1993, in the converted double garage of the owners' 14th-century hall house. Pipkin and Halcyon pale and crystal malts, plus a touch of black malt in the Strong Ale; Fuggles and Goldings whole hops, and no adjuncts or additives whatsoever.

Bitter (4%) cask
Polly's Folly (4.3%) cask
Best Bitter (4.9%) cask
Ale (5.5%) cask
Strong Ale (6.5%) cask

BULLMASTIFF

*Bullmastiff Brewery, 14 Bessemer Close, Leckwith, Cardiff CF1 8DL
Tel (01222) 665292*

Est. 1987 elsewhere, moving to Cardiff in 1992.

Bitter (3.5%) cask
Ebony Dark (3.8%) cask
Best Bitter (4%) cask
Son of a Bitch (6%) cask

BUNCES

Bunces Brewery, The Old Mill, Netheravon, Wilts SP4 9QB Tel (01980) 70631

Est. 1983, when Tony Bunce bought and converted this dinky little 'tower' brewery (which was actually built in 1914 as a mini power station). Sold on to new Danish owners, the Andersens, in 1993; successfully too, as they are about to add a further fermentation vessel. As we go to press they also plan to add a Viking herb beer to the range. Vice Beer is a wheat beer (Weissbier! geddit?). Full-mash brewing with all natural ingredients, including Goldings and Omega hops.

Vice Beer (3.2%) cask
Benchmark (3.5%) cask
Pigswill (4%) cask
Best Bitter (4.1%) cask
Old Smokey (5%) cask
Rudolph (5%) cask

BURTON BRIDGE

Burton Bridge Brewery, 24 Bridge Street, Burton-upon-Trent, Staffs DE14 1SY
Tel (01283) 510573

Est. 1982. Very well regarded for their bottled Burton Porter, and further bottle-conditioned beers are promised. Mostly (Pipkin) malt brewing, just using a little invert sugar, plus Challenger, Northdown and Target hops, though they ring the changes here, and also dry-hop with Styrian Goldings on some. Burton Porter uses torrefied barley, which is heated but not roasted, rather like torrefied wheat. They also brew Thomas Sykes Old Ale for Heritage.

Summer Ale (3.8%) cask
XL Bitter (4%) cask
Bridge Bitter (4.2%) cask
Burton Porter (4.5%) cask and bottled BC (4.6%)
Spring Ale (4.7%) cask
Knot Brown Ale (4.8%) cask (autumn)
Top Dog Stout (5%) cask (winter)
Burton Festival Ale (5.5%) cask
Old Expensive (6.5%) cask

BURTONWOOD

*Burtonwood Brewery PLC, Bold Lane, Burtonwood, Warrington, Cheshire WA5 4PJ
Tel (01925) 225131*

Est. 1867 by James Forshaw. Still family run, though a public company with millions of pounds' worth of investment in the last ten years. Now poised to break into the Take Home market (they hope). They also brew Chester's Best Bitter for Whitbread.

Mild (3%) cask/keg
Special Pale Ale (3.1%) keg
Bitter (3.8%) cask/keg and can
James Forshaw's Bitter (4%) cask
Top Hat Premium Bitter (4.8%) cask

BURTS

*Burts Brewery, Dodnor Industrial Estate, Newport, Isle of Wight P030 5FA
Tel (01983) 528098*

Est. 1842, went bust in 1992, then rematerialized as the new name for Island Brewery, who bought up the name and the

brands. The beers are all-malt (pale, crystal, chocolate and wheat), and use Target, Goldings and Challenger hops.
Nipper Bitter (3.8%) cask
VPA/Ventnor Premium Ale (4.2%) cask
Newport Nobbler (4.4%) cask
Tanner Bitter (4.8%) cask
Vectis Venom (5%) cask

BUSHY'S

Mount Murray Brewing Co. Ltd, Mount Murray, Castletown Road, Braddan, Isle of Man IM4 1JE Tel (01624) 661244
Est. 1986 as a brew pub, moving to this location in 1990. Pure Beers, as stipulated under Isle of Man law. Piston Brew (4.5%) is produced when the island races are held. They also make a Christmas Ale (6.2%) and a stout is planned as we go to press.
Dark Mild (3.7%) cask
Best Bitter (3.7%) cask
T.T. Pilsner (4%) keg
Old Bushy Tail (4.7%) cask

BUTCOMBE

Butcombe Brewery Ltd, Butcombe, Bristol BS18 6XQ Tel (01275) 472240
Est. 1978, at the forefront of the then new wave in small independents, but now, almost 20 years on, one of the most established names in the West Country. Splendidly purposeful, and sticking as ever to its one delicious, fruity-yeasty, clean and hoppy real ale. Made using 100% malt, and Goldings and Fuggles hop pellets.
Bitter (4%) cask

BUTTERKNOWLE

Butterknowle Brewery, The Old School House, Lynesack, Butterknowle, Bishop Auckland, Co. Durham DL13 5QF Tel (01388) 710373
Est. 1990, and quickly built a reputation for good, well-made beers. The bottle-conditioned beers can be ordered by the case direct from the brewery. Festival Stout is an occasional brew.
Bitter (3.6%) cask
Festival Stout (3.8%) cask
Banner Bitter (4%) cask
Fine Pale Ale (4%) bottled BC
Conciliation Ale (4.3%) cask and bottled BC
Black Diamond (4.8%) cask
Strong Brown Ale (4.8%) bottled BC
High Force (6.2%) cask
Old Ebenezer (8%) cask

CAINS

Robert Cain Brewery Ltd, Stanhope Street, Liverpool, Merseyside L8 5XJ Tel (0151) 709 8734
Est. 1850 as Robert Cain's Brewery, bought by Higsons in the twenties, and sold to Boddingtons in 1985. Boddingtons were in turn bought by Whitbread in 1990, who then closed Higsons (and moved the brands elsewhere). Denmark A/S brewery group now own the old brewery, and have revived its original name. Superior Stout (4.5%) is brewed on an occasional basis.
Dark Mild (3.2%) cask and can
Traditional Bitter (4%) cask and can
Formidable Ale (5%) cask, bottled and can

CALEDONIAN

Caledonian Brewing Co. Ltd, 42 Slateford Road, Edinburgh EH11 1PH Tel (0131) 337 2370
Est. 1869, when there were 30 breweries in Edinburgh, and remains the last brewery in Britain to use direct-fired open coppers to produce its fine beers, many of them made to original Victorian and Edwardian recipes. Originally called Lorimer & Clark, after its founders, then taken over by Vaux in 1919, it was finally acquired by a managment buy-out in 1987. All-malt, deep-bed infusion brewing using Golden Promise pale, crystal, amber and black malts, whole Goldings and Fuggles hops, their own well water and no additives. Bottled beers are cold-conditioned and pasteurized: of these, Golden Promise was Britain's first organic beer. Merman, typical of the late Victorian style, is creamy with crystal and roast malt flavours. Deuchars gets its ravishing dryness from late hopping. Edinburgh Real Ale, also late-hopped, gets its glorious ruby colour from the use of roast barley. Caledonian 125 is a new addition to

the cask list, originally brewed for their famous June beer festival in 1994, which was also their 125th anniversary.
60/- Ale (3.2%) cask
70/- Ale (3.5%) cask, and bottled
Murrays Summer Ale (3.6%) cask
Deuchars IPA (3.8%) cask and bottled (4.4%)
Golden Pale Organic Ale (4%) bottled
Edinburgh Real Ale/ERA (4.1%) cask
80/- 'Export' Ale (4.1%) cask and bottled
Porter (4.1%) cask
Murrays Heavy (4.3%) cask
Caledonian 125 (4.5%) cask
Campbell Hope & King Double Amber Ale (4.6%) cask
Merman XXX (4.8%) cask and bottled
Golden Promise Organic Ale (5%) cask and bottled
Edinburgh Strong Ale/ESA (6.4%) cask and bottled

CAMERONS

Cameron Brewery Co. Ltd, Lion Brewery, Hartlepool, Cleveland TS24 7QS Tel (01429) 266666
Now owned by Wolverhampton & Dudley, having first passed through the hands of Brent Walker. Beers were 'relaunched' in 1992. Harp lager is made under contract to Guinness (every second brewery in Britain seems to be brewing Harp – where does it all go, for heaven's sake?). Cameron's Crown Special, a new draught beer, is made with 100% pale malt.
Cameron's Best Scotch (3.5%) keg, and can
Bitter (3.6%) cask/keg and can
Crown Special (4%) cask/keg
Strongarm (4%) cask/keg and can

CANNON

Parker & Son Brewers Ltd, The Cannon, Cannon Street, Wellingborough, Northants NN8 4DL Tel (01933) 279629
Est. 1993 at the Cannon public house.
Light Brigade (3.6%) cask
Pride (4.2%) cask
Fodder (5.5%) cask
Old Nosey (6%) cask

CANNON ROYAL

Cannon Royal Brewery, Fruiterer's Arms, Uphampton, Ombersley, Hereford & Worcester WR9 0JW Tel (01905) 621161
Est. 1993 in the old cider house behind the pub. There are plans to brew (at least) two new beers: Fruiterer's Mild (3.7%) and Heart of Oak (5.6%), which will be oak-matured. Pure beer, using hops, water, barley malt and yeast only.
Arrowhead Bitter (3.9%) cask
Buckshot Bitter (4.5%) cask
Millward's Musket Ale (4.6%) cask
Olde Merrie (6%) cask (Xmas)

CARLSBERG-TETLEY

Carlsberg-Tetley Brewing Ltd, 107 Station Street, Burton-upon-Trent, Staffs DE14 1BZ Tel (01283) 531111
The old Allied Brewery, dating from the merger of Ansells, Ind Coope and Tetley Walker in 1961, has now transmogrified into Carlsberg-Tetley, which leaves one of our national brewing giants with a distinctly half-Danish, half-Yorkshire image. On the quite distinct Carlsberg side of the business, brands are still made using their own Carlsbergensis yeast strain, and Carlsberg Ice Beer is the first product they've launched in 20 years. It's a Danish version of a Canadian style, brewed in Northampton, and chilled in Wrexham: that's about the size of international brewing these days. Allied's Castlemaine 'Australian' lager is still made with imported Oz Cluster hops, at least. On the draught ale front, the sudden burst of energy that has surrounded cask beer development in all the big breweries of late has here resulted in a new Samuel Allsopps range, named after their founder. Taylor Walker now own and run the Firkin pub brewery chain, which is steadily expanding.

Cockleroaster and the Dartmoor beers are from their 'Furgusons' West Country brewery. Carlsberg-Tetley also brew Greenall's beers (including Davenports and Shipstone's brands). Additional bottled brands available in pubs/licensed premises: Alloa Sweet Stout, Friary Meux Light Ale, Ind Coope Light Ale,

Tetley Special Pale Ale, Tetley Brown Ale, Walker Brown Peter – all weak keg beers. On the lager front, there are two low alcohol brands: Swan Light (1%) and St Christopher (0.05%).

Alloa's Export 80/- (4.2%) keg, and can
Alloa's Original Light (2.8%) keg
Alloa's Special 70/- (3.6%) keg, and can
Ansells Best Bitter (3.7%) cask/keg, and can (3.5%)
Ansells Mild (3.4%) cask/keg, and can (3.2%)
Arrol's 80/- (4.4%) cask
Aylesbury Best Bitter/ABC (3.7%) cask
Barleycorn Pale Ale (3%) keg
Benskins Best Bitter (3.7%)
Benskins Pale Mild (3%) keg
Burton Ale (4.8%) cask and can
Cockleroaster (6%) cask
Dartmoor Best Bitter (3.9%) cask
Dartmoor Strong (4.6%) cask
Double Diamond (3.3%) keg and bottled (4%)
Dryborough Best Scotch (3.6%) keg
Dryborough Heavy (3.6%) keg
Falstaff Scotch (3.6%) keg
Friary Meux Bitter (3.7%) cask
HP&D 'Holt's' Bitter (3.7%) cask
HP&D 'Holt's' Entire (4.4%) cask
HP&D 'Holt's' Mild (3.7%) cask
Ind Coope Dark Mild (2.6%) keg
Ind Coope Pale (3%) keg
John Bull (3.4%) keg
Nicholson's Best Bitter (3.7%) cask
Samuel Allsopps Harvest Ale (4.2%) cask
Samuel Allsopps IPA (4.2%) cask
Samuel Allsopps Single Malt Ale (4.1%) cask
Samuel Allsopps Winter Warmer (5.5%) cask
Tamebridge Pale Bitter (3%) keg
Tetley Bitter (3.7%) cask/keg and can (3.6%)
Tetley Dark Mild (3.2%) cask; 'Drum Dark Mild' is keg
Tetley Falstaff Pale (3.2%) keg
Tetley Imperial (4.3%) cask/keg and can
Tetley Mild (3.3%) cask and can; 'Drum Mild' is keg
Walker Best Bitter (3.7%) cask
Walker Bitter (3.6%) cask
Walker Mild (3.2%) cask
Walker Winter Warmer (6.2%) cask
Wild Rover (5.6%) cask

LAGERS

Carlsberg Pilsner (3.4%) keg and can
Carlsberg Export (4.7%) keg and bottled
Carlsberg Ice Beer (5.6%) bottled
Carlsberg Special Brew (9%) bottled and can
Castlemaine XXXX (4%) keg and can
Castlemaine XXXX Export (4.8%) can (imported)
Elephant Beer (7.2%) bottled (imported)
Long Life (4.2%) keg and can
Oranjeboom (5%) bottled (imported) and can
Skol (3.4%) keg, bottled and can
Skol Special (4.6%) keg, bottled and can
Skol Super (9.2%) can
Tuborg Gold (5%) keg and can
Tuborg Pilsener (3.4%) keg and can
Wrexham Lager (3.4%) keg and can

CARTMEL

Cartmel Brewery, Cartmel, Cumbria
Tel (015395) 36240

New brewery, not connected to Mason's Arms/Lakeland brewery nearby.

Summer Ale (3.6%) cask
Buttermere (3.8%) cask
Lakeland Gold (4%) cask
Cartmel Thoroughbred (4.5%) cask
Winter Warmer (5.2%) cask

CASTLE

The Castle Brewery, Rhosmaen Street, Llandeilo, Dyfed SA19 Tel (01558) 823313

New brewery, founded by Simon Buckley, of the famous Welsh brewing family (their old concern is now known as Crown Buckley), who also co-organized the Ushers buy-out in 1989. A purpose-built 20-barrel plant has been installed at the rear of the Castle Hotel, a Georgian inn in central Llandeilo. As we went to press no beer names had been finalized.

Brewery Bitter (3.5%) cask
Old Style Best (3.9%) cask
Premium (4.3%) cask

CASTLE EDEN

see Whitbread

CHALK HILL

Chalk Hill Brewery, Rosary Road, Thorpe

Hamlet, Norwich, Norfolk NR1 4DA
Tel (01603) 620703
Est. 1993, by the Reindeer brew-pub ex-owner and team. Full-mash brewing in their 15 barrel plant.
Tap Bitter (3.6%) cask
CHB (4.2%) cask
Dreadnought (4.9%) cask
Old Tackle (5.6%) cask

CHARRINGTON

see Bass

CHERITON

Cheriton Brewhouse, Brandymount, Cheriton, Alresford, Hants SO24 0QQ
Tel (01962) 771166
Est. 1993 beside the Flowerpots Inn. An all-malt, full mash operation using Challenger hops and Halcyon malt. There are also at least three occasional brews, and a regular chilli beer.
Pots Ale (3.8%) cask
Cheriton Best (4.2%) cask
Diggers Gold (4.6%) cask

CHESTER'S

see Whitbread

CHILTERN

Chiltern Brewery, Nash Lee Road, Terrick, Aylesbury, Bucks HP17 0TQ
Tel (01296) 613647
Est. 1980 on a farm. They also have a thriving brewery shop, which sells their bottled beers among other ale-related and country groceries.
Ale (3.7%) cask
Beechwood Bitter (4.3%) cask and bottled BC
Three Hundreds Old Ale (4.9%) cask and bottled
Bodgers Barley Wine (8%) bottled BC

CHILTERN VALLEY

see Old Luxters

CHURCH END

Church End Brewery Ltd,The Griffin Inn, Church Road, Shustoke, Warwickshire B46 2LP Tel (01675) 481567
Est. 1994 in an old stable which had also been used as a coffin workshop; this may explain the gloomier beer names. All-malt brewing using Maris Otter, and a mix of hops including the rich and lemony Bramling Cross.
Gravediggers (3.8%) cask
What the Foxes Hat (4.2%) cask
Vicars Ruin (4.4%) cask
Pews Porter (4.5%) cask
Old Pal (5.5%) cask
Rest In Peace (7%) cask

CLARK'S

H. B. Clark & Co., Westgate Brewery, Westgate, Wakefield, W. Yorks WF2 9SW
Tel (01924) 372306
Est. 1905, though brewing was abandoned for a time in the seventies, and cask ale production only recommenced in 1982. Traditional brewing methods, using pale and crystal malts, roasted barley and torrefied wheat in various combinations. Around 75 barrels a week of cask ale, which appear in their own three pubs and all over the north and east of England.
Traditional Bitter (3.8%) cask
Festival Ale (4.2%) cask
Burglar Bill (4.4%) cask
Rams Revenge (4.8%) cask
Hammerhead (5.5%) cask
Winter Warmer (6.4%) cask
Dreadnought (9%) cask

COACH HOUSE

Coach House Brewing Co. Ltd, Wharf Street, Howley, Warrington, Cheshire WA1 2DQ
Tel (01925) 232800
Est. 1991. The Four Nations range is produced for Burn's Night, St David's Day, St Patrick's Day and St George's Day respectively. Also special occasion beers on high days and holidays. New Zealand hops feature in the spring ale, and German hops in the summer ale.
Coachman's Bitter (3.7%) cask
Gunpowder Strong Mild (3.8%) cask
Ostlers Summer Pale Ale (4%) cask (summer)
Squires Gold Spring Ale (4.2%) cask (spring)

Innkeeper's Special Reserve (4.5%) cask
Posthorn Premium Ale (5%) cask
Taverners Autumn Ale (5%) cask (autumn)
Blunderbus Old Porter (5.5%) cask (winter)

COMBE

Combe Brewery, Unit 5a, Mullacott Cross Industrial Estate, Ilfracombe, Devon EX34 8NY Tel (01271) 864020

New brewery. Brian Broughton started his micro on such a tiny scale it was virtually microscopic – with a quarter-barrel capacity, selling his beer in PET bottles. He's now bought a 5-barrel plant and taken on an industrial unit to make his all-malt, full-mash beers, which use Tuckers malt, plus Fuggles, Goldings and Challenger hops.
Combe Gold (4%) cask
Ship Wreckers (4.4%) cask
Combe Wallop (5%) cask

COMMERCIAL

Commercial Brewing Co. Ltd, Worth Brewery, Worth Way, Keighley, W. Yorks BD21 5LP Tel (01535) 611914

Est. 1992, with a huge variety of both permanent, seasonal and occasional beers, and looks to expand even further when new brewery plant is installed in autumn 1995. Alesman is the new name for the old Keighlian. The new wheat beer, Knobwillter, is supposed to be pronounced K-nob-villter (funny, yes?).
Alesman Traditional Bitter (3.7%) cask and bottled BC
Alesman Bitter (3.7%) cask
Neary's Stout (4%) cask
Wild Boar (4%) cask
Worth Best Bitter (4.5%) cask and bottled BC
OWorth Porter (4.5%) cask and bottled BC
Knobwillter (5.2%) cask
Old Toss (6.5%) cask and bottled BC
Master James (8%) bottled BC
Santa's Toss (8%) bottled BC

CONCERTINA

Concertina Brewery, The Mexborough Concertina Band Club, 9a Dolcliffe Road, Mexborough, S. Yorks S64 9AZ Tel (01709) 580841

Est. 1993 in a club cellar, and has since expanded its trade well beyond the band club walls.
Old Dark Attic (3.8%) cask
Best Bitter (3.9%) cask
Fitzpatricks Stout (4.3%) cask
Hackett VC (4.4%) cask
KW Special Pride (4.5%) cask
Bengal Tiger IPA (4.6%) cask
Bandsman Strong Ale (5.2%) cask

COOK'S

The Cook Brewery Co., 44 Burley Road, Bockhampton, Christchurch, Dorset BH23 7AJ Tel (01425) 673721

Est. 1991, though Nigel Cook, an ex-brewhouse engineer, had been brewing on a small scale for three years previously.
Priory 900 Ale (3.8%) cask
New Forest Gold Bitter (4.1%) cask
Yardarm Special Bitter (5.2%) cask

CORNISH

see Whitbread

COTLEIGH

Cotleigh Brewery, Ford Road, Wiveliscombe, Somerset TA4 2RE Tel (01984) 624086

Est. 1979 in a converted stable block, transferring to a purpose-built brewhouse in 1985, and much expanded in the years since. Cask-conditioned beers only, traditionally brewed, and a monthly changing special. Also makes 'Aldercote' beers for East-West Ales.
Harrier SPA (3.6%) cask
Tawny Bitter (3.8%) cask
Barn Owl Bitter (4.5%) cask
Old Buzzard (4.8%) cask

COTTAGE

Cottage Brewing Co., Little Orchard, West Lydford, Somerset TA11 7DQ Tel (01963) 240551

Est. 1993 by a former airline pilot, and has expanded threefold since (the brewery, not the airline pilot). Traditional methods, and ingredients from West Country suppliers where possible. Rail Ales reflect Chris

Norman's passion for old steam railway companies. Occasional beers: Wheeltappers and Xmas Cottage.
Southern Bitter (3.7%) cask
S&D Bitter (4.4%) cask
GWR (5.4%) cask

COURAGE

Courage Ltd, Ashby House, 1 Bridge Street, Staines, Surrey TW18 4TP
Tel (01784) 466199
One of our best known brewery dynasties, Courage is now actually part of the Australian giant Foster's empire. Unusually for a brewery of this size, since 1991 it's also been a company without pubs. It did, however, purchase all of Grand Metropolitan's breweries at the same time, in a giant, but essentially simple industry swap. They also own Beamish, of Cork, Ireland. John Smith's Extra Smooth, which was launched summer 1995, is one of the new breed of mixed gas (nitrogen joins carbon dioxide) keg beers with a creamy, foamy, smooth texture, an innovation developed from widget 'draught beer in cans' technology. There's a low alcohol product: John Smith's LA (0.9%).
Beamish Stout (4.1%) keg and can
Bulldog Strong Ale (6.3%) bottled
Courage Best Bitter (4%) cask and can
Courage Best Scotch (3.6%) keg
Courage Bitter Ale (3.3%) cask
Courage Dark Mild (3%) keg
Courage Directors (4.8%) cask and can
Courage Light Ale (3.2%) keg and bottled
Imperial Russian Stout (10%) bottled
John Courage (4.2%) keg and bottled
John Smith's Bitter (3.8%) cask/keg and can
John Smith's (Draught) (4%) can
John Smith's Chestnut Mild (3%) keg
John Smith's Extra Smooth Bitter (4%) keg
John Smith's Magnet (4%) cask/keg
John Smith's Strong Ale (5%) can
Magnet Pale Ale (4%) bottled
Manns Brown Ale (2.8%) bottled
Norwich Best Bitter (3.5%) keg
Norwich Mild (2.8%) keg
Prize Brew Dark (3%) keg
Simonds Bitter (3.3%) keg
Watney Truman Mild (2.9%) keg
Webster's Green Label (3.2%) cask/keg
Webster's Pennine Bitter (3.8%) cask/keg
Webster's Yorkshire Bitter (3.5%) cask/keg and can
Wilson's Original Bitter (3.5%) cask/keg
Wilson's Original Mild (3%) cask/keg
Wilson's Special Mild (2.7%) keg

LAGERS

AKA (7.5%) bottled
Budweiser (5%) bottled and can
Carlsberg Pilsner (3.4%) keg and can
Colt 45 (5%) can
Foster's (4%) keg and can
Foster's Export (5%) bottled and can
Foster's Ice Beer (5%) bottled
Hofmeister (3.4%) keg and can
Holsten Export (4.9%) keg and can
Kronenbourg 1664 (5%) keg, bottle (imported) and can
Miller Pilsner (4.2%) keg and can
Molson Special Dry (5.5%) bottled
Victoria Beer/VB (4.9%) can (imported)

CROPTON

Cropton Brewery Co., The New Inn, Cropton, Pickering, N. Yorks YO18 8HH
Tel (01751) 417330
Set up in 1984 in the New Inn basement, to put to rest finally the paranoid fear that one winter, snow and ice would prevent the beer wagon getting across the moors. Now much expanded: a full-mash brewery, using Challenger and Golding whole hops, pale malt only in King Billy, pale and crystal in the rest, plus 'dry roasted' malt in the stout.
King Billy Bitter (3.6%) cask
Two Pints Best Bitter (4%) cask
Scoresby Stout (4.2%) cask
Special Strong Bitter (6%) cask

CROUCH VALE

Crouch Vale Brewery Ltd, 12 Redhills Road, South Woodham Ferrers, Chelmsford, Essex CM3 5UP Tel (01245) 329082
Est. 1981, and expanded greatly in the last five years. Now almost ubiquitous in East Anglia, and fairly common in London, too. They also own just one rather good pub, the

Cap & Feathers, in Tillingham, Essex.
Woodham IPA (3.6%) cask
Best Bitter (4%) cask
Millenium Gold (4.2%) cask
Strong Anglian Special/SAS (4.8%) cask
Essex Porter (4.9%) cask
Santa's Revenge (5.7%) cask
Willie Warmer (6.4%) cask

CROWN BUCKLEY

Crown Brewery, Cowbridge Road, Pontyclun, Mid Glamorgan CF7 9YG Tel (01443) 225453

Est. 1989, when the 18th-century Buckley brewery and Crown brewery merged, a move financed by Guinness. A management buy-out followed in 1993. Their single canned beer is currently available in regional Spar shops only.

Brenin Bitter (3.4%) keg
Buckley's Dark Mild (3.4%) cask/keg
Crown Pale Ale (3.4%) cask
Buckley's Best Bitter (3.7%) cask/keg and can
Special Best Bitter/SBB (3.7%) cask
James Buckley Ale (3.9%) cask
Reverend James Original Ale (4.5%) cask

CUCKMERE HAVEN

Cuckmere Haven Brewery, Exceat Bridge, Cuckmere Haven, East Sussex BN25 4AB Tel (01323) 892247

New brewery. Beers are made with Bramling Cross and Fuggles (and dry-hopped with Goldings), pale and crystal malts; amber malt is used in the darker, tawnier beers. Invert sugar is also used in some cases, to compensate for the presently undersized mash tun.

Cuckmere Best (4.1%) cask
Saxon King Stout (4.2%) cask
Gentlemen's Gold (4.5%) cask
Guv'ner (4.7%) cask

DALESIDE

Daleside Brewery, Camwal Road, Starbeck, Harrogate, N. Yorks HG1 4PT Tel (01423) 880041

Est. 1988 as Big End Brewery, revitalized and renamed with a change of premises in 1992.

Bitter (3.7%) cask
Country Stile (4.1%) cask
Dalesman Old Ale (4.1%) cask
Monkey Wrench (5.3%) cask and bottled

DAVENPORTS

see Greenalls

DENT

Dent Brewery, Hollins, Cowgill, Dent, Cumbria LA10 5TQ Tel (01539) 625326

Est. 1990 in a converted barn. Beers are made using their own spring water.

Bitter (3.7%) cask
Ramsbottom Strong Ale (4.5%) cask
T'Owd Tup (6%) cask

DONNINGTON

Donnington Brewery, Stow-on-the-Wold, Gloucs GL54 1EP Tel (01451) 830603

Est. 1865, when it was converted from a 13th-century watermill; probably the most romantically set brewery in Britain. Still a small-scale, family-run affair.

BB (3.5%) cask
XXX (3.5%) cask, and bottled (as Brown Ale)
SBA (3.8%) cask, and bottled (as Double Donn)

DOROTHY GOODBODY

see Wye Valley

DYFFRYN CLWYD

Bracdy Dyffryn Clwyd Brewery, Chapel Place, Denbigh, Clwyd LL16 3TJ Tel (01745) 815007

Est. 1993. All-malt brewing using a mix of malts, and whole Northdown, Challenger and Styrian Goldings hops. Jolly Jack Tar is a porter; there's also a winter warmer at just over 6%. As we go to press Four Thumbs is about to be bottled. Beers are labelled in English and Welsh.

Comfort Bitter/Cysur (3.6%) cask
Druid/Derwydd (3.9%) cask
Castle Bitter/Cwrw Castell (4.2%) cask
Jolly Jack Tar (4.4%) cask
Four Thumbs/Pedwar Bawd (4.8%) cask

EARL SOHAM

Earl Soham Brewery, The Victoria, Earl Soham, Woodbridge, Suffolk IP13 7RL
Tel (01728) 685758

Est. 1985 to provide supplies for its pub, the Victoria, though the beers are now also seen elsewhere in the area.

Gannet Mild (3%) cask
Victoria (3.5%) cask
Albert Ale (4.3%) cask
Jolabrugg (5–5.4%) cask

EAST-WEST ALES

Non-brewing wholesaler. Aldercote brands are brewed for them by Cotleigh, and other, seasonal beers provided by Brewery on Sea.

EASTWOOD'S

Eastwood's Brewery, Unit 2a, Commercial Mill, Savile Street, Milnsbridge, Huddersfield, W. Yorks HD3 4PG Tel (01484) 656024

Est. 1993 by the former landlord of the Dusty Miller. The newest beer, Myrtle's Temper ('it had to be a very strong one'), is a rather unflattering reference to his wife.

Best Bitter (3.8%) cask
Black Stump (5.1%) cask
Nettlethrasher (5.1%) cask
Myrtle's Temper (7.2%) cask

ELDRIDGE POPE

Eldridge Pope & Co. PLC, Weymouth Avenue, Dorchester, Dorset DT1 1QT
Tel (01305) 251251

Est. 1837 by the Eldridges, who were joined by the Popes in 1880; Popes still run the company. Like most other well-known regional breweries at the moment, they have added a summer ale (Indian Summer), and a new winter beer; Blackdown Porter has been demoted to guest status. Their famous Thomas Hardy's Ale is the strongest bottle-conditioned beer in Britain. They also brew the bottle-conditioned Saxon Strong Ale for Ross.

Dorchester Bitter (3.3%) cask
Best Bitter (3.8%) cask/keg and can
Blackdown Porter (4%) cask
Indian Summer (4%) cask
Thomas Hardy Country Bitter (4.2%) cask and bottled BC
Royal Oak (5%) cask and bottled (4.8%)
Old Spiced Ale (6%) cask (winter)
Thomas Hardy's Ale (12%) bottled BC

ELGOOD'S

Elgood & Sons Ltd, North Brink Brewery, Wisbech, Cambs PE13 1LN
Tel (01945) 583160

Est. 1795, moving in 1878 to this 18th century riverside brewery premises, itself converted from an old mill. A visitor's centre has been opened to celebrate their bicentenary.

Black Dog Mild (3.6%) cask (spring)
Fenman Pale Ale (3.6%) bottled
Fenman Special (3.6%) keg
Mellow Mild (3.6%) keg
Cambridge Bitter (3.8%) cask
Bicentenary Pageant Ale (4.3%) cask
Barleymead (4.8%) cask (autumn)
North Brink Porter (5%) cask (winter)
Greyhound Strong Bitter/GSB (5.2%) cask
Wenceslas Winter Warmer (7.5%) cask (Xmas)

ENVILLE

Enville Ales, Enville Brewery, Cox Green, Enville, Stourbridge, W. Midlands DY7 5LG
Tel (01384) 873728

Est. 1993 by a bee-keeper: Enville ales get their unique character from being routinely primed with honey from his 320 hives. Maris Otter pale malt, plus Northdown, Challenger and Goldings pellets are used in varying combinations, plus Saaz for aroma. The bitter is dry-hopped with whole Goldings. Gothic is a black 'dinner ale', using black malt and sugars on a pale ale base; it will shortly be available bottled in champagne style halves.

Enville Bitter (3.8%) cask
White (4%) cask
Ale (4.5%) cask
Simpkiss Bitter (no abv) cask
Gothic Ale (5.2%) cask

EVERARDS

Everards Brewery Ltd, Castle Acres, Narborough, Leicester LE9 5BY
Tel (0116) 2814100

Est. 1849, but the present brewery, still family-owned and run, dates from 1982. Over 70% of their production is cask-conditioned, and uses Maris Otter pale and crystal malts, torrefied wheat, some malt extract for colour, Fuggles, Goldings and Challenger hop pellets, and dry-hopping in the cask.
Mild (3.3%) cask/keg
Beacon Bitter (3.8%) cask/keg
Tiger Best Bitter (4.2%) cask/keg and can
Old Original (5.2%) cask and can
Daredevil Winter Warmer (7.1%) cask and bottled

EVESHAM

Evesham Brewery, Oat Street, Evesham, Hereford & Worcester WR11 4BJ Tel (01386) 443462
Asum Ale (3.8%) cask
Asum Gold (5.2%) cask

EXE VALLEY

Exe Valley Brewery, Land Farm, Silverton, Exeter, Devon EX5 4HF Tel (01392) 860406
Est. 1984, formerly known as Barron's Brewery. Located in a converted barn. Brewing with the farm's own spring water.
Bitter (3.7%) cask
Dob's Best Bitter (4.1%) cask
Spring Beer (4.3%) cask (spring)
Devon Glory (4.7%) cask
Exeter Old Bitter (4.8%) cask

EXMOOR

Exmoor Ales Ltd, Golden Hill Brewery, Wiveliscombe, Somerset TA4 2NY Tel (01984) 23798
Est. 1980, in a defunct brewery premises first founded in 1807 by William Hancock, but which closed in 1959. Their traditional cask-conditioned beers are made with whole hops, West Country barley malt, and Brendon Hills water. Exmoor Gold was one of the trendsetting pale gold, summery beers of the 'single malt' sort. Exmoor Beast is almost porter-like.
Ale (3.8%) cask
Gold (4.5%) cask
Stag (5.2%) cask
Exmas (6%) cask (Xmas)
Beast (6.6%) cask (winter)

FEATHERSTONE

Featherstone Brewery, Unit 2, King Street, Enderby, Leicester Tel (0116) 2750952
Howes Howler (3.6%) cask
Best Bitter (4.2%) cask
Vulcan Bitter (5.1%) cask
ESB (6%) cask

FEDERATION

Northern Clubs Federation Brewery Ltd, Lancaster Road, Dunston, Tyne & Wear NE11 9JR Tel (0191) 460 9023
Est. 1919 as a co-operative to supply beer to its members in the post-war shortage. Still owned by local clubs, though it now also supplies pubs and clubs elsewhere. Three cask ales, but the emphasis is on club-friendly keg products, although a bottled ale, Federation Export IPA, was submitted to the Brewer's Heritage pack currently on supermarket sale; it's not available singly. They also make a bottled low alcohol product: Danish Light (0.9%).
Ace Lager (3%) can and PET
Brewer's Choice (3%) can
Legend Bitter (3.1%) keg
Pale Ale (3.2%) keg
Mild Ale (3.2%) keg
Light Ale (3.2%) keg
Scotch Ale (3.3%) keg
Buchanan's Best Bitter/70/- (3.6%) cask and keg
Extra Special/80/- (3.7%) keg
Medallion Lager (3.9%) keg
Buchanan's Special Ale (4%) cask/keg, bottled and can
Buchanan's High Level Brown Ale (4.3%) bottled
Buchanan's Original (4.4%) cask
LCL Pils (4.5%) keg, bottled, can and PET (5%)
LCL Super (8.5%) can

FELINFOEL

Felinfoel Brewery Co Ltd, Farmers Row, Felinfoel, Llanelli, Dyfed SA14 8LB Tel (01554) 773357
Est. 1878, and became famous in the thirties

when it was the first brewery to can beer in Britain. Has been almost gobbled up by larger concerns on several occasions, but despite this is still family-owned and independent.
Best Bitter (3.2%) cask
Dark (3.2%) cask
Double Dragon (4.2%) cask/keg and can

FIRKIN

The Firkin Brewery, 77 Muswell Hill, London N10 3PH Tel (0181) 356 2823
Est. 1979 and a pioneering brew-pub chain, now purchased and extended by a division of Carlsberg-Tetley. Easily identifiable pubs – all the something & Firkin (eg. Fox & Firkin) – now number 25 and still counting. Thirteen of them have breweries, and also supply the rest with the standard range of six beers, though seasonal brews like summer wheat beers are also made now. Two of the beers, the Bitter and Best Bitter, are named by the individual pubs. It's full-mash, whole hop brewing.
Firkin Mild (3.4%) cask
Bitter (3.5%) cask
Best Bitter (4.3%) cask
Dogbolter (5.6%) cask
Golden Glory (5%) cask
Firkin Stout (6%) cask

FLAGSHIP

The Flagship Brewery, Unit 2, Building 64, The Historic Dockyard, Chatham, Kent ME4 4TE Tel (01634) 832828
New brewery, a 5 barrel micro established in the restored old dockyard in Chatham. Visitors are encouraged. Beers are made using pale, crystal and chocolate malts, roast barley and Fuggles, Goldings and Progress hops.
Capstan (3.8%) cask
Ensign (4.2%) cask
Crow's Nest (4.8%) cask
Futtock (5.2%) cask
Gang Plank (6%) cask (winter)

FLOWERS

see Whitbread

FOX & HOUNDS

Barley Brewery, Barley, Royston, Herts SG8 8HU Tel (01763) 848459
Nathaniel's Special (3.5%) cask
Flame Thrower (4.1%) cask
Old Dragon (4.6%) cask

FOX & HOUNDS

Woody Woodward's Brewery, Fox & Hounds, High Street, Stottesdon, Shropshire DY14 8TZ Tel (01746) 718222
Wust Bitter (3.7%) cask
Bostin Bitter (4.2%) cask
Gobstopper (7%) cask

FOXLEY

Foxley Brewing Co. Ltd., Unit 3, Home Farm Workshops, Mildenhall, Marlborough, Wilts SN8 2LR Tel (01672) 515000
Est. 1992 by two keen home-brewers. They occasionally also make Roadhog (4.1%) for East-West Ales.
Best Bitter (3.8%) cask
Barking Mad (4.3%) cask
Dog Booter (4.6%) cask
Strong Bitter (4.8%) cask

FRANKLIN'S

Franklin's Brewery, Bilton Lane, Harrogate, N. Yorks HG1 4DH Tel (01423) 322345
Est. 1980 by Sean Franklin, who went on to set up Rooster's.
Bitter (3.9%) cask
Summer Blotto (4.7%) cask
Winter Blotto (4.7%) cask

FREEMINER

Freeminer Brewery Ltd, Sling, Coleford, Gloucs GL16 8JJ Tel (01594) 810408
Est. 1992 by ex-Firkin employees. All-malt brewing using Maris Otter, and local Worcestershire Fuggles and Goldings whole hops. Lots more bottling is planned. Slaughter, as in the Porter, is a local cave system. The new beer, Iron Brew, is made with American hops. Dead Ringer (4.8%), Stairway to Heaven (5%) and Low Rider (6%) are brewed for Blackbeard Trading.
Bitter (4%) cask

Iron Brew (4.4%) cask
Speculation Ale (4.8%) cask
Slaughter Porter (5%) cask
Deep Shaft Stout (6.2%) cask and bottled BC

FREETRADERS

Non brewing wholesaler, its Twelve Bore Bitter (3.7%) produced by King & Barnes.

FREMLINS

see Whitbread

FRIARY MEUX

see Carlsberg-Tetley

FULLER'S

Fuller, Smith & Turner PLC, Griffin Brewery, Chiswick Lane South, Chiswick, London W4 2QB Tel (0181) 995 0230

Est. 1845 in its present guise, when John Bird Fuller, Henry Smith and John Turner went into partnership, and a PLC since 1929. They use English malt and Fuggles and Golding hops. Their 1845 was launched for the 150th anniversary; India Pale Ale is the newest permanent addition to the range. They also own 63 wine merchants under the Fuller's name in the London/M25 area.

Brown Ale (3.2%) bottled
Hock (3.2%) cask
Pale Ale (3.2%) bottled
Chiswick Bitter (3.5%) cask/keg and can
Summer Ale (3.9%) cask
London Pride (4.1%) cask, bottled (4.7%) and can
India Pale Ale (4.8%) cask
Mr Harry (4.8%) cask
ESB (5.5%) cask, and bottled 'Export' (5.9%)
1845 Strong Ale (6.3%) bottled BC
Golden Pride (9.2%) bottled

FURGUSONS

see Carlsberg-Tetley

GALE'S

George Gale & Co. Ltd, Hampshire Brewery, Horndean, Hants P08 0DA Tel (01705) 571212

Est. 1847 and still family-owned. The tower, a local landmark, was added during rebuilding after a devastating fire in 1869. All the beers are made from Maris Otter barley, Fuggles, Goldings and Challenger hops. Gold, launched in 1994, is one of the new breed of pale summer refreshers, and uses 100% pale malt. Prize Old Ale is still bottled, corked and labelled by hand; 5X contains some blended-in Prize Old Ale. There's also a bottled low alcohol product, Wyvern (1%).

Butser Brew Bitter/BBB (3.4%) cask
Best Bitter (3.8%) cask
Gold (4%) cask
5X (4.2%) cask (winter)
Festival Mild (4.8%) cask
HSB (4.8%) cask and can
Prize Old Ale (9%) bottled BC

GIBBS MEW

Gibbs Mew PLC, Anchor Brewery, Gigant Street, Salisbury, Wilts SP1 2AR Tel (01722) 411911

Est. 1898, when the local Gibbs and Mew breweries merged. Two of its bottled beers are available in licensed premises only; the third, Bishop's Tipple, is now exported to France, Italy, Australia, New Zealand and North America. Ingredients used: barley malt, hops, torrefied wheat, yeast and water.

SPA (3%) keg
Supermild (3%) keg
Overlord (3.6%) cask
Wiltshire Special Bitter (3.6%) keg
Wiltshire Traditional Bitter (3.6%) cask
Salisbury Best Bitter (4%) cask
Wake Ale (5%) cask (winter)
Deacon (5%) cask
The Bishop's Tipple (6.5%) cask and bottled

GOACHER'S

P. & D. J. Goacher, Unit 8, Tovil Green Business Park, Tovil, Maidstone, Kent ME15 6TA Tel (01622) 682112

Est. 1983. Kentish hops and all-malt brewing. Special, which appears in Kent pubs under their own house names, is a 75/25 mix of Light and Dark.

Real Mild Ale (3.4%) cask
Fine Light Ale (3.7%) cask

Best Dark Ale (4.1%) cask
Gold Star (5.1%) cask
Maidstone Porter (5.1%) cask
Old 1066 Ale (6.7%) cask

GOFF'S

Goff's Brewery Ltd, 9 Isbourne Way, Winchcombe, Gloucs GL54 5NS
Tel (01242) 603383
Est. 1994. Beers are made with best Pipkin pale and crystal malts, Challenger and Fuggles hop pellets. White Knight is a straw-coloured summer bitter. A stronger seasonal will appear in the winter.
Jouster (4%) cask
White Knight Bitter (4%) cask

GOLDFINCH

Goldfinch Brewery, 47 High East Street, Dorchester, Dorset DT1 1HU
Tel (01305) 264020
Est. 1987 at Tom Brown's public house. Beers are all-malt, using pale and crystal malts, plus chocolate malt in M.B., and Goldings hops.
Tom Brown's Best Bitter (4%) cask
Flashman's Clout Strong Ale (4.5%) cask
Midnight Blinder (5%) cask

GOOSE EYE

Goose Eye Brewery, Ingrow Bridge, South Street, Keighley, W. Yorks BD21 5AX
Tel (01535) 605807
Est. 1991, a revival of a brewery that had closed four years earlier. All-malt brewing using Fuggles and Goldings. Pommie's Revenge should properly be called 5X; it was launched shortly after Castlemaine.
Black Goose Mild (3.5%) cask
Bitter (3.8%) cask
Bronte Bitter (4%) cask
Wharfedale (4.5%) cask
Pommie's Revenge (4.5%) cask

GREENJACK

Greenjack Brewing Co. Ltd, Oulton Broad Brewery, Harbour Road Industrial Estate, Oulton Broad, Suffolk NR32 3LZ
Tel (01502) 587905
Est. 1993 in the defunct Forbes Brewery. Traditional all-malt brewing (mostly Halcyon), plus Challenger and Goldings hops. There are also two occasional beers.
Bitter (3.5%) cask
Best Bitter (4.5%) cask
Golden Sickle (5%) cask
Norfolk Wolf Porter (5.2%) cask
Lurcher (6%) cask

GREENALLS

Greenalls Group PLC, Wilderspool House, Greenalls Avenue, Warrington, Cheshire WA4 6RH Tel (01925) 651234
Formerly a sizeable regional brewery, but now a non-brewing pub group. The beers are made by Carlsberg-Tetley.
Greenalls Mild (3.3%) cask/keg
Shipstone's Mild (3.4%) cask/keg
Greenalls Bitter (3.8%) cask/keg
Davenports Traditional Bitter (3.9%) cask/keg
Shipstone's Bitter (3.9%) cask/keg
Thomas Greenall's Original Bitter (4.6%) cask

GREENE KING

Greene King PLC, Westgate Brewery, Westgate Street, Bury St Edmunds, Suffolk 1P33 1QT Tel (01284) 763222
Est. 1799, and now a prosperous regional brewery that has won national recognition – certainly in branding and marketing terms – for its IPA and Abbot Ale. New seasonal ales include Sorceror (4.5%), Black Baron (4.3%) and a new summer beer, King's Champion (3.8%). There's also a low alcohol bottled product: Lowes LA (1%).
Dark Mild (3%) cask
Harvest Brown (3%) bottled
Pale Ale (3%) bottled
Pelham Light Ale (3%) bottled
Brewers Bitter (3.6%) keg
IPA (3.6%) cask/keg and can
King Keg (3.8%) keg
Crown Ale (4%) bottled
Rayments Special Bitter (4%) cask
Abbot Ale (5%) cask, bottled, can and PET
Strong Suffolk (6%) bottled
St Edmunds Special Brew (6.3%) bottled
Winter Ale (6.4%) cask

GREENWOOD'S

Greenwood's Brewery, Bell Farm, Bell Foundry Lane, Wokingham, Berks RG11 5QF Tel (01734) 793516

New brewery. Ten barrels a week, using 100% Maris Otter malt, Challenger and Goldings whole hops, with no adjuncts or additives. Now looking to add a mild to the list. They have also launched the now obligatory seasonal ales.

Hop Pocket Bitter (3.8%) cask
Temperance Relief (4.3%) cask
Prohibition (4.8%) cask
Amber Gambler (5.5%) cask

GUERNSEY

The Guernsey Brewery Co., South Esplanade, St Peter Port, Guernsey GY1 1BJ Tel (01481) 720143

Est. 1865 as the London Brewery, became Guernsey in 1920 (when it registered itself as an island company to avoid mainland income tax) and was taken over by Jersey's Ann Street brewery in 1988. There's also a bottled stout.

Braye Ale (3.7%) cask, and bottled (Pony Ale)
Pony Original (3.8%) keg
Britannia Bitter (4%) cask
Champion Bitter (4.2%) keg
Sunbeam Bitter (4.2%) cask
Captain's Special (5%) keg and can

GUINNESS

Guinness Brewing (GB), Park Royal Brewery, London NW10 7RR Tel (0181) 965 7700

Est. 1759 by Arthur Guinness, with an £100 legacy, in the old brewery at St James's Gate, Dublin, on a 9000-year lease. He switched from Dublin Ale to the then extremely fashionable Porter style in the 1770s. One hundred and fifty years later, Guinness was producing 3 million barrels a week, and needed a second brewery. Park Royal, London, opened in 1936. It is London which produces much of the packaged Guinness for the home market. Guinness also have a huge presence all around the world, but particularly in the Tropics: the strong, complex, sweet and fruity Guinness made for and by this market is now finding its way back home. Guinness own no pubs, but achieve their huge sales via saturation levels of advertising. All their brands are available retail apart from Satzenbrau lager, which is sold through pubs and clubs only.

Bottled Guinness Original used to be bottle-conditioned, but is no longer. The main difference between it and Draught Canned Guinness now is the tight creamy head, achieved with an award-winning widget that cost four years, 100 discarded prototypes and £5 million to produce. Draught Guinness sold by the pint in Irish pubs is 'real' in so far as it's not pasteurized, but is still served with the aid of gas pressure.

Cherry's Bitter (3.7%) can
Enigma lager (5%) can
Draught Guinness (4.1%) keg and can
Guinness Draught Bitter (4.3%) can
Guinness Original (4.3%) bottled
Guinness Foreign Extra Stout (7.5%) bottled
Harp lager (3.6%) can
Kronenbourg 1664 (5%) bottled and can
Premier Export Lager (5%) can

HP&D HOLT PLANT & DEAKIN

see Carlsberg-Tetley

HADRIAN

Hadrian Brewery Ltd, Unit 10, Hawick Crescent Industrial Estate, Newcastle upon Tyne NE6 1AS Tel (0191) 276 5302

Est. 1987, and moved to this industrial unit, and bigger premises, in 1991. All-malt brewing, using Halcyon, plus whole Target and Fuggles hops, added to which they have just started using the remarkably citrus-fruity Bramling Cross variety. They also (occasionally) brew Zetland Best Bitter for Village Brewer.

Gladiator Bitter (3.8%) cask
Legion Ale (4.2%) cask
Centurion Best Bitter (4.5%) cask
Emperor Ale (5%) cask

HALL & WOODHOUSE

Hall & Woodhouse Ltd, The Brewery, Blandford St Mary, Blandford Forum, Dorset

DT11 9LS Tel (01258) 454700
Est. 1777 as the Ansty Brewery by Charles Hall; Mr Woodhouse joined the company in 1847. Their current relationship with Hofbrauhaus, Munich, involves importing four bottled beers, and making two others (both lagers) under licence, using pilsner malt, Bavarian hops and Hofbrau yeast. The bottled and canned Hofbrau products are available in Woodhouse Wines off-licences. The 'Badger' ales are made with ale malt and sugar, and English hops.
Badger Best Bitter (4.1%) cask, and can (4%)
Badger Country Bitter (4.1%) keg version of BBB
Hofbrau Export (4.3%) keg, and can (4.2%)
Hofbrau Royal/Premium (5%) keg, and can (4.8%)
Tanglefoot (5.1%) cask, bottled and can (5%)

HAMBLETON

Hambleton Ales, Holme-on-Swale, Thirsk, N. Yorks YO7 4JE Tel (01845) 567460
Est. 1991, and has expanded rapidly: a new brewery is now being built to provide a 150-barrel-a-week capacity. Halcyon malt, Northdown and Styrian Golding hops, their own yeast, and water are the only ingredients. They also produce three beers for Village Brewer.
Bitter (3.6%) cask
Goldfield (4.2%) cask
Stallion (4.2%) cask
Nightmare (5%) cask
Thoroughbred (5%) cask (summer)

HAMPSHIRE

Hampshire Brewery, 5 Anton Trading Estate, Andover, Hants SP10 2NJ
Tel (01264) 336699
Est. 1992 with a purpose-built 25-barrel plant. Alfred the Great had a parliament in Andover.
King Alfred's (3.8%) cask
LionHeart (4.2%) cask
Pendragon (4.8%) cask
1066 (6%) cask and bottled

HANBY

Hanby Ales Ltd, New Brewery, Aston Park, Sorlton Road, Wem, Shropshire SY4 5SD
Tel (01939) 232432
Happy Jack (3%), Black Betty (4.4%), Queen Ann's Revenge (7.6%) and the ginger and cherry beers (Joybringer and Cherry Bomb, both Nutcracker variants) are supplied to Blackbeard Trading. Scorpio, a new beer, is a 'dark porter/bitter hybrid'.
Pale Ale (3%) cask
Black Magic Mild (3.3%) cask
Drawwell Bitter (3.9%) cask
Shropshire Stout (4.4%) cask
Scorpio (4.5%) cask
Treacleminer Bitter (4.6%) cask
Old Wemian Ale (4.9%) cask
Cherry Bomb (6%) cask
Joybringer (6%) cask
Nutcracker Bitter (6%) cask
Cocklewarmer Bitter (8%) cask

HANCOCK'S

see Bass

HANSEATIC

Hanseatic Trading, West Walk Building, 110 Regent Road, Leicester LE1 7LT
Tel (01572) 722215
Non-brewing beer company, which gets its concepts run up by others. In this case, the beers are brewed and bottled for them by McMullen.
Brewer James Crystal Ale (4.5%) bottled BC
James Pryor's IPA (4.5%) bottled BC
Vassilenski's Black Russian (4.8%) bottled BC

HANSON'S

see Banks's

HARDINGTON

Hardington Brewery, 4 Albany Buildings, Dean Lane, Bedminster, Bristol BS3 1BT
Tel (0117) 963 6194
Est. 1991. Unconnected with the defunct Somerset brewery of the same name.
Special Pale (3.5%) cask
Traditional Bitter (3.6%) cask
Best Bitter (4.2%) cask and bottled
Jubilee (5%) cask
Moonshine (5%) cask and bottled

Old Lucifer (5.5%) cask
Old Ale (6%) cask and bottled

HARDYS & HANSONS

Hardys & Hansons PLC, Kimberley Brewery, Kimberley, Nottingham NG16 2NS
Tel (0115) 938 3611
Est. 1930, when Hardys and Hansons Victorian breweries merged. The old Hansons building is now demolished, and its maltings closed down because, they say, there's a shortage of skilled maltsters. None of the products is pasteurized, because 'it gives the beer a cooked taste'. The brewery is still controlled by both families, and is a major pub owner in the area.
Best Mild (3.1%) cask and can
Best Bitter (3.9%) cask and can
Kimberley Classic (4.7%) cask and can

HARTLEYS

see Robinson's

HARVEYS

Harvey & Sons Ltd, The Bridge Wharf Brewery, 6 Cliffe High Street, Lewes, East Sussex BN7 2AH Tel (01273) 480209
Est. 1790, and refurbished in 1880, when the classic Victorian tower and brewhouse were added. All their bottled beers are packaged in returnable glass, so they have very little supermarket and off-licence trade. There are, however, a dozen bottled beers, including two low alcohol brands: John Hop and Bill Brewer, both 1% abv.
Sweet Sussex (2.8%) bottled
Nut Brown Ale (3%) bottled
XX Mild Ale (3%) cask
IPA (3.2%) bottled
Sussex Pale Ale (3.5%) cask
Blue Label (3.6%) bottled
Exhibition Brown Ale (3.6%) bottled
Sussex Keg Bitter (3.6%) keg
Sussex Best Bitter (4%) cask
XXXX/Old Ale (4.3%) cask
Armada Ale (4.5%) cask and bottled
1859 Porter (4.8%) bottled BC
Tom Paine (5.5%) bottled
Elizabethan Ale (8.1%) bottled
Christmas Ale (8.1%) bottled

HARVIESTOUN

Harviestoun Brewery Ltd, Devon Road, Dollar, Clackmannanshire FK14 7LX
Tel (01259) 742141
Est. 1985, in an old cow byre, in a former dairy. Typical ingredients: Pipkin pale malt, crystal (and in some cases chocolate) malt, Fuggles and Golding hops, though Northdown and Progress are also used in some beers. Schiehallion is a cask-conditioned lager-ale hybrid, made with lager yeast, fermented at low temperatures, but served with active yeast at cellar (ale) temperature, with no added gas. Wheat malt and Saaz hops are used in Ptarmigan; roasted barley in Waverley.
Waverley 70/- (3.7%) cask
Original 80/- (4.1%) cask
Montrose (4.2%) cask
Ptarmigan 85/- (4.5%) cask
Schiehallion (4.8%) cask
Old Manor (5%) cask

HEDGEHOG & HOGSHEAD

see Belchers

HERITAGE

Heritage Brewery Museum, Burton-upon-Trent
Their Thomas Sykes Old Ale (10% abv, cask and bottled BC) is produced by Burton Bridge, and Dark Amber (4.2%) by Lloyds brewery.

HESKET NEWMARKET

Hesket Newmarket Brewery, Old Crown Barn, Hesket Newmarket, Cumbria CA7 8JG
Tel (0169 74) 78288
This Lake District brewery names most of its beer after local hills. Their full mash, 99% malt brewing also uses Fuggles, Goldings and Hallertau hops. Catbells is a new beer.
Great Cockup Porter (2.8%) cask
Blencathra Bitter (3.1%) cask
Skiddaw Special Bitter (3.7%) cask
Doris's 90th Birthday Ale (4.3%) cask
Catbells Pale Ale (5.1%) cask
Old Carrock Strong Ale (5.6%) cask

HEXHAMSHIRE

Hexhamshire Brewery, Ordley, Hexham, Northumberland NE46 1SX
Tel (01434) 673031
Est. 1992 in converted farm steading, using recycled milk tanks. All-malt brewing, with some roast barley in the darker beers, plus Goldings hops, with a little Target and Styrian Goldings.
Low Quarter Ale (3.5%) cask
Shire Bitter (3.8%) cask
Devil's Water (4.1%) cask
Whapweasel/Strong (4.8%) cask
Old Humbug (5.5%) cask

HIGHGATE

see Bass

HIGSONS

see Cain's

HIGHWOOD

Highwood Brewery Ltd, Melton Highwood, Barnetby, South Humberside DN38 6AA
Tel (01652) 680020
New 10 barrel brewery, converted from a disused granary on a farm in the Lincolnshire Wolds. All-malt brewing, using pale, crystal and pale chocolate malts, Challenger and Fuggles whole hops.
Tom Wood Best Bitter (3.5%) cask
Tom Wood Old Timer (4.5%) cask

HILDEN

Hilden Brewery, Hilden House, Lisburn, Co. Antrim BT27 4TY Tel (01846) 663863
Est. 1981, and not merely the only microbrewery in Northern Ireland, but the only independent brewery in the whole of Ireland, Eire included. Otherwise, it's pretty much just Guinness and Bass (plus imports). All-malt brewing, using pale, crystal and black malts, Goldings and Hersbrucker hops.
Ale (4%) cask
Great Northern Porter (4%) cask
Special Reserve (4%) cask

HOBSON'S

Hobson's Brewery & Co., The Brewery, Cleobury Industrial Estate, Cleobury Mortimer, Shropshire DY14 8DP
Tel (01299) 270837
Est. 1993 in an ex-sawmill, full-mash brewing using Maris Otter and crystal malts, whole Challenger, Progress, Fuggles and Goldings hops, and routinely dry-hopping. Town Crier is bottled in a limited way. Distribution of all Hobson's beers is limited to a radius of one hour's drive.
Best Bitter (3.8%) cask
Town Crier (4.5%) cask
Old Henry (5.2%) cask

HOGS BACK

Hogs Back Brewery, Manor Farm, The Street, Tongham, Surrey GU10 1DE
Tel (01252) 783000
Est. 1992, in a converted farm building. Full mash, all-malt brewing, using whole English hops. They also have a brilliant brewery shop, offering around 400 Belgian imports and 100 English bottled beers, among others.
Dark Mild (3.4%) cask
A Pinta Bitter/APB (3.7%) cask
Traditional English Ale/TEA (4.2%) cask
Blackwater Porter (4.4%) cask
Hop Garden Gold (4.6%) cask
Ripsnorter (5%) cask
Olde Tongham Tasty/OTT (6.5%) cask
Brewsters Bundle (7.45%) bottled BC
Aromas Over Tongham (9%) cask, and bottled BC

HOLDEN'S

Holden's Brewery Co. Ltd, Hopden Brewery, George Street, Woodsetton, Dudley, W. Midlands DY1 4LN
Tel (01902) 665473
Est. 1916, and still in family hands. Big on bottling, for themselves and others in the Midlands. Typical ingredients: pale and coloured malts, hops, sugar, wheat.
Hazledown's Stout (3.3%) bottled
Hazledown's Mild (3.5%) bottled
Stout (3.5%) cask
Hazledown's Bitter (3.7%) bottled
Mild (3.7%) cask, and bottled
Bitter (3.9%) cask, and bottled (as 'Golden')

XB (4.1%) cask
Special Bitter (5.1%) cask, and bottled
Old Ale (6.9%) cask, and bottled

HOLT

Joseph Holt PLC, Derby Brewery, Empire Street, Cheetham, Manchester M3 1JD
Tel (0161) 834 3285
Est. 1849, a family brewery unconnected with the 'Holt's' brands of Carlsberg-Tetley. All-malt (Pipkin and Halcyon) brewing of the old-fashioned sort, using a wide variety of hops in combination. Bottled and canned products are presently only available in pubs.
Mild (3.2%) cask
Brown Stout (3.5%) bottled
Pale Ale (3.5%) bottled
Bitter (4%) cask and can
6X (6%) bottled

HOLT, PLANT & DEAKIN

aka HP&D, aka Holt's
see Carlsberg-Tetley

HOME

see Scottish & Newcastle

HOOK NORTON

Hook Norton Brewery Co. Ltd, Hook Norton, Banbury, Oxon OX15 5NY
Tel (01608) 737210
Est. 1850, and much of the old equipment is still in use. All three of its cask-conditioned, traditionally made ales are also bottled. Typical ingredients: Maris Otter malt, Fuggles, Goldings and Challenger hops.
Best Mild (3%) cask and bottled (as 'Hook Ale')
Best Bitter (3.4%) cask and bottled (as 'Jackpot')
Old Hooky (4.6%) cask and bottled

HOP BACK

Hop Back Brewery PLC, Unit 22, Batten Road Industrial Estate, Downton, Salisbury, Wilts SP5 3HU Tel (01725) 510986
Est. 1987 as a brew pub, and the little plant at the Wyndham Arms is still used for try-outs and small batch beers, though the bulk of the brewing transferred here in 1992. Their cask-conditioned wheat beer is made from 50/50 pale and wheat malts.
Mild (3.2%) cask
GFB (3.5%) cask
HBS/Special (4%) cask
Wilt Alternative (4%) cask
Entire Stout (4.5%) cask
Summer Lightning (5%) cask
Wheat Beer (5%) cask

HOSKINS

T Hoskins Ltd, Beaumanor Brewery, 133 Beaumanor Road, Leicester LE4 5QE Tel (0116) 266 1122
Est. 1877, and a family brewery until taken over in 1983, a development that led to the founding of Hoskins & Oldfield, in much the same way that Black Sheep came about from the sale of Theakston. Maris Otter pale and crystal malts, malted wheat and invert sugar, plus Challenger hops.
Bitter (3.7%) cask
Penn's Ale (4.6%) cask
Churchill's Pride (4.9%) cask
Premium (4.9%) cask
Old Nigel (5.8%) cask

HOSKINS & OLDFIELD

Hoskins & Oldfield Brewery Ltd, North Mills, Frog Island, Leicester LE3 5DH
Tel (0116) 251 0532
Est. 1984 by Philip and Stephen Hoskins after the sale of their family brewery. The beer range is growing like crazy. A raspberry beer is planned for the summer; they would do a cherry beer too, but as around 15lb of fruit is needed for an 18 gallon batch, this will probably prove prohibitively expensive. The stronger beers are going into bottled BC form shortly. Typical ingredients: Maris Otter malt (and a little sugar in some), whole Bramling Cross, Challenger and Mounthood (American) hops, and Hallertau in the wheat beer.
HOB Mild (3.5%) cask
Brigadier Bitter (3.6%) cask
HOB Bitter (4%) cask
Little Matty (4%) cask
White Dolphin (4%) cask
Tom Kelly's Stout (4.2%) cask

Supreme (4.4%) cask
Tom Hoskins Porter (4.8%) cask
EXS Bitter (5%) cask
Ginger Tom (5.2%) cask
Old Navigation Ale (7%) cask
Christmas Noggin (10%) cask

HULL

Hull Brewery Co. Ltd, 144–148 English Street, Hull, Humbs HU3 2BT
Tel (01482) 586364
Est. 1989, reviving a tradition that had died out 15 years earlier. New owners as of 1994. Full mash, all-malt brewing using a real mix of English malts and hops.
Traditional Dark Mild (3.3%) cask
Elwoods Best Bitter (3.8%) cask
Hull Brewery Best Bitter (3.8%) cask
Governor Strong Ale (4.4%) cask

HYDES ANVIL

Hydes Anvil Brewery Ltd, 46 Moss Lane West, Manchester M15 5PH Tel (0161) 226 1317
Est. 1863, and it remains a steadfastly all-malt, traditional family brewery, with no keg, bottled or canned beer production.
Mild (3.5%) cask
Dark Mild (3.5%) cask
Light (3.7%) cask
Bitter (3.8%) cask

IND COOPE

see Carlsberg-Tetley

ISLE OF MAN

Isle of Man Breweries Ltd, Kewaigue, Douglas, Isle of Man IM2 1QG
Tel (01624) 661120
Now the main Isle of Man brewery, after taking over and closing Castletown, its old rival. The island's very own Pure Beer Law (1874) still ensures that Manx beers are made from malt, hops, yeast, sugar and water only. Doolish is Manx for 'black water', the closest the old language comes to a word for stout.
Okells Mild (3.4%) cask/keg
Okells Bitter (3.7%) cask/keg
Doolish Manx Stout (4.1%) cask
Olde Skipper (4.5%) cask (occasional)

JENNINGS

Jennings Bros PLC, Castle Brewery, Cockermouth, Cumbria CA13 9NE
Tel (01900) 823214
Est. 1828, and has grown rapidly in the last five years. Latest plans include a range of 50cl bottled beers for supermarkets; the first of these will be Sneck Lifter (sneck is a Cumbrian word for a cottage latch). Beers are all-malt, using Fuggles, Goldings and Challenger whole hops. Only a small percentage goes into kegs. Bottled Cumbrian Ale (4.2%) and Sneck Lifter are currently available in pubs. Their Oatmeal Stout is brewed by Broughton.
Dark Mild (3.1%) cask
Bitter (3.5%) cask/keg
Cumberland Ale (4%) cask/keg
Cocker Hoop (4.8%) cask
Sneck Lifter (5.1%) cask

JOHN SMITH'S

see Courage

JOLLY ROGER

Jolly Roger Brewery, 31-33 Friar Street, Worcester WR1 2NA Tel (01905) 22222
Est. 1982 as a brew pub in Upton upon Severn, moving here in 1985. All-malt brewing using Maris Otter and Halcyon, with Challenger plus American Willamette and Mounthood hops. More beers and general expansion are expected for 1996.
Ale (3.8%) cask
Broadsword (3.9%) cask
Shipwrecked (4%) cask
Goodness Stout (4.2%) cask
Flagship (5.2%) cask
Winter Wobbler (11%) cask, and bottled BC (10%)

JUDGES

Judges Brewery, Unit 5, Church Lawford Business Centre, Church Lawford, Warwickshire CV23 9HD
Tel (01203) 545559
Barristers Bitter (3.5%) cask
Old Gavel Bender (4.8%) cask
Solicitor's Ruin (5.6%) cask

KELHAM ISLAND

Kelham Island Brewery, 23 Alma Street, Sheffield, S. Yorks S3 5SA Tel (0114) 278 1867

Est. 1990, originally to supply to the Fat Cat pub next door. The wheat beer is made 'Bavarian style' with wheat malt and Maris Otter, and Golden Eagle is intended to reflect the American micro ale style, using a mix of Continental and American ingredients.

Best Bitter (3.8%) cask
Golden Eagle (4.2%) cask
Wheat Beer (5%) cask
Pale Rider (5.2%) cask
Bete Noire (5.5%) cask

KEMPTOWN

Kemptown Brewery Co. Ltd, 33 Upper St James's Street, Kemptown, Brighton, East Sussex BN2 1JN Tel (01273) 699595

Named after the original Kemptown brewery (1849–1964), and a venture inspired by a 'lively evening' at the 1988 Great British Beer Festival. Full mash brewing using English malt and hops.

Budget Bitter (3.5%) cask
Mild (3.5%) cask
Best Bitter (4%) cask
Crewsaver (4.5%) cask
Celebrated Staggering Ale/CSA (5%) cask
Staggering in the Dark/SID (5%) cask

KING & BARNES

King & Barnes Ltd., Horsham Brewery, 18 Bishopric, Horsham, West Sussex RH12 1QP Tel (01403) 270570

An early Victorian brewery, but King & Barnes since 1906; Kings still run it. They use British malt and whole Goldings, Challenger and Whitbread Golding Variety hops, and their own artesian well, which provides their characteristic very soft water. Delicious bottled Festive, named after the Festival of Britain, is made from barley malts, maize, hops and maltose syrup. There's wheat malt and molasses in the Porter. Specials for 1995 included a corn beer and a wheat beer, and Wealdman was launched in May. They also brew Twelve Bore Bitter for Freetraders, and bottled Bajan (4.7%) under licence from Banks brewery, Barbados, as well as importing Hackerbrau Edelhell from Hacker-Pschorr, Munich.

Mild Ale (3.5%) cask
Sussex (3.5%) cask and bottled
Wealdman (3.8%) cask
Broadwood (4.2%) cask/keg
Harvest Ale (4.5%) cask
Old Ale (4.5%) cask
Spring Ale (4.5%) cask
Festive (5%) cask, bottled BC (5.3%) and can
Old Porter (5.5%) bottled BC
Christmas Ale (6.5%) cask and bottled BC (8%)

KING'S HEAD

King's Head Ale House and Brewery, 21 Bretonside, Plymouth, Devon PL4 0BB Tel (01752) 665619

King's Ransom (4%) cask

LARKINS

Larkins Brewery Ltd, Chiddingstone, Edenbridge, Kent TN8 7BB Tel (01892) 870328

Est. 1986, when the hop-growing Dockerty family bought the old Royal Tunbridge Wells Brewery. They opened their own farm brewhouse in 1990. Onwards and upwards, and now brewing two to three times a week, instead of once every three weeks. Traditional all-barley malt brewing, with Kent whole hops, including some of their own.

Traditional Bitter (3.5%) cask
Sovereign (4%) cask
Best Bitter (4.4%) cask
Porter (5.2%) cask

LASTINGHAM

Lastingham Brewery Co. Ltd, Unit 5, Westgate Carr Road, Pickering, N. Yorks YO18 8LX Tel (01751) 477628

Est. 1993, and doing very nicely thank you. A recent visit by HRH Prince Charles initiated the brewing of a new beer, Royal Oui.

Church Bitter (3.7%) cask
Curate's Downfall (4.3%) cask
Royal Oui (4.5%) cask
Amen (5.4%) cask

LEES

J W Lees & Co. Ltd, Greengate Brewery, Middleton Junction, Manchester M24 2AX
Tel (0161) 643 2487

Est. 1828 by a retired cotton mill owner, John Willie Lees, and still family run. Typical ingredients include Maris Otter barley malt and East Kent Goldings. The Mild is sweetened with cane sugar, and the lager, which they've been brewing since 1959, is made from lager malt, torrefied wheat and Styrian hops. This will be the 10th annual Harvest Ale.

Archer Sweet Stout (3.5%) bottled
GB Mild (3.5%) cask
Lees Pilsner Lager (3.7%) keg
Edelbrau Lite (3.9%) keg
Bitter (4%) cask/keg
John Willie Lees Premium Draught Bitter (4%) can
Export Ale (5%) bottled
Edelbrau Diat Pils (5.5%) can
Moonraker (7.5%) cask and bottled
Harvest Ale (11.5%) bottled

LICHFIELD

Lichfield Brewery, 3 Europa Way, Boley Park, Lichfield, Staffs WS14 9TZ
Tel (01543) 419919

Est. 1992, the first brewery in the city since the thirties. Typical ingredients: Maris Otter and amber or chocolate malt (plus crystal in Inspired and Expired), with Challenger and Styrian hops.

Steeplechase (3.7%) cask (summer)
Inspired (4%) cask
Sherrif's Ride (4.2%) cask
Steeplejack (4.5%) cask
Xpired (4.8%) cask
Mincespired (5.8%) cask (Xmas)

LINFIT

Linfit Brewery, Sair Inn, Lane Top, Linthwaite, Huddersfield, W. Yorks HD7 5SG
Tel (01484) 842370

Est. 1982, though brewing had been a Sair Inn tradition long before. Three new seasonal ales may join the permanent list next year. Bottling is also planned for 1996.

Mild (3%) cask
Summer Ale (3.2%) cask
Bitter (3.7%) cask
Special (4.3%) cask
Janet St. Porter (4.5%) cask (winter)
Autumn Gold (4.7%) cask
Springbok (4.7%) cask (autumn)
English Guineas Stout (5.3%) cask
Old Eli (5.3%) cask
Leadboiler (6.6%) cask
Enoch's Hammer (8.6%) cask

LITTLE AVENHAM

Little Avenham Brewery, Arkwright Mill, Hawkins Street, Preston PR1 7HS
Tel (01772) 555305

Est. 1992 after creating their successful real ale pub, Gastons. All-malt brewing, using whole hops; the new Hedgerow beer uses a local harvest of wild hops. Pierrepoints was a local hangman.

Arkwright Mild (3.5%) cask
Arkwright Ale (3.6%) cask
Hedgerow (3.5-4%) cask (autumn)
Clog Dancer (4%) cask
Porter (4%) cask
Pickled Priest (4.3%) cask
Torchlight (5%) cask
Stocking Filler (6%) cask
Pierrepoints Last Drop (7%) cask

LITTLE PUB COMPANY

Their Lumphammer is brewed by Carlsberg-Tetley.

LLOYDS

Lloyds Country Beers Ltd, John Thompson Brewery, Ingleby, Derbyshire DE7 1HW
Tel (01332) 863426

Est. 1977, and based at the John Thompson Inn brewery. Mostly all-malt brewing (though there's sugar in some beers), using Maris Otter and Challenger. They also brew Dark Amber for Heritage.

Classic (3.6%) cask
Gold (4%) cask
Vixen Velvet (4.2%) cask
Very Important Pint/VIP (4.8%) cask
Overdraught (7%) cask (Xmas)

LONDON BEER COMPANY

Non-brewing wholesaler. The old (sadly defunct) Pitfield brewery brands have settled here. Pitfield Bitter (3.6%), Hoxton Heavy (5.4%), Dark Star (5.6%) and London Porter (5.7%) are now brewed by Brewery on Sea, Sussex.

LONGSTONE

Longstone Brewery, Station Road, Belford, Northumberland NE70 7DT
Tel (01668) 213031
Est. 1991, bringing a much needed pep-up to the rather dreary Northumberland real ale scene. Old Grace commemorates local heroine Grace Darling.
Hotspur Bitter (3.7%) cask
Bitter (4%) cask
Old Grace (4.2%) cask

LORIMER & CLARK

see Vaux

LUCIFER

Lucifer Brewing Company, Hope & Anchor, 38 Jacob's Well Road, Clifton, Bristol BS8 1DR
Tel (0117) 929 2987
Est. 1994 in the Hope & Anchor pub.
Jack High (3.2%) cask
Eight Bore Special (4.2%) cask
O'Hooligan's Revolt (5.2%) cask

M&B MITCHELL & BUTLER

see Bass

McEWAN

see Scottish & Newcastle

THOMAS McGUINNESS

Thomas McGuinness Brewing Co., Cask & Feather, 1 Oldham Road, Rochdale, Greater Manchester OL16 1UA Tel (01706) 711476
Est. 1991 at the Cask & Feather public house. Full-mash brewing using whole Fuggles and Goldings hops, a dash of torrefied wheat, English Pipkin pale and crystal malts and roasted barley. The Stout was launched in April 1995.
Feather Plucker Mild (3.4%) cask
Best Bitter (3.8%) cask
Special Reserve (4%) cask
Stout (4%) cask
Junction Bitter (4.2%) cask
Tommy Todd Porter (5.2%) cask

MACLAY

Maclay & Co. Ltd, Thistle Brewery, East Vennel, Alloa, Clackmannanshire FK10 1ED
Tel (01259) 723387
Est. 1830, relocating to this tower brewery in 1869. The brewery has now passed from the hands of the Maclays into the ownership of the chairman's family, and a marketing and branding shake-up is under way. Hogmanay Special Brew is, as the name suggests, made once a year, specially for bottling. The 1995/6 Brew is to be 3.8% abv.
60/- Ale (3.4%) cask
70/- Ale (3.6%) cask/keg (as Special)
Broadsword (3.8%) cask
Porter (4%) cask
80/- Export Ale (4%) cask, and bottled (as Export)
Kane's Amber Ale (4%) cask
Hogmanay Special Brew 94/5 (4.5%) bottled
Oat Malt Stout (4.5%) cask and bottled
Wallace IPA (4.5%) cask
Fraoch Heather Ale (5%) cask, and bottled
Scotch Ale (5%) cask, and bottled

McMULLEN

McMullen & Sons Ltd, The Hertford Brewery, 26 Old Cross, Hertford SG14 1RD
Tel (01992) 584911
Est. 1827 and still in family hands. Aside from their core beer list, they brew McMullen Special Reserve cask ales, which are limited edition specials. They also produce bottle-conditioned beers for Hanseatic Trading Company, and bottled beers for Nethergate, among other brewing contracts. Typical ingredients: East Anglian barley malt, plus unmalted barley, and whole hops. Continental hops are used for the lagers.
Crafter LA (1%) bottled
Mac's Brown (3%) bottled
Hartsman Lager (3.6%) keg

Original AK (3.7%) cask
No 1 Pale Ale (3.8%) bottled
Country Best Bitter (4.3%) cask
Steingold Export lager (4.6%) keg
Castle Special Pale Ale (5%) bottled
Stronghart (7%) cask, and bottled

MALTON

Malton Brewery Co. Ltd, Crown Hotel, Wheelgate, Malton, N. Yorks YO17 0HP
Tel (01653) 697580
Est. 1985, and expanded since. Much of the brewing is now carried out by the founder's daughter, Cilla Parlett. All local malt-brewing, with Challenger hops, and no adjuncts or additives.
Pale Ale (3.2%) cask
Double Chance Bitter (3.8%) cask
Nut Brown (4%) cask
Pickwick's Porter (4%) cask
Owd Bob (5.9%) cask

MANSFIELD

Mansfield Brewery PLC, Littleworth, Mansfield, Notts NG18 1AB
Tel (01623) 25691
Est. 1855, and a major local pub owner. All its ales are fermented in traditional Yorkshire squares. The Drayman's beer range is made and packaged for the budget end of the retail trade. There's also a cask range of six week specials under the name Deakin's Ales.
Drayman's Best Bitter (3%) can, and PET
Drayman's Dark Mild (3%) can and PET
Jorvik Lager (3.1%) can and PET
Mansfield Mild (3.5%) keg
Riding Mild (3.5%) cask and can
Riding Bitter (3.6%) cask/keg can and PET (3.8%)
Bitter (3.9%) cask can and PET
Marksman Lager (4.1%) can and PET
Drayman's Draught Premium Bitter (4.5%) can
Old Baily (4.8%) cask/keg

MARCHES ALES

Unit 6, Western Close, Southern Avenue Industrial Estate, Leominster, Herefordshire HR6 0QD Tel (01568) 610063
Est. 1994, when the Solstice brewery got new owners and a new identity. Their up-to-date 16 barrel plant produces full mash ales using Maris Otter and crystal malts (plus a dash of amber and chocolate), whole local Goldings, plus Fuggles and Challenger hops.
Marches Best (3.8%) cask
Priory Ale (4.8%) cask
Jenny Pipes Summer Ale (5.2%) cask
Earl Leofricks Winter Ale (7.2%) cask

MARSTON MOOR

Marston Moor Brewery, Crown House, Kirk Hammerton, N. Yorks YO5 8DD
Tel (01423) 330341
Est. 1983, moved to the Crown public house in 1988, but closed the pub in 1993. Now looking to buy other pubs, elsewhere.
Cromwell Bitter (3.6%) cask
Brewers Pride (4.2%) cask
Porter (4.2%) cask
Merrie Maker (4.5%) cask
Black Tom Stout (4.5%) cask (winter)
Brewers Droop (5.1%) cask
Trooper (5.1%) cask

MARSTON'S

Marston, Thompson & Evershed PLC, Shobnall Road, Burton-upon-Trent, Staffs DE14 2BW Tel (01283) 531131
Est. 1835, and the last remaining brewer to use the traditional Burton Union fermentation system; the yeast from the 'sets' gives their beer its bitter-sweet pungency, and they spent £1 million on a new Union room in 1992. The all-natural beers use English hops, and their own well water and yeast. The tremendously influential 'Head Brewer's Choice' (HBC) bottled beers also appear as Tesco's Select Ales and are occasionally put out in cask. Marston also brew and bottle Victoria Ale for Victoria Wine off-licences.
Bitter (3.8%) cask
Low 'C' (4.2%) bottled
Oyster Stout HBC (4.5%) bottled
Pedigree (4.5%) cask, bottled and can
Albion Porter HBC (4.8%) bottled
India Pale Ale Export HBC (5.5%) bottled
Burton Strong Pale Ale HBC (6.2%) bottled
Owd Rodger (7.6%) cask, and bottled

MASON'S ARMS

Lakeland Brewing Co., Mason's Arms, Strawberry Bank, Cartmel Fell, Cumbria LA11 6NW Tel (0153 95) 68686

Splendid and well-loved pub with an excellent bottled beer selection, including its own three bottle-conditioned brands.

Amazon Bitter (4%) cask
Great Northern (5%) cask, and bottled BC
Big Six (6%) cask and bottled BC
Damson Beer (7%) cask, and bottled BC (9%)

MAULDONS

Mauldons Brewery, 7 Addison Road, Chilton Industrial Estate, Sudbury, Suffolk CO10 6YW
Tel (01787) 311055

Est. 1982 by an ex-Watney's brewer, reviving an old family business. Plenty of seasonals and special occasion beers are also produced.

Best Bitter (3.8%) cask
Porter (3.8%) cask
Old Eatanswill (4%) cask
Squires (4.2%) cask
Special Bitter (4.2%) cask
Suffolk Punch (4.8%) cask
Black Adder (5.3%) cask
White Adder (5.3%) cask
Suffolk Comfort (6.6%) cask

MILDMAY

Mildmay Brewery, Holbeton, Plymouth, Devon PL8 1NA Tel (01752) 830248

Est. 1993. Owns one pub. Also available in a few others locally.

Colours Best (3.8%) cask
SP Ale (4.5%) cask
50/1 (5.1%) cask
Old Horsewhip (5.7%) cask

MILL

Mill Brewery, 18c Bradley Lane, Newton Abbot, Devon TQ12 4JW
Tel (01626) 63322

Est. 1983. New owners 1994, with expansion plans. 'Janner' is local patois for the Devonshire-born. Typical ingredients: pale, crystal and chocolate malts, roasted barley (in Black Bushel) and Challenger hops.

Janner's Ale (3.8%) cask
Ruby Ale (4.5%) cask
Janner's Old Original (5%) cask
Black Bushel (6%) cask

MITCHELL'S

Mitchell's Ltd, 11 Moor Lane, Lancaster, Lancs LA1 1QB
Tel (01524) 63773

Est. 1880 in the old Yates and Jackson brewery, and still owned by the Mitchell family. Fuggles, Goldings and Challenger hops are used, and their own well water; capacity is now up to around 30,000 barrels a year. Single Malt is a single varietal ale made with pale malt only. They also do seasonal beers. Mitchell's Traditional Bitter (can) was actually brewed under licence by another brewery for George Barker International, but isn't available in the UK at present.

William Mitchell's Original Bitter (3.8%) cask keg
Brewer's Pride (4.2%) cask
Dark Stout (4.2%) cask
Lancaster Bomber (4.4%) cask
Single Malt (7.4%) cask

MOLE'S

Mole's Brewery, 5 Merlin Way, Bowerhill, Melksham, Wilts SN12 6TJ
Tel (01225) 704734

Est. 1982 by an ex-Ushers brewer, whose nickname is Mole. An enterprising and expanding company: plans include a new bottle-conditioned ale for sale in the USA (and here).

Tap Bitter (3.5%) cask
Best Bitter (4%) cask
Landlords Choice (4.5%) cask
Brew 97 (5%) cask
XB (6%) cask

MOORHOUSE'S

Moorhouse's Brewery Ltd, 4 Moorhouse Street, Burnley, Lancs BB11 5EN
Tel (01282) 422864

Est. 1865, though only a cask ale brewery since 1978.

Black Cat Mild (3.2%) cask
Premier Bitter (3.7%) cask
Pendle Witches Brew (4.1%) cask and bottled
Owd Ale (6%) cask

MORLAND

Morland & Co. PLC, The Brewery, Ock Street, Abingdon, Oxon OX14 5DD
Tel (01235) 553377
Est. 1711, moving to this site 150 years later. The beers are made using pale and crystal malts plus brewing sugar, and Goldings and Challenger hops. Independent IPA was launched to celebrate rebuffing the unwelcome advances of Greene King. Old Speckled Hen has been given masses of Macallan malt whisky-style broadsheet advertising, with great success. Jacks, as in Tanner's Jack, were old English leather tankards.
Independent IPA (3.4%) cask
Revival Dark Mild (3.5%) keg
Original Bitter (4%) cask
Tanner's Jack (4.4%) cask
Old Masters (4.6%) cask
Old Speckled Hen (5.2%) cask, bottled and can

MORRELLS

Morrells Brewery Ltd, The Lion Brewery, St Thomas' Street, Oxford OX1 1LA
Tel (01865) 792013
Est. 1782, Oxford's oldest brewery, and still in family hands. Traditional full mash infusion brewing, using British malt, hops and wheat products. They also brew for Whitbread, and make Harp lager for Guinness (but then who doesn't?).
Friar's Bitter (3.2%) keg
Oxford Light Ale (3.2%) bottled
Oxford Bitter (3.6%) cask
Oxford Mild (3.7%) cask
Brewery Gate Bitter (4.3%) keg, and bottled
Varsity (4.3%) cask
Oxford Castle Ale (4.5%) bottled
Graduate (5.2%) cask, and bottled
College (7.4%) cask

NENE VALLEY

Nene Valley Brewery, Unit 1, Midland Business Centre, Midland Road, Higham Ferrers, Northants NN9 8PN
Tel (01933) 412411
Union Bitter (3.6%) cask
Trojan Bitter (3.8%) cask
Shipmates Ale (4.4%) cask
Old Black Bob (4.7%) cask
Rawhide (5.1%) cask
Medusa Ale (7.8%) cask

NETHERGATE

Nethergate Brewery Co. Ltd, 11–13 High Street, Clare, Suffolk CO10 8NY
Tel (01787) 277244
Est. 1986 in a converted commercial vehicle workshop by an ex-Cambridge academic, botanist turned industrial microbiologist, initially with one of Peter Austin's (Ringwood Brewery) 10-barrel plants, now replaced by one of his 30-barrel models. The dark, delicious Bitter and Old Growler, which are currently made and bottled under contract by McMullen, benefit from the addition of black malt, plus Halcyon and Goldings hops. The rest of the range uses Maris Otter pale and crystal malts, Challenger pellets (for production reasons), and are late-copper hopped with whole Fuggles. Umbel Ale and Magna are based on an ancient recipe and involve an infusion of coriander seeds.
IPA (3.6%) cask
Umbel Ale (3.8%) cask
Bitter (4%) cask, and bottled ('Old Nethergate Special Bitter')
Old Growler (5.5%) cask and bottled
Umbel Magna (5.5%) cask

NEWALE

Newale Brewing Co., 6 Viscount Count, Walworth Industrial Estate, Andover, Hants SP10 5NW Tel (01264) 333310
Est. 1993. Purpose-built 7-barrel plant in an industrial unit. Typical ingredients: 90% pale malt, a little crystal, a dash of torrefied wheat, a pinch of chocolate malt in the Bitter, roast barley in Old Hatch Ale, and 50/50 Bramling Cross and Styrian Goldings hops (apart from

Clatford Clout, which is 75% Styrian).
Anna Valley Ale (4%) cask
Balksbury Bitter (4.5%) cask
Clatford Clout (5%) cask
Old Hatch Ale (6%) cask (winter)

NICHOLSON'S

see Carlsberg-Tetley

NIX WINCOTT

Nix Wincott Brewery, Three Fyshes Inn, Bridge Street, Turvey, Beds MK43 8ER
Tel (01234) 881264
Est. 1987 as a brew pub at the Three Fyshes, and much expanded since in response to demand. A new fermenting room was added in 1993.
Old Cock Up Mild (3.4%) cask
Turvey Bitter (3.4%) cask
Two Henrys Bitter (3.9%) cask
THAT (4.8%) cask
Old Nix (6%) cask
Winky Wobbler (7.5%) cask

NORTH YORKSHIRE

North Yorkshire Brewing Co., 80–84 North Ormesby Road, Middlesbrough, Cleveland TS4 2AG Tel (01642) 226224
Est. 1990, with a purpose-built plant, to make beers using traditional ingredients and methods. All-malt brewing, using Maris Otter and crystal malts, Northdown whole hops, chocolate malt in the darker beers, and roast barley in the porter. ABVs vary a bit, so average levels are given.
Best Bitter (3.6%) cask
Yorkshire Brown (3.9%) cask
Yorkshire Porter (3.9%) cask
Fools Gold (4.4%) cask
Flying Herbert (4.8%) cask
Dizzy Dick (7.9%) cask

OAK

Oak Brewing Co. Ltd, Phoenix Brewery, Green Lane, Heywood, Greater Manchester OL10 2EP Tel (01706) 627009
Est. 1982 in Ellesmere Port, relocating here in 1991. All-malt brewing using Halcyon malt, and a mixture of whole hops, including Brewer's Gold. At present seriously considering bottling: 'People want good bottled beer now, but they don't want to pay Belgian prices.' Midsummer Madness is available May–August, and Porter is now an occasional beer.
Bantam (3.5%) cask
Hopwood Bitter (3.5%) cask
Best Bitter (3.9%) cask
Tyke Bitter (4.3%) cask
Midsummer Madness (4.4%) cask
Old Oak Ale (4.5%) cask
Thirsty Moon (4.6%) cask
Bonneville (4.8%) cask
Double Dagger (5.1%) cask
Porter (5.1%) cask
Wobbly Bob (6.1%) cask
Humbug (6.5%) cask (Xmas)

OAKHAM

Oakham Ales, 12–13 Midland Court, Station Approach, Oakham, Rutland, Leics LE15 6QW Tel (01572) 755338
Jeffrey Hudson Bitter/JHB (3.8%) cask
Old Tosspot (5.2%) cask

OAKHILL

Oakhill Brewery, High Street, Oakhill, Somerset BA3 5AS Tel (01749) 840134
Est. 1984, in an ex-fermenting room of the original, defunct Oakhill brewery, which dominates this small Somerset village. Should have relocated to the Old Maltings by the time you read this. Hoping to start bottling there.
Somer Ale (3.5%) cask (summer)
Best Bitter (4%) cask
Black Magic Stout (4.5%) cask
Yeoman 1767 Strong Ale (5%) cask
Mendip Tickler (6.3%) cask

OKELLS

see Isle of Man

OLD BEAR

Old Bear Brewery, Old White Bear, 6 Keighley Road, Cross Hills, Keighley, W. Yorks BD20 7RN
Est. 1993 by the former owner of Goose Eye.
Bitter (3.9%) cask

Ursa Minor (4.7%) cask
Ursa Major (5.7%) cask

OLD LUXTERS

Old Luxters Farm Brewery, Hambleden, Bucks RG9 6JW Tel (01491) 638330

Est. 1990 by David Ealand, a retired City legal practitioner who set up Chiltern Valley vineyard in 1980, and added this small brewhouse on Old Luxters pig farm ten years later. Bottle-conditioned Barn Ale has now achieved exports of 42,000 to France, Holland and Sweden in just a year, and Luxters' sparkling new, hi-tech bottling plant is attracting other small (and medium) breweries. Barn Ale is made from pale, crystal and chocolate malt, hops, yeast and water only.

Barn Ale (4.4%) cask and bottled BC (5.4%)

OLD MILL

Old Mill Brewery Ltd, Mill Street, Snaith, Goole, E. Yorks DN14 9HS
Tel (01405) 861813

Est. 1983 in an old malt kiln, previously used as a clog factory until the end of the war. Much expanded, but still brewing the same four reliable cask ales (though a summer beer is being considered).

Traditional Mild (3.4%) cask
Traditional Bitter (3.9%) cask
Bullion (4.7%) cask
Traditional Porter (5%) cask

ORANGE BREWERY

Orange Pub Brewery, 37–39 Pimlico Road, Pimlico, London SW1W 8NE
Tel (0171) 730 5984

Est. 1983, and swiftly attracted lots of good notices for its fine quality beers. Now owned by Scottish & Newcastle (this is by far their most successful brew pub). Full mash brewing using Worcester Goldings hops. Ales are served direct from 180 gallon cellar tanks, so carbon dioxide tank breathers are used. Seasonal beers, including a summer wheat beer, are also produced.

SW1 (3.8%) cask
Pimlico Porter (4.5%) cask
SW2 (4.8%) cask

ORKNEY

Orkney Brewery, Quoyloo, Orkney KW16 3LT
Tel (01856) 84802

Est. 1988. Roger White, a teetotal civil engineer who'd been working abroad, bought an old school in Orkney and decided to turn it into a brewery. Originally intending to provide keg beer for the island, he was besieged by requests for cask-conditioned versions from the mainland, and now also exports to Canada. Beers are made using Golden Promise Scottish malt, a little crystal and chocolate malt (black malt and roasted barley in the stout), various hop pellet varieties, and a dash of torrefied wheat. Cane sugar, too, in Dark Island and Skullsplitter.

Raven Ale (3.8%) cask/keg and bottled
Dragonhead Stout (4%) cask/keg and bottled
Dark Island (4.6%) cask/keg and bottled
Skullsplitter (8.5%) cask/keg and bottled

OTTER

Otter Brewery, Mathayes, Luppit, Honiton, Devon EX14 0SA Tel (01404) 891285

Est. 1990. The beers are made using local malt and their own spring water. Bright, a summer beer launched in 1994, is one of the pale straw-coloured, refreshing and moreish West Country summer quaffers that are becoming a beer style in their own right.

Bitter (3.6%) cask
Bright (4.3%) cask (summer)
Ale (4.6%) cask
Dark (4.8%) cask (winter)
Head (8.5%) cask

PALMERS

Palmer Ltd, The Old Brewery, West Bay Road, Bridport, Dorset DT6 4JA
Tel (01308) 422396

Est. 1794, and Britain's only thatched brewery. IPA has 5% cane sugar and Tally Ho a little malt extract 'for colour', but the rest are all-malt (Pipkin), and seasoned with English Goldings. Not dry-hopped, though; the locals gave it the thumbs down during a recent trial. Bottled beers are mainly sold in

pubs, but are also available at the brewery shop.
Light Ale (3%) bottled
Nut Brown Ale (3%) bottled
Bridport Bitter (3.2%) cask
Best Bitter/IPA (4.2%) cask
Classic Pale Ale (4.7%) bottled
Tally Ho! (4.7%) cask and bottled
200 (5%) cask and bottled

PARISH

Parish Brewery, The Old Brewery Inn Courtyard, Somerby, Leics LE14 2PZ Tel (01664) 454781
Est. 1983, at the Stag & Hounds, Burrough on the Hill, moving here to a new 20-barrel plant in 1991. Desperate for recognition in the record books, forced to admit that their BBB was merely the 'strongest beer available on handpump in England', they have now produced a 23% abv ale (twice as strong as wine), only available in third of a pint glasses.
Mild (3.5%) cask
Special Bitter/PSB (3.5%) cask
Somerby Premium Bitter (4%) cask
Rainbow Porter (4.5%) cask
Poachers Ale (6%) cask
Baz's Bonce Blower/BBB (12%) cask
Baz's Super Brew (23%) cask

PASSAGEWAY

Passageway Brewing Co., Unit G8, Queens Dock Storage Yard, Norfolk Street, Liverpool L1 0BG Tel (0151) 708 0730
Est. 1994. The original cask beer, St Arnold, named after the Belgian patron saint of brewing and made with an abbey brewery yeast, has now been joined by two new beers. Redemption is made with 30% rye.
Dockers Hook (3.7%) Cask
Redemption (4%) cask
St Arnold (5%) cask

PEMBROKE

Pembroke Brewery Co., Eaton House, 108 Main Street, Pembroke, Dyfed SA71 4HN Tel (01646) 682517
Est. 1994 in an old stable block. The Darklin, a pond-dark mild, is the notorious alias of a local street (historically) of ill-repute.
The Darklin (3.5%) cask
Main Street Bitter (4.1%) cask
Golden Hill Ale (4.5%) cask

PETT

Pett Brewing Co. Ltd, The Old Forge Brewery, Pett Road, Pett, Hastings, East Sussex TN35 4HB Tel (01424) 813030
New brewery, owned by Pett village residents, who loyally managed to get through 20 casks in the first week of test marketing. A 5 barrel plant with two fermenters (but room for four more) has been installed in the village's old forge, which was on the point of falling down before a bar-room conversation inspired this brilliant wheeze.
Brothers Best (3.9%) cask
Petts Progress (4.6%) cask
Old Farnes (5.3%) cask

PILGRIM

Pilgrim Brewery, West Street, Reigate, Surrey RH2 9BL Tel (01737) 222651
Est. 1982, relocating to Reigate three years later. Bottled Pudding and Great Crusader (which was brewed summer 1995 only) are planned, if David Roberts can finally find the right bottle for them (it might be best not to hold your breath on this one). Summer, winter and seasonal ales are also produced. The Porter has an improved grist for 1995, apparently.
Surrey Pale Ale (3.7%) cask
Porter (4%) cask
Progress Best Bitter (4%) cask
Autumnal (4.5%) cask (autumn!)
Saracen Stout (4.5%) (winter)
Spring Bock wheat beer (4.5%) (spring)
Talisman Winter Warmer (5%) cask
Crusader Special Bitter (4.9%) cask (summer)
Pudding (7.3%) cask (Xmas)

PIONEER

see Rooster's

PLASSEY

Plassey Brewery, The Plassey, Eyton, Wrexham, Clwyd LL13 0SP Tel (01978) 80922

Est. 1955 on the 250-acre Plassey Estate. Now building a new brewery, with its own bottling plant, and shortly to add a stout to its beer range, to be based on a 1906 recipe from the now defunct Soames of Wrexham.
Bitter (4%) cask
Glyndwr's Revenge (4.8%) cask
Cwrw Tudno (5%) cask
Dragon's Breath (6%) cask

POOLE

The Brewhouse Brewery, 68 High Street, Poole, Dorset BH15 1DA
Tel (01202) 682345
Est. 1981, transferring to the Brewhouse pub in 1990.
Poole Best Bitter/Dolphin (3.8%) cask
Bosun Bitter (4.6%) cask

POWELL

see Wood

RCH

RCH Brewery, West Hewish, Weston Super Mare BS24 6RR Tel (01278) 783138
Est. 1993 as a commercial brewery, but only after ten years at the Royal Clarence Hotel in neighbouring Burnham-on-Sea, where the brewery was founded in order to supply a single bitter to the hotel bar. Their traditionally brewed beers, using malt, hops, yeast and water only, are now wholesaled to venues all over Britain.
PG Steam (3.9%) cask
Pitchfork (4.3%) cask
Old Slug Porter (4.5%) cask
East Street Cream (5%) cask
Firebox (6%) cask
Santa Fe (7.3%) cask (Xmas)

RANDALLS

R. W. Randall Ltd, Vauxlaurens Brewery, St Julian's Avenue, St Peter Port, Guernsey GY1 3JG Tel (01481) 720134
Est. 1868 as Randalls, when Mr Randall bought the brewery from Joseph Gullick. Not connected with Randalls Vaultier of Jersey, though the two companies have the same original root. Typical ingredients: malt, whole hops, hop extract, hop oil and sugar, in various combinations, except for the Traditional Bitter, which, true to its name, uses malt and whole hops only.
Original VB (3.3%) bottled
Triple X (3.3%) keg
Mild (3.8%) cask
Best Bitter (5%) keg
IPA (5%) bottled
Premium Bitter (5%) can
Traditional Bitter (5%) cask
Stout (5.1%) bottled

REBELLION

Rebellion Beer Co., Unit J, Rose Industrial Estate, Marlow Bottom Road, Marlow, Bucks SL7 3ND Tel (01628) 476594
Est. 1993, close to the old Wethereds brewery, by two friends who went to school together. They have ambitions to move into part of the now defunct building, and gain access to the brewery well; currently their water is treated to replicate the Marlow style. Over £60,000 investment has been made in gleaming new equipment. Currently 50 barrels a week are made, using pale, crystal and chocolate malts, and English hops.
IPA (3.9%) cask
ESB (4.5%) cask

RECKLESS ERIC'S

Reckless Brewing Co. Ltd, Unit 4, Albion Industrial Estate, Cilfynydd, Pontypridd, Mid Glamorgan CF37 4NX Tel (01443) 409229
Retribution (3.4%) cask
Renown (4%) cask
Restoration (4.3%) cask
'Recked 'Em (5.2%) cask
Rejoice (6%) cask

REDRUTH

Redruth Brewery Ltd, The Brewery, Redruth, Cornwall TR15 1AT Tel (01209) 212244
Est. 1792, but troubled in recent years with changes of ownership, failure and receivership. Meanwhile, Redruth makes a living as a contract brewer and packager, and brews 'Limited' products for retailer sale.
Bronx lager (5%) bottled

Limited Bitter (5%) can
Limited Lager (5%) can
Limited Stout (5%) can
Limited Superstrength Lager (9.5%) can

REEPHAM

Reepham Brewery, Unit 1, Collers Way, Reepham, Norfolk NR10 4SW
Tel (01603) 871091
Est. 1983 when the owner was made redundant by Watneys and bought a 7.5 barrel plant from Peter Austin at the Ringwood Brewery. Beers are made using whole Fuggles and Whitbread Golding Variety hops, and on average 90% malt, 10% brewing sugar/barley syrup. The cask lager uses Hallertau hops. Occasional beers: Smugglers Stout (4.4%), Reepham Dark (3.8%) and LA Bitter (2%).
Granary Bitter (3.8%) cask
Summer Velvet (4.1%) cask (summer)
Rapier Pale Ale (4.2%) caskand PET
Velvet Stout (4.2%) cask (winter)
Reepham Gold Natural Lager (4.4%) cask
Old Bircham Ale (4.6%) cask
Bittern Pale Strong Ale (5%)
Brewhouse Ale (5%) cask (winter)

REINDEER

Reindeer Trading Co. Ltd, 10 Dereham Road, Norwich, Norfolk NR2 4AY
Tel (01603) 666821
Est. 1987 as a brew pub, but now wholesaled all over the country. Full mash brewing using Maris Otter, crystal, chocolate and wheat malts, Kent Goldings hops, yeast and water only. Its 10-barrel plant is now reaching bursting point.
Moild (3.4%) cask
Pale Ale/RPA (3.7%) cask
Bevy (3.9%) cask
Gnu Bru (4.4%) cask
Bitter (5%) cask
Red Nose (6%) cask

RIDLEYS

T. D. Ridley & Sons Ltd, Hartford End Brewery, Hartford End, Chelmsford, Essex CM3 1JZ Tel (01371) 820316
Est. 1842 by Thomas Dixon Ridley, a miller. They also make seasonal ales. The bottle-conditioned Chelmer Gold is a new beer.
Essex Light (3.1%) bottled
Essex Brown Ale (3.4%) bottled
IPA (3.5%) cask
Mild (3.5%) cask
ESX Best Bitter (4.3%) cask
Witchfinder Porter (4.3%) cask
Spectacular (4.6%) cask
Chelmer Gold (5%) bottled BC
Winter Ale (5%) cask
Old Bob (5.1%) bottled
Bishops Ale (8%) bottled

RINGWOOD

Ringwood Brewery Ltd, 138 Christchurch Road, Ringwood, Hants BH24 3AP
Tel (01425) 471177
Est. 1978, and at the very forefront of the British microbrewery revival. Its name is now known all over the world, thanks to the pioneering work of Ringwood's Peter Austin. Otherwise known as the father of the small brewery revolution in England, Austin has also provided purpose-built small plant to new ventures all over the world. All-malt (Maris Otter) brewing, with a dash of torrefied wheat, and Goldings, Challenger and Progress hops. Ringwood Bitter PET is available in local off-licences. True Glory was a VE Day bitter, with Fuggles and Goldings only, which may join the permanent range.
Ringwood Bitter (3.7%) PET
Best Bitter (3.8%) cask
True Glory (4.5%) cask and bottled
XXXX Porter (4.7%) cask
Fortyniner (4.8%) cask
Old Thumper (5.8%) cask and bottled

RISING SUN

Rising Sun Inn, Shraley Brook, Audley, Stoke-on-Trent, Staffs ST7 8DS
Tel (01782) 720600
Est. 1989 as a brew pub, but now popular in the local free trade too. The original 5-barrel plant doubled capacity in 1994. Sunstroke and Total Eclipse use malt extract, but otherwise pale, crystal and chocolate malts

are used, plus Goldings, Fuggles and Challenger hops.
Mild (3.3%) cask
Rising (3.8%) cask
Setting (4.4%) cask
Sunstroke (5.6%) cask
Total Eclipse (6.8%) cask
Solar Flare (10%) cask

ROBINSON'S

Frederic Robinson Ltd., Unicorn Brewery, Lower Hillgate, Stockport, Cheshire SK1 1JJ Tel (0161) 480 6571
Est. 1838. Robinson's took over and closed down Cumbrian brewers Hartley's. Hartley's XB, all that remains from their old list, is now brewed at Stockport.
Brown Ale (3%) bottled
Three Shires Mild (3%) keg
Cock Robin (3.2%) keg
Dark Best Mild (3.3%) cask
Hatters Mild (3.3%) cask
Old Stockport Bitter (3.5%) cask
Einhorn Lager (4%) keg
Fellrunners Gold (4%) keg
Hartleys XB (4%) cask
Pale Ale (4%) bottled
Best Bitter (4.2%) cask, and can (4%)
Frederic's (5%) cask and bottled
Old Tom (8.5%) cask and bottled

ROOSTER'S

Rooster's Brewery, Unit 20, Claro Court, Claro Business Centre, Claro Road, Harrogate, N. Yorks HG1 4BA Tel (01423) 561861
Est. 1993 by Sean Franklin. Currently 20 barrels a week and expanding. Pale, crystal, black, chocolate and wheat malts are used, plus smoked malts from Bamburg, as well as Styrian and English Goldings, Fuggle and Challenger hops. Plus more esoteric varieties in the experimental Pioneer Brewery range, their other brandname. The popular Cream, which came into the main list via the Pioneer test marketing route, contains some wheat.
Mayflower II (3.7%) cask
Jak's (3.9%) cask
Special (3.9%) cask
Yankee (4.3%) cask
Cream (4.7%) cask
Hop Along (4.7%) cask (Easter)
Rooster's (4.7%) cask and bottled BC
Nector (5.8%) cask (Xmas)

ROSE STREET

Rose Street Brewery, 55 Rose Street, Edinburgh EH2 2NH Tel (0131) 220 1227
Est. 1983. Owned by Alloa Brewery (Carlsberg-Tetley), and supplies ten other Edinburgh outlets. Cask-conditioned beers only, using English malt and hops.
Auld Reekie 80/- (4.1%) cask
Auld Reekie 90/- (5.3%) cask

ROSS

Ross Brewing Company, Bristol Brewhouse, 117–119 Stokes Croft, Bristol BS1 3RW Tel (0117) 942 0306
Est. 1989, and best known outside Bristol for their Saxon Strong Ale, which was the first to use organic grade malt. It's now brewed by Eldridge Pope, but owing to disappointing sales may be discontinued. Sam Pepys Rowan Ale is made with rowanberries, and Old Kingsdowner with elderflowers and meadow sweet. The latest 'strongest beer' contender, from Parish brewery, has led Ross to (informally) label their Uncle Igor's 'the strongest nice beer in the world'. Full-mash, all-malt brewing with a variety of malts, and mostly Goldings hops.
Old Kingsdowner (3.8%) cask
Picton's Pleasure (4.5%) cask
Hartcliffe Bitter (4.5%) cask
Porter (5%) cask
SPA (5%) cask
Double Bowler (6%) cask
Numbskull (6%) cask
Sam Pepys Rowan Ale (6%) cask
Ginger Beer (12%) cask
Uncle Igor's (21%) cask

ROTHER VALLEY

Rother Valley Brewing Co., Gate Court, Northiam, Rye, East Sussex TN31 6QT Tel (01797) 252444
Est. 1993. One beer only, available in local

pubs here and in West Kent. Seventy-five per cent local ingredients used, typically pale ale, crystal malt, a little wheat, and their own Goldings hops. Ambitions include sinking their own brewery well, and bottling a new golden bock style beer of around 5% abv.
Level Best (4%) cask

RUDDLES

Ruddles Brewery Ltd, Langham, Oakham, Leics LE15 7JD Tel (01572) 756911
Est. 1858, taken over by Grand Met in 1986, and sold to Dutch brewery Grolsche in 1992. There may be one or two more products to add to the list by the end of 1995, including a new bottled bitter intended for the supermarket trade (for which they already contribute own brand products). Typical ingredients are listed as: malt, plus Goldings, Fuggles and Bramling Cross hops.
Best Bitter (3.7%) cask/keg, bottled, can and PET
County (4.9%) cask, bottled, can and PET

RUDGATE

Rudgate Brewery Ltd, 2 Centre Park, Marston Business Park, Rudgate, Tockwith, York YO5 8QF Tel (01423) 358382
Est. 1992, close to this most Viking-conscious of English cities (what – no Jorvik Ale?). Full-mash brewing, using Yorkshire malt, whole English hops, and fermenting in traditional Yorkshire squares.
Viking (3.8%) cask
Battleaxe (4.2%) cask
May Pole (4.5%) cask (spring)
Pillage Porter (4.5%) cask (autumn)
Thor's Hammar (5.5%) cask

RYBURN

Ryburn Brewery, Mill House, Mill House Lane, Sowerby Bridge, Halifax, W. Yorks HX6 3LN
Tel (01422) 835413
Est. 1990, as a tiny 2-barrel brewhouse in a former dyeworks, and now expanded to 10-barrel capacity. Their traditional gravity-fed three tier brewing system uses whole Goldings, Fuggles and Northdown hops, and Halcyon pale, crystal and wheat malts.
Best Mild (3.3%) cask
Bitter (3.8%) cask
Rydale Bitter (4.2%) cask
Old Stone Troff (4.7%) cask
Luddite (5%) cask
Stabbers Bitter (5%) cask
Coiners (6%) cask

ST AUSTELL

St Austell Brewery Co. Ltd, 62 Trevarthian Road, St Austell, Cornwall PL25 4BY
Tel (01726) 74444
Est. 1851 by Walter Hicks, relocating to this site in 1893, and still a family affair. Typical ingredients: English and crystal malts, torrefied wheat, Fuggles, Goldings and Challenger whole hops, Styrian hop pellets, and water from their own supply. There's a visitors centre.
Pilsner Lager (3.3%) keg/can
Bosun's Bitter (3.4%) cask
XXXX Mild (3.6%) cask
Duchy Bitter (3.7%) keg
Tinners Ale (3.7%) cask, and can
Export Gold lager (5%) keg/can
Hicks Special Draught/HSD (5%) cask
Wreckers Bitter (5%) keg, and can
Smugglers Strong Ale (7.8%) bottled
Crippledick (11.7%) bottled

SAMUEL SMITH

Samuel Smith Old Brewery, Tadcaster, N. Yorks LS24 9SB Tel (01937) 832225
Est. 1758, and a neighbour of cousin John Smith's now Courage-owned brewery, but Sam's remains staunchly independent and firmly small-scale (relatively speaking). All brewing makes the most of natural ingredients, using well-water, Yorkshire stone square fermentation, and wooden barrels, but they're also down to just one cask beer (farewell, Museum Ale). Bottled beers are much more the modern focus of the brewery.
Old Brewery Bitter/OBB (4%) cask and can
Nut Brown Ale (5%) bottled
Oatmeal Stout (5%) bottled
Old Brewery Strong Pale Ale (5%) bottled
Pure Brewed Lager (5%) can
Taddy Porter (5%) bottled
Imperial Stout (7%) bottled

SARAH HUGHES

Sarah Hughes Brewery, Beacon Hotel, 129 Bilston Street, Sedgley, Dudley, West Midlands DY3 1JE Tel (01902) 883380

Est. 1988, reopening after 30 years enforced idleness. The bottled Dark Ruby Mild is available by mail order direct from the brewery.

Sedgley Surprise Bitter (5%) cask
Dark Ruby Mild (6%) cask and bottled BC

SCOTTISH & NEWCASTLE

Scottish & Newcastle PLC, Abbey Brewery, 111 Holyrood Road, Edinburgh EH8 8YS Tel (0131) 556 2591

Est. 1960 when the former Scottish Breweries (itself a merger of Younger and McEwan) and Newcastle Breweries amalgamated. National breweries are classified as those with over 2000 pubs; S&N left the fold of the giants for a time after the 'guest beer law' was instituted (which decrees that Nationals must allow landlords to choose a guest beer), but is now back in the premier league, having acquired the Chef & Brewer group. They operate breweries in Edinburgh, Newcastle, Nottingham, Manchester and Ripon; this last being Theakston, though most of Theakston's beers are now produced over the border in Newcastle. Home Mild is now brewed for them by Mansfield.

Newcastle Brown is the biggest selling bottled (and canned) ale in the country. Kestrel Super Strength – now referred to as Younger's Kestrel – is the third best-selling superstrength lager, in a market worth over £300 million a year. S&N also brew Coors Extra Gold under licence, and Harp under licence from Guinness (but then who doesn't?), and imports Becks from Germany and Jupiler from Belgium. They also own a clutch of successful brew pubs and are keen to develop this side of their 'portfolio', as they would put it.

Gillespie's Stout (4%) keg and can
Home Bitter (3.5%) cask/keg
Home Mild (3.6%) cask/keg
Matthew Brown Bitter (3.5%) cask/keg
Matthew Brown Mild (3.1%) cask/keg
McEwan's 60/- (3.2%) keg
McEwan's 70/- (3.7%) cask/keg
McEwan's 80/- (4.5%) cask/keg, and bottled
McEwan's 80/- Special (4.5%) keg
McEwan's 90/- (5.5%) cask, and bottled
McEwan's Best Scotch (3.6%) keg, and can
McEwan's Export (4.5%) cask/keg, and can
McEwan's Pale Ale (3.2%) keg, and can
Newcastle Bitter (3.7%) keg
Newcastle Brown (4.7%) bottled, and can
Newcastle Exhibition (4.3%) cask/keg, and can
Newcastle IPA (3.3%) keg
Theakston Best Bitter (3.8%) cask/keg, bottled and can
Theakston Black Bull (3.9%) cask
Theakston Hogshead (4.1%) cask
Theakston Masham Ale (6.6%) cask
Theakston Mild (3.5%) cask/keg
Theakston Old Peculier (5.6%) cask, and bottled
Theakston XB (4.6%) cask/keg, and can
Younger's Best Bitter (3.7%) cask/keg
Younger's Heavy/70/- (3.7%) keg, and can (3.5%)
Younger's IPA (4.5%) is McEwan's 80/-
Younger's Light Mild/Pale Ale (3.1%) keg
Younger's Mild (dark) (3.2%) keg
Younger's No 3 (4.5%) cask, and bottled
Younger's Scotch (3.7%) is McEwan's 70/-
Younger's Tartan Special Bitter (3.7%) keg, and can
Younger's Welsh Bitter (3.2%) keg

LAGERS

Coors Extra Gold (5%) keg, bottled and can
McEwan's Extra (5%) keg
McEwan's Lager (4.1%) keg, and can
Younger's Kestrel Pilsner (3.4%) can
Younger's Kestrel Super Strength (9%) can

SCOTT'S

Scott's Brewing Co., Crown Hotel, 151 High Street, Lowestoft, Suffolk NR32 1HR
Tel (01502) 537237

Est. 1988 behind the Crown Hotel. William French brewed here in the 16th century.

Golden Best Bitter (3.4%) cask
Blues and Bloater (3.7%) cask
East Point Ale (4%)

Mild (4.4%) cask
William French (5%) cask
Dark Oast (5%) cask

SELBY

Selby Brewery Ltd, 131 Millgate, Selby, N Yorks Y08 OLL Tel (01757) 792826

Est. 1972, though the family had previously brewed right up until the 1950s. Going against the modern micro tide, they make just one beer, and are happy to be small. Old Tom is made with Maris Otter pale and crystal malts, and Whitbread Golding Variety hops. They also do specials from time to time.

Old Tom (6.5%) cask

SHARDLOW

Shardlow Brewery Ltd, Ground Floor, Kiln Warehouse, British Waterways Yard, Cavendish Bridge, Leics DE72 2HL Tel (01332) 799188

Est. 1993 in the kilnhouse of the old Cavendish Bridge Brewery. There are three varieties of hops in the Bitter. Cavendish uses a high proportion of crystal malt. There's lots of chocolate malt in Sleighed.

Session (3.6%) cask (summer)
Bitter (4.2%) cask
Cavendish 47 Bridge (4.7%) cask
Sleighed (5.7%) cask (winter)

SHARP'S

Sharp's Brewery, Rock, Wadebridge, Cornwall PL27 6NU Tel (01208) 862121

Est. 1994 by a former silversmith.

Cornish Coaster (3.6%) cask
Own Cornish (4.4%) cask

SHEPHERD NEAME

Shepherd Neame Ltd, 17 Court Street, Faversham, Kent ME13 7AX
Tel (01795) 532206

Est. 1698, so easily Kent's oldest brewery. But probably also Britain's oldest brewing company, with a history stretching back into the early middle ages and possibly beyond. Situated in the very heart of hop-growing country, and still Neame family controlled. Bishops Finger is the biggest selling British bottled beer in Sweden and France. They also import Kingfisher lager, as well as brewing Hürlimann under licence.

Masons Pale Ale (3.3%) cask
Steinbock (3.6%) keg and can
Master Brew Bitter (3.7%) cask/keg, bottled and can (4%)
Best Bitter (4.1%) cask
Spitfire Ale (4.7%) cask and bottled BC
Hürlimann (5%) keg, bottled and can
Bishops Finger (5.2%) cask, bottled and can (5.4%)
Original Porter (5.2%) cask and bottled

SHIPSTONE'S

see Greenalls

SMILES

Smiles Brewing Co. Ltd, Colston Yard, Colston Street, Bristol BS1 5BD
Tel (0117) 929 7350

Est. 1978 as a commercial operation, and known in the area for its excellent pubs.

Brewery Bitter (3.7%) cask
Best Bitter (4.1%) cask
Bristol Stout (4.7%) cask (Xmas)
Exhibition Bitter (5.2%) cask

SOLSTICE

see Marches Ales

SOUTH YORKSHIRE

South Yorkshire Brewing Co., Elsecar Workshops, Wath Road, Elsecar, Barnsley, S. Yorks S74 8HJ Tel (01226) 741010

Est. 1994. A 20-barrel plant with a 60-barrel fermenting capacity, which uses the original yeast culture from the defunct Oakwell Brewery. Full-infusion mash brewing, using pale and coloured malts.

Barnsley Bitter (3.8%) cask
Heritage Bitter (4.2%) cask
Black Heart Stout (4.6%) cask

SPRINGHEAD

Springhead Brewery, Main Street, Sutton on Trent, Newark, Notts NG23 6PE
Tel (01636) 821000

Est. 1990. A tiny brewhouse, originally single-

barrel, has now expanded to seven and a half, and will have to move if demand grows any further. (NB: As Yet Untitled isn't the name of the beer, it just doesn't have a name as we go to press.)
As Yet Untitled (3.5%) cask
Bitter (4%) cask
The Leveller (4.8%) cask
Roaring Meg (5.5%) cask
Cromwell's Hat (6.5%) cask

STANWAY

Stanway Brewery, Stanway, Cheltenham, Gloucs GL54 5PQ Tel (01386) 584320
Stanney Bitter (4.5%) cask
Old Eccentric (5.5%) cask

STEAM PACKET

Steam Packet Brewery, The Bundles, Racca Green, Knottingley, W. Yorks WF11 8AT Tel (01977) 674176
Est. 1990, initially as a brew pub. Full-mash, all-English malt brewing, but with American Willamette hops among the Target. They find American hop quality much more consistent, and feel English varieties are going through a particularly ropey and diseased phase. (NB: Craam is not a misspelling.)
Summer Lite (3.5%) cask
Mellor's Gamekeeper Bitter (3.6%) cask
Chatterley (3.9%) cask
Foxy (3.9%) cask
Bit o Black (4%) cask
Brown Ale (4.5%) cask
Ginger Beer (4.5%) cask
Packet Porter (4.5%) cask
Bargee (4.8%) cask
Poacher's Swag (5%) cask
Craam Stout (5.2%) cask
Giddy Ass (8%) cask

STILTON FEN

Stilton Fen Brewery, Inn on the Green, Watton Road, Datchworth, Herts HG3 6TB Tel (01438) 812496
New brewery. Planning to be up and running by the end of 1995; no product names available as we go to press.

STOCKS

Stocks Brewery, The Hallcross, 33–34 Hallgate, Doncaster, S. Yorks DN1 3NL Tel (01302) 328213
Est. 1981, initially as a brew pub. The beers have been reformulated recently. Golden Wheat is a new wheat beer.
Best Bitter (3.9%) cask
Golden Wheat (4.7%) cask
Select (4.7%) cask
St Leger Porter (5.1%) cask
Old Horizontal (5.4%) cask

STONES

see Bass

STRONG

see Whitbread

SUMMERSKILLS

Summerskills Brewery, Unit 15, Pomphlett Farm Industrial Estate, Broxton Drive, Billacombe, Plymouth, Devon PL9 7BG Tel (01752) 481283
Est. 1983, moved here in 1985, closed in 1988, reopening with new owners in 1990. If you think the beer names are terrible, you should see the posters – adolescent record sleeve art, every one. Nice beer though, and traditional methods, using local malt and whole hops.
Best Bitter (4.3%) cask
Whistle Belly Vengeance (4.7%) cask
Ninjabeer (5%) cask
Indiana's Bones (5.6%) cask

SUTTON

Sutton Brewing Co., 31 Commercial Road, Plymouth, Devon PL4 OLE Tel (01752) 255335
Est. 1994, and has rapidly expanded its capacity and business.
Plymouth Pride (3.8%) cask
XSB (4.2%) cask
Eddystone Light (5%) cask
Plymouth Porter (5.5%) cask

TALLY HO

Tally Ho Country Inn and Brewery, 14 Market

Street, Hatherleigh, Devon EX20 3JN
Tel (01837) 810306
Est. 1990, and recently changed hands. The draught beers are still only available at the Tally Ho, but the bottle-conditioned beers (hand-filled and with signed labels!) pop up in shops and delis hereabouts. Just 3–5 barrels per brew, using twice filtered water, a mix of local malts, Kent Goldings and yeast only.
Dark Mild (2.8%) cask (summer)
Potboiler's Brew (3.5%) cask
Tarka's Tipple (4%) cask, and bottled BC (4.6%)
Nutter (4.6%) cask
Thurgia (5.7%) cask and bottled BC
Thurgia Premium (6%) bottled BC
Janni's Jollop (6.6%) cask (winter)

TAYLOR

Timothy Taylor & Co. Ltd, Knowle Spring Brewery, Keighley, W. Yorks BD21 1AW
Tel (01535) 603139
Est. 1858, and still family owned. All cask-conditioned ales, excepting a small quantity available unpasteurized in bottle. No canning, no sales to supermarkets. Typical ingredients: English malt, their own Pennine spring water, Hereford & Worcester Fuggles, and Kent and Styrian Goldings hops. For a largeish, established regional independent of great fame (Taylor's Landlord appears on most beer buffs Desert Island Ales list) they only own a surprisingly modest 29 pubs. They also have a beer shop in Leeds.
Golden Best (3.5%) cask
Dark Mild (3.5%) cask
Best Bitter (4%) cask
Porter (3.8%) cask
Landlord (4.3%) cask
Ram Tam/XXXX (4.3%) cask

TAYLOR WALKER

see Carlsberg-Tetley

TEIGNWORTHY

Teignworthy Brewery, Tuckers Maltings, Teign Road, Newton Abbot, Devon TQ12 4AA Tel (01626) 332066
Est. 1994. A 15-barrel plant on the Tuckers Maltings complex; bottle-conditioned Reel Ale was produced for sale to its many summer visitors. Tuckers malt is used in the beers, along with Hereford hops and Dartmoor water. No adjuncts or additives used.
Reel Ale (4%) cask and bottled BC
Springtide (4.3%) cask (spring)

TENNENTS

see Bass

TETLEY

see Carlsberg-Tetley

THEAKSTON

see Scottish & Newcastle

THOMPSON'S

Thompson's Brewery, Unit 4, Exhibition Way, Pinhoe Trading Estate, Exeter, Devon EX4 8HX Tel (01392) 464760
Thompson's got started when Mel Thompson began making Thompson's Aysheburton Bitter in what is now the function suite of the London Hotel. They built a spanking new 5000-barrel brewhouse in 1992. Man o' War is the pale West Country summer refresher of the list.
Black Velvet Stout (4%) cask
Celebration Porter (4%) cask
Best Bitter (4.1%) cask
IPA (4.4%) cask
Man o' War (5.1%) cask
Figurehead (5.1%) cask

THWAITES

Daniel Thwaites PLC, PO Box 50, Star Brewery, Blackburn, Lancs BB1 5BU
Tel (01254) 54431
Est. 1807. The following beer names and abv percentage rates may well be out of date; Thwaites would not confirm any details we requested.
Best Mild (3.3%) cask and can
Bitter (3.6%) cask and can
Craftsman (4.5%) cask

TISBURY

Tisbury Brewery Ltd., Church Street, Tisbury,

Wilts SP3 6NH Tel (01747) 870986
New brewery, established in the wake of the closure and dismemberment of the old Wiltshire Brewery. The new 20-barrel brewery uses only traditional ingredients: Maris Otter pale and crystal malts, Fuggles and Bramling Cross hop pellets, and late copper-hopped with Goldings (Styrians in Old Wardour, as well as a sprinkling of chocolate malt).
Tisbury Best (3.8%) cask
Archibald Beckett (4.3%) cask
Old Wardour (4.8%) cask

TITANIC

Titanic Brewery, Unit G, Harvey Works, Lingard Street, Burslem, Stoke- on-Trent, Staffs ST6 1ED Tel (01782) 823447
Est. 1985, relocating and expanding in 1992. They're now brewing 52 barrels a week. Beers are made from Maris Otter malt, with a small percentage of flaked wheat (Lifeboat is all-malt), brewing sugar in the stronger beers, and Goldings, Fuggles and Northdown hop pellets. A little 12-months-matured Wreckage is available in bottle. White Star is the permanent name for the old Anniversary Ale.
Best Bitter (3.5%) cask
Lifeboat Ale (3.9%) cask
Premium Bitter (4.1%) cask
Stout (4.5%) cask, and bottled BC
White Star (4.8%) cask
Captain Smith's Strong Ale (5.2%) cask
Wreckage (7.8%) cask, and bottled BC
Christmas Ale (7.8%) bottled BC

TOLLY COBBOLD

Tolly Cobbold Brewery Ltd, Cliff Road, Ipswich, Suffolk IP3 0AZ Tel (01473) 231723
Est. 1723, as Cobbold's, merging with Tollemache's in 1957 – 1996 sees their 250th anniversary of brewing in Ipswich. Taken over and closed down by Brent-Walker in 1989, Tolly reopened triumphantly the following year thanks to a management buy-out. Two further bottled beers, Tolly Light & Brown Ale (3%) and Cobnut Brown Ale (3.2%), are seldom seen outside pubs. Tollyshooter commemorates the televised visit of Sir John Harvey-Jones; Tolly's Strong is a new edition of 1993's Cantab, relabelled.
Mild (3.2%) cask
Bitter (3.5%) cask
Original Best Bitter (3.8%) cask
Cobbold's IPA (4.2%) bottled
Old Strong (4.5%) cask (winter)
Tolly's Strong (4.6%) bottled
Tollyshooter (5%) cask

TOMINTOUL

Tomintoul Brewery Co Ltd, Mill of Auchriachan, Tomintoul, Ballindalloch, Aberdeenshire AB37 9EQ
Tel (01807) 580333
Est. 1993 in a bit of a beer desert (though not a desert in any other sense). Actually, what with Borve as well, and Aberdeenshire Ales turning up, Grampian is beginning to look almost crowded. Full-mash, all-malt brewing. Ginger Tom, a ginger beer, is an occasional. Look out for the new bottled Stag in local outlets.
Caillie (3.6%) cask
Stag (4.1%) cask and bottled BC
Ginger Tom (4.5%) cask
Wild Cat (5.1%) cask

TOMLINSON'S

Tomlinson's Old Castle Brewery, Unit 5, Skinner Lane, Pontefract, W. Yorks WF8 1HU
Tel (01977) 780866
Est. 1993. Just 5 barrels capacity, brewing three times a week, produces a versatile (and all individually brewed) range of beers, named after historic Pontefract associations. All-malt, using Maris Otter, roast malts, Challenger, Goldings and Styrian hops. The newer, lighter beers have proved very popular, Sessions in particular. Femme Fatale was brewed for International Women's Day, but may return.
Sessions (4%) cask
Down With It! (4.3%) cask
Femme Fatale (4.4%) cask
Fractus XB (4.5%) cask
De Lacy (4.6%) cask
Deceitful Rose (5%) cask
Richard's Defeat (5%) cask
Three Sieges (6%) cask

TOWNES

Townes Brewery, Bay 9, Suon Buildings, Lockoford Lane, Chesterfield, Derbyshire S41 7JJ Tel (01246) 277994

Est. 1994 to return traditional, all-malt cask-conditioned brewing to Chesterfield. Pynot is the old local name for a magpie.

Muffin Ale (3.5%) cask
Sunshine (3.6%) cask (summer)
Best Lockoford Bitter (4%) cask
IPA (4.5%) cask
Pynot Porter (4.5%) cask (winter)
Double Bagger (5%) cask

TRAQUAIR

Traquair House Brewery, Innerleithen, Peebleshire, Borders EH44 6PW Tel (01896) 830323

Est. 1965, although the brewhouse itself is an 18th-century one, located in one of the great houses of the Scottish borders. The 20th laird, the late Peter Maxwell Stuart, unearthed this miniature working museum in 1965; his daughter Catherine now continues the Traquair tradition. Ninety five per cent of Traquair House Ale is bottled, and 60% exported. It's fermented in oak, using a bottom-fermenting yeast, and is cold-conditioned. All natural ingredients: malt, Kent Goldings hops, yeast and their own spring water. Jacobite Ale will be a limited edition, for the 1745 anniversary. Fair Ale is only available at Traquair festivals.

Bear Ale (5%) cask
Fair Ale (6%) cask
Traquair House Ale (7.2%) cask, and bottled
Jacobite Ale (8%) cask

TRING

Tring Brewery Co. Ltd, 81–82 Akeman Street, Tring, Herts HP23 6AF Tel (01442) 890721

Est. 1992. All-malt brewing using Maris Otter pale, crystal and wheat malts, Challenger, Goldings and Styrian hops. Bottled Death or Glory is only available in pubs at present. Old Cantankerous is a porter.

Finest Summer Ale (3.7%) cask
The Ridgeway Bitter (4%) cask
Old Cantankerous (4.8%) cask (autumn)
Old Icknield Ale (5%) cask
Death or Glory Ale (7.2%) cask (Xmas), and bottled BC

ULEY

Uley Brewery Ltd, The Old Brewery, Uley, Dursley, Gloucs GL11 5TB Tel (01453) 860120

Est. 1985, in the old Price's Brewery (1833), which had long been defunct. Devon malt, Herefordshire hops, and water from the original brewery spring go into their delicious range of ales, which are conditioned in the vaulted cellars of the old brewery.

Bitter (3.8%) cask
Old Ric (4.5%) cask
Old Spot Ale (4.8%) cask
Pig's Ear Strong Pale Ale (4.8%) cask
Pigor Mortis (6%) cask

UNITED BREWERIES

United Breweries of India – non-brewing former owners of the old Pitfield and Wiltshire brewery brands – is now concentrating on its pub estate.

USHERS

Ushers of Trowbridge PLC, Directors House, 68 Fore Street, Trowbridge, Wilts BA14 8JF Tel (01225) 763171

Est. 1824, bought out by Watney in 1960, regained independence 1991, and now embarked on a huge investment programme. They began brewing the Four Seasons Ales (FSA) in 1994, the idea being to create short-season beers that reflect the grains available at that time of year. Manns Brown Ale is the best-selling brown ale brand in Britain. All Ushers beers are brewed with Goldings hops.

Manns Original Brown Ale (2.8%) bottled
Light Ale (3.2%) bottled
Triple Crown (3.2%) keg
Best Bitter (3.8%) cask and can
Special Bitter (3.8%) keg
Autumn Frenzy FSA (4%) cask
Spring Fever FSA (4%) cask
Summer Madness FSA (4%) cask
Founders Ale (4.5%) cask, bottled and can
IPA (4.5%) keg and bottled (5%)

Dark Horse Porter (5%) bottled
1824 Particular FSA (6%) cask and bottled

VAUX

Vaux Breweries Ltd, The Brewery, Sunderland, Tyne & Wear, SR1 3AN
Tel (0191) 567 6277

Est. 1837, and still independent, though it also owns Wards (and is increasingly rebranding their beers as its own), and did have the old Lorimer & Clark brewery in Edinburgh, until selling it to Caledonian in 1987. The new Vaux cask beer (actually made in Sheffield), Waggle Dance, is primed with honey – a waggle dance is the excited little bop a bee does when it's spotted a nectary flower. Vaux makes Labatt and Heineken brands under licence, and also brews for supermarkets. Vaux ESB (also made by Wards) is also the beer in Tesco's own label canned Strong Yorkshire Bitter. There's a low alcohol product: Maxim Light (0.9%).

Light Ale (3.3%) keg and can
Mild (3.4%) cask/keg
Cooper's Best Bitter (3.6%) can
Lorimer's Best Scotch (3.6%) cask/keg, and can
Bitter (3.9%) cask/keg, and can
Samson (4.2%) cask/keg and can
Double Maxim (4.2%) cask/keg, bottled and can
ESB/Extra Special Bitter (5%) cask
Leiter Pils (5%) can
Scorpion Dry lager (5%) bottled and can
Waggle Dance (5%) cask
Scorpion Super (8.5%) can

VILLAGE BREWER

Non-brewing wholesaler. Most of the beer is supplied by Hambleton.

White Boar (3.7%) cask
Bull (4%) cask
Zetland Best Bitter (4.2%) cask
Old Raby (4.8%) cask

WADWORTH

Wadworth & Co. Ltd, Northgate Brewery, Devizes, Wilts SN10 1JW
Tel (01380) 723361

Est. 1885, a red brick Victorian tower brewery that still dominates Devizes market place. Still using the original open copper, too. Their new bottled beer, 6X Export, has been jinxed by setbacks, and may or may not be launched by the time you read this. Malt and Hops '95, this year's harvest ale, is a unique green hop beer made from the new, unkilned season's flowers. They also make a Valentine's Day Ale, and an Easter Ale (4.5%). Saaz hops are used in the brewing of Summersault, which is only available in June and July.

Henry's Original IPA (3.8%) cask
6X (4.3%) cask, bottled (5%), and can
Farmer's Glory (4.5%) cask
Malt and Hops '95 (4.5%) cask
Summersault (4.5%) cask
Old Timer (5.8%) cask and bottled (5.5%)

WARDS

S. H. Ward & Co. Ltd, Sheaf Brewery, Eccleshall Road, Sheffield, S. Yorks S11 8HZ
Tel (0114) 275 5155

Now part of the Vaux empire. Among other contract jobs, Wards supplies the contents of two Tesco canned own brands, Tesco Strong Yorkshire Bitter (ESB) and Tesco Best Bitter, as well as making Vaux ESB, and the new Waggle Dance honey beer (see p. 293).

Thorne Best Bitter (3.9%) cask/keg
Best Bitter (4%) cask/keg and can

WATNEY

see Courage

WEBSTER'S

see Courage

WEETWOOD

Weetwood Ales Ltd, Weetwood Grange, Weetwood, Tarporley, Cheshire CW6 0NQ
Tel (01829) 752337

Est. 1993 at an equestrian centre. Weetwood Old Dog is a new beer, with a further new one planned for late 1995.

Best Bitter (3.8%) cask
Old Dog (4.5%) cask

WELLS

Charles Wells Ltd, The Eagle Brewery, Havelock Street, Bedford, Beds MK40 4LU
Tel (01234) 272766
Est. 1876, a family brewery still run by Wells descendants, and a major pub owner in the area. Their cask ale brands have now been joined by a third name in Fargo, which is in fact a revival, and now considered their flagship ale; it's made with English barley malt, Goldings and Challenger hops. A wide sphere of influence and a strong track record in contract brewing (they make Scandia lagers for Spar, among other things) has now brought contracts to produce Kirin, Japan's number one beer brand, and Bitburger, Germany's number two.
Crest lager (3%) can and PET
Eagle IPA (3.6%) cask/keg
Bombardier (4.3%) cask, bottled and can
Bitburger (4.6%) bottled
Kirin (4.8%) bottled
Fargo (5%) cask, and bottled
Crest Super (10%) can

WESTBURY ALES

Non-brewing wholesaler, its monthly changing beers supplied by Hop Back

WETHERED'S

see Whitbread

WHIM

Whim Ales, Whim Farm, Hartington, Buxton, Derbyshire SK17 0AX Tel (01298) 84702
Est. 1993 in a converted farm building.
Hartington Bitter (3.8%) cask
Magic Mushroom Mild (3.8%) cask
Special (4.4%) cask
Old Izaak (4.8%) cask
Black Christmas (5.8%) cask
Black Bear (6.8%) cask

WHITBREAD

Whitbread PLC, Porter Tun House, Capability Green, Luton, Beds LU1 3LS
Tel (01582) 391166
Ubiquitous giant which owns thousands of pubs, and had become notorious by the 1980s for its buy 'em up, close 'em down approach to well-placed independents. Some of these breweries' names survive in the beer portfolio – Chester's, Wethered's and Higsons among them. Boddingtons, another takeover, has instead been preserved, and its brands thrust into the mass market. More recently, one interesting development in the cask-conditioned range has been the devising and promotion of 'New Classic Ales' (try-outs) under the 'Beer Thinkers' banner, and single varietal hop beers, an innovation which will either spawn a host of exciting new names on the permanent range or sink without trace.

Fuggles Imperial IPA, which uses 100% Fuggles hops, is the first 'varietal' to make it onto the A list. Summer Ale, another innovation, uses Czech Saaz hops, and 50/50 pale ale and lager malts, for a refreshing lager-ale effect. Bottled Gold Label is unpasteurized, and has its very own yeast, as does Heineken, which is also lagered for several weeks. The Porter is in the modern style, using more chocolate malt and less 'burnt' black malt, for more mellow coffee richness. Only a sixth of the hop quantity dictated in the original recipe is used; apparently modern hop varieties have such greater tannins and acid levels. It's also dry-hopped with Goldings. White Label, the low alcohol product, is produced by arrested fermentation: brewed conventionally for a short time, and then halted at 1% alcohol by volume. Heineken and Stella Artois are brewed under licence. In addition, the following beers are contract-brewed by other companies: Chesters Best Bitter (Burtonwood); Chesters Best Mild (Everards); English Ale (Marston's); Higson's Double top (Robinson's); Oldham Bitter (Burtonwood); Pompey Royal (Gales); Strong Country Bitter (Morrells); Wethereds Bitter (Gales and McMullen).
Bentley's Bitter (3.8%) cask/keg, bottled and can (3%)
Boddingtons Bitter (3.8%) cask/keg, can and PET
Boddingtons Mild (3%) cask/keg
Campbells 70/- (3.4%) keg
Campbells 80/- (4%) keg

Castle Eden Ale (4.2%) cask and can (4%)
Chesters Best Bitter (3.6%) cask/keg
Chesters Best Mild (3.5%) cask/keg
Chesters Light (3.4%) keg
Eden Bitter (3.7%) cask/keg
English Ale (5.4%) bottled
Flowers Best Bitter (3.4%) cask/keg
Flowers IPA (3.6%) cask/keg, and can
Flowers Original Bitter (4.5%) cask and can (4.4%)
Forest Brown Ale (2.7%) bottled and can
Fremlins AK (2.7%) cask
Fremlins Bitter (3.5%) cask
Fuggles Imperial IPA (5.5%) cask
Gold Label Strong Ale (10.9%) bottled and can
Higsons Bitter (3.8%) cask/keg
Higsons Double Top (3.1%) bottled
Higsons Mild (3.1%) cask/keg
John Groves Bitter (3.4%) keg
Mackeson Stout (3%) bottled and can
Murphy's Irish Stout (4%) keg and can
Newquay Steam 3X (3.4%) keg
Newquay Steam Bitter (3.8%) keg, bottled and can (4%)
Old Dambuster (4.3%) cask
Oldham Bitter (3.8%) cask/keg
Oldham Mild (3%) cask/keg
Poacher Bitter (3.4%) keg
Pompey Royal (4.5%) cask
Royal Wessex Bitter (4%) cask
Saxon Bitter (3.4%) keg
Strong Country Bitter (3.9%) cask
Summer Ale (3.6%) cask
Trophy Bitter (3.8%) cask/keg and can
Welsh Bitter (3.4%) keg
West Country Pale Ale (3%) cask
Wethereds Bitter (3.6%) cask
Whitbread Best Bitter (3.6%) cask/keg and can (3.3%)
Whitbread Best Mild (2.6%) cask/keg and can
Whitbread Best Scotch (3.4%) keg
Whitbread Light (3.4%) keg
Whitbread Light Ale (3.1%) bottled and can
Whitbread Pale Ale (3.4%) bottled and can
Whitbread Porter (4.5%) cask
Whitbread Winter Royal (5.5%) cask
White Label (1%) bottled and can

LAGERS

Brewmaster (3.8%) bottled
Gold Label lager (3.9%) keg
Heineken Export (5%) keg, bottled and can
Heineken Lager Beer (3.4%) keg, bottled, can and PET
Heldenbräu (3.2%) can and PET
Heldenbräu Super (8.9%) can
Kaltenberg Diat Pils (6%) bottled and can
Newquay Steam Lager (5.3%) bottled and can
Newquay Steam Pils (4.4%) keg
Stella Artois (5.2%) keg, bottled and can

WHITBY'S

Whitby's Own Brewery Ltd, St Hilda's, The Ropery, Whitby, N. Yorks YO22 4ET
Tel (01947) 605914

Est. 1988, and expanded into neighbouring buildings in 1992. Its beers have won local (and even national) admiration, with special mention for the Nut Brown, which deserves to be better known. The pale, strong winter beer, Demon, has been successfully tapped and tasted after six months' maturation in the barrel! (And yes, Woblle is spelt like that – an adjusted acronym from Whitby's Own Brewery Limited.)

Golden Pale Bitter (3.3%) cask
Wallop (3.6%) cask
Nut Brown (4.5%) cask
Woblle (4.5%) cask
Force Nine (5.5%) cask
Demon (6.6%) cask

WICKWAR

Wickwar Brewing Co., The Old Cider Mill, Station Road, Wickwar GL12 8NB
Tel (01454) 294168

Est. 1990 by two former Courage tenants, who were asked to sign up for 20-year leases on their pubs, or get out. They got out. Wickwar's located in an ex-cider mill, which was itself an ex-brewery; the new enterprise is based in the old Arnold's cooperage. Capacity has now doubled to 60 barrels a week.

Coopers WPA (3.5%) cask
Brand Oak Bitter/BOB (4%) cask
Olde Merryforde Ale (5.1%) cask
Station Porter (6.1%) cask

WILD'S

Wild's Brewery, Unit 3e, Spa Fields Industrial Estate, Slaithwaite, Huddersfield HD7 5BB Tel (01484) 648387

Est. 1994 in the *Last of the Summer Wine* village. All-malt beers using Maris Otter pale and crystal malts, Fuggles and Challenger hops; chocolate malt and (American) Cascade hops are used in Wild Redhead. There are plans to bottle a four-pack, The Wild Bunch, in 1996.

Wild Session (3.8%) cask
Wild Oats (4.1%) cask
Wild Blonde (4.5%) cask
Wild Redhead (4.5%) cask
Wild Thing (5%) cask and bottled

WILLY'S

Willy's Brewery, 17 High Cliff Road, Cleethorpes DN35 8RQ
Tel (01472) 602145

Est. 1989, originally to supply a seafront pub, but now enjoying a thriving wholesale trade.

Original Bitter (3.7%) cask
Burcom Bitter (4.2%) cask
Coxswains Special Bitter (4.8%) cask
Old Groyne (6.2%) cask

WILSON'S

see Courage

WOLVERHAMPTON & DUDLEY

see Banks's and Camerons

WOOD

Wood Brewery Ltd, Wistanstow, Craven Arms, Shropshire SY7 8DG Tel (01588) 672523

Est. 1980, by the Wood family, in a small brewhouse adjoining their pub, the Plough. Sam Powell brands have been produced here since the Powell brewery went to the wall in 1991.

Sam Powell Best Bitter (3.4%) cask
Wallop (3.4%) cask
Sam Powell Original (3.7%) cask
Parish Bitter (4%) cask
Special Bitter (4.2%) cask
Woodcutter (4.2%) cask (autumn)
Shropshire Lad (4.5%) cask (spring)
Sam Powell Original Bitter (4.6%) cask
Wonderful (4.8%) cask

WOODFORDE'S

Woodforde's Norfolk Ales Ltd, Broadland Brewery, Woodbastwick, Norwich, Norfolk NR13 6SW Tel (01603) 720353

Est. 1980 in Norwich, relocating here in 1989. Traditional full-mash infusion brewing, using only pale and coloured malts, except in the case of Headcracker, which also uses 7% brewing syrup. Porter (4.1%) and John Browne's Ale (4.3%) are also brewed on an occasional basis.

Broadsman Bitter (3.5%) cask
Mardler's Mild (3.5%) cask
Wherry Best Bitter (3.8%) cask
Old Bram (4.1%) cask
Great Eastern Ale (4.3%) cask
Nelson's Revenge (4.5%) cask
Norfolk Nog (4.6%) cask
Baldric (5.6%) cask
Headcracker (7%) cask, and bottled
Norfolk Nips (8.5%) bottled BC

WORLDHAM

Worldham Brewery, Smith's Farm, East Worldham, Hants GU34 3AT Tel (01420) 83383

Est. 1991, a 10-barrel plant in a converted hop kiln. Traditionally brewed, all-malt cask ales, using East Kent Golding hops. A fourth ale is planned as we go to press.

Session Bitter (3.6%) cask
Old Dray (4.4%) cask
Barbarian (5.2%) cask

WORTHINGTON

see Bass

WYCHWOOD

Wychwood Brewery Ltd, Eagle Brewery, The Crofts, Witney, Oxon Tel (01993) 702574

Est. 1983 as 'Glenny's', a one-man band making 8–10 barrels a week. Now it's 150 barrels, in a 500 barrel capacity brewery, situated within the old Clinch's brewery buildings, where new and old equipment happily rub shoulders – the mash tun is

Edwardian cast iron, but the fermentation rooms, complete with Yorkshire squares, are brand new.
Shires Bitter (3.4%) cask
Fiddlers Elbow (4%) cask
Best (4.2%) cask
Black Wych Stout (5%) cask
Dr Thirsty's Draught (5.2%) cask
Hobgoblin (6%) cask
The Dog's Bollocks (6.5%) cask

WYE VALLEY

Wye Valley Brewery, 69 St Owen Street, Hereford HR1 2JQ Tel (01432) 342546
Est. 1985. Traditionally brewed ales, using Golden Promise malt and local Herefordshire hops. They also produce seasonal beers under the Dorothy Goodbody (DG) brandname, which aims to create a 1950s atmosphere of wholesome simplicity. A range of malts (including wheat malt) and hops are used in this second range.
Bitter (3.5%) cask
HPA/Hereford Pale Ale (4%) cask
DG Springtime Bitter (4%) cask
DG Golden Summertime Ale (4.2%) cask
Supreme (4.3%) cask
DG Glowing Autumn Ale (4.5%) cask
DG Wholesome Stout (4.6%) cask (Jan–March)
Brew 69 (5.6%) cask
DG Wintertime Ale (5.6%) cask
Father Xmas Ale (8%) cask

WYLYE VALLEY

Wylye Valley Brewery, Dove Inn, Corton, Warminster, Wilts BA12 0S2
Tel (01985) 850109
New brewery. Building wasn't finished, and products not finalised as we go to press.

YATES

Yates Brewery, Ghyll Farm, Westnewton, Aspatria, Cumbria CA5 3NX
Tel (0169 73) 21081
Est. 1986 by Peter and Carol Yates in a steading on their wee farm. Full-mash brewing using English and Scots malt and English whole hops. Yates is brewing 33 barrels a week at present, and with no plans to expand whatsoever; they're happy to be small and in personal control of things. Also own the Ship hotel in Allonby.
Bitter (3.7%) cask
Premium (5.5%) cask
Best Cellar (6%) cask (Xmas)

YOUNGER'S

see Scottish & Newcastle

YOUNG'S

Young & Co.'s Brewery PLC, The Ram Brewery, High Street, Wandsworth, London SW18 4JD Tel (0181) 870 0141
Est. 1675, becoming Young's proper in 1884, after 50 years of partnership. It's been a public company since 1898, and, along with Fuller's, the joint-premier brewery of London. Their biggest seller is the 'ordinary', Young's Bitter, which is made from Maris Otter barley malt, crystal malt, enzymic malt, flaked barley, and glucose sugar; these ingredients are fairly typical of the range. Oatmeal Stout, originally brewed for the USA, now available here, also has roasted barley, and opts for dark sugar; Winter Warmer and Brown Ale use a special syrup mix. Young's also make lagers; they invested in their own conical lager vessels in 1979. There's a bottled low alcohol product: Young's Extra Light (1%).
Brown Ale (3.1%) bottled
Light Ale (3.2%) bottled
Bitter (3.7%) cask/keg, and can
London Lager (3.9%) keg
Special (4.6%) cask
Ram Rod (4.8%) keg, and bottled
Premium Lager (4.9%) keg
Oatmeal Stout (5%) keg
Winter Warmer (5%) cask
Export Bitter (6.4%) bottled
Old Nick (6.8%) bottled

The Retailers

THE SPECIALISTS

Independent and regional stores and small retailers that stock specialist beers

These are just some of the specialist shops now dotted around the country. If you know of others, please do write in, so that the list is more comprehensive in the second edition. Not all the beers (by any means) listed as being available from specialists will be available in the following shops. Some only take one or two favoured imports; others are more dedicated to the World Beers cause, carrying a large and impressive permanent stock. Almost all will be happy to order beers for you, as long as they are plugged into that particular import/wholesale company. Many beers are carried by several wholesalers.

The Ale Shop, 205 Lockwood Road, Huddersfield HD1 3TG
The Ale Shop, 79 Raglan Road, Leeds
Army & Navy Store, Victoria Street, London SW1
Beer Hunter's Paradise, Old Malthouse, 5 Avison Yard, Kirkgate, Wakefield WF1 1UA
Beer Paradise Ltd, Unit 11, Riverside Place, Bridgewater Road, Leed LS9 ORQ (*see also* Mail Order, below)
The Beer Shop, 8 Pitfield Street, Shepherds Market, London N1 6HA
Beers in Particular, 151 Highgate, Kendal, Cumbria LA9 4EN
Beers Unlimited, 500 London Road, Westcliffe on Sea, Essex
Billy Bunters Beer Shop, St Edward Street, Leek, Staffs
Binns Department Store Wine Shop, 7 High Row, Darlington DL3 7QE
Bitter Experience, 129 Lee Road, Blackheath, London SE3
The Bottle Stop, 136 Acre Lane, Bramhall, Stockport
The Bottle Store, 66 London Road, Leicester LE2 0QD
Brodie & Brodie Ltd, 11 The Square, Kelso, Borders TD5 7HF
Butler's Wine Cellar, 247 Queens Park Road, Brighton, Sussex BN2 2XJ
D Byrne & Co., 12 King Street, Clitheroe, Lancs BB7 2EP
Canterbury Beer Shop, 83 Northgate, Canterbury, Kent CT1 1BA
Churnet Wines & Beers, Cheadleton, Leek, Staffs
I. T. Coloquhoun, 92 Shenley Avenue, Ruislip Manor, Middx HA4 6BY
Cooks Delight, 360–364 High Street, Berkhampstead, Herts HP4 1HU
Cork & Cask, 3 Bourne Parade, Bexley, Kent DA5 1LQ
Corks of Cotham, 54 Cotham Hill, Redland, Bristol BS6 6XJ
Corkscrew Wine & Ale, Carlisle
Czerwiks, 82 Commercial Street, Brighouse, W. Yorks HD6 1AQ

The Dram Shop, 21 Commonside, Sheffield, S. Yorks S10 1GA
Elliotts, 27 Watlands View, Porthill, Stoke on Trent
Farmhouse Kitchen, 16 Market Place, Otley, W. Yorks
Fuller, Smith & Turner wine merchants, London area (branches)
Gales Wine Merchants, 204 The High Road, Woodford Green, Essex IG8 9EF
Gloucester Wines, Maidenhead, Kent
Goodies Delicatessen, 2a St Saviours Road, Larkhill, Bath BA1 6RT
Gourmet Vintners Ltd, Billingshurst, Sussex
Goyt Wines, 1 Canal Street, Whaley Bridge, nr Stockport, Cheshire SK12
Grapevine, Hebden Bridge, W. Yorks
Grassington Wine Shop, 13 Main Street, Grassington, N. Yorks
Peter Green, Warrender Park Road, Edinburgh
Grog Blossom, 253 West End Lane, London NW6
Grog Shop, 13 Kingston Road, Oxford OX2 5EF
Grosvenor Wines, 22b Belle View, Bude, Cornwall
Guildford Wine Market, 216 London Road, Guildford, Surrey
J Hall & Co., 303 Eaves Lane, Chorley, Lancs
Harbour Wine Lodge, 4 Harbour Street, Whitstable, Kent CT5 1AG
Harbourside Beers, Poole Quay, Poole, Dorset BH15 1HJ
Harpenden Wines, Harpenden, Beds
Harrods, Knightsbridge, London SW1
Hart Lane Off Licence, 12 Hart Lane, Luton, Beds
Heaton Drinks, 200 Heaton Road, Heaton, Newcastle NE6 5HP
Hopkins-Porter Ltd, Old Stable Shop, Ripley Castle, Harrogate HG3 3AY
Jug & Firkin, 90 Mill Road, Cambridge, Cambs CB1 2BD
Karls Beer House, Unit 10, Chaser Court, Greyhound Park, Chester
J C Karn & Son, Cheltenham, Glos
Kings Off Licence, 61/63 Hamlet Court Road, Westcliffe on Sea, Essex
Lancaster World Beers, 100 Penny Street, Lancaster
Liquor Store, 10 London Road, London SE1 6JZ
Lupe Pintos, 24 Leven Street, Edinburgh EH3 9LZ
Marble Arch World Beers, 57 Manchester Road, Chorton-cum-Hardy, Lancs
Martinez Fine Wines, The Grove, Ilkley, W. Yorks
Mason's Arms (pub), Strawberry Bank, Cartmel Fell, Cumbria CA11 6NW
McLeod's Off Licence, Bridge Street, Louth, Lincs LN11 0DR
Meanwood Supermarket, 569 Meanwood Road, Leeds LS6 4AY
Melvin Moffat & Co., Skegness
Norris Stores, 26/27 Quay Road, Halesworth, Suffolk IP19 8ER
The Offie, 142 Clarendon Park Road, Leicester
Osbornes, Burton-on-Trent, Staffs
Peckham & Rye Ltd, 18 Bognor Place, Glasgow GS1 4TQ, and branches
Pop Inn Off Licence, 43 Boughton, Chester, Cheshire
Porters Provisions, Boroughbridge, N. Yorks
Quenchers, 59 Norman Lane, Eccleshill, Bradford BD2 2LB
Quentin Johnstone, 16–20 East Trinity Road, Edinburgh EH5 3DY
Rackhams, Corporation Street, Birmingham
The Real Ale Shop, 47 Lovat Road, Preston, Lancs PR1 6DQ
Rhythm & Booze, Barnsley
Richardsons, Sunderland
I. G. Robertson Ltd, Hemel Hempstead, Herts
Saltaire Wines, 32 Bingley Road, Saltaire, Bradford BD18 4RU
Sandiway Wine Co, The Old Post Office, Sandiway, Cheshire
Selfridges, 400 Oxford Street, London W1 1AB
Simpkin & James, 5 Cank Street, Leicester
Small Beer, 91 Newland Street West, Lincoln

Small Beer, 57 Archer Road, Sheffield, S. Yorks S8 OJT
Southbury Wines, 34 Southbury Road, Enfield, Middx
Springfield Wines, Springfield Mill, Norman Road, Denby Dale, Huddersfield HD8 8TH
Stephans Cellar, 1 Lewis's Walk, Lewis's Lane, Abergavenny NP7 5BA
Stephensons, Nelson, Lancs
Villeneuve Wines Ltd, 1 Venlaw Crescent, Peebles, Borders EH45 8AE
Wardwick Hop & Vine, 63 The Wardwick, Derby
Wells Wine Cellar, 94/100 St Thomas Street, Scarborough
Whitstable Oyster Fishery Co., Royal Native Oyster Stores, The Horsebridge, Kent CT5 1BV
The Wine Bank, 532 Mansfield Road, Nottingham NG5 2RF
The Wine Basket, 144 Dundas Street, Edinburgh EH3 5DQ
The Wine Cellar, 15 Tabbs Lane, Scholes, Cleckheaton, W. Yorks BD19 6DY
Wine Centre, Tavistock, Devon
Wycombe Wines, 20 Crendon Street, High Wycombe, Bucks
York Beer Shop, 28 Sandringham Street, off Fishergate, York YO1 4BA

MAIL ORDER

The Beer Cellar, 31 Norwich Road, Strumpshaw, Norwich, Norfolk NR13 4AG Tel (01603) 714884
Over 200 beers from over 40 countries, in an informative full-colour brochure, complete with illustrations and tasting notes. Beers are sold by the case, though cases can be mixed. Mail order only.

Beer Paradise Ltd., Unit 11, Riverside Place, Bridgewater Road, Leeds LS9 0RQ Tel (0113) 235 9082
A huge catalogue of Belgian, as well as British and international bottled beers. Their Belgian selection is unsurpassed in Britain. Membership costs £1 a year, and members can buy beers direct from the showroom, in single bottles as well as cases.

Scottish Gourmet, The Thistle Mill, Station Road, Biggar ML12 6LP Tel (01899) 21268
Aside from their delicious mail order foodstuffs and upmarket ready meals service, the Scottish Gourmet also lists a limited range of beers available by post.

Selfridges, 400 Oxford Street, London W1A 1AB Tel (0171) 318 3730
Aside from being a very useful central London beer shop in its own right, Selfridges now lists beers of the world in its mail order drinks catalogue.

Wine Society, Gunnelswood Road, Stevenage, Herts SG1 2BG Tel (01438) 741177
As well as their mail order wine selection, the Wine Society carries a smaller list of beers. You need to join before you can order.

IMPORTERS AND WHOLESALERS

The following companies are those which very kindly supplied samples and information for this guide, and between them are responsible for most of those beers tasted and listed as available from specialist outlets. They do not supply beer direct to the general public, but will probably be helpful in directing you to retailers if a particular beer is being sought.

Beer Direct
10 Farndale Close, Warrington, Stoke on Trent ST9 0PW Tel (01782) 303823

Beers International
Bridge House, Summer Hill, Goudhurst, Kent TN17 1JT Tel (01580) 211388

Cave Direct
20 Danson Mead, Welling, Kent DA16 1RU Tel (0181) 303 2261

Classic Ales
4 Ascot Road, Bedfont, Feltham, Middx TW14 8QH Tel (01784) 248475

James Clay & Sons
Unit 7, Thorpe Garage Triangle, Sowerby Bridge, W. Yorks HX6 3DL Tel (01422) 822659

CV Sales & Marketing
South Sefton Business Centre, Canal Street, Bootle L20 8AH Tel (0151) 933 0511

Global Beer Company
Old Hasland Road, Chesterfield, Derbyshire S41 0RW Tel (01246) 233777

Maison Caurette
144–152 Bermondsey Street, London SE1 3TQ Tel (0171) 403 9191

Nectar Imports
The Old Hatcheries, Bell's Lane, Zeals, Wiltshire BA12 6LY Tel (01747) 840100

Premier Worldwide Beers
42 Beddington Lane, Croydon, Surrey CR0 4TB Tel (0181) 684 7682

NATIONAL RETAILERS

Asda, the Co-op, Marks & Spencer, Majestic, Oddbins, Safeway, Sainsbury, Somerfield, Spar, Tesco, Thresher, Victoria Wine and Waitrose all submitted samples of their British and imported beers for the listings in this guide. Safeway and Sainsbury have decent selections in their favoured areas, and Asda is to be applauded in making a concerted effort to improve its previously trailing-in-fourth position. The first fruits of this push, seven new Asda own brands, were launched as the Guide went to press. All the national supermarkets are too conservative, and too big-brand conscious when it comes to beer, as I have already moaned elsewhere in this book. Sainsbury is the top supermarket for own brands, but Tesco is probably a whisker ahead with its general selection, and is also to be applauded for insisting that its beers list all the ingredients on the label, always an enlightening process, and one that other big stores should follow. Tesco is the *Guide*'s Beer Supermarket of the Year.

Following closely behind is Waitrose, which has a much smaller, more intimate selection, but is also the most daring and eclectic of all supermarkets. Perhaps, with a little push, Waitrose could become the Oddbins of the supermarket world. Derek Strange, its beer-buyer, feels that Eastern Europe is set to become the next major beer exporter, if it can only get its investment and marketing sorted out, so with any luck there will be a whole new section in Waitrose's Beers of the World range before too long.

The Off Licence of the Year has to be Oddbins. It has quite a small list, but its beer range is also packed tight with absolute gems (as well as a few mass-market nasties, which hopefully it'll have the courage to drop entirely as its beer retailer role develops). Parallel to its pioneering role in the wine world, Oddbins is often the first retailer to stock an exciting bottled import, or British beer come to that. Where it leads, others follow. It is now perfectly poised to expand its range. With more pro-active beer buying all over the globe, and more descriptive shelf tickets and editorializing (just as they have done with their excellent wine list) Oddbins could easily become the high street focus of the beer renaissance in Britain. We could do with one of those.

It had better not dither too long, though, as Victoria Wine is currently beefing up its world beer list. Now presiding over 1531 retail outlets all over Britain (Augustus Barnett having been absorbed), including Haddows in Scotland, Victoria Wine is directing part of this estate towards a more upmarket look, with more than half an eye on the Oddbins style. 'Premium' beers are to be shown in Victoria Wine Cellars, as well as fine wine; the new 'Destination Wine Shops' will have the Victoria Wine fascia but will also have a new wood-and-wicker look within, with more wine on offer, and more beer too. On the premium beer front, they say they are looking to enhance regional variations, with more local bottled beers on offer. The company might also increase its exclusives list, and commission more own brands, like the excellent, Marston-brewed Victoria Ale. It is also intending to use its new Victoria Wine Cellars shops to offer limited parcels of unusual imports from time to time.

If you know what you want, and you prefer to buy it cash-and-carry style, Majestic is a good place to try. Its beer range is pretty limited – though it does have one or two exclusives, too – but the better products look particularly attractive when sold at discount price, by the case only. Price is almost the biggest factor in its buying policy, because of this quality-at-a-discount image; it is even prepared to source its own beers from the continent if necessary, to get a better deal. For instance, Beck's Bier, which is only usually available in 275ml bottles in Britain, is specially imported (some half a million bottles a year) by Majestic in the 330ml size, and is much better value. There's increasing emphasis on seasonal costcutter promotions, with special offers particularly congregating in the busiest months (June, July, November, December).

It's odd that Marks & Spencer should have such a limited range of beers, when it is so well placed to promote expensive and delicious imported and home bottled products. But for some reason it seems to think that people popping in to Marks's to buy smoked salmon and freshly squeezed OJ will also want to buy Whitbread beers: St Michael Best Bitter, Wethereds Draught, St Michael Draught Lager and Schonbrau lager are all produced by Whitbread in Lancashire. Though there are also genuine lager imports: St Michael Original Pils hails from St Pauli Girl in Hamburg, who also make one of the 25cl ten-packs (St Michael German Pilsener Lager). The other comes from Fischer, Strasbourg, who also package one of their better lagers as Alsace Gold for M&S. The home contingent may feature four Whitbread beers, but at least it also features two of the best bottled bitters in Britain: Caledonian 80/- and 'Traditional Yorkshire Bitter' (Black Sheep Ale).

OTHER NATIONALS

In addition to the supermarkets, wine shops and off-licences listed in the main beers directory, the following might be fertile ground for beer hunting: Army & Navy stores; Bentalls; Binns; Cavendish House; D. H. Booth's; Corney & Barrow; Davies; Europa; Kwik Save; Leo's; Makro; Morrisons; Savacentre; Unwins; Winerite. Littlewoods and BHS also carry a restricted supply of beer. Kwik Save, Littlewoods and Morrisons were encouraged to supply information and samples for this guide but declined to participate.

The Beers Index